❖ The AS/400 Owner's Manual for V4 ❖

The AS/400 Owner's Manual for V4

Mike Dawson

First Edition

Second Printing—March 2000

ISBN: 1-58347-001-8

Midrange Computing
5650 El Camino Real, Suite 225
Carlsbad, CA 92008
www.midrangecomputing.com

V4R3

Acknowledgments

The best part of being in the AS/400 world is the friends we make. I feel I'm particularly blessed in this area. I'd like to thank those friends at J.J. Croney and Associates, Phoenix, Arizona, for their help and support in producing *The AS/400 Owner's Manual for V4.*

From January 1998 through September 1998, I was a senior AS/400 consultant at J.J. Croney and Associates. For much of that time, client demands took away those "extra" hours I used for my writing about the AS/400. For a while, it looked like this book wouldn't happen. But the folks came through, lightened my schedule, and allowed me to pretty much write at the office and have free rein over their AS/400.

From the bottom of my heart, thanks for the support to Jerry, Emily, Janice, Wally, Murray, Tom, and everyone at J2C+A. And I don't want to forget to thank Bob W., who kept the machine healthy when I occasionally "screwed up"—and for the great lunches!

CONTENTS

PREFACE

Welcome to the wonderful world of the AS/400!

It's hard to believe I wrote that two years ago.

Also hard to believe was the overwhelming response to this book's first version. I don't mean it to seem like a cliché, but I was truly humbled.

It has been good to see that so many fellow AS/400 advocates also needed the same information I needed, and that my once-overflowing file folder of scratched notes about how to do this and that did indeed contain information equally valuable to many others.

Like with my own children, it's hard to say I prefer one to the other, but I have to say that *The AS/400 Owner's Manual* has become the favorite of my books. Two reasons come to mind.

First—soon after the first edition came out—Midrange Computing's ace phone solicitor, (Acquisitions Editor) Leah Wilbur, happened to call me. I was on the phone with her a good 10 minutes getting hooked on this great new book before I realized she was talking about my own book! I had never heard one of my books pitched to me as if I were a customer and the experience was a new perspective. It really drove home what a great service this book provided.

Second, unlike my other books, a copy of *The AS/400 Owner's Manual* is always located next to my workstation. Technical books age quickly and my copy grew wrinkled with many notes inked in the margins. I don't know about other readers, but I can't get through a typical day without using it.

About a year ago, Merrikay Lee (my good friend and publishing guardian angel) suggested that I update the book. I demurred because the AS/400 always supports all the old stuff. The book was pretty basic (I thought) and didn't have anything that IBM would be upgrading (I thought). Boy, was I wrong.

In early 1998, I agreed to a rewrite and quickly realized how different the point of view is between day-to-day computer work and book writing. When I work on an AS/400 every day, I kind of grow with it. A little new thing today, another next week, then another—I really don't notice anything special going on.

But, when I write a book, I focus all my energies on it and, in this case, I realized that Version 4 introduces a lot of cool stuff for the AS/400 that just didn't exist when *The AS/400 Owner's Manual* first came out.

For example, consider Internet access. Version 4 gives the AS/400 tremendous Internet server power. But that's only half the equation. The other half is that the Internet has grown to a point where at least the consideration of the AS/400's almost native connectivity to this medium is of prime importance to any customer. When I wrote that new section (chapter 12), I was particularly proud to be a part of the AS/400 phenomenon.

Frankly, I can't wait for this new book to replace the battered copy on my own desk.

And I sincerely hope you find *The AS/400 Owner's Manual for Version 4* as useful as you found the first version. Like I also wrote two years ago:

Enjoy this book.

More importantly, enjoy the AS/400.

1 Starting the AS/400

1.1 Overview

Booting up an AS/400 is referred to as IPLing the AS/400. The abbreviation comes from the term *initial program load* (IPL). This is similar to booting or rebooting a personal computer (PC) except that an IPL does many more tasks. Compared to a PC boot, an IPL takes a lot more time and it is done less frequently.

1.2 License Key

New with Version 4 is the requirement for a license authorization code, or *license key,* to be entered into AS/400s upgrading from V3 and prior to V4. (Note: New AS/400 customers don't have to worry about this as IBM loads the password and provides a 70-day grace period.) An AS/400 without a license key will power up and IPL for 70 days. After 70 days, the AS/400 will not IPL again, although it will keep running until it is taken down for a re-IPL.

There is an ongoing penalty for running the AS/400 without a license key. Within the 70-day grace period, the AS/400 will issue a message every four hours to the system operator (and possibly the users as well) stating that a valid key has not been supplied. After the 70th day, the AS/400 will issue the message every hour.

To add the license key, just type in ADDLICKEY on any command line on the AS/400 and press the F4 key. Fill in the blanks on the screen and press the Enter key. If you forgot your code or for any reason don't have one, contact the company that sold you your AS/400 as soon as possible. For more information, refer to section 1.8 System Password.

1.3 What an IPL Does

An AS/400 IPL does more than just start the operating system. Additionally, it:

- Resets disk storage. This results in increasing available disk storage.
- Recognizes new licensed-program products.
- Optionally applies delayed PTFs.
- Recognizes some changes in system values.
- Unused addresses are returned to the system.

1.4 WHEN TO IPL

In general, if your AS/400 runs 24 hours per day, 7 days per week, schedule a routine IPL at least monthly. If you do this, performance will stay healthy. You will IPL any time:

- You power on the AS/400. After a power failure or any abnormal end, expect your IPL to take a very long time.
- After you've installed delayed PTFs. For additional information, see chapter 2, section 2.5 Program Temporary Fixes.
- After you've installed a new licensed program product (LPP) from IBM.
- You have a problem with the system (at IBM support's direction).
- Your ADDRESSES USED reaches 90 percent.
- Your SYSTEM AUXILIARY STORAGE reaches 95 percent.

Of the preceding items, the last two require some discussion. Check them both with the Work System Status (WRKSYSSTS) command. Just type on the command line:

```
WRKSYSSTS
```

When you do, you'll get a screen similar to the one shown in Figure 1-1.

```
                          Work with System Status                       TEST400
                                                             08/12/98  07:13:04
% CPU used . . . . . . . :            .9    Auxiliary storage:
Elapsed time . . . . . . :      00:00:28      System ASP . . . . . . :    14.55 G
Jobs in system . . . . . :           401      % system ASP used  . . :    39.9451
% addresses used:                             Total  . . . . . . . . :    14.55 G
  Permanent  . . . . . . :          .007      Current unprotect used :     360 M
  Temporary  . . . . . . :          .009      Maximum unprotect  . . :     368 M

Type changes (if allowed), press Enter.

System     Pool    Reserved    Max    -----DB-----  ---Non-DB---
 Pool    Size (K)  Size (K)  Active   Fault  Pages  Fault  Pages
   1      40920     22800     +++++     .0     .0     .9    1.8
   2      81972         0        20     .0     .0     .0     .0
   3       1308         0         1     .0     .0     .0     .0
   4       6872         0         6     .0     .0    3.2    5.4
```

Figure 1-1: Sample of WRKSYSSTS command.

Note that the permanent and temporary address percentages are shown as the fourth and fifth items in the upper left column. Together these should not exceed 90 percent.

The system auxiliary storage is shown as an absolute number and as a percentage on the top two fields of the right column. Don't let the percentage get above 95 percent or you'll start to experience serious system degradation.

An additional factor with the system auxiliary storage is that, although an IPL will return some storage to you, you might not regain enough storage. If this occurs, you will be forced to re-IPL soon. In this case, check the contents of the system auxiliary storage for libraries and files that aren't system related. I'm referring here to objects in ASP 1. Your system should be set up with ASP 1 dedicated to system objects and at least one other, ASP 2, to hold all non-system objects. For more information on ASPs, see chapter 3, section 3.4 DASD and User Auxiliary Storage Pools.

On a heavily utilized AS/400, addresses will creep up to 90 percent fairly quickly. Of course, upgrading to a larger model will solve that problem. While you're waiting for upgrade money to be available, schedule an IPL often enough to keep the addresses under control. Many at-capacity shops do a daily IPL.

1.5 Attended/Unattended and Manual/Normal IPLs

IPLs are designated as one of two broad categories: attended or unattended. An unattended IPL will, if it can, bring up sign-on displays on all attached terminals. In other words, it will attempt to get the whole system up. The attended IPL will bring up a sign-on display on the system console before it brings up the rest of the system. This is your chance to get in and make changes to the system before it gets all the way up.

Before I go any further, take note that the *control panel* is the flat panel physically on the front of every AS/400, old and new. The panel has a place to insert a physical key, some LCDs, and green lights. The *system console* is a workstation through which you access the AS/400. This workstation gets dubbed the "system console" because it is physically connected to the first address of the first input/output processor capable of supporting workstations. In addition, the system console is named DSP01. It runs at a higher priority than other workstations, and data entry (or programming) is not done on it.

You tell the AS/400 which IPL you'd like by changing the IPL *mode* on the AS/400 control panel. To set the mode on an AS/400, you must have the key in the slot. On older, gray-colored AS/400s, there was an actual key. On the black models the key is a black, rectangular piece of plastic with a chip inside called a *keystick*. To change mode on these AS/400s, insert the keystick and press the MODE switch until a light illuminates next to the word MANUAL. On the gray models, turn the key to the MANUAL position.

An IPL done with the AS/400 in manual mode is an attended IPL. The sign-on display will come up only on the system console and you'll have to sign on to continue the IPL.

Most AS/400 IPLs are done in *normal mode* (sometimes referred to as *auto* or *automatic mode*), which is another way of saying unattended IPL. If you ever have a need to do a manual IPL, return the system's mode setting to NORMAL when you're through. And remove and store the key if that is part of your security procedures.

If you're going to do an unattended IPL, check first that the System Value, QIPLTYPE, is set to 0 (allowing an unattended IPL). Use the WRKSYSVAL (Work with System Values) to display or change this variable. Keep the following tips in mind:

TIP: MANUAL = ATTENDED
NORMAL = UNATTENDED

Make it a standard practice to leave the mode in NORMAL and the System Value QIPLTYPE = 0.

1.6 STARTING THE IPL

An AS/400 IPL starts when the system is powered up after it has been powered off. There is no soft-boot command. Simple enough? Consider then the two states an AS/400 could be in at any time:

- It is powered off. Start the IPL through the control panel. Insert the key, set the mode, and press the Power button.
- It is powered on. Start the IPL by issuing the following command from any command line. (Security permitting, this command might be restricted to just the system console or it might be restricted to just the Security Office [SECOFR] or Security Administrator [SECADM]): P WRDWNSYS OP TION (*IMMED) RESTART (*YES)

In addition to these two planned states, the AS/400 could experience a power failure. When power is restored with PWRDWNSYS OPTION(*IMMED) RESTART (*YES), an IPL might be automatically started, but only if system value QPWRRSTIPL is set to 1. For more information, refer to section 1.7 System Values Important to IPLs.

1.6.1 What You Can Change with a Manual IPL

When you sign on to the display console during a manual IPL, you are presented with a menu of options. If you take Option 1, you'll have a chance to change several system options. Figure 1-2 shows the screen you'll see.

```
                         IPL Options

Type choices, press the Enter key.

  System date . . . . . . . . . . . . . . . .  XX / XX / XX    MM / DD
  System time . . . . . . . . . . . . . . . .  XX : XX : XX    HH / MM
  Clear job queues . . . . . . . . . . . . . . N               Y=Yes,
  Clear output queues  . . . . . . . . . . . . N               Y=Yes,
  Clear incomplete job logs  . . . . . . . . . N               Y=Yes,
  Start print writers  . . . . . . . . . . . . Y               Y=Yes,
  Start this device only . . . . . . . . . . . N               Y=Yes,
  Start the system to a restricted state . . . N               Y=Yes,
  Run #STRTUP1 procedure . . . . . . . . . . . Y               Y=Yes,
  Run #STRTUP2 procedure . . . . . . . . . . . Y               Y=Yes,
  Set major system options . . . . . . . . . . N               Y=Yes,
  Define or change system at IPL . . . . . . . N               Y=Yes,
```

Figure 1-2: IPL options that can be changed.

To change an option, simply position the cursor over it and type the new value. What you see next depends on what you entered for the last two parameters of the screen shown in Figure 1-2 (SET MAJOR SYSTEM OPTIONS and DEFINE OR CHANGE SYSTEM AT IPL). If you left them both No (N), you will see the menu/program/ procedure indicating that either you typed on the sign-on display or that it is a part of your user profile. For more information on user profiles, see chapter 5, section 5.2 Managing User Profiles.

If you put a Y on SET MAJOR SYSTEM OPTIONS, you'll see the menu discussed in section 1.5.1.1 Set Major System Options. If you put a Y on DEFINE OR CHANGE SYSTEM AT IPL, you'll get a menu with six options to change system configuration. Of these six, Option 3 allows you to change system values; it is the most useful of these options. For another, simpler, way to change system values, see section 1.7 System Values Important to IPLs.

1.6.1.1 Set Major System Options

If you indicated (with a Y on the SET MAJOR SYSTEM OPTIONS parameter) that you wanted to set some system options, you'll get the screen as shown in Figure 1-3.

```
                    Set Major System Options

Type choices, press the ENTER key.

  Enable automatic configuration . . . . . . . Y         Y=Yes, N=No
  Device configuaration naming . . . . . . . . *NORMAL   *NORMAL, *S36,
  Default special environment  . . . . . . . . *NONE     *NONE, *S36
```

Figure 1-3: Set major system options menu.

ENABLE AUTOMATIC CONFIGURATION tells the AS/400 to automatically configure any devices that start communicating with it that it doesn't recognize. Most AS/400 shops leave this at the default value Y (YES). If automatic configuration is selected, the AS/400 will want to know how you would like it to name the devices it creates. You can specify one of three options on the DEVICE CONFIGURATION NAMING parameter:

- *NORMAL (most common in AS/400 shops) names devices with a three-character prefix and a rotating numeric suffix. For example, displays are named DSP01, DSP02, etc., while printers are named PRT01, PRT02, etc.
- *S36 names devices with System/36 naming conventions. For example, displays are W1, W2, etc., while printers are P1, P2, etc.
- *DEVADR names devices using the device resource name. Examples would be DSP010203, PRT010204, etc. For additional information on resource names, see chapters 11 and 12.

The DEFAULT SPECIAL ENVIRONMENT sets up a System/36 environment for customers, migrating from a System/36, who need to run the SSP operating system on the AS/400.

1.7 System Values Important to IPLs

There are several system values that pertain specifically to IPLs on the AS/400. Display the current values of these and change them if you want by using the WORK WITH SYSTEM VALUES (WRKSYSVAL) command. Appendices A and B provide an overview of system values.

- QIPLDATTIM—IPL date and time. This is the date and time when the system will IPL itself automatically. Default value: *NONE.
- QIPLSTS—IPL status. Displays the way the system did the last IPL. You cannot change this value; you can only display it. Here are the codes and what they mean:
  - ✔ 0—an IPL from the control panel of the AS/400.
  - ✔ 1—an unattended IPL after a power failure (refer to system value QPWRRSTIPL).
  - ✔ 2—an unattended IPL after the PWRDWNSYS command with the RESTART(*YES) parameter.
  - ✔ 3—an unattended scheduled IPL as a result of system value QIPLDATTIM being used.
  - ✔ 4—an unattended remote IPL, with system value QRMTIPL being set to 1.

- QIPLTYPE—Defines the type of IPL the system will do from the control panel:
  - ✔ 0—an unattended IPL. No one needs to be there. However, if the control panel is set to manual mode, the IPL will be attended, manual.
  - ✔ 1—an attended IPL with dedicated service tools (DST). However, if the IPL is done via a remote AS/400, due to a value in QIPLDATTIM being reached, or after a power failure, an unattended, normal mode IPL will be done regardless of this system value.
  - ✔ 2—an attended IPL in debug mode. Set this only if you are experiencing problems with your AS/400 and only at the direction of the IBM CE or Rochester support.
- QPWRRSTIPL—Will the system automatically restart itself after a power failure?
  - ✔ 0—No automatic IPL after a power failure (most common setting).
  - ✔ 1—Automatic IPL after a power failure.
- QRMTIPL—Can a remote system start the AS/400?
  - ✔ 0—A remote system cannot start the AS/400.
  - ✔ 1—A remote system can start the AS/400.
- QUPSDLYTIM—If the AS/400 is connected to a smart, uninterruptible power supply (UPS), there is a set amount of time it will wait before it starts saving main storage and entering a controlled shutdown.
  - ✔ *BASIC or *CALC—*CALC is the default. Neither of these are very popular options. A numeric value is preferred.
  - ✔ *NOMAX—Is used when a user-written program controls the shutdown or when a generator will take over for the UPS after a few seconds.
  - ✔ 0—Automatic system shutdown starts as soon as the UPS kicks in.
  - ✔ 1-99999—The delay time in seconds before the system starts to shut itself down. This is the preferable method in most shops that rely only on a UPS. Work with your UPS engineer about the power consumption of your AS/400 and the rating of the UPS for a good time-delay figure.
- QUPSMSGQ—The message queue that receives messages about a power interruption. You can specify this as library/message queue.

1.8 System Password

New with Version 4, AS/400s have an internal password. It doesn't come up much and most people don't even know an internal password exists. When it does come up, you could have a problem. An internal password will come up anytime during an IPL when the system senses that either:

- The AS/400 model has changed.
- Certain service conditions appear.
- AS/400 ownership has changed

It helps to have your system password ready in case you're asked. If you don't have it, here's what you do.

Press the Enter key to get the VERIFICATION OF SYSTEM PASSWORD FAILED display. Take Option 2 (bypass the system password). After reading the information on the screen that the AS/400 presents, press F9 to continue with the IPL.

1.8.1 Request a New Password

Don't forget to request a new password from your sales rep because you are now running on borrowed time. You can help your sales rep by asking him or her to order RPQ S40345 (for United States, Asia Pacific, Canada, Latin America, or Japan) or RPQ S40346 (Europe, Middle East, or Asia).

If you bypassed your password, when you finally get one, you must enter it and the only way to do that is to perform an attended (manual) IPL. When the system asks you, take Option 1 (change the system password).

One final thing about system passwords—if you don't know yours, don't guess more than four times or you'll have to start the IPL again.

1.9 Is the IPL Progressing?

Most of the time, your IPLs are unattended routine events. Sometimes, however, IPLs are done as a result of a problem. In case there is a problem, it is important for you to be able to read the LCD lights on the AS/400 console. Here are the main items (italicized X's represent any letter or number):

- C1*XX* B*XXX*—Input/Output processor testing (1-5 minutes).
- C1*XX* 1*XXX*—Input/Output processor loading (1-10 minutes).
- C3*XX* 3*XXX*—System processor testing (2-10 minutes).
- C1*XX* 2*XXX*—System processor loading (2-10 minutes).
- C1*XX* 202E—Testing system main storage (30 seconds-10 minutes).
- C1*XX* D009 —System power hardware ready (10 seconds).
- C1*XX* 2034—IPL control passed to system processor (10 seconds).
- C6*XX* 4*XXX*—Testing system configuration (1-10 minutes).

If attended, the display will appear on the system console. Sign on and make any changes. After this point, the length of time of each step depends on the size of your system and its condition when it went down.

- C6*XX* 4*XXX*—IPLing the system.
- C6*XX* 4260—System disk data recovery.
- C9*XX* 2*XXX*—Operating system starting.
- C900 29C0—Operating system recovering.

1.10 IPL Storage Areas

An IPL can be made from one of two system storage areas: the A side or the B side. For the most part, you'll always be on the B side. Storage areas come into play when working with PTFs. For additional information, see chapter 2. To change the IPL storage area on the AS/400 physical console:

- Put the machine in manual mode (with the key in the slot, press the Mode button).
- Select Function 02 (with the Increment/Decrement button).
- Press the Enter button.
- Select storage area A, B, or D (with the Increment/Decrement button).
- Press the Enter button.
- Return the machine to the normal mode (with the key in the slot, press the Mode button).

1.11 Start a Remote AS/400 from a Host AS/400

On the remote system, make sure you have set system value QRMTIPL to a 1. This allows the system to be powered off, but it is able to accept a remote power-on command. For additional information, see section 1.7, System Values Important to IPLs.

Make sure the remote system's mode is set to NORMAL. Using the ECS (Electronic Customer Support) modem, dial the remote system from your local system. Wait while you hear the dial tone, ringing, and modem tone. After the modem tone, there will be silence. At this point, it is acceptable to break the connection to the remote system if you want. There are a few areas where problems occur with remote systems' startup.

- The remote modem is turned off. Therefore, you can't start it remotely.
- The remote modem is turned off and then on. The system might start to bring itself up.
- The local system operator breaks the phone connection too soon. Be certain to wait while the connection is made.

1.12 Powering the AS/400 Down

Be careful when powering down your AS/400. If you don't do it properly, the system will be said to have ended abnormally and the IPL will take longer. Depending on the size of your system and the damage from the abnormal end, it can take many hours to recover.

Before powering down your AS/400, make sure all batch jobs are ended and all users are signed off. Use the Work Active Jobs (WRKACTJOB) command to verify this. You might have to end some jobs yourself. When you do, use Option 4 on the WRKACTJOB screen, but press F4 before you press the Enter key. Override the *CNTRLD value with *IMMED on the screen you get, and then press the Enter key.

Remove any tapes or diskettes from their drives. Use either the PWRDWNSYS command or GO POWER.

If you're really in a bind where there is just no way to power down the AS/400, you can use the power button on the control console. But consider this a last resort only! Chances are very high that the IPL that follows such a step will be considered an abnormal IPL and will take additional recovery time.

To turn the AS/400 off with the power switch, make sure tapes and diskettes are out of their drives and the control panel mode is set to manual. Then press the power button. The control panel will give you a cryptic warning by displaying 0?. If you want to continue with the power down, press the power button again. If you want to stop the power down, press any other button on the control console.

After pressing the power button a second time, the power light on the console will flash as the AS/400 powers down. When the power is off, the light will go off. If the light flashes for approximately 30 minutes and still hasn't powered down, the System Attention light will light on the panel. If that happens, you've got a problem beyond the scope of this book. Call for service.

1.13 AUTOMATICALLY POWERING YOUR SYSTEM ON AND OFF

While automatically powering your system on and off isn't strictly an IPL issue, I will discuss it here. You can have your AS/400 power itself on and off using any schedule you like. This method isn't used very much in 24-hour AS/400 shops or even 16-hour shops. A problem can occur if the automatic power-off happens in the middle of a nightly process that, for some reason, goes beyond its scheduled end time. Automatic power on and off is better suited for weekend and holiday shutdowns and for 8-hour shops.

To set your own power on-and-off schedule, type GO POWER on any command line and take Option 2 (CHANGE POWER ON AND OFF SCHEDULE). From that screen, immediately press the F10 (CHANGE POWER ON/OFF DEFAULTS). The screen you'll get is shown in Figure 1-4.

```
                      Change Power On/Off Defaults
                                                          System:   TEST400
Type choices below, then press Enter.

First day of week . . . . . . . . .   1    1=Sunday, 2=Monday, 3=Tuesday,
                                           4=Wednesday, 5=Thursday, 6=Friday,
                                           7=Saturday

Minutes before power off to send
  message . . . . . . . . . . . . .   30   0-60

                        Default       Default
Week                    Power         Power
Day                     On            Off
Sunday                  ________      ________
Monday                  05:30:00      ________
Tuesday                 ________      ________
Wednesday               ________      ________
Thursday                ________      ________
Friday                  ________      20:00:00
Saturday                ________      ________
```

Figure 1-4: Change automatic power on/off defaults.

Actually, I put in the times 05:30:00 and 20:00:00. Normally the command would display these lines blank or a previously entered schedule.

The "schedule" is predicated on the same thing happening each day of the week. In the example, the system is set to power off at 8:00 P.M. Friday and to power itself back on at 5:30 A.M. Monday. Prior to going down on Friday evening, the system will send a message to all users 30 minutes prior to shutting down. Note the MINUTES BEFORE POWER OFF TO SEND MESSAGE parameter in the upper part of the figure. The value can be changed from no message (0 minutes) to 60 minutes.

When the message appears, a security administrator (SECADMIN) or security officer (SECOFR) can delay shutdown for up to three hours. But that's the last opportunity to delay a shutdown before the system comes down. For additional information on the role of security administrators and security officers, see chapter 6.

Return to the CHANGE POWER ON/OFF SCHEDULE screen (the screen used earlier to set defaults) by pressing F12. Figure 1-5 shows what it looks like with defaults set up.

```
                         Change Power On/Off Schedule                  TEST400
                                                             08/12/98  07:21:55
Start list at  . . . . . . . .   ________          Date

Change times and descriptions below, then press Enter.  To change defaults,
  press F10.

                    Power      Power
Date       Day      On         Off        Description
08/12/98   Wed      ________   ________   ______________________________________
08/13/98   Thu      ________   ________   ______________________________________
08/14/98   Fri      ________   20:00:00   ______________________________________
08/15/98   Sat      ________   ________   ______________________________________

08/16/98   Sun      ________   ________   ______________________________________
08/17/98   Mon      05:30:00   ________   ______________________________________
08/18/98   Tue      ________   ________   ______________________________________
08/19/98   Wed      ________   ________   ______________________________________
08/20/98   Thu      ________   ________   ______________________________________
08/21/98   Fri      ________   20:00:00   ______________________________________
08/22/98   Sat      ________   ________   ______________________________________
                                                                        More...
```

Figure 1-5: Automatic power on/off schedule.

You can make schedule changes on this screen. Also, you can document why you made changes. You could even do all your on/off schedules on this screen. For the most part, however, power schedules are meant to be driven by the defaults screen.

Before you assume everything will go on and off on schedule, double-check that the AS/400 control panel mode is set to NORMAL. If it is left in MANUAL, even an automatic IPL will hang up with a sign-on screen on the system console. Also verify that System Value QIPLTYPE is set to 0.

1.14 REFERENCES

AS/400 Basic System Operation, Administration, and Problem Handling V4R3 (SC41-5206-02)

AS/400 System Operation V3R6 (SC41-4203-00)

2 Operating Systems, Licensed Program Products, and PTFs

2.1 Overview

The software on your AS/400 consists of the IBM-supplied software and software from other vendors. This book focuses on only the IBM-supplied software, and that software consists of three main parts:

- The operating system, called OS/400.
- Any number of optional Licensed Program Products (LPPs).
- Any number of optional Programming Request for Price Quotations (PRPQs).

The basic OS/400 has quite a lot in it: you can run many applications without purchasing anything else. LPPs are other software items that you purchase in addition to OS/400. LPPs include things like compilers, Office Vision, Backup/Recovery Management System (BRMS), and many others. PRPQs are basically something that either IBM developed on its own or, more likely, a customer felt was so necessary that the customer paid for IBM to develop it. In each case, IBM then decided the product would be profitable to sell to other customers, but not profitable enough to support. So PRPQs are offered to everyone for a generally low price and are unsupported.

All three basic pieces of software are continually improved through periodic releases of the software and through ongoing Program Temporary Fixes (PTFs).

2.1.1 New Releases

Let's start with new releases of software. Generally, new releases of LPPs and PRPQs are combined within a new release of the OS/400 operating system. When you decide it's time to upgrade your OS/400 to a new release, you'll also get new releases of all your IBM-supplied software.

There are three levels of the name of an OS/400 release: version, release, and modification levels. When AS/400 people speak of a new release, they often drop the modification level. They also refer to the version and release simply by the letters V and R. For example, Version 4, Release 2, Modification 00 is just called "V 4 R 2."

New releases are generally offered in roughly 18-month intervals. When they are available, they come with lots of fanfare from your local branch and every AS/400 news medium. It's almost impossible to miss a new release of OS/400.

Because they are available for years, you can decide when you would like to install a new operating system release. A good rule of thumb when dealing with anything from IBM is never be the first to get it and never be the last. Give all releases a while to settle in. Let other customers find out how stable the release is and, when you're comfortable, order and install it.

2.1.2 PTFs

PTFs are replacements for specific objects within OS/400 or LPPs. PTFs come out at any time in any frequency. They become available with little fanfare and you can go a long time without even being aware of them. They have weird codified names and you'll have to make an effort to know what problem each one fixes.

The two types of PTFs are normal and high-impact pervasive PTFs (better known as HIPER). HIPERs are PTFs that are quite serious. If you ever learn about a HIPER PTF that you haven't installed on your system, do so as soon as is humanly possible.

If you don't know when they're available or what they do, how do you keep on top of PTFs? IBM offers a service known as Preventive Service Planning (PSP) and it offers lots of help for keeping up with PTFs. PSP has general information about licensed program products, their cumulative PTF tapes, new releases of the operating system, and so on. The service tells you the HIPERs discovered on the operating system or LPPs and will tell you if any previous PTFs were found to be in error. Also, the service gives you tips and techniques about installing releases and PTFs. The tips and techniques should be reviewed prior to installing a cumulative PTF tape and from time to time just to review what Rochester is doing about the software on your system.

PSPs are available from IBM as a free service. Contact your marketer for information about signing up. Another way to keep current with HIPERs is through the Internet at:

www.as/400service.ibm.com

All that PTF jargon sounds intimidating, but keeping up with PTFs in reality can be a low-impact job. IBM always has a cumulative tape available that contains all the PTFs for a given release. Unless you're having a problem, just order the latest tape about every six months and install whatever is on it.

Sometimes, a new release of OS/400 or an LPP is a little "rough." In those cases, order and install the cumulative tape more frequently. If you do wait six months, problems can be unwieldy.

PRPQs generally don't have PTFs. But if they do, the PTFs are for something fairly serious. Make sure you get them. PTFs are discussed in more detail in section 2.5 Program Temporary Fixes.

2.2 Ordering New Releases

When you order a new release of the operating system, you will get:

- OS/400 and licensed internal code (LIC).
- All current PTFs for new OS/400 and LIC.
- Licensed product program(s).
- All current PTFs for licensed product program(s).
- PRPQs and all current PTFs for them.

You place your order directly with your independent reseller (IR), value-added reseller (VAR), or direct from IBM. You usually will talk to someone over the phone and then follow up with a letter specifying the order in writing.

This sounds simpler than it is. When you originally purchased your AS/400, whomever you purchased it from is the holder of your customer profile. As far as IBM is concerned, this is the company that will handle all your future purchases. That's all right until your profile gets out of date. If you shop around for the best deals and add to your system from other dealers of AS/400 equipment and software, your profile could become out of date.

Consequently, when you order a new release of the operating system, the organization holding your profile might not know what equipment and software you currently own. It's your responsibility to ensure the release you are ordering will cover everything currently on your system. Hence, the initial discussion with the marketer prior to ordering new software. Always ask for a list of what the marketer thinks you have on your AS/400 and what is being ordered. Double-check that against what you really do have on your machine.

I can't stress enough that you should make a double-check of your configuration before making the order and to double-check the release again before starting its installation. This is especially true on the first order after you've initially installed the licensed program product. Frequently, your first OS release upgrade after a LPP has been installed will come minus the LPP.

When you order a new release of the operating system, PRPQs might not be automatically shipped with that release. Even if they are shipped with the release, they usually come with their own installation instructions. Ask specifically and triple-check for PRPQs and their PTFs when you order a new release.

2.3 OS/400 Release Installation

Installing a new release isn't to be taken lightly. Plan to spend at least a weekend at it. If you have enough people, you can divide the weekend up so the installation process continues round the clock until it is finished.

First, do all your preparation. Then immediately prior to the installation weekend, contact IBM software support or your IR and ask them to double-check your planning just to see if you missed anything.

2.3.1 Planning

The planning part of installing a new release is as crucial as the actual installation. Release installation generally means spending weekend-time, and the process is quite lengthy. You don't want any surprises when you are doing a release installation. If the release fails to install, you'll have to reinstall the old system. It's your weekend. Do as much work as you can up-front to ensure you encounter no surprises.

Probably, the first thing you should determine is whether it is even possible to install the new release. This little matter will hinge on two things:

- The release level already on your system compared with the release level you want to install.
- The size of your system, how much of the system you have been using, and how much additional system space the new release will require.

First, check the release installation instructions for previous releases on your system so that you won't have a conflict when you load the new release. For example, when V3R1 came out, it could be installed only on AS/400s that already had V2R1M0, V2R2M1, V2R2M0, or V2R3M0. At that time, any Version 1 machines had to go to one of those V2Rx releases before it could go to V2R3. If you do not know what release level is currently on your machine, see section 2.3.1.2 Planning—What Release Level Am I on Now?

New releases come with installation sizing, timing, and performance information. This information is in the *Installation Guide* that comes with the release, and it is also included as a utility. The utility is a program you run on your AS/400. Its purpose is to give you very accurate sizing and timing information—as those factors can be highly dependant on the model and current capacity of the AS/400.

Use the timing figures from the utility intelligently. If your window for installation is a weekend (it usually is), make sure a weekend will be long enough to do the work and assign people to handle different aspects of the installation during that time.

Use whatever resources are available to ensure that you'll have enough memory and DASD to support the new release. Prior to installing a new release is a perfect time to look over your system and clean up libraries, files, and programs you no longer need.

Make sure you have received a copy of the current PTF cumulative package if one is available. Or, if the release is very fresh, there will be no outstanding PTFs so there won't be a cumulative package. Check this out with your marketing person, through the PSPs, or over the Internet before you commit to an upgrade date. Check the release instructions for:

- PTFs that need to be applied before the new relase can be installed. Don't continue if the minimum-required PTFs aren't installed. Apply the PTFs a week or so prior to the release installation.
- If your AS/400 connects to one or more other AS/400s on a network of any kind, and they are not being upgraded together, check for the *interoperability* of the two releases. Interoperability refers to the capability of the two machines to send/receive or save/restore each other's data. This is also a good idea if you are upgrading two or more networked AS/400s and you plan to do them together. This research will tell you what your exposure will be if one completes the installation but the other doesn't.

If you are installing from a tape:

- Clean the drive before you begin.
- Ensure the drive is designated ONLINE AT IPL. To do this, use the DSPDEVD command. Enter the tape-device description name and check the screen that displays. It will have the words, ONLINE AT IPL and either a *YES or *NO with them. If *NO appears, select another device that is online at IPL or change the one with the CHGDEVD command.

2.3.1.1 Planning—Appropriate Directories

Enter DSPDIRE (Display Directory Entry) on the command line. This will display all the users on your system. Verify that QSECOFR and QLPINSTL are there. See Figure 20-1.

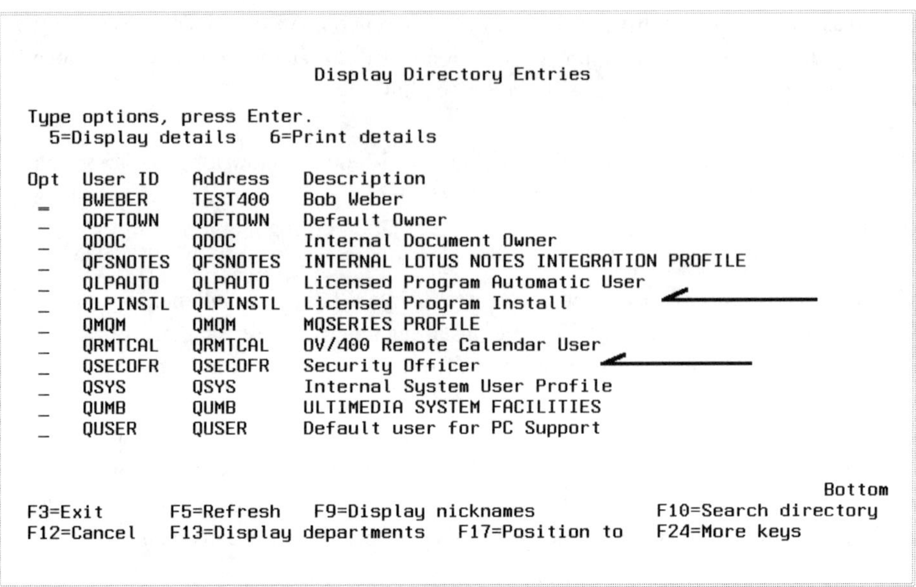

```
                     Display Directory Entries

Type options, press Enter.
  5=Display details   6=Print details

Opt  User ID   Address   Description
 _   BWEBER    TEST400   Bob Weber
 _   QDFTOWN   QDFTOWN   Default Owner
 _   QDOC      QDOC      Internal Document Owner
 _   QFSNOTES  QFSNOTES  INTERNAL LOTUS NOTES INTEGRATION PROFILE
 _   QLPAUTO   QLPAUTO   Licensed Program Automatic User
 _   QLPINSTL  QLPINSTL  Licensed Program Install
 _   QMQM      QMQM      MQSERIES PROFILE
 _   QRMTCAL   QRMTCAL   OV/400 Remote Calendar User
 _   QSECOFR   QSECOFR   Security Officer
 _   QSYS      QSYS      Internal System User Profile
 _   QUMB      QUMB      ULTIMEDIA SYSTEM FACILITIES
 _   QUSER     QUSER     Default user for PC Support

                                                                Bottom
F3=Exit      F5=Refresh   F9=Display nicknames          F10=Search directory
F12=Cancel   F13=Display departments   F17=Position to  F24=More keys
```

Figure 2-1: Output from DSPDIRE command.

If either is not present, add the missing data with the following appropriate command:

```
ADDDIRE USRID(QSECOFR QSECOFR) USRD( 'Security Officer') +
     USER(QSECOFR)
ADDDIRE USRID(QLPINSTL QLPINSTL) USRD( 'Licensed Program +
     Install')  USER(QLPINSTL)
```

2.3.1.2 Planning—What Release Level Am I on Now?

Enter GO LICPGM (Go to Licensed Programs) on the command line. See Figure 2-2.

```
LICPGM                      Work with Licensed Programs
                                                          System:   TEST400
Select one of the following:

  Manual Install
     1. Install all

  Preparation
     5. Prepare for install

  Licensed Programs
    10. Display installed licensed programs
    11. Install licensed programs
    12. Delete licensed programs
    13. Save licensed programs


                                                                  More...
Selection or command
===> 10_
```

Figure 2-2: Initial menu for GO LICPGM.

Take Option 10 from the menu. From that screen, press F11—Display Release. This gives you the release level of OS/400 for that machine. See Figure 2-3.

```
_                      Display Installed Licensed Programs
                                                                System:
 Licensed  Installed
 Program   Release     Description
 5769SS1   V4R2M0 L00  OS/400 - Library QGPL
 5769SS1   V4R2M0 L00  OS/400 - Library QUSRSYS
 5769SS1   V4R2M0 L00  Operating System/400
 5769SS1   V4R2M0      OS/400 - Extended Base Support
 5769SS1   V4R2M0      OS/400 - Online Information
 5769SS1   V4R2M0      OS/400 - Extended Base Directory Support
```

Figure 2-3: Detail of OS/400 and LICPGM installed.

The release level is in the column labeled "Installed Release." There is one for each piece of OS/400. If you happen to scroll through and see different versions of the release level, determine if they are for support of previous versions of programming languages (described something like *PRV). If they are for different versions of the release level, don't worry about them. If they aren't for different versions, check with your marketer. Note the release level listed for the bulk of your OS/400 modules.

2.3.1.3 Planning—Traps

If you've made changes to IBM-supplied objects in libraries other than QGPL and QUSRSYS, those changes will be lost. Some examples are:

- Changes to subsystem descriptions.
- Changes to IBM-supplied printers (like QPRINT) for things like rotation, lines-per-inch, and characters-per-inch.
- Some customers make duplicates of IBM commands. If you have duplicates and these are stored in Q-libraries other than the two mentioned above, those commands will be lost.
- If you've built your own logical files over IBM-supplied physical files (created on the fly when using commands that have OUTPUT(*OUTFILE) capability).

The preceding are just some of the examples. You will want to brainstorm with your staff for others. If you have any of these changes, either save the objects for separate restoration later or document the changes so you can redo them after the installation.

2.3.2 Saving the System

After you've done adequate planning, and immediately before you start installing a new release, always save your system with the SAVSYS command. If there is any problem with the installation, you will have to use this tape to restore your system. Of course, this step is not for customers installing OS/400 on new machines.

To save your system, you must be user QSYSOPR, QSECOFR, or be a user with the specific SAVSYS authorities (see chapter 5). Select the tape drive that is online at IPL (see section 2.3.1 Planning). Set aside a number of scratchable tapes, mount one of those tapes on a tape device, and enter the command:

```
SAVSYS <tape device name>
```

2.3.3 Installing the Release

You'll find that after all the preparation, actually installing the release can be boring, and that's good—you don't want exciting.

2.3.3.1 Automatic/Manual Installation

There are two modes of release installation: AUTOMATIC and MANUAL. You will use AUTOMATIC (sometimes called NORMAL) most of the time. AUTOMATIC is the faster method.

Like the name implies, AUTOMATIC will install the new release (plus optional licensed program products already installed on your system). If you are planning to do one or more of the following, use MANUAL release installation to:

- Add DASD using mirroring, device parity, or user ASP (auxiliary storage pool).
- Change the primary language (national, not programming) of the machine.
- Change the environment of the AS/400 (to S/36 for example) or change system default values or system configuration.
- Use tapes that were created with the SAVSYS (Save System) command.
- See if you have duplicated IBM libraries (the ones that start with a Q) on your system.
- Install for the first time one or more licensed program product on your machine.

Your new release package will contain release instructions in a document called the *Installation Guide*. Within that document are checklists for doing each step of the installation. Depending on which method you use, make sure you pull the checklist for AUTOMATIC or MANUAL installation. If you follow those steps, you shouldn't have a problem. But be careful! Sometimes waiting for the installation is so tedious that you forget a step from the checklist.

The *Installation Guide* even indicates which steps are fairly long. Therefore, you can allocate your installation activities efficiently. Most of the time, release loading is flawless, but always be prepared for the worst. Make sure you've done your homework and that you have your system saved just in case.

2.3.3.2 Installation—Tips to Save Time When Installing a New Release

Use automatic mode if you can. Delete all QHST files to prevent them from being saved as system files. Enter on the command line:

```
WRKOBJ QSYS/QHST* *FILE
```

When the files are displayed, use a 4 and delete them all.

End all subsystems before starting. Enter on the command line:

```
ENDSBS *ALL
```

2.4 Installing New Licensed Products

Sometimes you need to add new products to your AS/400. You initially install these manually. Later, when you install a new operating system release, new product versions should be included on the release media. This section is about how to do the initial installation of these products.

First, perform the planning steps outlined in section 2.3.1 Planning. Sign on to the system as QSECOFR. Load the media containing the new licensed program product on the appropriate drive. Change the message queue with the following command:

```
CHGMSGQ QSYSOPR *BREAK SEV(60)
```

End all subsystems with the command:

```
ENDSBS  *ALL  *IMMED
```

Change the message queue again with the command:

```
CHGMSGQ  QSYSOPR  *BREAK  SEV(95)
```

Enter the command:

```
GO  LICPGM
```

Take Option 11, INSTALL LICENSED PROGRAMS. See Figure 2-4.

```
                              Install Licensed Programs
                                                            System:   TEST400
 Type options, press Enter.
   1=Install

        Licensed  Installed
 Option Program   Status        Description
   _    5769SS1   *COMPATIBLE   OS/400 - Library QGPL
   _    5769SS1   *COMPATIBLE   OS/400 - Library QUSRSYS
   _    5769SS1   *COMPATIBLE   OS/400 - Extended Base Support
   _    5769SS1   *COMPATIBLE   OS/400 - Online Information
   _    5769SS1   *COMPATIBLE   OS/400 - Extended Base Directory Support
   _    5769SS1   *COMPATIBLE   OS/400 - S/36 and S/38 Migration
   _    5769SS1   *COMPATIBLE   OS/400 - System/36 Environment
   _    5769SS1   *COMPATIBLE   OS/400 - System/38 Environment
   _    5769SS1   *COMPATIBLE   OS/400 - Example Tools Library
   _    5769SS1   *COMPATIBLE   OS/400 - AFP Compatibility Fonts
   _    5769SS1   *COMPATIBLE   OS/400 - *PRV CL Compiler Support
   _    5769SS1   *COMPATIBLE   OS/400 - S/36 Migration Assistant
   _    5769SS1   *COMPATIBLE   OS/400 - Host Servers
                                                                     More...
```

Figure 2-4: Detail of INSTALL LICENSED PROGRAM menu.

Install the new LPP by placing a 1 next to it. Next, install any PTFs that came with the LPP. If the LPP you plan to install is not listed on the Figure 2-4 screen, check the installation instructions that came with the LPP.

If the LPP is large enough, it might span multiple media volumes. If this is the case, you'll get a message when the system is ready for the next volume. When you get the message, first insert the volume and then respond to the message with the appropriate response (usually a "G" but always read the message first).

The new product won't run until you re-IPL the AS/400. An IPL is required to run the Initialize System (INZSYS) process. Without this step, the new product won't work.

Make a fresh save of your system after the IPL is complete (see section 2.3.2 Saving the System). Although you don't have to use manual installation if you have PRPQs, keep in mind that they generally require special installations and, therefore, are done manually. They come with their own instructions to do this.

2.5 Program Temporary Fixes

As I mentioned at the beginning of this chapter, PTFs are fixes to bugs discovered in the operating system or in program products. Sometimes they are enhancements. They are a way of life on any computer software.

Always follow the instructions that come with your PTFs. Learn how they are applied and how previous, temporary PTFs are to be treated. Temporary PTFs might have to be permanently applied or they might have to be removed before applying any new PTFs.

This section refers to several specific commands. An optional path to the same commands is to type GO PTF on the command line. You will get a menu from which you can easily get to the PTF functions (ordering, loading, applying, etc.).

2.5.1 Keeping Current with and Ordering PTFs

PTFs take more effort to keep up with than new OS releases. You can order PTFs through:

- Your marketing representative.
- Via a telephone call to AS/400 Service.
- On your AS/400 through the ECS modem (this may be the most convenient way).
- Over the Internet at: www.as400service.ibm.com/

But first you still have the problem of keeping up with PTFs so that you'll know what to order. Fortunately, you use the same command to keep updated and to order PTFs.

2.5.1.1 Keeping Current and Ordering through the AS/400

You will probably want to know two things about PTFs:

- What PTFs are currently on your AS/400 and their status (temporarily or permanently applied).
- What PTFs are currently available and their relative importance (normal or HIPER).

Check the PTFs already on your own AS/400 with the WRKPTF command. Just type WRKPTF on any command line, press Enter, then press the F11 key twice, and you'll get a screen similar to the one shown in Figure 2-5.

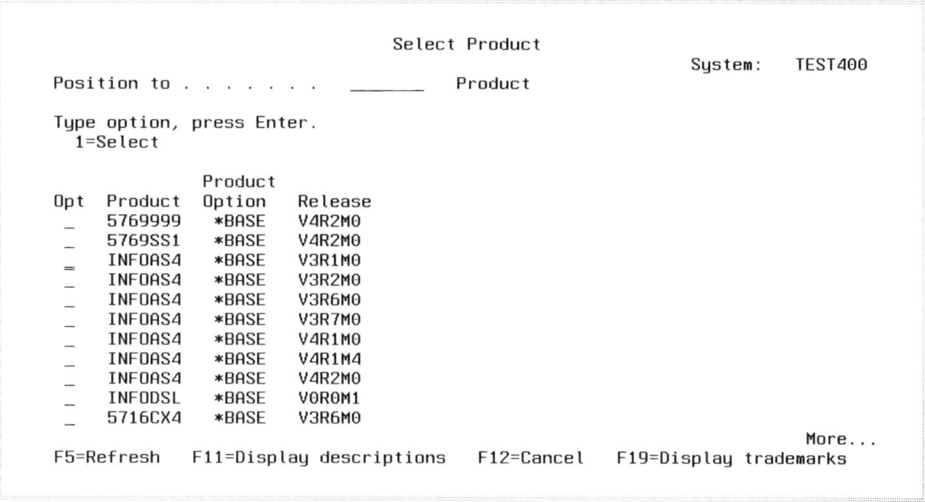

```
                         Select Product
                                                      System:   TEST400
Position to . . . . . . .  _______  Product

Type option, press Enter.
  1=Select

              Product
Opt  Product  Option   Release
 _   5769999   *BASE   V4R2M0
 _   5769SS1   *BASE   V4R2M0
 _   INFOAS4   *BASE   V3R1M0
 _   INFOAS4   *BASE   V3R2M0
 _   INFOAS4   *BASE   V3R6M0
 _   INFOAS4   *BASE   V3R7M0
 _   INFOAS4   *BASE   V4R1M0
 _   INFOAS4   *BASE   V4R1M4
 _   INFOAS4   *BASE   V4R2M0
 _   INFODSL   *BASE   V0R0M1
 _   5716CX4   *BASE   V3R6M0
                                                                More...
F5=Refresh   F11=Display descriptions   F12=Cancel   F19=Display trademarks
```

Figure 2-5: The PTFs currently installed on my AS/400.

The current release is in the fourth column. To find out what PTFs are available, use one of the four PTF ordering codes. Those four codes are PTFs designed to order general products for you. You use them through the command SNDPTFORD (Send PTF Order). Here is its general form:

```
SNDPTFORD SFyyvrm
```

Where yy is one of the following:

yy value	to order
97	*PTF Summary List*
98	*PSP for Software*
99	*Cumulative PTF Package*

The values *v, r,* and *m* stand for the version, release, and modification level you will want to specify. For example, V4R1M5 would be 415 and V4R3 would be 420.

One other order code is used to order PSPs for hardware:

```
SNDPTFORD MF98vrm
```

Where VRM has the same meaning described above.

To use these to keep current by using these commands is to issue a PTF "order":

```
SNDPTFORD SF97vrm
```

But when you get the resulting screen, fill it out similar to how it's shown in Figure 2-6. You won't get any PTFs, but you'll get a printout of summaries of each available PTF. This isn't a bad thing to obtain and review from time to time.

```
                          Send PTF Order (SNDPTFORD)

 Type choices, press Enter.

 PTF description:
   PTF identifier . . . . . . . . > SF97420        Character value
   Product  . . . . . . . . . . .   *ONLYPRD       F4 for list
   Release  . . . . . . . . . . .   *ONLYRLS       *ONLYRLS, VxRxMx
                + for more values _
 PTF parts  . . . . . . . . . . . > *CVRLTR        *ALL, *CVRLTR
 Remote control point . . . . . .   *IBMSRV        Name, *IBMSRV, *SELECT
 Remote network identifier  . . .   *NETATR        Name, *NETATR
```

Figure 2-6 Screen to order PTFs.

2.5.1.2 Ordering Cumulative PTF Package and Cross-Reference PTF

The cumulative PTF used to come on a set of tapes. Today it comes on CD-ROM.

```
SNDPTFORD SF99vrm
```

The contents of VRM are described above.

When you press Enter after typing the command, you'll get a screen that gives you a chance to verify or change the mailing address and contact name. Figure 2-7 shows the screen.

Refer to section 2.5.1.4, Common Order Screens, for two additional screens common to all PTF orders.

When upgrading to a new release, you'll also order the current cumulative PTF package and install it. After all, you want all the known problems fixed, right? But sometimes problems fixed by PTFs on your older release are not part of the new release. In such cases, another PTF number will still be required to fix the same problem.

```
                          Verify Contact Information
                                                           System:    SYS02
 Type changes, press Enter.

   Company . . . . . . . . . .   World Wide Widgets, Inc.
   Contact . . . . . . . . . .   Mike Dawson
   Mailing address:
     Street address  . . . . .   999 N. Any Drive


     City/State  . . . . . . .   Scottsdale, AZ
     Country . . . . . . . . .   USA
     Zip code  . . . . . . . .   85999
   Telephone numbers:
     Primary . . . . . . . . .   602-555-1234
     Alternative . . . . . . .
   Fax telephone numbers:
     Primary . . . . . . . . .
     Alternative . . . . . . .
   National language version     2924    F4 for list
                                                                     Bottom
 F3=Exit   F4=Prompt   F5=Refresh   F12=Cancel
```

Figure 2-7: Screen to change delivery information for the cumulative PTF tape.

Just to make sure you're covered, you can order the *Cross-Reference PTF.* This is a list of PTF numbers from an old release and their new PTF numbers on the new release. Use this list to cross-check the PTF numbers, applied on your new release, just to make sure you didn't fix anything.

Imagine, a year ago, you had a problem and fixed it by downloading and applying a PTF. You've since forgotten all about the original problem. Now you're upgrading to V4R3 of the operating system and have it and the cumulative PTF package. If that PTF has not been made part of V4R3 and is not in the PTF package, your old problem will come back to haunt you again.

There are five new order commands to cover possible cross-references to V4R3M0. They are:

```
SNDPTFORD SF97075 (from V2R3M0)
SNDPTFORD SF97023 (from V3R2M0)
SNDPTFORD SF97052 (from V3R7M0)
SNDPTFORD SF97057 (from V4R1M0)
SNDPTFORD SF97095 (from V4R3M0)
```

2.5.1.3 Ordering Non-Cumulative PTFs

After you've checked for available PTFs by reviewing their cover letters, you can order through the Electronic Customer Support (ECS) modem on your AS/400. Enter the command:

```
SNDPTFORD  SF97vrm
```

If you prompt the command, and ask for additional parameters, you will get a screen like the one shown in Figure 2-8.

```
                         Send PTF Order (SNDPTFORD)

 Type choices, press Enter.

 PTF description:                 _
   PTF identifier . . . . . . . . > SF97420        Character value
   Product  . . . . . . . . . . .   *ONLYPRD       F4 for list
   Release  . . . . . . . . . . .   *ONLYRLS       *ONLYRLS, VxRxMx
              + for more values _
 PTF parts  . . . . . . . . . . .   *ALL           *ALL, *CVRLTR
 Remote control point . . . . . .   *IBMSRV        Name, *IBMSRV, *SELECT
 Remote network identifier  . . .   *NETATR        Name, *NETATR

                          Additional Parameters

 Delivery method  . . . . . . . .   *LINKONLY      *ANY, *LINKONLY
 Order  . . . . . . . . . . . . .   *REQUIRED      *REQUIRED, *PTFID
 Reorder  . . . . . . . . . . . .   *NO            *NO, *YES
 Check PTF  . . . . . . . . . . .   *NO            *NO, *YES
```

Figure 2-8: Ordering PTF through the AS/400's ECS modem.

As shown in Figure 2-8, you can order one PTF (by entering its number in PTF IDENTIFIER). By entering a plus sign (on the + FOR MORE VALUES parameter), you can order many PTFs. You can order complete PTFs (PTFs with cover letters) or only cover letters so you can review them and decide if you want the PTF. If you're reviewing cover letters, they contain the release they are valid for starting with V4R3M0.

If you order a PTF that requires prerequisite PTFs before it can be installed, you'll get them automatically. Don't be confused if you order one PTF and receive three or four.

On the other hand, if you order a PTF that has been superseded, you won't get the higher level. For example, if you order PTF 5 and it requires that PTF 3 and 4 be installed before 5 can be installed, you'll get PTFs 3, 4, and 5. However, if a PTF has been superseded by PTF 6, you won't get PTF 6. Two things to keep in mind are:

- Know the whole set of available PTFs by reviewing cover letters or investigating on the Internet.
- Always work from a current cumulative package.

IBM will attempt to send your PTF order using the ECS link. If you specified *ANY for DELIVERY METHOD and what you ordered is too large to ship by the link, IBM will make you a tape or CD-ROM. If what you ordered is also too large for a single volume, you'll hear from your marketing representative.

If you specified *LINKONLY for DELIVERY METHOD and what you ordered is too large to ship using the link, you'll get a message right away at the bottom of the order screen. You then can break the order into several smaller orders.

Normally, you don't get PTFs that you've previously received. This control can be nice. However, if you've lost the previous PTFs (as often happens), and you want those PTFs, specify *YES on the REORDER keyword.

The CHECK PTF keyword specifies whether the order program should check if the PTF being ordered is already installed or supported on your machine. Refer to section 2.5.1.4 Common Order Screens, for two additional screens common to all PTF orders.

2.5.1.4 Common Order Screens

Whether you order cover letters only, cumulative packages, or specific PTFs, you use the SNDPTFORD command as described above. When you press the Enter key, you'll get two verification screens. The first screen (as shown in Figure 2-9) allows you to change the shipping address and contact person:

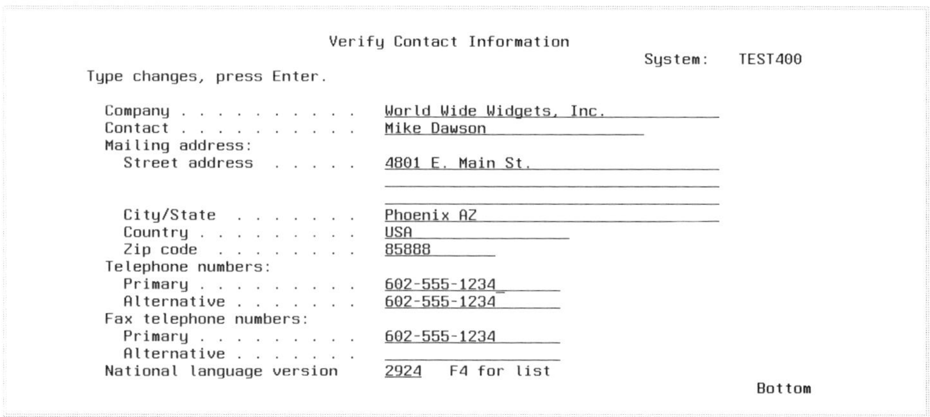
```
                         Verify Contact Information
                                                         System:   TEST400
 Type changes, press Enter.

   Company . . . . . . . . . .   World Wide Widgets, Inc.
   Contact . . . . . . . . . .   Mike Dawson
   Mailing address:
     Street address  . . . . .   4801 E. Main St.


     City/State  . . . . . . .   Phoenix AZ
     Country . . . . . . . . .   USA
     Zip code  . . . . . . . .   85888
   Telephone numbers:
     Primary . . . . . . . . .   602-555-1234
     Alternative . . . . . . .   602-555-1234
   Fax telephone numbers:
     Primary . . . . . . . . .   602-555-1234
     Alternative . . . . . . .
   National language version     2924    F4 for list
                                                                 Bottom
```

Figure 2-9: Shipping and contact information change after SNDPTFORD.

After you press the Enter key from the screen shown in Figure 2-9, you'll have one last chance to really send or not send the order. Refer to the screen shown in Figure 2-10:

```
                    Select Reporting Option
                                                   System:   TEST400
Problem ID . . . . . . . . . . :     9822847136
Current status . . . . . . . . :     READY
Problem  . . . . . . . . . . . :     PTF summary information requested.


Select one of the following:

     1. Send service request now
     2. Do not send service request
     3. Report service request by voice


Selection
     _
```

Figure 2-10: Confirmation screen before the order is sent.

If you want to proceed with ordering, just type 1 and press the Enter key.

2.5.1.5 Verifying PTFs on Order

If you've ordered anything other than the cumulative tape, it can be delivered through the ECS into your computer. To display delivered PTFs, PTF summary lists, or general PSP documents, enter the command on the command line:

```
DSPPTF
```

Now press F4. You'll get a prompted screen that looks like the example shown in Figure 2-11.

```
                 Display Program Temporary Fix (DSPPTF)

Type choices, press Enter.

Product . . . . . . . . . . . .   *ALL        F4 for list
PTF numbers to select . . . . .   *ALL        Character value, *ALL...
Release . . . . . . . . . . . .   *ALL        *ALL, VxRxMx
Cover letter only . . . . . . .   *NO         *NO, *YES
Output  . . . . . . . . . . . .   *           *, *PRINT, *OUTFILE
```

Figure 2-11: The prompted version of command DSPPTF.

Prompt (press F4) at the PRODUCT keyword because you'll never remember all the product codes. Figure 2-12 shows a product screen.

```
                    Specify Value for Parameter LICPGM

Type choice, press Enter.

Type . . . . . . . . . . . . . . :   CHARACTER
Product  . . . . . . . . . . . . .   *ALL

*ALL                                   5716SV2 V3R7M0 ADSTAR Distributed
5769999 V4R2M0 AS/400 Licensed Int     5716US1 V3R6M0 Client Access/400 U
5769SS1 V4R2M0 Operating System/40     5716VG1 V3R6M0 VisualGen Host Serv
INFOAS4 V3R1M0 Information APARs       5763JC1 V3R2M0 AS/400 Toolbox for
INFOAS4 V3R2M0 Information APARs       5763XB1 V3R1M1 Client Access/400 f
INFOAS4 V3R6M0 Information APARs       5763XC1 V3R1M1 Client Access/400 f
INFOAS4 V3R7M0 Information APARs       5763XD1 V3R1M3 Client Access/400 O
INFOAS4 V4R1M0 Information APARs       5763XF1 V3R1M0 Client Access/400 f
INFOAS4 V4R1M4 Information APARs       5763XG1 V3R1M1 Client Access/400 O
INFOAS4 V4R2M0 Information APARs       5763XK1 V3R1M0 Client Access/400 f
INFODSL V0R0M1 Information APARs       5763XL1 V3R1M0 Client Access/400 f
5716CX4 V3R6M0 Visualage C++ for O     5769BR1 V4R1M0 Backup Recovery and
5716CX5 V3R7M0 VisualAge for C++ f     5769CB1 V4R2M0 ILE COBOL for AS/40      +
```

Figure 2-12: The prompted product information for the DSPPTF command.

Note the product number under which your PTF would fall. Most of the time, it'll be a PTF for the operating system so the number would be 5769SS1. Press the F3 or F12 key and return to the screen shown in Figure 2-11 and enter this number for the PRODUCT keyword.

In the field PTF NUMBERS TO SELECT as shown in Figure 2-11, enter the number you ordered when you did the SNDPTFORD command. For example, if you ordered the PTF summary list for V4R3M0 and now want to look at it, you would enter SF97420.

Enter the release number as V4R3M0 and *NO or *YES for COVER LETTER ONLY. Cover letters are a quick way to browse the highlights of the PTFs. Later, you can ask for specific PTFs in their entirety. Additionally, these summaries can be quite large. Therefore, I prefer to get a hard copy of them by entering *PRINT for the OUTPUT keyword.

New with V4R3M0, Cumulative PTF packages are indicated on the DSPPTF command encoded starting with the letter T. The second letter indicates:

- "C" is an applied cumulative PTF package.
- "A" means applied HIPERs.
- "L" means applied HIPER LLC fixes.

Following the Tx is the Julian date.

Figure 2-13 shows a screen to determine if the summary PTF information you ordered has been delivered. From the report on this screen, you get a summary of all the PTFs by product that have been received on your AS/400 through the ECS modem.

```
                    Display Program Temporary Fix (DSPPTF)

Type choices, press Enter.

Product . . . . . . . . . . . . . > 5769SS1       F4 for list
PTF numbers to select . . . . . .   SF97420       Character value, *ALL...
Release . . . . . . . . . . . . .   V4R2M0        *ALL, VxRxMx
Cover letter only . . . . . . . .   *YES          *NO, *YES
Output . . . . . . . . . . . . . .  *             *, *PRINT, *OUTFILE
```

Figure 2-13: Completed command DSPPTF.

2.5.2 Loading/Applying PTFs

Before loading or applying any PTFs, do the following:

- Make a backup of your system with the SAVSYS command.
- Have all users sign off the AS/400. It's also important to make sure no batch jobs are running.
- Make sure you have signed onto the AS/400 with SECOFR authority.

There are two operations needed to install a PTF:

- Load PTF (LODPTF).
- Apply PTF (APYPTF).

2.5.2.1 Loading PTFs

You can order one or many PTFs, and you can load all or some of those received PTFs. Due to the varied relationships of the PTFs, you might be asked to perform different specific tasks.

Because instructions change all the time, always follow the instructions that come enclosed with the PTF order. The instructions can be quite complex and require that you first load/apply some PTFs before you load/apply other PTFs. The following example is the general mechanism to load PTFs. Use this command to load PTFs:

```
LODPTF
```

Figure 2-14 shows a sample of that prompted command. You should know which PTFs are for what products. If you don't, check the documentation that comes with the PTF or press F4. You'll get a product display similar to Figure 2-14.

```
                     Load Program Temporary Fix (LODPTF)

 Type choices, press Enter.

 Product . . . . . . . . . . . .   _______       F4 for list
 Device . . . . . . . . . . . . .  *SERVICE      Name, *SERVICE, *SAVF
 PTF numbers to select . . . . .   *ALL          Character value, *ALL
                + for more values  _______
 PTF numbers to omit . . . . . .   _______       Character value
                + for more values  _______
 Superseded PTFs . . . . . . . .   *APYPERM      *APYPERM, *NOAPY
 Release . . . . . . . . . . . .   *ONLY         *ONLY, VxRyMz
```

Figure 2-14: The prompted version of command LODPTF.

The DEVICE is where you tell the system where it can find the PTF to load. It can be in *SERVICE (delivered from the ECS), *SAVF (a save file, from another AS/400), or a device such as a CD-ROM drive. PTFs are on *SERVICE when they were received by the ECS modem. They can be in a *SAVF in a multiple-CPU system. In that case, they were loaded from a device, then saved, and physically moved to your system (or sent via SNDNETF). Another possibility is that the PTFs arrived on a CD-ROM or tape. Just load the media and specify the device on which it is loaded. This is the common way of loading cumulative PTFs, but not necessarily individual PTFs (which are usually on *SERVICE).

For the most part, customers take the defaults on the rest of the keywords when installing individual PTFs. When installing PTFs from a cumulative tape, you'll make more use of these fields. Here is a summary of what they do. With PTF NUMBERS TO SELECT, you select only specific PTFs from a cumulative package.

Note that PTFs are sent with their own Mandatory Special Instructions. If IBM really wants you to read those instructions, those PTFs won't be installed from the command when you USE PTF NUMBERS TO SELECT(*ALL).

With PTF NUMBERS TO OMIT, you omit specific PTFs from a cumulative tape. You will do a lot of this for superseded PTFs. If it has been a long time since you installed any PTFs and the cumulative tape contains earlier PTFs, you will have PTFs that have been superseded by newer PTFs. This is why the individual cumulative tape installation instructions are crucial.

Finally, the field SUPERSEDED PTFS refer to PTFs that have been applied to your system prior to this load. This field instructs the system to apply them permanently or to not apply them. Remember, PTFs that have been permanently applied cannot be removed. Follow any installation instructions to the letter.

2.5.2.2 Applying PTFs

After PTFs are loaded, they must be applied. PTFs are applied in two conditions:

- Temporary:
  - ✔ Takes a little longer when they run.
  - ✔ Can be removed in the future.
- Permanent:
  - ✔ Becomes a permanent part of the program product.
  - ✔ Runs fast.
  - ✔ Cannot be removed.

Most customers apply PTFs temporarily at least for a few weeks to see how they affect the system. Before any PTFs are applied permanently, make a system backup. In the unlikely event you have to back out the permanent PTF, the only way you can do it is to restore the system from a SAVSYS taken prior to making the PTF permanent. PTFs are further defined as two types:

- Immediate—Once applied, they take effect immediately.
- Delayed—Once applied, the don't take effect until after the next IPL. PTFs become delayed when the program they are fixing is active—PTFs can't be applied to active programs. At IPL time, the program will not be active.

The command to apply PTFs is APYPTF. Figure 2-15 shows an example of its prompted screen.

```
                    Apply Program Temporary Fix (APYPTF)

 Type choices, press Enter.

 Product . . . . . . . . . . . .     ________      F4 for list
 Release . . . . . . . . . . . .     *ONLY         *ONLY, VxRxMx
 PTF numbers to select . . . . .     *ALL          Character value, *ALL
                + for more values    ________
 PTF numbers to omit . . . . . .     ________      Character value
                + for more values    ________
 Extent of change . . . . . . . .    *TEMP         *TEMP, *PERM
 Delayed PTFs . . . . . . . . . .    *NO           *NO, *YES, *IMMDLY
```

Figure 2-15: Prompted command APYPTF.

Type the product name and press the Enter key. If you don't know the product, press the F4 key for a product list. After filling in the product code and pressing Enter, you'll get the screen shown in Figure 2-16.

```
                    Apply Program Temporary Fix (APYPTF)

 Type choices, press Enter.

 Product . . . . . . . . . . . . > 5769SS1        F4 for list
 Release . . . . . . . . . . . .   *ONLY          *ONLY, VxRxMx
 PTF numbers to select . . . . .   *ALL           Character value, *ALL
                + for more values  ________
 PTF numbers to omit . . . . . .   ________       Character value
                + for more values  ________
 Extent of change . . . . . . . .  *TEMP          *TEMP, *PERM
 Delayed PTFs . . . . . . . . . .  *NO            *NO, *YES, *IMMDLY
```

Figure 2-16: Command APYPTF after supplying the product code.

In the example shown in Figure 2-16, the product is OS/400 itself. If you're applying an individual PTF, put that number in PTF NUMBERS TO SELECT. If you're loading a cumulative tape, follow the instructions shipped with the tape. Generally, you'll only have one release of the operating system installed. Therefore, *ONLY is sufficient for the RELEASE keyword. You'll want to select *ALL PTFS and not OMIT any (next two keywords). However, specific cumulative tape instructions could and probably will change this.

The EXTENT OF CHANGE keyword determines whether the PTF(s) applied will be temporary or permanent.

This command will immediately apply any PTFs it can. If a PTF cannot be immediately applied because the operating system or licensed program product is active, it will be marked as not applied and designated as a delayed PTF.

The DELAYED PTFS keyword concerns applying PTFs that have been previously designated as delayed. These can be applied at the next IPL. In the case of licensed program products, delayed PTFs can be applied anytime that the particular product is inactive.

Most of the time you will have to re-IPL in order to make applied PTFs take effect. Note: There is a power menu on the AS/400 that will power the system down. Don't use this when you are IPL-ing to apply PTFs; it doesn't invoke the APYPTF command. When you IPL to apply delayed PTFs, use the following command after you have ended all subsystems:

```
PWRDWNSYS *IMMED RESTART(*YES) IPLSRC( x )
```

In the preceding command, X means the system storage area. As far as applying PTFs is concerned, see Table 2-1.

Table 2-1: Applying PTFS.

Storage Area	Description
*PANEL	Uses the Storage area (A, B, or D) currently shown on the control panel.
A	Temporarily applies unapplied PTFs or removes specific previously temporarily applied PTF.
B	Permanently applies previously temporarily applied PTFs.
D	System is started from a tape device.

If you have delayed PTFs that you want permanently applied, you will first have to IPL with storage area A. That will apply them temporarily. Then you will have to re-IPL from storage area B to get them applied permanently.

After entering the command PWRDWNSYS and pressing the Enter key, you should see an INSTALL THE SYSTEM display. Enter Option 1 for PERFORM AN IPL on that screen and press Enter.

You will get a WORK WITH PTFS display if you have any outstanding PTFs that have not been applied (they were delayed) or have been temporarily applied. From this screen, you can apply PTFs permanently or remove them temporarily or permanently.

PTF application might not work every time. There are many ways to start an IPL; the PWRDWNSYS is only one method. PTFs are applied only when the IPL is a result of a PWRDWNSYS command. Even then they will not apply if:

- The system came down from a power failure.
- The power-down part of the PWRDWNSYS command didn't complete normally (power to the machine failed before it successfully powered down).
- Any abnormal condition existed in the AS/400 prior to issuing the PWRDWNSYS command. This can be due to:
  - ✔ A job ending at any time using the End Job Abnormal (ENDJOBABN) command.
  - ✔ The system ending previously with any function check in the controlling subsystem.
  - ✔ The system going down previous while rebuilding database files during another abnormal IPL.

For additional information on IPL, see chapter 1, section 1.5 Starting the IPL.

2.5.3 Removing PTFs

Occasionally, you will have a problem with a PTF and you'll want to remove it. Or you'll be instructed to remove a previous PTF before you can load a new one.

Only PTFs that have not been applied permanently can be removed. Like applications, PTF removal can be done temporarily or permanently. When a PTF is removed, the original object the PTF replaced is restored. When the PTF is removed temporarily, it reverts back to being loaded but non-applied. When the PTF is removed permanently, it disappears, non-loaded, non-applied.

There are a couple of rules about removing PTFs.You can't remove one that has another PTF that is dependent on it. You also can't remove a PTF that has its related operating system or licensed program product active. Finally, operating system PTFs can only be removed permanently. Table 2-2 summarizes these and other rules.

Table 2-2: PTF Remove—Temporary/Permanent Rules Grid.	
Condition/Type of PTF	**Remove Description**
Permanently applied	Cannot remove
Operating system PTF	Remove permanently only
Delayed PTF, applied temporarily	Remove temporarily only
Delayed PTF, applied temporarily, then removed temporarily	Remove permanently
Immediate PTF, applied temporarily	Remove temporarily or permanently
Immediate PTF, loaded but not applied	Remove permanently

The command to remove PTFs is RMVPTF. Figure 2-17 shows a prompted version of it.

```
                    Remove Program Temporary Fix (RMVPTF)

 Type choices, press Enter.

 Product . . . . . . . . . . . . > 5769SS1       F4 for list
 Release . . . . . . . . . . . .   *ONLY         *ONLY, VxRxMx
 PTF numbers to select . . . . .   *ALL          Character value, *ALL
                + for more values  _______
 PTF numbers to omit . . . . . .   _______       Character value
                + for more values  _______
 Extent of change . . . . . . . .  *TEMP         *TEMP, *PERM
 Delayed PTFs . . . . . . . . . .  *NO           *NO, *YES
```

Figure 2-17: The RMVPTF command.

Filling this out is similar to filling out the APYPTF command. When removing a PTF that was delayed when it was originally applied (that is, it could not be fully applied until an IPL was performed) you will have to likewise perform an IPL (with the IPL Storage Area set to B) to complete the removal. If you are in doubt, check the status of the PTF after RMVPTF completes.

2.6 References

AS/400 Basic System Operation, Administration, and Problem Handling V4R3 (SC41-5206-02)

AS/400 Software Installation V4R3 (SC41-5120-02)

Getting Your AS/400 Working for You V4R3 (SC41-5161-01)

3 CONFIGURE YOUR SYSTEM

3.1 OVERVIEW

Any AS/400 will run fine as soon as the operating system (see chapter 1) and applications are installed, and some user profiles are created (see chapter 5). You can sign onto a workstation right away, but don't really try to use the system this way. Sign on and do some configuring. The AS/400 comes with defaults that you can use to quickly bring up a basic, workable system.

If you are new to the AS/400 and going it alone, just make the basic configuration outlined in this chapter. Come back later, when you understand the system better, and make adjustments.

3.2 JOBS: THE AS/400 WORK UNIT

Every task the AS/400 does is a *job*. Each job has an external name and a unique internal name. All jobs (except some system jobs) run in *subsystems*. Jobs can only enter subsystems in these ways:

- Job queues (part of job descriptions).
- Workstation entry (defined in subsystem descriptions).
- Communication entry (defined in subsystem descriptions).
- Autostart job entry (defined in subsystem descriptions).
- Prestart job (defined in subsystem descriptions).

There are implications with this reliance on jobs. For example, system-level activities automatically happen when jobs start and end. Probably the more important area is when jobs end. Database record locks are automatically released when a job ends. If you're expecting these automatic things to happen, it's important to know the definition of a job and when it ends.

For example, if you submit a job, PGMA, and it starts, runs, and stops, that's a job unit. If you sign onto a workstation in the morning, you've started a job that will continue until you sign off your workstation in the afternoon. If you run the same program, PGMA, interactively from your workstation, it is no longer a job in its own right; it is just a piece of your long workstation job. If you are relying on PGMA's completion for things like record locks to be released, they won't be completed—because the workstation job is the controlling job—until you sign off the workstation. As you can see, programs may behave differently depending on how they are executed.

Jobs are labeled by their type. Three broad types of jobs are:

- Interactive.
- Batch.
- Communication (new with Version 4).

Interactive jobs are those that use the workstation at least for their data entry. Their output is often directed back to the workstation but can be directed to a printer. Interactive jobs are bound by a person working the keyboard. The job will wait until the person presses the Enter key. It will stay active until the person ends it.

Batch jobs run in the "background" (which is another way of saying they aren't dependent on a workstation or a person) of the computer until they are finished. They usually don't take any user involvement. Because batch jobs can be long running, sometimes for hours, you don't want them tying up a workstation.

A communication job is a job started on the AS/400 by a remote system.

New with Version 4 is the concept of *threads*. Every job has one or more threads. The one thread every job has is referred to as its *initial thread*. Subsequent threads are referred to as *secondary threads*. A thread is a dispatched independent unit of work. This isn't a big deal most of the time. You will come across references to threads when you encounter a few job-controlling functions that are directed at the thread level. However, most functions still are directed at the job level. Threads become most significant when you are dealing with storage pool activity levels.

3.3 Memory: Storage Pools and Activity Levels

3.3.1 Storage Pools

Any *storage pool* is a pool of memory where one type of program/application runs. You ordered your AS/400 with a certain amount of memory. When you got your machine, that memory was divided into two special shared storage pools: *MACHINE and *BASE.

*MACHINE is the storage pool where the system tasks that you have no control over run. *BASE can be where everything else runs until you build other pools and assign jobs to run in them.

Your AS/400 comes with the optimum memory assigned to *MACHINE. You can reset this, but you don't have to and probably shouldn't initially. Later, if you suspect problems with *MACHINE pool, you can adjust its memory within parameters. See chapter 9, Section 9.2.4.1 Memory.

*MACHINE's memory can never be below a base of 256Kb plus what the machine thinks it needs (based on the size and model); the system will not allow it. Memory adjustments to *MACHINE can be made by changing the system value (see appendix A, AS/400 System Values) QMCHPOOL.

The amount of memory in *BASE cannot be adjusted directly because it is the total memory available on the system (less the memory used by *MACHINE and any other *private pools* or *shared pools*). You can, however, set system value QBASPOOL to a value below which the system will not allow *BASE to fall. QBASPOOL comes with an IBM-set value you shouldn't change until you're accustomed to using the AS/400. In addition to the minimum you can set, the system has a built-in minimum limit for *BASE memory (like *MACHINE: 256Kb plus what the machine thinks it needs) below which you cannot go. Keep the following tip in mind:

TIP

*MACHINE	= QMCHPOOL	: Set memory.
*BASE	=QBASPOOL	: Set memory lower limit.

*MACHINE and *BASE are sufficient to run your AS/400. Beyond them, however, you might want to consider using private or shared pools in your system for better performance.

Dividing memory into pools is like fencing the range. Although at first it might look like something is being lost, it isn't. Actually, the control will make an AS/400 with a broad job mix run better. Fencing the range allows dissimilar animals to graze "together" within fences better than they would on the open range. Cattle could graze in their space, sheep in theirs, and goats in other places. Similarly, dividing memory into pools allows interactive jobs to coexist with batch jobs without either eating all the other's grass. The term *pool* is actually an amount of memory fenced in.

Here's how to use memory pools and enhance performance. You will have your interactive jobs running in an interactive subsystem (see section 3.7 Subsystems). You will also have your batch jobs running in a batch subsystem. If you do nothing with the configuration, both will use memory in *BASE.

There are two things that happen in any virtual machine's memory—paging and faulting. I have to define these before going any further. *Paging* is when memory pages for a relatively inactive program are written out to DASD so the system can load memory pages for the program (or its data) on which it is currently working. *Faulting* is when the AS/400 is working on a program (or its data) and attempts to go to a new memory page and doesn't find it. The system has to go look for the page and determine if it was either moved out to DASD to support another program or if it hasn't been loaded from DASD the first time, yet.

Now that you have a grasp of paging and faulting, I'll return to performance and storage pools. My example is interactive and batch jobs running in their own subsystems, but using *BASE as the memory. Interactive jobs typically run at a higher priority than batch jobs, and, therefore, get system attention much more often. The system might run through all interactive jobs—working on them two or three times—before it goes to any batch job.

With all jobs using the same storage pool, when the system needs memory for interactive jobs, it will probably take it from batch jobs. Because batch jobs run at a lower priority, they are "inactive" and their memory gets stolen. After several iterations of this, the system decides to work on a batch job. None of its previously loaded pages are around anymore. By the time the system finds them and returns them to memory, the time is up for working on the batch job and the system returns to the interactive jobs. This is called *thrashing*. It means a lot of work goes on and nothing gets done.

One way around this is to have interactive and batch jobs running in their own subsystems (each having its own private memory pools). In this scenario, paging for interactive jobs occurs only between interactive jobs. Meanwhile, paging for batch jobs occurs only between batch jobs.

The AS/400 makes some further distinctions concerning pools. Any AS/400 can have these types of pools:

- Shared Pools
  - ✔ *Special shared pools.* The two pools that come with the AS/400, *MACHINE and *BASE, are special shared pools. These are the only special shared pools.
  - ✔ *General shared pools.*
- Private Pools

You can only have a total of 64 pools on your system. Because the system insists on using *MACHINE and *BASE, you can add only 62 to your system. As far as creating and naming pools, keep the following points in mind:

- Private pools are created and named on the subsystem description (see section 3.7 Subsystems). Their names are simple: 1 through 62. A private pool can only support one subsystem. A shared pool can support multiple subsystems and still maintain thrashing protection from other subsystems' jobs not using the pool. Example: If subsystem HOTRPTS has a private pool and it's name is pool 1, no other subsystem can use or refer to pool 1. If an AS/400 has two interactive subsystems, QINTER01 and QINTER02, they can both use shared pool *INTERACT.
- The AS/400 comes with predetermined names and, in two cases, predetermined uses, for shared pools. Here's the list:
  - ✔ *INTERACT —Supports interactive subsystems' jobs.
  - ✔ *SPOOL—Supports spool writers (printing).
  - ✔ *SHRPOOL1 through *SHRPOOL60—Names you can use for your own shared pools.

Whether you use private or shared pools, you can adjust their memory at any time you like. The more memory you assign to a pool the more work it can do. It is common to put more memory in the interactive subsystem's pool and take some away from the batch subsystem's pool during the day. By reversing the procedure in the evening, you take memory away from the interactive pool and give it to the batch pool.

Because it contains all the system's memory that isn't taken by all the other pools, *BASE plays a major part in moving memory around the AS/400. When you take from one pool and give to another, you do so by:

- Adjusting one pool down; the adjustment returns memory to *BASE, making it bigger.
- Increasing the other pool; the increased memory comes out of *BASE, making it smaller.

3.4 Activity Level

Before getting into activity levels, you need to know that AS/400 jobs have three states:

- Active—the job is running or waiting for disk I/O.
- Wait—the job is waiting for something to happen. This can be waiting for a:
  - ✔ User to press the Enter key at the workstation.
  - ✔ File open or close.
  - ✔ Device allocation.
  - ✔ Locked record to become unlocked.
  - ✔ Message.
- Ineligible—
  - ✔ The job is ready to run but the system is too busy for it.
  - ✔ The system has spent its allocated time (measured in time slices) on the job and will work on some other jobs for a while.

Every storage pool has an activity level associated with it. An activity level limits the number of job threads the computer will work on at one time within the pool. This is a confusing subject to most experienced AS/400 people because there is a similar system value that limits the maximum number of jobs it can run at one time. These are not the same values. Keep the following tips in mind:

Tip: Job queue's MAXACT (Maximum Active Jobs) = Number of jobs from that queue that can be active in the subsystem at one time.

Storage pool's MAXACTLVL (Maximum Activity Level) = Number of jobs active in the subsystem that the system will work on at the same time.

In the batch subsystem, QBATCH, you could easily have a maximum of six active jobs, but an activity level of 3. If you had six jobs in the subsystem, three would be active and three would be present (but either waiting or ineligible). When an active job goes into a wait or ineligible state, the system makes one of the ineligibles active. If the job that entered the wait state returned from that state and the system is working on three other jobs, it goes ineligible until one of the others goes to wait or ineligible.

This isn't as choppy as it sounds because jobs go into and out of states all the time and do so very quickly. If you were monitoring the system I just described, you would mostly see six active jobs. You would see many waits and only occasionally catch ineligible statuses.

Overall throughput of any subsystem can be increased greatly by carefully setting the activity level. The exception to all this is the *MACHINE pool. It's the system's pool for its tasks and you can't change its activity level.

3.4.1 Using Memory and Activity Levels

3.4.1.1 Creating Private Pools/Assigning Shared Pools

Although you would think a private memory pool is closely associated with some kind of memory management command, it isn't. On the AS/400, it's associated closely with the subsystem and is created or changed by creating or changing the subsystem's description.

You create the subsystem description with the CRTSBSD command. Figure 3-1 shows the format for that. This command is discussed in more detail in section 3.7 Subsystems.

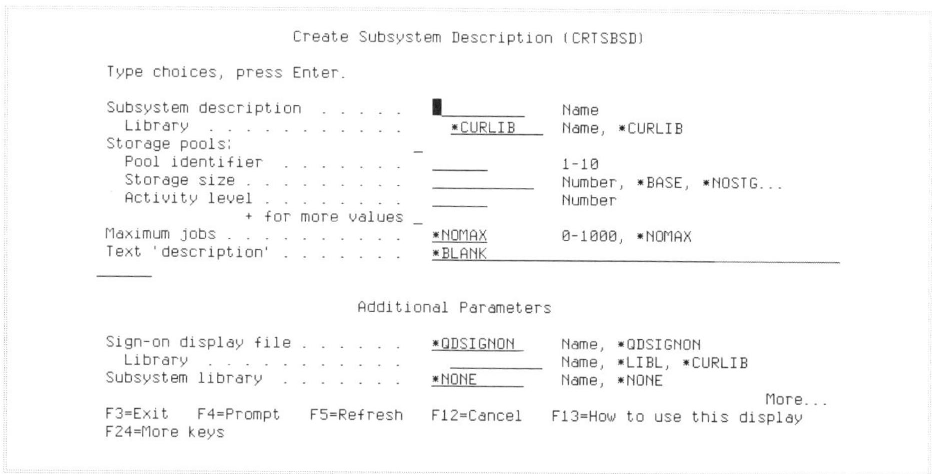

```
                    Create Subsystem Description (CRTSBSD)

 Type choices, press Enter.

 Subsystem description . . . . .   _________    Name
   Library . . . . . . . . . . .     *CURLIB    Name, *CURLIB
 Storage pools:                  _
   Pool identifier . . . . . . .   _____        1-10
   Storage size . . . . . . . . .  __________   Number, *BASE, *NOSTG...
   Activity level . . . . . . . .  _____        Number
              + for more values _
 Maximum jobs . . . . . . . . . .  *NOMAX       0-1000, *NOMAX
 Text 'description' . . . . . . .  *BLANK

                          Additional Parameters

 Sign-on display file . . . . . .  *QDSIGNON    Name, *QDSIGNON
   Library . . . . . . . . . . .     ________   Name, *LIBL, *CURLIB
 Subsystem library . . . . . . .   *NONE        Name, *NONE
                                                                 More...
 F3=Exit   F4=Prompt   F5=Refresh   F12=Cancel   F13=How to use this display
 F24=More keys
```

Figure 3-1: Prompted version of the CRTSBSD command.

For now, notice the area you use to specify the pools. You can define up to 10 pools for each subsystem description. These are referred to as the subsystem storage pools. There are three fields on this screen relevant to storage pools:

- *Pool identifier.* This field is the subsystem pool number (1-10) within the subsystem; it is not the system name-number of the pool. Subsystems can have up to 10 pools assigned to them. Actually, you don't see many subsystems with more than three pools assigned to them, and most have two. For more information see section 3.7 Subsystems.
- *Storage size.* This field has two forms:
  - ✔ If you want a private pool (no other subsystems can use it), do specify the amount of memory to be in the pool. When you start the subsystem (STRSBS), you will have a private pool started for that subsystem with that amount of memory. Don't specify a pool name on the pool identifier. The name of that private pool will be assigned by the system and it'll be the next available number between 1 and 62.
  - ✔ If you want to use a shared storage pool, do specify the name of the shared pool (e.g., *INTERACT or SHRPOOL5) in the pool identifier. Don't specify the storage size; that is defined on the shared pool itself. You adjust shared pools' memory with the WRKSYSSTS or CHGSHRPOOL commands.
- *Activity level* is the activity level for that pool.
- For more pools, put a plus sign (+) in the + FOR MORE VALUES parameter and the system will prompt you for up to 10 subsystem pools.

How do you know starting values if you've never configured a subsystem before? See the IBM manual *OS/400 Work Management V4R2* (Section 14.6.14.2 Using Dynamic Tuning Support to Determine the Minimum Storage Pool Size) for a table of these values.

3.4.1.2 Changing Pool Memory/Activity Levels

There are three commands that will change memory and activity level settings on pools. Each has its place. Table 3-1 shows the commands and where they are used.

Table 3-1: Memory Activity Level Commands.

Pool Name	Adjustments to Memory	Adjustments to Activity Level
*MACHINE	QMCHPOOL (SV) WRKSYSSTS	— — n/a — —
*BASE	— — n/a — —	QBASACTLVL (SV) WRKSYSSTS
All private pools	WRKSYSSTS CHGSBSD	WRKSYSSTS CHGSBSD
All shared pools	WRKSYSSTS CHGSHRPOOL	WRKSYSSTS CHGSHRPOOL
(sv) = System Value. Use CHGSYSVAL command to change these.		

Figure 3-2 shows an example of using the CHGSHRPOOL command to change attributes of a shared pool. Type the command (CHGSHRPOOL) on a command line and press Enter. Just type in the new values for memory or activity levels and the change will take effect immediately.

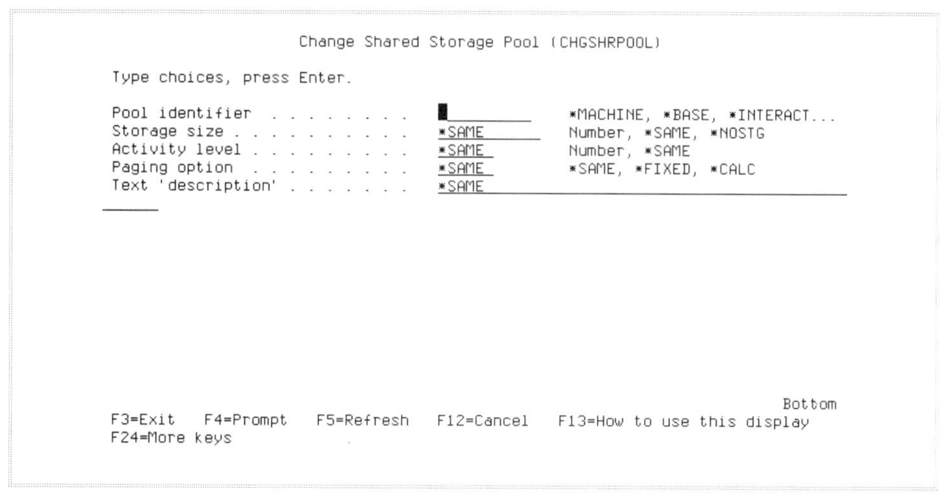

```
                  Change Shared Storage Pool (CHGSHRPOOL)

Type choices, press Enter.

Pool identifier . . . . . . . . . _________   *MACHINE, *BASE, *INTERACT...
Storage size . . . . . . . . . .  *SAME       Number, *SAME, *NOSTG
Activity level . . . . . . . . .  *SAME       Number, *SAME
Paging option  . . . . . . . . .  *SAME       *SAME, *FIXED, *CALC
Text 'description' . . . . . . .  *SAME

                                                                    Bottom
F3=Exit   F4=Prompt   F5=Refresh   F12=Cancel   F13=How to use this display
F24=More keys
```

Figure 3-2: The CHGSHRPOOL command.

If you don't want to change one or both, don't enter anything. The *SAME value means it won't make any change. Private pools are changed within their subsystems. Figure 3-3 shows the prompted version of the CHGSBSD command.

```
                  Change Subsystem Description (CHGSBSD)

Type choices, press Enter.

Subsystem description . . . . . . _________   Name
  Library  . . . . . . . . . . .    *LIBL     Name, *LIBL, *CURLIB
Storage pools:                  _
  Pool identifier  . . . . . . .  *SAME       1-10, *SAME
  Storage size . . . . . . . . .  _________   Number, *BASE, *NOSTG...
  Activity level . . . . . . . .  _____       Number
               + for more values _
Maximum jobs . . . . . . . . . .  *SAME       0-1000, *SAME, *NOMAX
Text 'description' . . . . . . .  *SAME

                        Additional Parameters

Sign-on display file . . . . . .  *SAME       Name, *SAME, *QDSIGNON
  Library  . . . . . . . . . . .  _________   Name, *LIBL, *CURLIB
Subsystem library  . . . . . . .  *SAME       Name, *SAME, *NONE
                                                                    Bottom
F3=Exit   F4=Prompt   F5=Refresh   F12=Cancel   F13=How to use this display
F24=More keys
```

Figure 3-3: The CHGSBSD command.

You can only make changes to private pools on this command. Specify the subsystem pool identifier (see section 3.4.2 Pool Names) and its new memory or activity level.

3.4.1.3 Deleting Pools

- You cannot delete or remove pools *MACHINE and *BASE.
- Delete private pools by ending the subsystem in which they run.
- Make shared pools inactive by ending the subsystems in which they run. They still will appear on the WRKSYSSTS command, but they will have zeros for memory and activity level, and you won't see a pool identification associated with them.

3.4.2 Pool Names

Nothing confuses AS/400 customers as much as storage pool names. First, the system names pools and it's not very creative. Second, pools are sometimes referred to by their relative pool number within a subsystem and sometimes by their system-generated pool number-name, and, in the case of shared pools, by their shared pool names. Is that confusing? As an example, Figure 3-4 shows the command Work with Subsystems (WRKSBS).

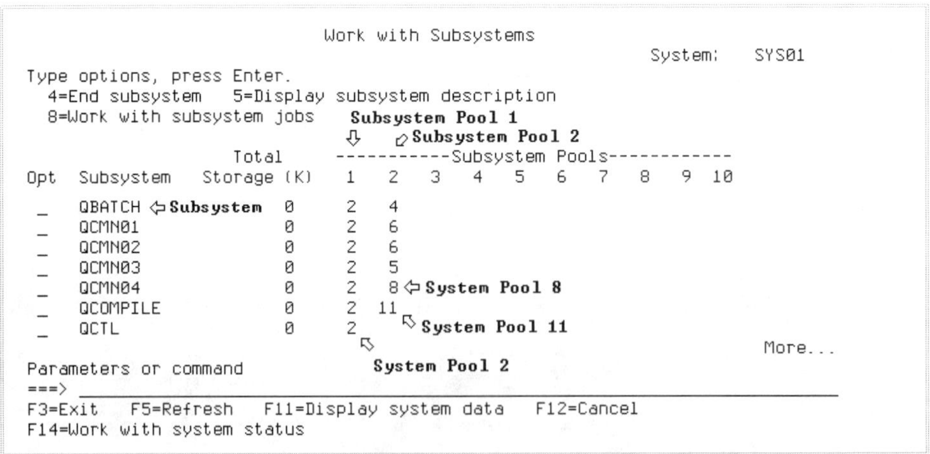

```
                          Work with Subsystems
                                                       System:   SYS01
Type options, press Enter.
  4=End subsystem   5=Display subsystem description
  8=Work with subsystem jobs   Subsystem Pool 1
                               ⇩   ⇗Subsystem Pool 2
                  Total        -----------Subsystem Pools------------
Opt  Subsystem   Storage (K)   1   2   3   4   5   6   7   8   9  10

 _   QBATCH ⇦Subsystem  0      2   4
 _   QCMN01             0      2   6
 _   QCMN02             0      2   6
 _   QCMN03             0      2   5
 _   QCMN04             0      2   8 ⇦System Pool 8
 _   QCOMPILE           0      2  11
 _   QCTL               0      2     ⇖System Pool 11
                                 ⇖                           More...
Parameters or command          System Pool 2
===> ____________________________________________________________
F3=Exit   F5=Refresh   F11=Display system data   F12=Cancel
F14=Work with system status
```

Figure 3-4: The WORK WITH SUBSYSTEMS command.

Here's a list of subsystems and their pools. The columns 1 through 10 refer to the subsystem pools. The numbers under those columns are the system pool names that occupy those subsystem pool slots. Take a further look at subsystem QCOMPILE. It has two subsystem pools: 1 and 2. It's number 1 pool contains system pool identification 2 (which is always *BASE) and its number 2 pool is system pool identification 11. If you put a 5 option on DISPLAY SUBSYSTEM DESCRIPTION, you can look at the subsystem's pool definitions. See Figure 3-5 for a sample of the Work with Subsystems (WRKSBS) command, showing a display of QCOMPILE'S pool definitions.

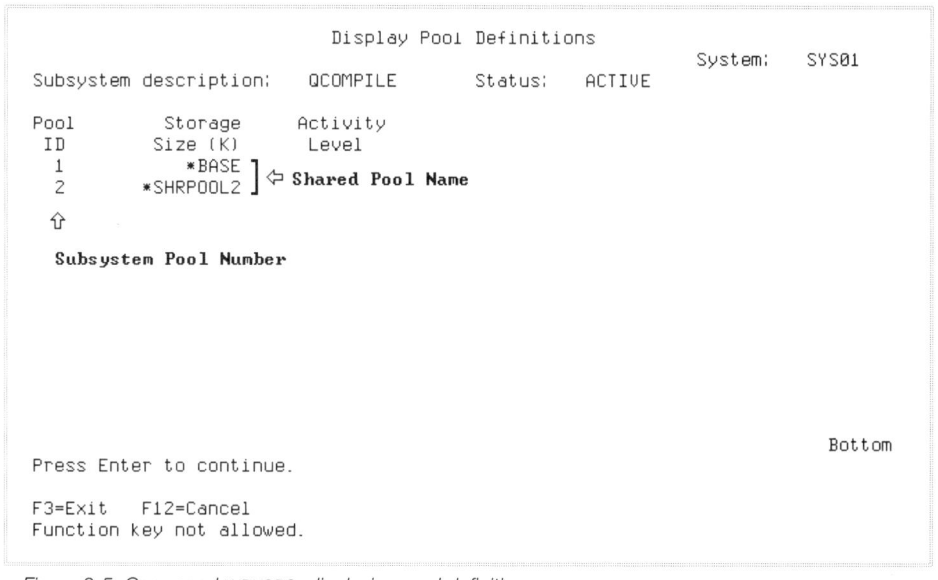

Figure 3-5: Command WRKSBS, displaying pool definitions.

Each row shows information about each of QCOMPILE's pools. Each row is a subsystem's pool number. Here you can verify that *BASE is the shared pool for QCOMPILE's subsystem pool 1. The shared pool name for QCOMPILE's subsystem pool 2 is *SHRPOOL2. Remember (from Figure 3-4) that the subsystem's pool 1 contains system pool number 2? Figure 3-5 shows that subsystem pool 1 is the shared pool, *BASE. By applying a little logic, you can infer that system pool 2 is shared pool *BASE.

Moving on, Figure 3-4 shows subsystem pool 2 containing system pool 11. Figure 3-5 shows subsystem pool 2 is really *SHRPOOL2. Apply the same logic and system pool 2 is a shared pool called *SHRPOOL2.

You can focus on memory pools—if you know the system pool number—with the Work with System Status (WRKSYSSTS) command. Figure 3-6 shows a sample of the WRKSYSSTS command.

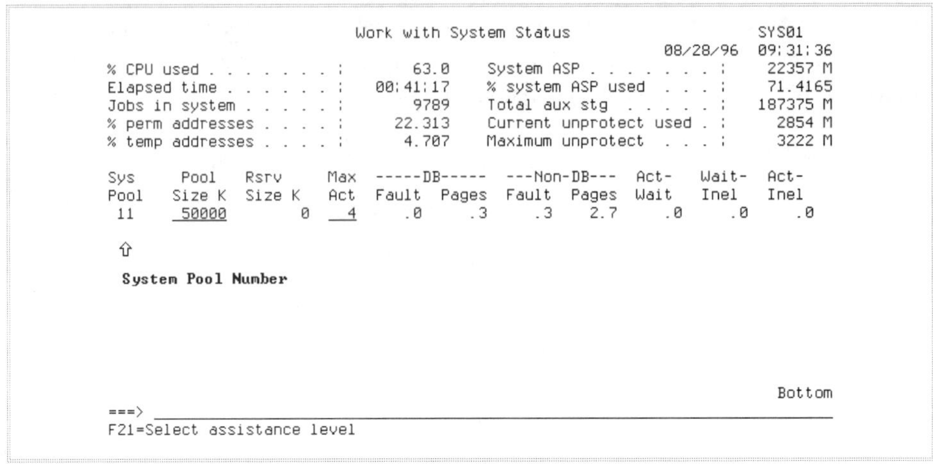

```
                          Work with System Status                      SYS01
                                                           08/28/96  09:31:36
% CPU used . . . . . . . :        63.0    System ASP . . . . . . . :    22357 M
Elapsed time . . . . . . :    00:41:17    % system ASP used  . . . :    71.4165
Jobs in system . . . . . :        9789    Total aux stg  . . . . . :   187375 M
% perm addresses . . . . :      22.313    Current unprotect used . :     2854 M
% temp addresses . . . . :       4.707    Maximum unprotect  . . . :     3222 M

Sys     Pool    Rsrv     Max  -----DB-----  ---Non-DB---  Act-    Wait-   Act-
Pool   Size K  Size K    Act  Fault  Pages  Fault  Pages  Wait    Inel    Inel
 11    _50000       0   __4     .0     .3     .3    2.7     .0      .0      .0

 ⇧

 System Pool Number



                                                                         Bottom
===> ____________________________________________________________________________
F21=Select assistance level
```

Figure 3-6: Command WRKSYSSTS includes information about system pools.

Here is the memory and activity level allocated to system pool name 11. It has 50,000Kb of memory and an activity level of 4. These lines are underscored to indicate that you can make changes to the pools from this screen.

If you weren't comfortable with the logic in connecting system pool numbers to shared pools, you could take the direct approach with the Work with Shared Pools (WRKSHRPOOL) command. Figure 3-7 contains a sample of it.

```
                          Work with Shared Pools
                                                           System:    SYS01
Main storage size (K)  . :         655360

Type changes (if allowed), press Enter.

             Defined     Max    Allocated    Pool  -Paging Option--
Pool         Size (K)  Active   Size (K)      ID   Defined  Current
*MACHINE       90000     +++       90000       1   *FIXED   *FIXED
*BASE          88360      32       88360       2   *FIXED   *FIXED
*INTERACT      10000       7       10000       8   *FIXED   *FIXED
*SPOOL         12000       7       12000       3   *FIXED   *FIXED
*SHRPOOL1     200000      10      200000       4   *CALC    *CALC
*SHRPOOL2      50000       4       50000      11   *FIXED   *FIXED
*SHRPOOL3      50000       4       50000      10   *CALC    *CALC
*SHRPOOL4      40000      10       40000       5   *FIXED   *FIXED
*SHRPOOL5      70000       7       70000       6   *FIXED   *FIXED
*SHRPOOL6          0       0                       *FIXED
          ⇖                                     ⇧                         More...
Command    Shared Pool Name                   System Pool Number
===> ____________________________________________________________________________
F3=Exit   F4=Prompt   F5=Refresh   F9=Retrieve   F11=Display text
F12=Cancel
```

Figure 3-7: Command WRKSHRPOOL.

Here are the shared pool names and the system pool names (pool ID) to which they correspond. Notice three things about the screen shown in Figure 3-7.

- Like WRKSYSSTS, in Figure 3-6, the memory and activity levels are underscored (meaning you can make changes to them).
- *SHRPOOL6, at the bottom of the screen, has no memory or activity level assigned to it. Apparently, its subystem was stopped at the time this was taken. Also, it has no system pool assigned to it. Therefore, it is dormant and uses no memory.
- The system pool numbers 7 and 9 are missing. These must have been used as private pools for some subsystem(s). The command WRKSHRPOOL only shows shared pools (not private). Another thing you can get from the omission of 7 and 9 is how the AS/400 is really only going to allow a total of 16 pool IDs (including all private, specific shared pools, and general shared pools).

3.5 DASD and User Auxiliary Storage Pools

If you order new DASD for your AS/400 at any time (and you probably will, most customers outgrow their DASD), you'll probably arrange with someone to come out and install it. That will probably be a representative from the company that supplied the DASD.

Be very careful that you know that the installer is going to leave your new DASD nonconfigured, configured but not assigned, or configured, assigned, and ready for use. Adding new DASD to the AS/400 used to be cut-and-dried but that is no longer true. Installers tend more and more to leave the final configuration up to the customer.

If the DASD is to be left in any condition other than up-and-running, you have some work to do. Refer to the IBM manual *OS/400 Backup and Recovery V4R3, Procedures for Configuring Disks and Disk Protection* for detailed information.

The AS/400 stores data and programs on disk with a process called *data striping*. This is one of the benefits of the AS/400's single-level store architecture. With data striping, the customer doesn't allocate files to specific disk volumes. Actually, the customer isn't even aware of disk volumes. When the system writes to a file, it finds the least-used disk volume and writes it there. Therefore, pieces of any file are located all over the system. The benefits of striping are:

- All volumes are always balanced, with no effort from the customer.
- Read/write activities automatically make use of multiple arms, resulting in faster throughput.

The disadvantages of data striping are:

- If a disk drive is lost, the whole system is lost. The customer must have adequate backup.
- The objects from some tasks, such as keeping a journal or saving, would perform better if they could be dedicated to specific disk volumes.

User auxiliary storage pools (ASPs) ameliorate these disadvantages. An ASP is a way to assign physical drives for specific applications or functions. Typically, specific objects are stored in specific ASPs. If you're new to the AS/400 and fond of dedicating every volume to a specific set of files, don't try to use ASPs to duplicate the environment to which you're accustomed. You'll dig a hole you'll never get out of.

ASPs reduce the impact to the system due to a single drive failure. If you had an ASP of one or several drives to hold a library and all its files and one of the drives failed, you would replace the drive and only have to worry about restoring that library and its files. The rest of the system would be untouched.

Two very popular uses of ASPs on AS/400s are:

- An ASP dedicated to save files (type *SAVF).
  - ✔ Backups can be done faster to a *SAVF than to tape, and that minimizes the time a library is held up during backups.
- An ASP could be designated to hold only journals and receivers. There are two advantages to this:
  - ✔ Performance improves on a machine using journaling heavily because the journaling DASD operations are always assured of dedicated read/write arms and heads.
  - ✔ Backups are more efficient. Typically, you save journal receivers to tape and you save library data to tape in separate times and operations. By keeping journaling physically out of the data library, this function is easier to manage.

Creating ASPs is not as easy as making memory adjustments described in the previous sections. ASPs are created only after a manual IPL, using the DST. Also, ASPs are usually created with lots of thought given to the physical hardware. Therefore, make that part of your consideration. There are different types of ASPs:

- ASP 1 is always referred to as the system ASP. The system creates this automatically whenever it IPLs. All configured disk drives that are not otherwise assigned to an ASP are placed in ASP 1.

- You can configure ASPs 2 through 16. These are called user ASPs and they come in two types:
  - ✔ Library user ASPs.
  - ✔ Non-library user ASPs.

How do you create each type of ASP? Well, first you create the ASP using the DST. If the first thing you move into the ASP when your machine comes up is a library, you have a library user ASP. If the first thing you move into the ASP is a journal, journal receiver, or save file, then you have a non-library user ASP. This library/non-library business will be more meaningful after you read chapter 8, Journaling.

3.5.1 Controlling ASPs

Never let the system ASP fill up. If it does, the AS/400 shuts down and the ASP is labeled as "damaged." You must IPL the AS/400 (and it'll be a longer IPL than usual), remove excess objects that caused the ASP to overflow, and re-IPL again to get it right.

For that matter, don't let a non-system ASP fill up. If one does, it overflows into the system ASP. If it causes the system ASP to overflow, the system will come down. You'll have to "repair" the overflowed user ASP as it will be considered damaged. There are two areas to protect yourself so that an ASP doesn't overflow:

- You can set a threshold percentage so that when the ASP capacity exceeds that percentage, the system will send a system operator message every hour until the condition is fixed (objects removed from the ASP).
- Two system values, QSTGLOWLMT and QSTGLOWACN will allow you to tell the system how to actively monitor the System ASP.

3.5.1.1 Setting ASP Thresholds

Set ASP thresholds through either the SST (System Service Tools) or DST (Dedicated Service Tools).

Both are similar but DST can only be started by performing a manual IPL (refer to chapter 1, Section 1.5 Attended/Unattended and Manual/Normal IPL). When the system menu comes up, take Option 3, Use Dedicated Service Tools, and take the menu options from there.

To start SST, simply type the command STRSST on any command line. Take Option 3, Work with Disk Units, then Option 2, Work with Disk Configuration, then Option 3, Work with ASP Conversion. You'll get a screen similar to the one shown in Figure 3-8.

```
                    Select ASP to Change Threshold

Type option, press Enter.
  1=Select

                                           ----Protected---   ---Unprotected--
Option   ASP   Threshold   Overflow           Size  %Used          Size  %Used
  1       1        90%     No                14550 39.87%             0  0.00%
```

Figure 3-8: Display of the ASPs and their thresholds (all ASPs will display).

If you want to change the threshold percentage, enter a 1 on the selection line to the left of the ASP on which you would like to work. When you do, you'll get a screen similar to the one shown in Figure 3-9.

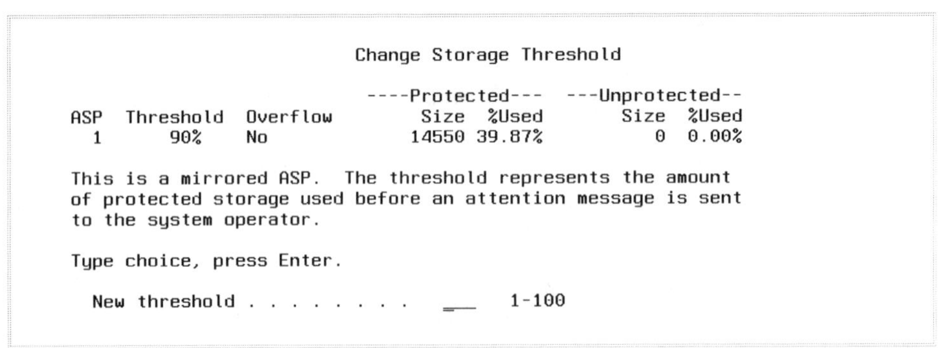

```
                        Change Storage Threshold

                                ----Protected---   ---Unprotected--
ASP   Threshold   Overflow         Size  %Used          Size  %Used
  1       90%     No              14550 39.87%             0  0.00%

This is a mirrored ASP.  The threshold represents the amount
of protected storage used before an attention message is sent
to the system operator.

Type choice, press Enter.

  New threshold . . . . . . . .   ___    1-100
```

Figure 3-9: Screen to change the ASP threshold.

Just enter the new percentage you would like the threshold to be at and press the Enter key.

3.5.1.2 Making System ASP Proactive

Thresholds only issue warnings. If you really want to keep your system intact, you need to play with the following two system values:

- QSTGLOWLMT—Sets the System ASP limit. This has nothing to do with the threshold. Set it anywhere you want. I like to set the threshold to 90 percent and this value to 95. If the operator doesn't respond quickly enough to the message, the system will kick in at 95 percent.

- QSTGLOWACN—Tells the AS/400 what action to take when the percentage specified in QSTGLOWLMT is reached. Possible values are:

    - ✔ *MSG—The system sends message CPI099C to the QSYSMSG and QSYSOPR message queues. (It sends this anyway when you choose any of the other options.)

    - ✔ *CRITMSG —Sends the message CPI099B to the user specified to receive crucial messages.

    - ✔ *REGFAC —The system calls the program registered for the QIBM_QWC_QSTGLOWACN exit point.

    - ✔ *ENDSYS—The system comes to a restricted state.

    - ✔ *PWRDWNSYS—The system is powered down immediately and restarts.

*PWRDWNSYS may seem the same as if you had no protection, but there is a big difference. It's better to power down the system before the system ASP gets labeled as damaged. Recovery is easier. Many times, ASPs fill up due to runaway programs. In these cases, either *ENDSYS or *PWRDWNSYS will stop the offending program and you'll have a chance to identify the program and alert the developers before allowing it to start again.

3.5.2 Creating User ASPs

There are many ways to create or change ASPs (I won't go into them here). For more information, refer to the *OS/400 Backup and Recovery V4R3, Procedures for Configuring Disks and Disk Protection* and *Working with Auxiliary Storage Pools* for more information.

The problem is there are different steps you go through if you are setting up ASPs on a new AS/400, adding new disk units to existing ASPs, moving disk units from one ASP to another, or removing disk units.

If you want to create a new ASP, refer to the section in the *OS/400 Backup and Recovery V4R3, Procedures for Configuring Disks and Disk Protection* manual regarding adding disk units to an ASP. You don't create ASPs directly. If you add disk units to an ASP that doesn't exist, the system will create the ASP for you. In general, do this:

- Have a plan. Know what you're going to do before you do it.
  - ✔ Know the disk units currently on your system. Use the WRKHDWRSC *STG command to get this information.
  - ✔ Have a current system backup.
  - ✔ If you are adding new disks, know if they are configured yet or not. If not, you'll have some extra steps to go through. Nonconfigured disk units are not seen by the system.
- You can use SST or DST to do the ASP work. Although SST is easier to start, you'll have to do an IPL anyway. For this reason, I prefer just to IPL the system and use DST.

3.5.3 Other ASP Considerations

- Not every type of object can exist in a user ASP. Section 4 of the *OS/400Backup and Recovery V4R2* manual has a list of object types that are not allowed in a user ASP.
- Be especially careful of ASPs used for journals/journal receivers. They are most apt to overflow unexpectedly.
- User ASPs cause developers headaches in two areas:
  - ✔ You cannot have dependent database files across ASPs. Therefore, all logical files that belong to a physical file must reside in the same ASP as the physical file.
  - ✔ You cannot MOVOBJ or CRTDUPOBJ across ASPs.
- A disk drive on the AS/400 can actually have several storage devices within one physical unit. If you are creating an ASP to enhance recovery, include all the devices within each unit as part of the ASP.

3.6 Things That Make Jobs Run

Once you have considered all the things you can do with memory and storage, there are still plenty of system settings that come together to make a functional AS/400 computer. It's helpful to know the default setting you can set for the AS/400. Also, it's nice to know what the AS/400 does to start a job.

3.6.1 Overview

The system is shipped with lots of defaults for all these pieces. In the basic system configuration, however, most of the defaults are unused. Such a system only contains one subsystem (QBASE) and two memory pools (*MACHINE and *BASE). You can sign onto the AS/400 even with this minimum setup.

But you should at least configure the system beyond the base. Configuration can be done just using other default objects. For example, you have QINTER, QBATCH, and QCTL subsystems that you should set up. Within those subsystems, you should specify some memory pools to be shared.

Remember, though, that everything you have to build for the AS/400 comes with a default. Check the default objects as you go. Use them unless there is something horrible about them (in which case, you can just copy and change them). For example, for job descriptions every AS/400 comes with QDFTJOBD in library QGPL. Use it or copy, rename, and change it. To help you get a perspective of all the pieces, the following section is an overview of the flow of batch and interactive jobs.

3.6.1.1 How the System Starts an Interactive Job

An interactive job is a real-time job performed at a workstation. The job's name is the same as the workstation name that the user signs onto. The interactive subsystem, through its workstation entries, does double duty.

- It projects the sign-on screen to the workstation.
- After the user signs on, it receives the sign-on screen and starts the subsystem's job initiation.

When the user signs on, the user's authority is checked before the incoming screen gets to the subsystem. Assuming it passes authority, the job goes first to the subsystem's workstation entry. From there, the subsystem has the job name (the name of the workstation) but not much else. It needs to know two things in order to run the job:

- Job attributes.
- Runtime attributes.

The workstation entry (WSE) within the subsystem tells the subsystem where to look for a job description. It has three possibilities:

- A job description name—the subsystem looks no further, it retrieves the job description and takes the job attributes it needs.
- *USRPRF—the subsystem looks in the user profile for a job description name to retrieve.
- *SBSD—The subsystem itself may have a default job description specified. If so, that's where the subsystem finds the job description from which to pull the job attributes.

Once the subsystem has the job description in hand, it also has the job attributes it needs. The job description also has a reference to a job class. The subsystem gets this to determine two things:

- The runtime attributes to assign to the job.
- The program that will support the job. (Most always this is QSYS/QCMD. You'll recognize this as the AS/400 main menu.)

At this point, the interactive job begins. There is just one last piece to clean up and that is with the program that supports the job. If that program is a non-system program (an application menu for example), when the user ends the application, the user will be automatically signed off. If the supporting program was QSYS/QCMD, the user must sign off to end the job.

Interactive jobs exist as jobs until the user signs off. When the user signs off, the workstation entry resumes displaying a sign-on screen. To put it another way, to have an interactive subsystem, you need:

- A workstation known to the system (probably courtesy of autoconfiguration).
- A valid user identification and password (see chapter 5).
- A subsystem (default QINTER) that has:
  - ✔ A job description (default QGPL/QDFTJOBD will do).
  - ✔ A job class (default classes have the same name as the default subsystems: QINTER).
- A subsystem (probably called QINTER, another default).

In addition to those objects, you need some "glue" to connect them:

- One or more workstation entries (WSE) in the subsystem. These connect the subsystem with a specific terminal and, when a user signs on, the job with a job description.
- One or more routing entries in the subsystem. When a match is found between the job description's routing data to one of these entries, the job is connected to a class and an initial program (usually QSYS/QCMP). A workstation entry with either the workstation's name or generic name will catch the workstation's name.
- A routing entry with *ANY for CMPVAL or a match of the data in the routing data in the job description. The routing entry should have:
  - ✔ Reference to a job class or *SBSD.
  - ✔ An initial program to call:
    - ➢ Use QSYS/QCMP for a general AS/400 main menu.
    - ➢ Specify a program or application for users.

3.6.1.2 How the System Starts a Batch Job

A batch job runs in the background; in other words, it doesn't tie up a workstation. Batch jobs are started in one of four ways:

- A user or program issues the SBMJOB (Submit Job) command.
- A user issues a communication program start request.
- A subsystem is started and it starts one or more autostart jobs.
- A subsystem is started and it starts one or more preliminary or so-called prestart jobs.

Autostart and prestart jobs are jobs that have been added to the subsystem description with the Add Autostart Job Entry (ADDAJE) or Add Prestarted Job Entry (ADDPJE) commands.

Prestarted jobs start right away within the subsystem, but they take no resources until they are activated. For more information, see chapter 11, Prestart Jobs, in the *OS/400 Work Management V4R2*.

Autostart jobs and jobs submitted (with SBMJOB) go into a job queue before entering a subsystem to run. They might have to wait for other jobs to complete before they can enter the subsystem or they can fall right through, but they have to enter a job queue before they can enter a subsystem.

When a batch job is submitted to the subsystem, the subsystem must do a search for job and runtime attributes similar to what it did with interactive jobs.

When the subsystem first encounters a job, it has the job name (the name specified by the user or program within the SBMJOB command or the autostart job itself) and maybe a job description. The subsystem must determine the job's:

- Job attributes.
- Runtime attributes.

The subsystem finds job attributes from one of several places in this order:

- Specified on the SBMJOB command itself.
- The SBMJOB names a job description to use. The subsystem simply retrieves that job description and pulls the job attributes from it.
- The current user's user profile.
- The job description of the job submitting the job.

Once the subsystem has the job description and the job attributes, it also looks into the job description for the routing data. Routing data makes a match to the subsystem's routing entries, yielding the:

- Supporting program to run.
- Storage pool to run in.
- Class.

From the last item (the class), the subsystem can get the job's runtime attributes. To run a batch job, you need:

- A valid user or executing program or autostart job.
- A SBMJOB command.

Presuming you have the preceding two items, you will need to build or use the defaulted objects for:

- A job description (or the default QDFTJOBD).
- A job queue (default job queues supplied with same names as default subsystems they serve).
- A subsystem (probably called QBATCH, another default).

After those objects are available, you need some "glue" to connect them.

- One or more routing entries in the subsystem. When a match is found between the job description's routing data to one of these entries, the job is connected to a class and an initial program (usually QSYS/QCMP).
- One or more uses of the ADDJOBQE (Add Job Queue Entry) command to connect one or more job queues to the subsystem.
- Additionally, your subsystem should have enough memory to run an active subsystem with:
  - ✔ One routing entry with a CMPVAL of:
    - ➢ *ANY.
    - ➢ A match with the routing data from the job description.
    - ➢ A match with the routing data from the SBMJOB command.
    - ➢ Enough memory to run the job.

3.6.1.3 How the System Starts a Communication Job

Think of a communication job as a kind of hybrid between interactive and batch. It is a job started on one system by another system. The remote system needs to send a program start request down an established communication link and the target system does the rest.

The program start request is a string of routing data. Position 29 of this string must contain the value PGMEVOKE. It must also contain the name of the supporting program the subsystem is to start. This name must start in position 37 of the routing data. The library of that supporting program can be specified starting in position 47.

The subsystem knows to look for these kinds of requests only if it has an appropriate communications entry. As with interactive subsystems, first you build the basic description with the CRTSBSD command. Then add what you need (in this case use the ADDCMNE to Add Communication Entries). The communication entry can specify the job description so the subsystem can get job attributes. The subsystem must also have appropriate routing entries for the job so the subsystem can assign runtime attributes.

Subsystems with communication entries will receive the incoming request and attempt to route it using the routing data. Usually, just one subsystem handles communication jobs.

When the subsystem has the request and it matches the routing data to its internal routing entry, it can figure out the job's runtime attributes. Like batch subsystems, it gets the job class and pool to run in. However, the supporting program to run and its library are specified in positions starting at 37 and 47 of the program start request (used as routing data).

Communications jobs, however, have a unique twist over batch jobs. If you want the supporting program to run in a special environment, you can create another routing entry just for it in the subsystem description. Routing entries are sequentially numbered; just number the routing entry for the supporting program lower than the routing entry that matches PGMEVOKE. Yes, they both have to be present.

With that special environment tool, the supporting program still runs in the subsystem, but it runs with its own class and storage pool.

3.6.2 All Together Now

It should be obvious that you have to have six things for any AS/400:

- Devices (done by autoconfiguration).
- Job descriptions.
- Job classes.
- Job queues.
- Subsystems with:
    - ✔ Routing entry(s).
    - ✔ Job queue entries. For batch subsystems only.
    - ✔ Workstation entry(s). For interactive subsystems only.
    - ✔ Communication entry(s). For communication subsystems only.
    - ✔ Storage pools.
- A valid user ID or password (see chapter 5).

After you read what each item is and what it does for you, you might want to refer to appendix C of the *OS/400 Work Management V4R3* for a list of these defaulted items and the IBM-supplied generic objects you can use.

3.6.2.1 Devices

All devices on an AS/400 need to be made known to it. This is done through *device configuration*. Here is a partial list:

- Workstations.
- Printers.
- Diskette.
- Controllers:
    - ✔ Drives.
    - ✔ Tapes.
    - ✔ Controllers.
- Communications devices:
    - ✔ Lines.
    - ✔ Controllers.

3.6.2.1.1 Automatic Configuration

Let's get right to the nitty-gritty of AS/400 device configuration. You don't have to do anything if you switch on the automatic configuration when you first start up your AS/400. When your AS/400 comes up from the IPL the first time, you'll see a SET MAJOR OPTIONS display. The default for ENABLE AUTOMATIC CONFIGURATION is YES. Therefore, you don't have to do anything if you want it on. See chapter 1, section 1.6.1.1 Set Major System Options.

With automatic configuration to add things like workstations, all you have to do is attach them and turn them on. The AS/400 configures a new device as soon as it senses its presence. If you don't use automatic configuration, you'll have to calculate a name for a device, describe it, then re-IPL before the system will recognize it.

When you enable automatic configuration, you'll be asked to choose among three naming schemes. Choose NORMAL NAMING because it's the most straightforward method. If you're coming from a System/36 shop and prefer its names, choose SYSTEM/36 STYLE.

3.6.2.2 Job Descriptions

Job descriptions define job attributes. All jobs have a job description even if they use the IBM-supplied default, QDFTJOBD. The primary elements of a job description are outlined as follows. Note: The items marked with an asterisk are job-attribute information.

- Job description name.
- Job date.
- Job date format.*
- User ID.*
- Starting information:
  - ✔ Job queue in which the job will be placed (for batch jobs).*
  - ✔ Priority of the job while it is on the job queue (but not its run priority).*
  - ✔ Status on job queue (it can be on HOLD, in which case it won't run until it is released).*
- Output information.
  - ✔ Output queue.*
  - ✔ Print device.*
  - ✔ Output queue priority.*
- Routing data.*
- Accounting code.*
- Message logging level. Whether to log lots of stuff to the job log or a little, see chapter 4.

Don't forget that you can make use of the system default job description, QDFTJOB. Figure 3-10, Figure 3-11, and Figure 3-12 show how to create one of your own descriptions with the Create Job Description (CRTJOBD) command.

```
                    Create Job Description (CRTJOBD)

 Type choices, press Enter.

 Job description . . . . . . . .   __________   Name
   Library . . . . . . . . . . .     *CURLIB    Name, *CURLIB
 Job queue . . . . . . . . . . .   QBATCH       Name
   Library . . . . . . . . . . .     *LIBL      Name, *LIBL, *CURLIB
 Job priority (on JOBQ) . . . . .  5            1-9
 Output priority (on OUTQ)  . . .  5            1-9
 Print device . . . . . . . . . .  *USRPRF      Name, *USRPRF, *SYSVAL...
 Output queue . . . . . . . . . .  *USRPRF      Name, *USRPRF, *DEV, *WRKSTN
   Library . . . . . . . . . . .     ________   Name, *LIBL, *CURLIB
 Text 'description' . . . . . . .  *BLANK

                        Additional Parameters

 User . . . . . . . . . . . . . .  *RQD         Name, *RQD
 Print text . . . . . . . . . . .  *SYSVAL
                                                                More...
 F3=Exit   F4=Prompt   F5=Refresh   F12=Cancel   F13=How to use this display
 F24=More keys
```

Figure 3-10: Prompted version of the CRTJOBD command (part 1 of 3).

```
                    Create Job Description (CRTJOBD)

 Type choices, press Enter.

 Accounting code . . . . . . . .   *USRPRF
 Routing data . . . . . . . . . .  QCMDI

 Request data or command  . . . .  *NONE



 CL syntax check . . . . . . . .   *NOCHK       0-99, *NOCHK
 Initial library list . . . . . .  *SYSVAL      Name, *SYSVAL, *NONE
                + for more values  __________
 End severity . . . . . . . . . .  30           0-99
 Message logging:
   Level . . . . . . . . . . . .   4            0-4
   Severity . . . . . . . . . . .  0            0-99
   Text . . . . . . . . . . . . .  *NOLIST      *NOLIST, *MSG, *SECLVL
 Log CL program commands  . . . .  *NO          *NO, *YES
                                                                More...
 F3=Exit   F4=Prompt   F5=Refresh   F12=Cancel   F13=How to use this display
 F24=More keys
```

Figure 3-11: Prompted version of the CRTJOBD command (part 2 of 3).

```
                        Create Job Description (CRTJOBD)

 Type choices, press Enter.

 Inquiry message reply  . . . . .   *RQD           *RQD, *DFT, *SYSRPYL
 Hold on job queue  . . . . . . .   *NO            *NO, *YES
 Job date . . . . . . . . . . . .   *SYSVAL        Date, *SYSVAL
 Job switches . . . . . . . . . .   00000000       Character value
 Device recovery action . . . . .   *SYSVAL
 Time slice end pool  . . . . . .   *SYSVAL        *SYSVAL, *NONE, *BASE
 Authority  . . . . . . . . . . .   *LIBCRTAUT     Name, *LIBCRTAUT, *CHANGE...
 Job message queue maximum size     *SYSVAL        2-64, *SYSVAL
 Job message queue full action  .   *SYSVAL        *SYSVAL, *NOWRAP, *WRAP...
 Allow multiple threads . . . . .   *NO            *NO, *YES




                                                                         Bottom
 F3=Exit   F4=Prompt   F5=Refresh   F12=Cancel   F13=How to use this display
 F24=More keys
```

Figure 3-12: Prompted version of the CRTJOBD command (part 3 of 3).

Sure there is a lot of stuff but all you really have to put in is the JOB DESCRIPTION.

New with Version 4 are three parameters. They and their possible values are:

- Job Message Queue Maximum Size (JOBMSQMX).
  - ✔ *SYSVAL.
  - ✔ Maximum size of job message queue.
- Job Message Queue Full Action (JOBMSQFL).
  - ✔ *SYSVAL.
  - ✔ *NOWRAP.
  - ✔ *WRAP.
  - ✔ *PRTWRAP.
- Allow Multiple Threads (ALWMLTTHD).
  - ✔ *NO.
  - ✔ *YES.

You can change anything later with either the CHGJOBD or the WRKJOBD command. CHGJOBD looks a lot like the CRTJOBD. Some customers prefer the WRKJOBD because it can give a quick overview of many job descriptions. This is especially helpful if you've forgotten the exact spelling or you are just browsing for a job description. Figure 3-13 shows a sample of WRKJOBD.

```
                         Work with Job Descriptions

 Type options, press Enter.
   1=Create   2=Change   3=Copy   4=Delete   5=Display

        Job
 Opt  Description  Library    Text
  _   __________   _________
  _   QCTL         QSYS       Controlling Subsystem Job Description
  _   QDIRJOBD     QSYS       Job description for Directory Services
  _   QESAUTON     QSYS       Job Description for Automatic Problem Notificati
  _   QFSIOPWK     QSYS       File Sever I/O Processor job description
  _   QIZAJOBD     QSYS       UPGRADE ASSISTANT FOR OS/400 JOBD
  _   QIZAJOBR     QSYS       UPGRADE ASSISTANT FOR OS/400 JOBD
  _   QJSCCPY      QSYS       COPY SCREEN
  _   QLPINSTALL   QSYS       Job description for LP Install
  _   QMSF         QSYS       Job description for QMSF job
  _   QPASVR       QSYS       Target Pass-through Server Job Description
                                                                    More...
 Parameters for options 1, 2, 3 and 5 or command
 ===> _______________________________________________________________________
 F3=Exit      F4=Prompt   F5=Refresh   F9=Retrieve   F11=Display names only
 F12=Cancel   F16=Repeat position to   F17=Position to   F24=More keys
```

Figure 3-13: The WRKJOBD command.

Pick the job description you want to change and put a 2 to the left of it, press F4, and you can change any of its parameters.

The AS/400 comes with several job descriptions made for you. They are listed in appendix C of *OS/400 Work Management V3R6.*

3.6.2.3 Job Classes

A *job class* is a way of providing job attributes. Where job descriptions supply jobs with job attributes, job classes provide runtime attributes. Runtime attributes consist of three primary elements:

- *Runtime priority.* Runtime priority is the priority the job will have when it is active in the subsystem.
- *Time slice.* Time slice in milliseconds is how long the CPU can work on this job before going on to another one.
- *Eligible for purge.* Always leave this setting at the default *YES. If the system needs to purge a job, it will regardless of this value. The difference is that if this parameter is *YES, the system will purge it and later restore it cleanly. When this parameter is *NO, the system will hack it to pieces when it purges it and have to work harder finding and reassembling those pieces.

Figure 3-14 shows the command to create a job class, CRTCLS.

```
                          Create Class (CRTCLS)

 Type choices, press Enter.

 Class . . . . . . . . . . . . .   _________   Name
   Library . . . . . . . . . . .     *CURLIB     Name, *CURLIB
 Run priority . . . . . . . . . .   50          1-99
 Time slice . . . . . . . . . . .   2000        Milliseconds
 Eligible for purge . . . . . . .   *YES        *YES, *NO
 Default wait time  . . . . . . .   30          Seconds, *NOMAX
 Maximum CPU time . . . . . . . .   *NOMAX      Milliseconds, *NOMAX
 Maximum temporary storage  . . .   *NOMAX      Kilobytes, *NOMAX
 Text 'description' . . . . . . .   *BLANK

                                                                   Bottom
 F3=Exit   F4=Prompt   F5=Refresh   F10=Additional parameters   F12=Cancel
 F13=How to use this display        F24=More keys
```

Figure 3-14: Prompted version of CRTCLS.

IBM has filled in some fairly decent default values (enough to make the class work). Before you start creating your own classes, however, you might want to try the IBM-supplied ones. They are listed in appendix C of the *OS/400 Work Management V4R2.*

3.6.2.4 Job Queues (Batch Jobs Only)

Before a job becomes active in a batch subsystem, it must pass through a job queue. A *job queue* is simply a holding place for jobs entering the system. Sometimes a queue is empty and a job falls right through into the subsystem where it starts running. Other times a queue will be full of pending jobs and a new job entering will take its place in the queue.

Each job has a job queue priority assignment that comes from its job description. Jobs in the queue will be released to the subsystem in ascending order of these priorities. If all jobs have equal priority, they will be released in first-in-first-out order.

You can manipulate jobs on a queue. If you had five jobs on a queue with equal priority and a sixth one entered with the same priority, the sixth one won't start until the other five have started (and the subsystem is ready to accept another job). If the sixth job is very important, you could change its priority to a number lower than any of the other five jobs' priorities to get it to start sooner. Another thing you can do is to hold all five jobs until after the sixth starts.

To manipulate jobs on a queue, however, you must have special authority JOBCTL (Job Control) on your user ID. For more on user IDs see chapter 5.

You create a job queue with the Create Job Queue (CRTJOBQ) command. Figure 3-15 shows its format.

```
                          Create Job Queue (CRTJOBQ)

Type choices, press Enter.

Job queue  . . . . . . . . . . .   █__________  Name
  Library  . . . . . . . . . . .     *CURLIB    Name, *CURLIB
Text 'description' . . . . . . .   *BLANK

                           Additional Parameters

Operator controlled  . . . . . .   *YES         *YES, *NO
Authority to check . . . . . . .   *OWNER       *OWNER, *DTAAUT
Authority  . . . . . . . . . . .   *USE         Name, *USE, *ALL, *CHANGE...




                                                                        Bottom
F3=Exit   F4=Prompt   F5=Refresh   F12=Cancel   F13=How to use this display
F24=More keys
```

Figure 3-15: Prompted version of the CRTJOBQ command.

All you really have to put in is the job queue name and its library; that is all most AS/400 customers actually do. There are some authority things at the bottom. You can read more about them in the *OS/400 CL Reference*. Their default values are adequate for most installations.

Creating a job queue is only half the job, though. You have to assign it to a batch subsystem. Do this with the ADDJOBQE (Add Job Queue Entry) command. Its basic format is simple:

ADDJOBQE <library>/<batch subsystem><library>/<job queue name>

Prompt it by pressing the F4 key and you will get more parameters you can set.

As an aid to getting started, the AS/400 comes with several job queues for you to use or modify as you wish. They are listed in appendix C of the *OS/400 Data Management V3R6, OS/400 Work Management V3R6.*

3.7 Subsystems

Subsystems are environments where jobs run. The best part is they are environments the customer defines. You get to create the optimum environment in which to run your batch jobs and the optimum environment in which to run your interactive jobs. You can even have separate environments for different departments' users and shift computer resources around as needed.

AS/400 jobs only run in subsystems. You create a subsystem by creating its description. The command is Create Subsystem Description (CRTSBSD). See Figure 3-16.

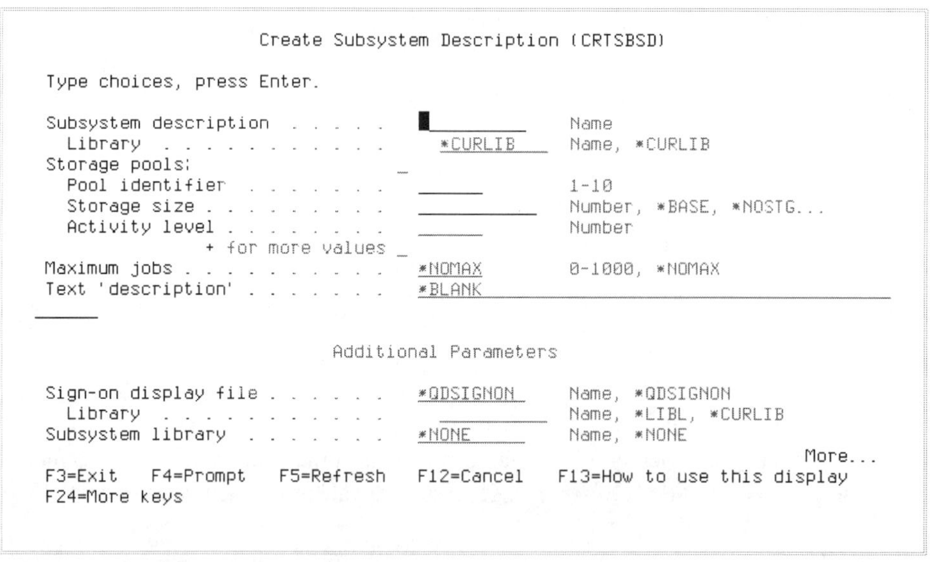

```
                    Create Subsystem Description (CRTSBSD)

Type choices, press Enter.

Subsystem description . . . . .   ________      Name
  Library . . . . . . . . . . .     *CURLIB     Name, *CURLIB
Storage pools:                  _
  Pool identifier . . . . . . .   ______        1-10
  Storage size . . . . . . . . .  ___________   Number, *BASE, *NOSTG...
  Activity level . . . . . . . .  ______        Number
             + for more values _
Maximum jobs . . . . . . . . . .  *NOMAX        0-1000, *NOMAX
Text 'description' . . . . . . .  *BLANK

                         Additional Parameters

Sign-on display file . . . . . .  *QDSIGNON     Name, *QDSIGNON
  Library . . . . . . . . . . .     ________    Name, *LIBL, *CURLIB
Subsystem library . . . . . . .   *NONE         Name, *NONE
                                                                More...
F3=Exit   F4=Prompt   F5=Refresh   F12=Cancel   F13=How to use this display
F24=More keys
```

Figure 3-16: Prompted CRTSBSD command.

You don't have to do much more than just put in the subsystem name and library. That's the beauty of the AS/400—it has enough built-in defaults that it kind of knows what you want to do.

However, you should at least specify some memory storage pools. Section 3.3, Memory: Storage Pools and Activity Levels, introduces the topic, but the practical side is covered here.

Section 3.3 describes how a subsystem can have up to 10 memory pools in which to run its jobs. What I didn't discuss is that the first pool, whatever it is, also always has the subsystem driver running. You really don't want that activity in a private or general shared pool. You want it in *BASE for any subsystem. So here is a rule: Any subsystem's number 1 pool is *BASE (referred to its system name, 2).

Reading down in Figure 3-16, the next parameter, MAXIMUM JOBS, is the maximum number of jobs that the subsystem will allow active at any one time. Remember, jobs come into the subsystem from one or more job queues. It wouldn't be very efficient if you could just flood a subsystem. Therefore, this value sets a limit on the number of jobs that can be in the subsystem at any one time. This value is crucial. How many jobs you allow in also helps determine how much memory the subsystem should have assigned to it.

Don't confuse maximum jobs with the subsystem's activity level. MAXIMUM JOBS specify how many jobs are in the subsystem at one time while activity level specifies how many of those jobs the subsystem will actually be working on at one time. For performance, the big difference between the two is this:

- Maximum Jobs:
  - ✔ Set too low and job queues back up.
  - ✔ Set too high and throughput goes down.
- Activity Level:
  - ✔ Very little impact on the casual observer because jobs frequently change states.
  - ✔ High impact on overall throughput of the subsystem. Even if MAXIMUM JOBS are set too high, if activity levels are set correctly, throughput will be good.

Usually you don't enter anything more than that. You could go back to storage pools and put a "+" on the + FOR MORE VALUES parameter and create at least one additional storage pool.

3.7.1 Routing Entries

After working on the main STRSBSD command, you need to add at least routing entries. These give the subsystem a place to find any job's runtime attributes.

There are no routing objects on the system that you can directly create or change. You add routing entries to an already created subsystem description with the ADDRTGE command. You do further maintenance on them with the CHGRTGE and RMVRTGE commands.

You control a job's *routing* indirectly, through these routing entries, and the routing-data parameter on the JOB DESCRIPTION (see section 3.6.2.2 Job Descriptions).

The system attempts to make a match between literals held in the routing data to those in the routing entries. Theoretically, a job has a description that contains a code or statement or something in its routing data. The subsystem also has a list of routing entries. Each entry has a corresponding code or statement that the system uses to match to the job's routing data. When there is a match, the subsystem reads what class to make the job, what supporting program to invoke, and what it's runtime attributes are. Figure 3-17 shows a sample of the routing data on a job description.

```
                        Display Job Description
                                                       System:   SYS02
Job description:   QINTER         Library:   QGPL

Message logging:
  Level  . . . . . . . . . . . . . . . . . . . :   4
  Severity . . . . . . . . . . . . . . . . . . :   0
  Text . . . . . . . . . . . . . . . . . . . . :   *NOLIST
Log CL program commands  . . . . . . . . . . . :   *NO
Accounting code  . . . . . . . . . . . . . . . :   *USRPRF
Print text . . . . . . . . . . . . . . . . . . :   *SYSVAL

Routing data . . . . . . . . . . . . . . . . . :   QCMDI
```

Figure 3-17: A sample of the routing data for a job description.

Figure 3-18 shows a sample of some routing entries from a subsystem. I got this by using the DSPSBSD command and taking the option for Routing Entries.

```
                        Display Routing Entries
                                                          System:   SYS01
Subsystem description:   QINTER01       Status:   ACTIVE

Type options, press Enter.
  5=Display details

                                                                     Start
Opt    Seq Nbr    Program       Library       Compare Value           Pos
 _       10       QCMD          QSYS          'QCMDI'                  1
 _       20       QCMD          QSYS          'QS36MRT'                1
 _       22       QCMD          QSYS          'QRPTY25I'               1
 _       24       QCMD          QSYS          'QRPTY30I'               1
 _       26       QCMD          QSYS          'QRPTY35I'               1
 _       40       QARDRIVE      QSYS          '525XTEST'               1
 _      700       QCL           QSYS          'QCMD38'                 1
 _     9999       QCMD          QSYS          *ANY

                                                                    Bottom
F3=Exit   F9=Display all detailed descriptions   F12=Cancel
```

Figure 3-18: Routing entries in the subsystem description.

Notice that the value to match is specified on the column under Compare Value (CMPVAL). To the right of that is the compare position of 1. You can compare different starting positions of the routing data. If a match is found, in most cases, the initial program the subsystem will call will be QSYS/QCMD. This is an AS/400 command processor program (CPP) that is able to execute commands. Generally, it is named as a routing entry's initial program.

For more information about a routing entry, put a 5 on the option line and press the Enter key. See Figure 3-19.

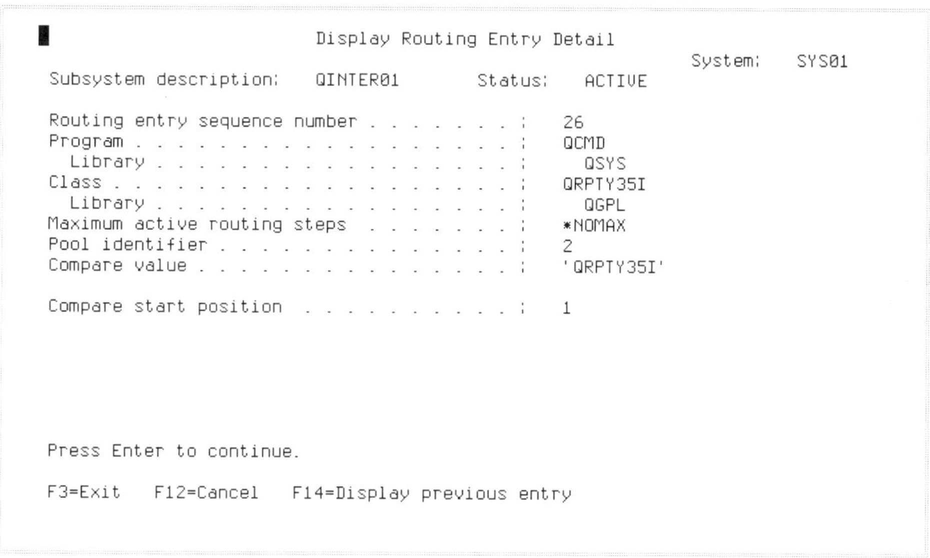

```
                        Display Routing Entry Detail
                                                              System:   SYS01
 Subsystem description:    QINTER01       Status:   ACTIVE

 Routing entry sequence number . . . . . . . . :   26
 Program . . . . . . . . . . . . . . . . . . . :   QCMD
   Library . . . . . . . . . . . . . . . . . . :     QSYS
 Class . . . . . . . . . . . . . . . . . . . . :   QRPTY35I
   Library . . . . . . . . . . . . . . . . . . :     QGPL
 Maximum active routing steps  . . . . . . . . :   *NOMAX
 Pool identifier . . . . . . . . . . . . . . . :   2
 Compare value . . . . . . . . . . . . . . . . :   'QRPTY35I'

 Compare start position  . . . . . . . . . . . :   1



 Press Enter to continue.

 F3=Exit   F12=Cancel   F14=Display previous entry
```

Figure 3-19: Expanded routing entries in the subsystem description.

Note the use of this routing entry (a clue to which is provided on the routing data) QPTY35. Any job with this routing data would get runtime attributes from class QPTY35, which is a modified version of job class QINTER. The only difference is that the runtime priority is 35 (not 20). It is for low-priority interactive jobs.

Using multiple routing entries and job classes like this is a fairly advanced procedure. If you're new to the AS/400, you can get by not specifying routing data information on any job description. Instead, specify a single routing entry on subsystem descriptions with a compare value of *ANY. No check is made because the specification considers any job to be a match.

3.7.2 Workstation Entries (Interactive Jobs Only)

AS/400 workstations are devices. Workstation entries (WSE) are listed with the subsystem description and are similar to routing entries. They contain the name of specific displays or generic displays that the subsystem will support. It also has a job description to use when a user attempts to sign on from that display.

If you're using the system's autoconfiguration, it will have named your display station devices something like DSP01, DSP02, DSP03, and so on. You can identify every display station in your shop to the interactive subsystem by leaving those names and specifying one workstation entry with the generic name: D*.

Most AS/400 shops just use the generic name and have one line that serves as a WSE for every display on the system. The WSE can be used to associate a job description with each terminal. The WSE's main jobs are:

- Associate valid workstations that the interactive subsystem will support.
- Associate a job description with a user signing on. This is either done by specifying on the WSE:
  - ✔ A job description.
  - ✔ *USRPRF, which tells the subsystem to go to the user profile of the signing-on user and get the job description.
  - ✔ *SBSD, which tells the subsystem to look at the job description specified on its description.

3.8 STARTING/ENDING SUBSYSTEMS

Section 3.6 describes creating subsystem descriptions; subsystems do not become active until you start them. The command for that is STRSBS. See Figure 3-20.

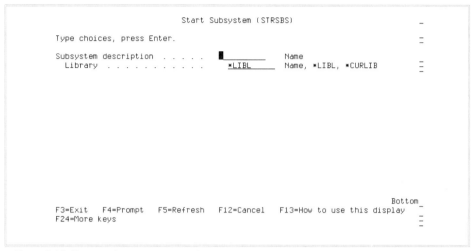

```
                           Start Subsystem (STRSBS)

 Type choices, press Enter.

 Subsystem description . . . . .   __________   Name
   Library . . . . . . . . . . .     *LIBL      Name, *LIBL, *CURLIB












                                                                Bottom
 F3=Exit   F4=Prompt   F5=Refresh   F12=Cancel   F13=How to use this display
 F24=More keys
```

Figure 3-20: Prompted STRSBS command.

The only parameter that you have to specify is the subsystem to start. When you bring up the AS/400 from an IPL, you need to have a program start all your subsystems or you need to start them yourself. Figure 3-21 contains a sample of such a program.

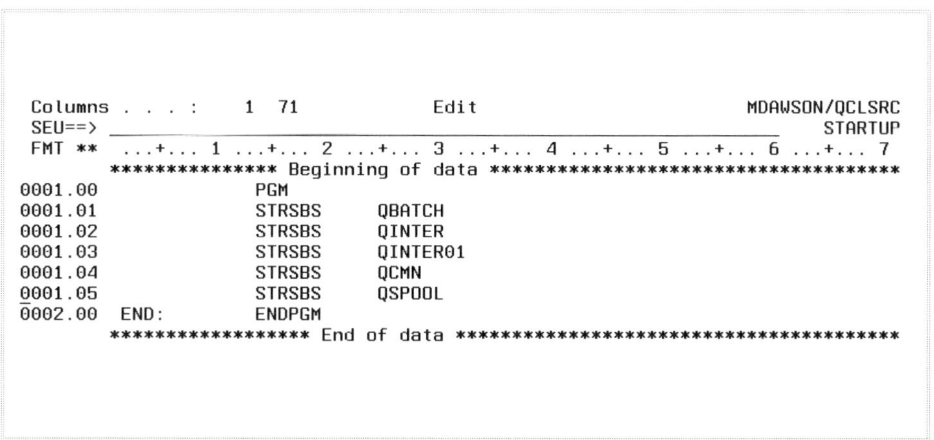

```
 Columns . . . :    1  71            Edit                        MDAWSON/QCLSRC
 SEU==> ____________________________________________________________  STARTUP
 FMT **  ...+... 1 ...+... 2 ...+... 3 ...+... 4 ...+... 5 ...+... 6 ...+... 7
        *************** Beginning of data *************************************
0001.00               PGM
0001.01               STRSBS      QBATCH
0001.02               STRSBS      QINTER
0001.03               STRSBS      QINTER01
0001.04               STRSBS      QCMN
0001.05               STRSBS      QSPOOL
0002.00  END:         ENDPGM
        ****************** End of data ****************************************
```

Figure 3-21: Sample of a program to automatically bring up subsystems when the AS/400 comes up from an IPL.

To have the program execute automatically every time the AS/400 comes up, put it's library and name on the QSTRUPPGM system value using the WRKSYSVAL command.

When you want to end a subsystem, use the ENDSBS command. See Figure 3-22.

```
                         End Subsystem (ENDSBS)

Type choices, press Enter.

Subsystem . . . . . . . . . . .   _________     Name, *ALL
How to end . . . . . . . . . . .  *CNTRLD       *CNTRLD, *IMMED
Delay time, if *CNTRLD . . . . .  *NOLIMIT      Seconds, *NOLIMIT








                                                                Bottom
F3=Exit   F4=Prompt   F5=Refresh   F12=Cancel   F13=How to use this display
F24=More keys
```

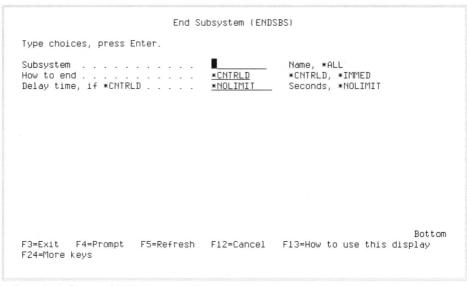

Figure 3-22: Prompted ENDSBS command.

You need to specify either a subsystem or the general *ALL. The second parameter, HOW TO END, will accept either *CNTRLD or *IMMED. *CNTRLD is for a controlled shutdown. It will have the system properly close any active jobs before it ends. The *IMMED is for an immediate end to the subsystem. You might think *CNTRLD is the way to close a job, but in real life *CNTRLD can take a long time.

Most customers end a subsystem by using the WRKACTJOB command to check it first for active jobs. If you find active jobs, you do whatever will end them normally. Once all jobs in a subsystem are ended, then do an ENDSBS with the *IMMED option.

3.9 OUTPUT QUEUES

Any job on the AS/400 that produces printed output must put that output into an output queue. This printed output on the queue is called a *spooled output file*. A printer (called a *writer* on the AS/400) must be connected with an output queue before it can print anything.

Create an output queue with the CRTOUTQ command. See Figure 3-23.

```
                     Create Output Queue (CRTOUTQ)

 Type choices, press Enter.

 Output queue . . . . . . . . . .   __________     Name
   Library  . . . . . . . . . . .    *CURLIB___    Name, *CURLIB
 Maximum spooled file size:        _
   Number of pages  . . . . . . .   *NONE______    Number, *NONE
   Starting time  . . . . . . . .   ________       Time
   Ending time  . . . . . . . . .   ________       Time
                 + for more values _
 Order of files on queue  . . . .   *FIFO_         *FIFO, *JOBNBR
 Remote system  . . . . . . . . .   *NONE_____________________________



                                                                Bottom
 F3=Exit   F4=Prompt   F5=Refresh   F10=Additional parameters   F12=Cancel
 F13=How to use this display        F24=More keys
```

Figure 3-23: Prompted CRTOUTQ command.

This is one of those simple commands. Just supply the output queue name and the rest of the defaults are fine. Change any of those parameters with the CHGOUTQ command.

New with Version 4 is the MAXIMUM SPOOLED FILE SIZE parameter set. It refers to the maximum number of pages that can be printed within a particular time range. The time range is expressed in terms of the 24-hour clock.

The NUMBER OF PAGES parameter specifies the maximum number of pages. The STARTING TIME and ENDING TIME specifies the time range within which the pages will be counted. If a user exceeds this number, the output will not be lost, it will be held in a deferred status until the next time period starts.

3.10 New Systems—Where to Now?

By now, you know the building blocks that make up job control and job environments on the AS/400. You also have a pretty good idea of interactive and batch-job flow.

The AS/400 comes with two subsystems up and running: QBASE and QCTL. As a minimum, you should also configure and start the following subsystems that are generic to the AS/400:

- QCMN to handle communication jobs. If your network is LAN-based, your terminals will come in through this subsystem before being handed off to QINTER.
- QINTER subsystem for interactive jobs.
- QBATCH subsystem for batch jobs.
- QSPL subsystem for printing jobs.

Review these subsystems. Also, review the generic job descriptions, classes, queues, and so on that came with your machine. Add some memory and routing information to the subsystems. Add some WSE entries to the QINTER subsystem description. Then start the subsystems.

As you configure user profiles and allow your users online, the jobs they run will be pretty much where you want them. Later, as you get used to the AS/400, you'll make changes to most of this. You'll even be cloning new subsystems from the AS/400-supplied ones. For now, just build this basic configuration.

3.11 References

AS/400 Programming Reference Summary V4R3 (SX41-5720-02)

OS/400 Backup and Recovery V4R3 (SC41-5304-02)

OS/400 CL Programming (SC41-5721-01)

OS/400 CL Reference (SC41-5722-02)

OS/400 Work Management V4R3 (SC41-5306-02)

4 Logs, Messages, and Cleanup

4.1 Overview

The AS/400 keeps four types of logs for you. Some are automatic—they are just there for you to use—but with others you have to do something to start them. Logs record information about events as they happen. The four logs and a brief description of how automatic they are and where they are kept include:

- History (QHST):
  - ✔ Automatic.
  - ✔ Is kept in a physical file.
- Job:
  - ✔ Automatic, but you can change what is logged.
  - ✔ Is kept within active jobs or in spooled output files for completed jobs.
- Job accounting:
  - ✔ Not automatic; requires that you start it.
  - ✔ Is kept in a journal.
- Security audit:
  - ✔ Not automatic; requires that you start it.
  - ✔ Is kept in a journal.

Much of the data in logs are actually captured messages. The AS/400 uses messages quite extensively both internally and externally. Messages notify the user or the system operator that something is happening. But messages also start and stop tasks within the AS/400.

Logs and messages are nice but they quickly take up lots of DASD space. If you ask it to, the AS/400 automatically will organize messages with a utility called Cleanup.

4.2 History Logs (QHST)

History logs are:

- ◆ Automatic.
- ◆ Are kept in a physical file.

Everything that the AS/400 does results in a message going somewhere around the system. In addition to their intended destinations, one place all high-level messages (system activities, job information, device status, operator messages, and more) go to is a history message queue (see section 4.6 Messages) named QHST.

A program receives those messages and writes them to a physical file called the history log. This history log is named QHST*yyjjjn* where:

- ◆ *yy* is the year on which the physical file was created.
- ◆ *jjj* is the Julian date on which the physical file was created.
- ◆ *n* is a sequence number (0-9, A-Z).

The maximum number of records in this physical file is set in system value QHSTLOGSIZ. You can find out what history logs are currently on your system with the command:

```
WRKOBJ QSYS/QHST* *FILE
```

You can display current history log information with command DSPLOG. You can specify that you only want messages issued during a specific time period, by a specific job, or certain message IDs. Figures 4-1 and 4-2 show the prompted version of the command DSPLOG.

```
                           Display Log (DSPLOG)

Type choices, press Enter.

Log . . . . . . . . . . . . . . . > QHST          QHST
Time period for log output:
  Start time and date:
  Beginning time . . . . . . . .   *AVAIL        Time, *AVAIL
  Beginning date . . . . . . . .   *CURRENT      Date, *CURRENT, *BEGIN
  End time and date:
  Ending time  . . . . . . . . .   *AVAIL        Time, *AVAIL
  Ending date  . . . . . . . . .   *CURRENT      Date, *CURRENT, *END
Output . . . . . . . . . . . . .   *             *, *PRINT




                                                                 More...
F3=Exit   F4=Prompt   F5=Refresh   F12=Cancel   F13=How to use this display
F24=More keys
```

Figure 4-1: Prompted version of DSPLOG command (part 1 of 2).

```
                          Display Log (DSPLOG)

 Type choices, press Enter.

                          Additional Parameters

 Jobs to display . . . . . . . .   *NONE          Name, *NONE
   User . . . . . . . . . . . .     __________    Name
   Number . . . . . . . . . . .     ______        000000-999999
               + for more values   __________
                                    __________
                                    ______
 Message identifier . . . . . . .  *ALL           Name, *ALL
               + for more values   _______



                                                                    Bottom
 F3=Exit   F4=Prompt   F5=Refresh   F12=Cancel   F13=How to use this display
 F24=More keys
```

Figure 4-2: Prompted version of DSPLOG command (part 2 of 2).

Figure 4-3 shows a sample of a screen of history log data.

```
                       Display History Log Contents

 Job 005392/QPM400/Q1PDR started on 08/12/98 at 00:00:15 in subsystem Q1PGSCH
 Job 005392/QPM400/Q1PDR ended on 08/12/98 at 00:01:39; 51 seconds used; end c
 Job 005393/QPM400/Q1PPMSUB started on 08/12/98 at 00:01:39 in subsystem Q1PGS
 Job 005393/QPM400/Q1PPMSUB ended on 08/12/98 at 00:01:39; 1 seconds used; end
 Job 005394/QPGMR/QPFRMON started on 08/12/98 at 00:01:39 in subsystem Q1PGSCH
 Performance monitor 005394/QPGMR/QPFRMON started at 00:01:39 08/12/98.
 Job 005395/QIJS/QIJSCCC started on 08/12/98 at 00:14:02 in subsystem QSYSWRK
 Job 005396/QIJS/RMVHSTJS started on 08/12/98 at 00:14:03 in subsystem QSYSWRK
 Job 005395/QIJS/QIJSCCC ended on 08/12/98 at 00:14:03; 1 seconds used; end co
 Job 005397/QIJS/RMVLOGEJS started on 08/12/98 at 00:14:03 in subsystem QSYSWR
 Job 005396/QIJS/RMVHSTJS ended on 08/12/98 at 00:14:04; 1 seconds used; end c
 Job 005397/QIJS/RMVLOGEJS ended on 08/12/98 at 00:14:04; 1 seconds used; end
 Job 005398/QPM400/Q1PPMSUB started on 08/12/98 at 01:00:17 in subsystem Q1PGS
 Job 005398/QPM400/Q1PPMSUB ended on 08/12/98 at 01:00:17; 1 seconds used; end
 Job 005399/QPM400/Q1PPMCHK started on 08/12/98 at 02:00:20 in subsystem Q1PGS
 Job 005399/QPM400/Q1PPMCHK ended on 08/12/98 at 02:00:20; 1 seconds used; end
 Job 005400/QPM400/Q1PPMSUB started on 08/12/98 at 02:00:20 in subsystem Q1PGS
                                                                      More...
 Press Enter to continue.

 F3=Exit   F10=Display all   F12=Cancel
```

Figure 4-3: Results of DSPLOG command.

At first glance, it looks confusing and without much substance. However, if you put the cursor over any line and press the Help key or F1 key, you'll get more information. Figure 4-4 shows an expanded line from Figure 4-3.

```
                      Additional Message Information

Message ID . . . . . . :   CPF0A51
Date sent  . . . . . . :   08/12/98      Time sent  . . . . . . :   00:01:39

Message . . . . :   Performance monitor 005394/QPGMR/QPFRMON started at
  00:01:39 08/12/98.

Cause . . . . . :   The job was started from job queue Q1PSCHQ2 in QMPGLIB.
  The performance monitor was submitted to the job queue by
  005393/QPM400/Q1PPMSUB.  The data will be put into the performance data
  collection database files located in library QMPGDATA with member name
  Q982240001.

                                                                   Bottom
Press Enter to continue.

F1=Help   F3=Exit   F6=Print   F9=Display message details   F12=Cancel
F21=Select assistance level
```

Figure 4-4: Expansion of the line marked on Figure 4-3 with cursor.

There is a lot of stuff in the QHST file. Sometimes when things happen that don't get into other logs like the job log, they end up here. If you know how to quickly wade through all those records, you can pull out a lot of information.

The best way to routinely scan the QHST file is to write a program to do it. Sections 5.11.15 through 5.11.17 of *OS/400 Work Management V4R2* provide a sample of program and QHST record layouts. A very useful scanning program to write is one that scans the file for security messages, which are all prefixed by CPI, CPF, CPC, CPD, and CPA. They are suffixed with the numeric range 2200 through 22FF.

When one history file fills up, the system creates another one. It doesn't take much time for history logs to take up quite a bit of system space. The best way to keep the logs manageable is to have the system automatically clean them up for you (see section 4.7 System Cleanup).

Any time you're going to do a SAVSYS, particularly prior to installing a new release of the operating system (OS), save yourself some time by deleting all history files before you start. For additional information on operating systems, see chapter 2.

4.3 Job Logs

Job logs are:

- Automatic, but you can change what is logged.
- Kept:
  - ✔ Within active jobs.
  - ✔ In spooled output files for completed jobs.

Every job that runs on the AS/400 collects messages in an internal log while it is running. AS/400 customers don't normally think of the job log as part of a running job. When the job finishes, the contents of the job log are written to a spooled-output file in queue QPJOBLOG or QEZJOBLOG.

You can limit the types of messages that any job logs. You can even turn off job logs if you want. However, when a job terminates abnormally, you get a job log anyway. It's somewhat risky turning off job logging altogether because that can be the only audit of what happened within the job. Many jobs terminate normally, but—if you happen to encounter a problem—your only source for what went wrong could be the job log.

Job logs come down to this: Most of the time you don't need them and they take up valuable DASD space. The temptation is to not collect them. But the one time a crucial program fails, the only audit of what happened will probably be the job log. Job logs are a pain but when you need them, you really need them. Your task is to balance DASD space against the need for an audit trail.

A job may not produce a job log for any of several reasons. This is no big deal most of the time. If you're watching a "problem" job and it completes without producing a job log, you can find out why by looking in the history log (refer to section 4.2 History Logs (QHST)) for message CPF1164. The reason no log was produced will be encoded in the message. The codes are listed in *OS/400 Work Management V4R3*.

4.3.1 Logging Level

You specify what messages you want collected for any job through the logging level. The parameter for this is LOG and it is on both the JOB DESCRIPTION and on the SBMJOB command. You can also change this parameter on an active job with the CHGJOB commands. Or you can change it on a job description with the CHGJOBD or

WRKJOBD commands. There are three parts to the LOG parameter. Figure 4-5 shows a representation of it.

```
Message logging:
  Level . . . . . . . . . . . . .   4           0-4, *JOBD
  Severity . . . . . . . . . . .   0           0-99, *JOBD
  Text . . . . . . . . . . . . .   *MSG        *JOBD, *MSG, *SECLVL, *NOLIST
```

Figure 4-5: Sample LOG parameter.

- Level accepts a numeric code from 0 to 4.

  ✔ 0 Nothing is logged.

  ✔ 1 Only messages sent to the job's external message queue and that have a severity greater than or equal to that specified under Severity (discussed as follows). Examples are a job's start/stop time and its completion status.

  ✔ 2 Level 1 messages plus.
  Any requests/command from a CL program that have a severity greater than or equal to that specified under Severity (discussed as follows). All messages associated with those requests/commands as long as the messages have a severity greater than or equal to that specified under Severity (discussed as follows).

  ✔ 3 Level 1 messages plus.

  Level 2 messages plus.
  All requests/commands from a CL program.
  All messages associated with those requests/commands as long as the messages have a severity greater than or equal to that specified under Severity (discussed below).

  ✔ 4 Level 1 messages plus.

  Level 2 messages plus.
  Level 3 messages plus.
  Any message that has a severity greater than or equal to that specified under Severity.

- Severity specifies the severity level of the requests/commands/ messages logged. On the AS/400, message have *severities* that range from 00 to 99. The 00 messages are informational only. The 99 messages tend to be the last message before a program abnormally terminates. Most serious job messages are level 30 or higher. That means if you specify a severity of 30, a level greater than 0, and text other than *NOLIST, you'll get all messages of severity 30 through 99.

- *Text* is the amount of message text to be written to the job log. All messages on the AS/400 have two levels.

  - ✔ Level 1 is the short, 80-bytes-or-less version.

  - ✔ Level 2 is the long version for those new to the system or the particular message. This is sometimes referred to as the *second level message*.

The possible values for TEXT are:

- *MSG—Only the Level 1 text of the message is written to the log.

- *SECLVL—Level 2 or Second Level messages are written to the log.

- *NOLIST—No messages are logged unless the program ends abnormally.

Most AS/400 shops specify a 4 for level and 0 for severity. After that, *NOLIST is fairly standard for stable, established shops and *MSG is used for others or for new applications. For AS/400-supplied job description objects, QCTL, QINTER, QBATCH, and QPGMR come with LOG(4 0 *NOLIST). You can create your own or change these with the CHGJOBD command.

There is one trap about message logging for interactive jobs. An interactive job ends only when the user signs off with the SIGNOFF command. A parameter on that command, LOG, can have a default of *NOLIST that allows no logging to occur no matter to what level your job-description logging level is set.

If you want logging to occur, you need to set the command's default to LOG(*LIST). Do so with the following command:

```
CHGCMDDFT SIGNOFF NEWDFT( 'LOG(*LIST)')
```

4.3.2 Displaying the Job Log

From time to time, you will want to look at the job log. The log can be a part of a running job or on the spool file for a completed job. To display the job log from:

- Current interactive job, do any of the following:
  - ✔ Type DSPJOBLOG on command line and press Enter, followed by F10.
  - ✔ Type WRKJOB on command line and take option 10, press F10.
  - ✔ Press F10.
  - ✔ If a job is still active on the system, do either:
    - ➢ WRKUSRJOB. (You have to know who the user is).
    - ➢ WRKACTJOB. Find the job and select Option 5 (WORK WITH JOB), then select option 10 (DISPLAY JOB LOG).
  - ✔ Press System Request key, Option 3 (DISPLAY CURRENT JOB). Take option 10 (DISPLAY JOB LOG) and press F10.
  - ✔ Sign off from your session, making sure LOG(*LIST) is set on the sign-off command. Then sign onto a new session and browse your job log from QEZJOBLOG.
- Any other job, do any of the following:
  - ✔ If the job is no longer active in the system, do WRKUSRJOB, select Option 8 (DISPLAY SPOOLED FILE) find last (which will be the latest) QPJOBLOG. Select Option 5 (DISPLAY JOB LOG).
  - ✔ WRKOUTQ QPJOBLOG (or QEZJOBLOG). The resulting list can be hundreds of screens long. Use F18 to quickly go to the bottom where the most current job logs are.

4.4 Job Accounting

Job accounting:

- Is not automatic; it requires that you start it.
- Data is kept in a journal receiver.

Job accounting captures information about jobs that tell you who uses what on your computer. It tracks usage of processing unit, printer, display stations, database, and communications functions.

A key distinction of job accounting is the use of the *accounting code*. A job's accounting code can be loaded into the job description or the user profile. The accounting code is optional because it's only a grouping device; you actually don't have to use it at all. But the accounting code helps make job accounting more meaningful when you want to study computer resource usage not by one job but by all jobs in a particular department (or by an individual).

For example, you could identify all the jobs accounting runs as ACC. You could further separate receivables from payables with the codes ACCAR and ACCAP. You have up to 15 characters to use for accounting codes.

What's interesting about job accounting information is that it has basic information to monitor other things about the jobs on your system. It contains response-time information, DASD I/O information, user, and start/stop times. For this reason, you can use it to monitor job performance without having to use Performance Monitor (see chapter 9). Or, if you have had a performance degradation and Performance Monitor wasn't on but job accounting was, you can use it to give you a pretty good idea of what happened to your system to cause the degradation.

You can also capture statistics—such as the number of pages a job prints, the time a job entered the system, and the time it started (from which you can calculate the queue wait time)—Performance Monitor can't do. I've written programs just to scan the job accounting data and calculate by department for this information during month-end processing. I filed that information to create a library of the relative work being done during this processing over a long period of time.

With job accounting, you can uniquely identify groups of jobs, either through their job descriptions or the profiles of the users using them.

4.4.1 Set Up Job Accounting

Job accounting is really a kind of journaling. An overview of how to set up journaling is included here but, if you want more information, refer to chapter 8, Journaling.

To set up job accounting, start by creating a journal and journal receiver. These will be in a library (logically enough) and it is a good idea to create a special library and receiver unique for job accounting. For performance reasons, it's a lot smarter to create your own job accounting library. Create the library with this command:

```
CRTLIB <library name of your choice>
```

Create a journal receiver. Receiver names should be 10 characters long (6 alpha characters followed by 4 numeric, and generally start with 0001 as the numeric). This is an accounting journal; therefore, ACCJRN0001 would be a good name.

```
CRTJRNRCV JRNRCV(<your library name/ACCJRN0001
```

Create the journal. In this case, you have no choice about the library or journal name. Here's the command you use:

```
CRTJRN QSYS/QACGJRN
```

Set system value QACGLVL, which controls job accounting logging. Use the WRKSYSVAL command to reset its contents as needed to one of the following values:

- *NONE Turns off job accounting.
- *JOB Captures the performance portion of each job on a JB entry.
- *PRINT Captures each job's printing information on a DB or SP entry.
- *JOB *PRINT Combines *JOB and *PRINT entries.

It might seem silly to have a value of *NONE. But one strategy for a shop that doesn't intend to use job accounting all the time is to set up the journal and journal receiver to control data collection simply by changing this system value.

When a journal receiver fills up or if you want to use job accounting sporadically, you'll want to change journals. Use the command:

```
CHGJRN  JRNRCV(*GEN)
```

4.4.2 Displaying Job Accounting Journal

Because job accounting information is in a journal, you have two ways of getting to the data:

- DSPJRN—if you're capturing many records from the journal. It is best to use this command's parameter, OUTFILE(*OUTFILE) to collect the extracted records into a physical file. From there you can browse the entries or write a program or query to analyze their contents.
- RCVJRNE—if you are looking for specific, real-time journal entries. RCVJRNE is usually used within a CL program.

When you display journal entries, you might notice that you have two sets of fields:

1. Lots of fields that make up the journal header.
2. A big blank field for the original contents of the journaled data. In other words, it has no record definition.

If you do work with accounting journal entries, they appear in three formats:

1. JB for job related records.
2. DP for directly printed files.
3. SP for spooled files.

You don't see many direct print jobs on an AS/400. Therefore, you don't see a lot of DP records. You'll be working mainly with JB and SP.

The AS/400 comes with two skeleton files and formats that contain the field layouts for these entries. They are known as the *field reference files* for the journal entries:

- QSYS/QAJBACG (format QWTJAJBE).
- QSYS/QAPTACG (format QSPJAPTE).

If you want to read those journal entries (and you are a masochist), you could take the fields from those reference files and create a DDS for them. It's more realistic to just create duplicates of each (CRTDUPOBJ command) in your library. Name the duplicates whatever you like. Then, when you display the journal entries, use this command to extract job records:

```
DSPJRN JRN(QACGJRN) JRNCDE(A) ENTTYP(JB) +
       OUTPUT(*OUTFILE) +
       OUTFILE(<your library>/<your job file (the duplicate)>)
```

That would extract the job records into your new physical file. From there, you'll be able to build one or more logical files or a join logical over the physical files to process the data with a query or a program.

4.5 Security Audit Journal

The security audit journal:

- Is not automatic; it requires that you start it.
- Data is kept in a journal receiver.

While system history logs and job logs are always there, you must set up and activate the AS/400 Security Audit Journal if you want to use it. The Security Audit Journal audits security-related activities. You get to set what you want logged. It keeps the log in a journal (see chapter 8).

You can use security audit to focus on activities of an individual user, a specific object, or one individual's contact with a specific object. There are system-wide things you can monitor for and user-specific things.

Security auditing on the AS/400 is a powerful tool for detecting security problems because it doesn't just log the successful completion of a function; it'll log any attempt at a function. In other words, if you suspect a user of trying to use System Service Tools (SST) to circumvent the AS/400 security, you can monitor that user just for *SERVICE and you will see all the suspect user's unsuccessful attempts (and, hopefully, no successful ones).

Typically, security audit is turned on and off for relatively brief periods of time and is focused on specific problems: user(s) or object(s). Security audit is a tightly focused problem-solving tool. You turn it on for a day or two, turn it off, and review the results. You really don't need it running all the time.

To set up security auditing on your system, perform the tasks in sections 5.2.2 and 5.2.2.1 in the order they are given.

4.5.1 Set Up the System for Security Auditing

To set up your security auditing:

- Create a library for the journal receiver with the CRTLIB command. Name it anything you like, but it should be a library just to hold this journal. Do not use any production libraries.

- Create a journal receiver in this library. Use 10 characters for its name (the first six of which are alpha characters and the last four are "0001"). For example, SECAUD0001. Use this command:

```
CRTJRNRCV JRNRCV(<your library>/SECAUD0001) +
   AUT(*EXCLUDE) TEXT('Security Auditing Journal Receiver ')
```

- The security journal must be named QAUDJRN and it must reside in QSYS. Create the journal with the CRTJRN command (use the library/file names as indicated):

```
CRTJRN QSYS/QAUDJRN +
       JRNRCV(<your library>/SECAUD0001) +
       AUT(*EXCLUDE) TEXT('Security Auditing Journal')
```

4.5.2 Set the System Values

There are four system values that affect security auditing. Use the WRKSYSVAL command to display or change them:

- QAUDCTL (Audit Control)—starts and stops security auditing. Change this to possible values other than *NONE and you will start capturing security audit information. Change it back to *NONE to stop capturing security audit information.

- QAUDLVL (Audit Level)—specifies what actions are audited on objects. See section 5.2.2.2 Set Security Auditing. Because an audit level usually contains more than one value and there are many values, refer to appendix A in this book for a list of them or refer to the IBM manual *OS/400 Security-Reference V4R3, Planning the Auditing of Actions* for a description of all possible actions.

- QAUDFRCLVL (Audit Force Level)—is a performance thing; it blocks the audit records before they are written to the journal. There is a trade-off here. If you want absolute protection so that you won't lose any security journal records in the event of a system failure, set this value to 1. However, performance can be degraded. Rather than try to figure out optimum blocking, use the value *SYS and the system will calculate some optimum value for you. You won't lose any records if the AS/400 doesn't go down.

- QAUDENDACN (Audit End Action)—tells the system what to do if it is unable to write an audit record to a journal. The default is *NOTIFY and the system just sends a message to the system operator. However, if your organization requires that the security audit be active in order for the AS/400 to even be up, you can specify *PWRDWNSYS. The instant the system is unable to write a record to the security audit journal, it does a PWRDWNSYS *IMMED. Because it can wreak havoc with your users, don't do this unless you absolutely must. Also, if you do select this value, ensure you have good journal change/backup/cleanup procedures in place. There are two reasons security audit won't be able to write to a journal:

    ✔ It is full and needs to be changed.

    ✔ It is damaged—in most cases an IPL is necessary to resume monitoring.

There are also two values, one on every object and one on every user profile, that affect what is audited.

- AUDLVL (Audit Level)—a parameter on the user profile specifies what actions are audited for that user. See section 5.2.2.2 Set Security Auditing. Here are the possible values:
  - ✔ *NONE turns off auditing this user.
  - ✔ *CMD logs all the commands used by this user.
  - ✔ *CREATE logs all objects created by this user.
  - ✔ *DELETE logs all objects deleted by this user.
  - ✔ *JOBDTA logs all job actions by this user.
  - ✔ *OBJMGT logs all objects moved or renamed by this user.
  - ✔ *OFCSRV logs some OfficeVision tasks by this user.
  - ✔ *OPTICAL logs all optical tasks performed by this user.
  - ✔ *PGMADP logs when this user runs programs that adopt authority.
  - ✔ *SAVRST logs save/restore functions performed by this user.
  - ✔ *SECURITY logs security functions performed by this user.
  - ✔ *SERVICE logs attempts by this user to access SST or DST.
  - ✔ *SPLFDTA logs spool file activity performed by this user.
  - ✔ *SYSMGT logs system management tasks performed by this user.
- OBJAUD (Object Audit)—a parameter on object descriptions that specify what actions are audited for that object. See section 5.2.2.2 Set Security Auditing. Here are the possible values:
  - ✔ *NONE turns off auditing for this object.
  - ✔ *USRPRF only reports the auditing information called for by the user profile parameter AUDLVL.
  - ✔ *CHANGE reports any changes (or change attempts) made to the object.
  - ✔ *ALL audits any attempts to change or even use the object.

See *OS/400 Security-Reference V4R3* for more discussion on these values.

4.5.3 Set Security Auditing on Objects/Users

The AUDLVL and OBJAUD parameters work together to provide an auditing picture. Although many scenarios are possible, the following sections contain three typical ones.

4.5.3.1 Specific File—Any User

- Use the CHGOBJAUD command to change the specific file object's Object Auditing Value (OBJAUD) to *CHANGE or *ALL.
- Ensure the system value, QAUDCTL, is set to *OBJAUD.

4.5.3.2 Many Files—One User

- Use the CHGOBJAUD command to change the file objects' Object Auditing Value (OBJAUD) to *USRPRF. (Note: the CHGOBJAUD command accepts generic library and file names; use these to save time. However, don't use *ALL/*ALL because it can take hours to implement. Also, carrying that much security auditing could degrade your system. It's better to specify any subset or *ALL files within a library.)
- Use the CHGUSRAUD command to set the user profile's OBJAUD value to *CHANGE or *ALL.
- Ensure the system value, QAUDCTL, is set to *OBJAUD.

4.5.3.3 One File—One User

- Use the CHGOBJAUD command to change the specific file object's Object Auditing Value (OBJAUD) to *USRPRF.
- Use the CHGUSRAUD command to set the user profile's Object Auditing Value (OBJAUD) to *CHANGE or *ALL.
- Ensure the system value, QAUDCTL, is set to *OBJAUD.

4.5.4 Managing Security Audit Journal Receivers

The Security Audit Journal is just a journal. For more information on the subject, refer to chapter 8, Journaling. Because of the extra security on it (through the AUT(*EXCLUDE) parameter on the CRTJRNRCV and CRTJRN commands), only the security officer or object owner can get to the information. Also, the system puts an exclusive lock on the journal while monitoring is taking place. Therefore, not everyone can get to the journal, and—even when the security officer can—many normal journal commands can't be done because of this system lock.

For these reasons, only use this journal and its receivers to journal security audit records. Do not use it to do any regular database file journaling.

If the value you specified in system value QAUDENDACN is *PWRDWNSYS, you really don't want this receiver to fill up. Create a special message queue for audit messages and associate that queue with the QSYS/QAUDJRN journal. Then write a message-handling program that monitors this queue. If it gets a "threshold reached" message, it should change receivers and pass the message onto the system operator.

For normal operation, you must periodically:

- Change receivers: CHGJRN JRN(QAUDJRN) JRNRCV(*GEN).
- Save the receiver with the SAVOBJ command, specifying object type *JRNRCV.
- Delete the old receiver after it is saved with the DLTJRNRCV command.
- If you want to look at the contents of a receiver, but don't know which one is current, WRKJRNA QAUDJRN will tell you which receiver is currently attached.

4.5.5 Viewing Security Audit Journal Receivers

You can view or use the contents of the security audit journal receivers by:

- Command DSPJRN QAUDJRN. This allows you to view the contents of the journal receiver.
- Command DSPJRN QAUDJRN OUTPUT(*OUTFILE). Access the resulting outfile with a query or a program.

4.5.6 Planning

Many AS/400 shops make the same set of mistakes when implementing security auditing. They ask for too much data so it becomes unusable. Or they set up elaborate auditing rules and never review the data.

Security auditing is nice and it gets rave reviews from auditors. But if you're not going to use it, don't bother. There is a performance cost to using it and it uses up DASD. Plan very carefully what it is about security you want to monitor. Ask yourself:

- Who am I concerned about?
- What objects am I concerned about?
- What types of security failures would I like to know about?

Then implement only these things and use the data. Unlike other logging, security audit journaling is sometimes activated for a short period of time just to monitor for a suspected problem. Then the monitor is turned off and the results are reviewed.

4.6 Messages

The AS/400 lives and dies on messages. Messages are sent to everybody, including most of its internal functions (which rely on messages as triggers). History, job log, and security-audit journal entries all start life as mere messages.

For this section, I stay away from the esoteric, under-the-covers messages and just focus on the ones that mean something to us lowly humans.

The command to send a message is Send Message (SNDMSG). Type it on the command line and prompt it with the F4 key.

Messages can be informational (require no answer) or inquiry (require an answer). They are sent to queues called *message queues*.

Every user currently signed on to the system has his or her own message queue (usually the message queue has the same name as the user profile). When a user signs off, the message queue goes away. Each workstation, on the other hand, also has a message queue and that queue is active as long as the workstation is active. You can see a difference between these two in a common AS/400 scenario.

The system operator at night wants to bring down the computer and sends a message asking the users to please sign off in five minutes. If the system operator sends the message to *ALL user queues, only those users currently signed on will see it. If the system operator sends the message to *ALL workstation queues, when people sign on in the morning, they'll get the message, "System coming down, please sign off in five minutes." This can be confusing to say the least.

Messages can be sent to the system operator, whoever that is, by sending the messages to the system operator message queue. Programs running on the system have their own message queues and other programs can send messages to them. The fifth queue you can send messages to could be one you create yourself with the CRTMSGQ command.

In real life, you will get a lot of messages from the system and programs running within the system.

4.6.1 Messages to You

The messages you receive while you are on an AS/400 workstation will be in one of three forms: break, notify, or program.

4.6.1.1 Break Messages

You can't miss a *break message* because it interrupts you to display a full screen of just MESSAGE. Although a message can be sent as a break message, your workstation can be set up to treat all messages as break messages. Therefore, you'll be interrupted for even benign messages.

4.6.1.2 Notify Messages

You might miss a *notify message* because you'll only get a small icon on the lower left corner of your screen when you have received a notify message. These icons vary in shape according to the terminal emulation and workstation manufacturer. Ask your system administrator what your icon will look like.

When you get a notify message, you can view it by entering the DSPMSG command on any command line. You will see what is known as your first-level message. If you would like more information about the message, use the arrow keys to move the cursor to the message itself and press the F1 or Help key. You'll get the second-level message.

4.6.1.3 Program Messages

The third message you may receive is a *program message*. When it appears, it'll appear on the bottom line of your screen when you complete a command or program. Like notify messages, it is only the first-level message. If you want more information, put the cursor on it and press the F1 or Help key.

Also, look for a small plus sign on the far right side of the program messages. The plus sign indicates that there are more messages for you. You can look at the other messages by putting the cursor on the message and pressing the Page Down key. If you want to go back up the list, press the Page Up key. You can press the F1 or Help key on any of them to get the second-level message.

4.6.2 Message Constructions

Messages on the AS/400 are coded. The codes are keys to text and data stored in message files. The system comes with several message files, and you can create one for your own application. Many customers do that.

As previously discussed, the job log is mostly captured messages. When you look at the job log, you will see messages, their IDs, and texts.

Message texts are fairly readable as they are, but they can contain variables that make them more cryptic. Variables are passed along with message texts in the MSGDTA area of each message.

To see what a message looks like, use the Work with Message Description (WRKMSGD) command like this:

```
WRKMSGD CPA4002
```

After the command gives you a menu, take Option 1 and you will get the message text. Then take Option 2 to see the MSGDTA variables. Option 2 will give you an idea of the construction of the variable fields. See Figures 4-6 through 4-8 for examples of these screens.

4.6.3 System Operator Message Queue: QSYSOPR

In most AS/400 shops, the most important message queue comes with the AS/400 as a default and is called the system operator message queue. It is always named QSYSOPR. Here is where all the really important system stuff goes. All batch jobs and any problems on the system, unless otherwise handled, go to message queue QSYSOPR. When the system itself feels the need to burp, it sends a message to QSYSOPR. There are two problems with this queue:

- Important things can get lost among many unimportant messages.
- Operators take lunch breaks and can miss time-crucial things.

The AS/400 has a way around these problems. You can create a special message queue just for really hot system messages. Also, you can write a program to intercept these hot messages and handle them. Create this special message queue with this command:

```
CRTMSGQ QSYS/QSYSMSG TEXT( 'System operator really important +
          message queue')
```

You must name the message queue QSYSMSG and you must place it in the QSYS library. Once this message queue is in existence, the AS/400 has a predetermined list of messages it will send to this queue instead of the QSYSOPR message queue. For a complete list of these messages and what they mean, see *OS/400 CL Programming*.

You can write a simple program to monitor and handle some of these messages. The messages it can't handle it forwards to the system operator. Messages it can handle are forwarded to the system operator and from there a copy is forwarded to the security officer for review. A sample of such a program can be found in *OS/400 CL Programming*.

4.6.4 System Reply List

Some inquiry system messages start to get in the way because they come up constantly and hang up programs until the user or system operator responds to them. Because the response to these messages is almost always the same, all they do is delay processing.

For these situations, the AS/400 has a *System Reply List* that consists of inquiry-only messages to which the system will respond. An example would be a message to change forms on a laser printer that only ever contains blank white stock. However, a message to change forms on a line printer in the computer room won't be so predictable.

With the System Reply List, you can have the system give the same response every time the question comes up. In the case of the two printers, you can also parse out sections of the message to determine which ones to have the system respond to and which ones to pass on to the user or system operator.

Not all jobs use the System Reply List. A job has to have the parameter INQMSGRPY(*SYSRPYL) specified or it will ignore this list. Most jobs do not have this set. The AS/400 comes with a basic System Reply List as outlined in Table 4-1.

Table 4-1: System Reply List.

Sequence Number	Message Identifier	Compare Value	Reply	Dump
10	CPA0700	*NONE	D	*YES
20	RPG0000	*NONE	D	*YES
30	CBE0000	*NONE	D	*YES
40	PLI0000	*NONE	D	*YES

Table 4-1 is a little difficult to decipher. It means that any error starting with the error number's trailing zeros and going to the 9s in those spaces will receive a response. In other words, all messages CPA07<u>00</u> through CPA07<u>99</u> from any job with INQMSGRPY(*SYSRPYL) will be answered automatically with a "D" (for a program dump).

You add reply list entries with the ADDRPYLE command. To illustrate, assume you want the AS/400 to automatically respond when an align-forms message (CPA4002) is received for any printer except the line printer in the computer room (which in the example, you should presume is designated QSYSPRT).

- If the align-forms message is not for QSYSPRT, it must be for a laser printer and the system will just reply with an "I" for ignore.
- If the align-forms message is for QSYSPRT, it is for the line printer and the message will be passed on through to the intended destination.

No problem. You just have to look inside the message identification, CPA4002, at its MSGDTA area. The command is WRKMSGD CPA4002. Figure 4-6 shows its first menu screen.

```
                        Select Message Details to Display
                                                          System:   TEST400
 Message ID . . . . . . . . . :   CPA4002
 Message file . . . . . . . . :   QCPFMSG
   Library  . . . . . . . . . :     QSYS
 Message text . . . . . . . . :   Verify alignment on printer &3. (I G N R E C)


 Select one of the following:

      1. Display message text
      2. Display field data
      3. Display reply specifications
      4. Display special reply values
      5. Display message attributes

     30. All of the above


 Selection
      _
```

Figure 4-6: The WRKMSGD menu.

Take Option 1 to look at the full message text. See Figure 4-7.

```
                         Display Formatted Message Text
                                                          System:   TEST400
 Message ID . . . . . . . . . :   CPA4002
 Message file . . . . . . . . :   QCPFMSG
   Library  . . . . . . . . . :     QSYS

 Message . . . . :   Verify alignment on printer &3. (I G N R E C)
 Cause . . . . . :   The forms may not be aligned correctly.  The first line
   for the file is &4.
 Possible choices for replying to message . . . . . . . . . . . . . . . :
   I -- To continue printing aligned forms starting with the next line of the
     file, type an I.
   G -- To continue printing aligned forms skipping to the next form and
     printing the first line again, type a G.
   N -- To print the first line again on the next form and to verify the
     alignment,
     1. Press Stop only if Start and Stop are two keys, or press Reset.
     2. Advance the paper to the next form by pressing Form Feed/New Page.
     3. Adjust the alignment with the forms adjust control.
                                                                    More...
 Press Enter to continue.

 F3=Exit   F11=Display unformatted message text   F12=Cancel
```

Figure 4-7: Message text for message ID CPA4002.

Press the F12 key to go back to the WRKMSGD menu (see Figure 4-6) and take Option 2 to see the MSGDTA layout. This is where you obtain the compare value. See Figure 4-8.

```
                         Display Field Data

Message ID . . . . . . . . . :   CPA4002
Message file . . . . . . . . :   QCPFMSG
  Library  . . . . . . . . . :     QSYS


                                  Decimal      Vary
Field     Data Type     Length    Positions    Length     Dump
 &1       *CHAR           10                              *NO
 &2       *CHAR           10                              *NO
 &3       *CHAR           10                              *NO
 &4       *BIN             2                              *NO
 &5       *CHAR           10                              *NO
 &6       *CHAR           10                              *NO
 &7       *CHAR            0                              *NO
 &8       *CHAR            0                              *NO
 &9       *CHAR            0                              *NO
 &10      *CHAR            0                              *NO
                                                                    More...
Press Enter to continue.

F3=Exit   F12=Cancel
```

Figure 4-8: Layout of MSGDTA for message ID CPA4002.

Now add two reply-message entries to the system reply list outlined in Table 4-1. One entry for the laser printer always gets an answer of "G" and the other entry is for the line printer you want the user or system operator to see and respond to. Add message CPA4002 immediately after CPA0700. Here's the command:

```
ADDRPYLE SEQNBR(12) MSGID(CPA4002) RPY(*RQD) CMPDTA( 'QSYSPRT' 21)
```

The message text in Figure 4-7 has a &3 as the variable that contained the printer name. On Figure 4-8, that variable is the third one in the list, and it starts on column 21. (The first two fields are 10 characters each, 10 + 10 is 20; the third field must start on 21). When the message is sent, column 21 will have the name of the printer and that's where I specified the comparison for value QSYSPRT.

This reply list entry will take care of a requirement that system printer, align-form messages are forwarded to an operator who will have to respond (*RQD). Here's one without the compare message to catch CPA4002's for the other printers:

```
ADDRPYLE SEQNBR(14) MSGID(CPA4002) RPY(G)
```

This reply list entry makes no comparison for the printer device name. I had to put the message for QSYSPRT first because the no-compare message would have passed anything (even QSYSPRT). Table 4-2 shows the system reply list after those changes.

Table 4-2: System Reply List after Changes.				
Sequence Number	Message Identifier	Compare Value	Reply	Dump
10	CPA0700	*NONE	D	*YES
12	CPA4002	'QSYSPRT' 21	&RQD	*NO
14	CPA4002	*NONE	G	*NO
20	RPG0000	*NONE	D	*YES
30	CBE0000	*NONE	D	*YES
40	PLI0000	*NONE	D	*YES

That was easy. For other messages, be very careful about their placement. Remember that RPG0000, on sequence 20, implicitly includes all RPG messages (RPG0000 through RPG9999). The trailing zeros automatically create that range. Therefore, a message RPG0120 would include RPG0120 through RPG0129. In this case, any new RPGxxx would have to be placed prior to the RPG0000 ahead of sequence 20. Once a message traps, the system quits looking any further.

4.7 System Cleanup

If people cleaned up their homes like they clean up their computers, we would have to buy new homes every year just to escape the cluttered homes. Obviously, this wouldn't work; it's a ridiculous idea. However, that is how most computer installations approach cleanup. It's fortunate that computer garbage doesn't smell.

The AS/400 has several tools available to help you clean up; use them. A "clean" AS/400 IPLs faster, it's overall performance is much better, and you don't have to buy new DASD so often.

4.7.1 Automatic Cleanup

The AS/400 comes with an automatic system cleanup program that works fairly well for keeping the amount of old messages and logs down to a manageable size. To get into the cleanup screen, type GO CLEANUP on your command line and take Option 1 from the Cleanup menu. You'll get a screen like the one shown in Figure 4-9.

```
                        Change Cleanup Options                    TEST400
                                                        08/12/98  16:04:43
Type choices below, then press Enter.

Allow automatic cleanup . . . . . . . . . . . . .   Y              Y=Yes, N=No

Time cleanup starts each day  . . . . . . . . . .   22:00:00       00:00:00-
                                                                   23:59:59,
                                                                   *SCDPWROFF,
                                                                   *NONE

Number of days to keep:
  User messages . . . . . . . . . . . . . . . . .   7              1-366, *KEEP
  System and workstation messages . . . . . . . .   4              1-366, *KEEP
  Job logs and other system output  . . . . . . .   7              1-366, *KEEP
  System journals and system logs . . . . . . . .   30             1-366, *KEEP
  OfficeVision for AS/400 calendar items  . . . .   30             1-366, *KEEP




F1=Help   F3=Exit   F5=Refresh   F12=Cancel
```

Figure 4-9: Automatic cleanup menu.

The first parameter, ALLOW AUTOMATIC CLEANUP, accepts a Y or N and tells the system to do the clean up automatically. Put a Y here to allow the system to do automatic cleanup.

The TIME CLEANUP STARTS EACH DAY tells the system when to do the clean up. In the example, this customer wants the automatic cleanup to start at 1:00 A.M. every day. Because these times are in military time, that means 0100 (or 1:00 A.M.).

The parameters under NUMBER OF DAYS TO KEEP are the really interesting items. To the right of each is a number for the days.

- User messages. All old user messages are purged after the allowed time (in this case, after seven days). This does not clean up the system-operator messages or security-officer messages.
- System and workstation messages. All old messages that belong to the system operator or to any device-message queue are erased after the allowed time.
- Job logs and other system output. All old job logs are purged after the allowed number of days.
- System journals and system logs. The system keeps its own journals to assist it in many tasks. This parameter says they will be purged after the allowed number of days. Included in system logs are the history logs (QHST) and problem logs generated by the AS/400 self-diagnostics. Also, included in this category are PTF cleanup.
- OfficeVision/400 calendar items. Such items are purged after the allowed number of days.

4.7.2 Cleanup User Profiles

I've been in audits where active user profiles were found on an AS/400 two years after the people had left the company (and even when a person had been asked to leave). User profiles can build up quickly. This is an audit issue as well as important for capacity and performance.

To clean up old user profiles, type GO SECTOOLS on any command line and press the Enter key. Take Option 4 (ANALYZE PROFILE ACTIVITY) from that menu. You'll get a screen similar to the one shown in Figure 4-10:

```
                      Analyze Profile Activity (ANZPRFACT)

   Type choices, press Enter.

   Number of inactive days . . . .   ______          1-366, *NOMAX
```

Figure 4-10: Screen to analyze user profiles

Enter the number of inactive days on this screen. This tells the analyzer how many inactive days a profile can have before you want it considered inactive.

When you press the Enter key, the system will schedule a job to run once a month (starting at 1:00 A.M. the current day). This program will mark any profile as *DISABLED that has not been used within the number of days you specified. You'll also get a report with this command.

From this report, you can delete old user profiles. Use the Work with User Profiles (WRKUSRPRF) command, scroll to the user profile you want to delete, and put a 4 on the Option line. Press Enter and the profile disappears.

If you have a user profile you want to keep active (even after a long absence)—like for someone who is on sick leave or a leave of absence—take Option 3 from the SECTOOLS menu and you can name profiles that will be exempt from the inactive analysis.

When you delete a user profile, its owned objects may still be on the system. On command WRKUSRPRF, enter a 12 on the option line to the left of the user profile targeted for deletion (but before you delete the profile with an Option 4). The system will display a list of objects owned by that user. Figure 4-11 contains a sample of this object screen.

```
                         Work with Objects by Owner

User profile . . . . . . . :    MDAWSON

Type options, press Enter.
  2=Edit authority          4=Delete   5=Display authority    7=Rename
  8=Display description     9=Change owner

Opt  Object                 Library       Type         Attribute
 _   CUSTMAST               MDAWSON       *FILE        PF
 _   QCLSRC                 MDAWSON       *FILE        PF
 _   QDDSSRC                MDAWSON       *FILE        PF
 _   QRPGSRC                MDAWSON       *FILE        PF
 _   MIKE0001               QGPL          *JRNRCV
 _   JOURNAL                QGPL          *JRN
 _   MDAWSON                QSYS          *LIB         PROD
 _   WLSLIN                 QSYS          *LIND        WLS
 _   WLSCTL                 QSYS          *CTLD        LWS
```

Figure 4-11: Screen to control objects owned by an expired user profile.

You'll have two options here:

- Change the object's ownership to another profile. To do this, type a 2 in the option column.
- Delete the object. To do this type a 4 in the option column.

Finally, the user can still own spool files. Type on any command line:

```
WRKSPLF SELECT(old user profile name)
```

Press the Enter key. On the work with spooled files display (refer to Figure 4-12), type a 4 on the option line for any spool files you want deleted.

```
                        Work with Printer Output
                                                     System:    TEST400
User . . . . . .    MDAWSON       Name, *ALL, F4 for list

Type options below, then press Enter.  To work with printers, press F22.
  2=Change    3=Hold    4=Delete    5=Display            6=Release    7=Message
  9=Work with printing status      10=Start printing    11=Restart printing

      Printer/
Opt     Output        Status
      Not Assigned
___     CUSTMAST      Not assigned to printer (use Opt 10)
```

Figure 4-12: Sample of the WRKSPLF command.

Keep the following tip in mind:

TIP: When you delete spool files, the space doesn't necessarily return to the system automatically. To really retrieve the space, first do the delete, then type the RCLSPLSTG command, and press the Enter key.

4.7.3 Clean Up Licensed Programs

You might have loaded licensed programs some time in the past and forgotten about them. I've done this when programs have been sent to me on a trial basis. To properly remove these, type GO LICPGM and press the Enter key.

Depending on the licensed program, you might want to save it before deleting it. Either take Option 1 (Save) from the LICPGM menu or use the SAVLICPGM command to save the program.

To delete the program, just type a 4 (Delete) on the option line and press the Enter key. For an alternative to the GO LICPGM menu, you can delete a licensed program directly with the DLTLICPGM command.

4.7.4 Clean Up Old Device Descriptions

One thing I'm really bad at is creating device descriptions and then forgetting about them. To clean up old device descriptions, use the command WRKHDWRSC *XXX. Where XXX will be:

- CMN for communications devices.
- LWS for local workstation devices.
- STG for storage resources.

You should see a display that includes the device statuses. If it does not, you might have to press F11; check the bottom of the display.

Device descriptions with a status of "Not Detected" deserve your attention. First, verify that the device is not on the system, and then type a 4 on the option line to delete the description.

There are two other device types that can be included on this command, but I just mentioned the three that get most of us in trouble. For more information, refer to *AS/400 Basic System Operation, Administration, and Problem Handling V4R3, Cleaning up Your Hardware Configuration.*

4.7.5 Miscellaneous Cleanup Tasks

There are a few other things that are simple to do and can return a lot of space to your AS/400. Here they are with caveats where necessary:

- If you save files or libraries to a save file prior to saving to tape, free up the space with the Clear Save File (CLRSAVF) command.
  - ✔ You might want to think about this one, though. Some customers leave the files intact and clear them immediately prior to the next save—thus ensuring enough DASD space available for the save.
- Use the Display File Description (DSPFD) to determine files that have a large number of deleted records. Return the space these deleted records occupy to the system by issuing the RGZPFM or by saving/restoring them.
  - ✔ If a file relies on physical sequence of records for ordering, do not do a RGZPFM to reclaim deleted records. In fact, I'd say leave it alone until it can be modified for a more positive ordering strategy.
- When a message queue suddenly gets a lot of messages, it expands in increments. Although the messages get deleted, the increments still exist, taking DASD. Message queues do not get returned to their original size until the Clear Message Queue (CLRMSGQ) is issued.
- If you are journaling, make sure you delete the journal receivers as soon as you save them. Refer to chapter 8 for more information.

4.8 References

AS/400 Basic System Operation, Administration, and Problem Handling V4R3 (SC41-5206-02)

AS/400 Programming Reference Summary V4R3 (SX41-5720-02)

OS/400 CL Programming (SC41-5721-01)

OS/400 Security-Reference V4R3 (SC41-5302-02)

OS/400 Work Management V4R3 (SC41-5306-02)

Tips and Tools for Securing Your AS/400 V4R3 (SC41-5300-02)

5 People

5.1 Overview

The AS/400 can support as simple or as complex a set of users as the customer needs. A very small shop will have one or two people who have access to everything. Large shops will have many subsets of users, each with a unique set of rights and accesses.

In one sense, any person known to the AS/400 is a *user*. He or she becomes known to the AS/400 through something called the *user profile*. The user profile contains items specific to a person:

- Basic security information about the person.
- Special authorities granted to the person.
- Job processing information specific to the person, such as:
  - ✔ Job queue.
  - ✔ Output queue.
  - ✔ Initial program or menu to call.
  - ✔ Current library.

The security level of your AS/400 affects user profiles. Security levels are set in the system value QSECURITY with the Work with System Value (WRKSYSVAL) command. The lowest security level is 10. When a user signs onto an AS/400 with a security level of 10, the AS/400 will accept anything as a user ID. If the AS/400 can't find a user profile for the ID, it'll build one automatically. AS/400s with security levels higher than 10 require users to sign on with a user ID that already exists as a user profile.

5.1.1 The New AS/400

A brand new AS/400 comes with several user profiles from IBM already loaded in library QSYS:

- QPGMR — Programmer and batch-user profile.
- QSECOFR — Security officer-user profile.
- QSRV — Services (all functions). This is the profile the person who services your AS/400 will use.
- QSRVBAS — Services (limited functions). This is the profile the person who services your AS/400 will use.
- QSYSOPR — System operator.
- QUSER — General user.

Except for QSECOFR, these user profiles have *NONE for their passwords. Although you theoretically could assign a password to user profile QPGMR and sign on the system, IBM recommends against that.

It's better to use the QPGMR as a model for your first programmer user profiles. Just copy QPGMR with the Create Duplicate Object (CRTDUPOBJ). Call it by some naming strategy that your shop likes and store the object in a library other than QSYS. If you do that, you inherit a lot of already filled out fields in the user profile; you only have to change the name, password, and status fields. Do the same with QUSER and you can blast through your first bunch of user profiles.

There are several additional IBM-supplied user profiles that you definitely do not want to try to turn into user profiles with which you can sign onto the system. These are internal user profiles that help the AS/400 do special functions as needed.

For example, when you delete a user profile, any objects that user owned stand a chance of either being owned by an invalid user profile or not being owned by anyone. The AS/400 takes care of that by using the special user profile, QDFTOWN, as the owner of those objects. You'll see system-level jobs running all the time that have a user of QSYS. You don't have to do anything with these user profiles. Just recognize them when you see them from time to time.

- QAUTPROF — IBM general authority profile.
- QBRMS — Backup Recovery Media (BRM) profile.
- QDBSHR — Database share profile.
- QDFTOWN — All objects on the AS/400 must be owned by a legitimate user. If a user profile is no longer valid its objects' ownership changes to QDFTOWN.
- QDOC — Document profile.
- QDSNX — Distributed system node executive.
- QFNC — Finance profile.
- QGATE — User profile to bridge into PROFS (VM/MVS on mainframes).
- QLPAUTO — Licensed program auto-installation user (see chapter 2).
- QLPINSTALL — Licensed program installation user (see chapter 2).
- QMSF — Mail server framework profile.
- QNETSPLF — Network spooling profile.
- QNFSANON — NFS user profile.
- QSNADS — SNADS user.
- QSPL — Spooling user.
- QSPLJOB — Spooling readers/writers job user profile.
- QSYS — Internal system user.
- QTCP — TCP/IP user.

These profiles are not used for signing onto the system. Do not attempt to change or delete these profiles. If you do, you might find internal functions suddenly not working.

5.1.1.1 Changing Passwords to IBM-Supplied Profiles

The security officer user profile, QSECOFR, comes with the password QSECOFR, but that password is set to *EXPIRED on the user profile. Therefore, the first time anyone uses it, they must change the password. Use a little planning in your department so that one person doesn't change it and leave the others hanging.

You can change many of the IBM-supplied profiles from something called the *setup menu*. To get to the menu, type GO SETUP on the command line and press the Enter key. Take Option 11, CHANGE PASSWORDS FOR IBM-SUPPLIED USERS, and change all the passwords from the same screen. See Figure 5-1.

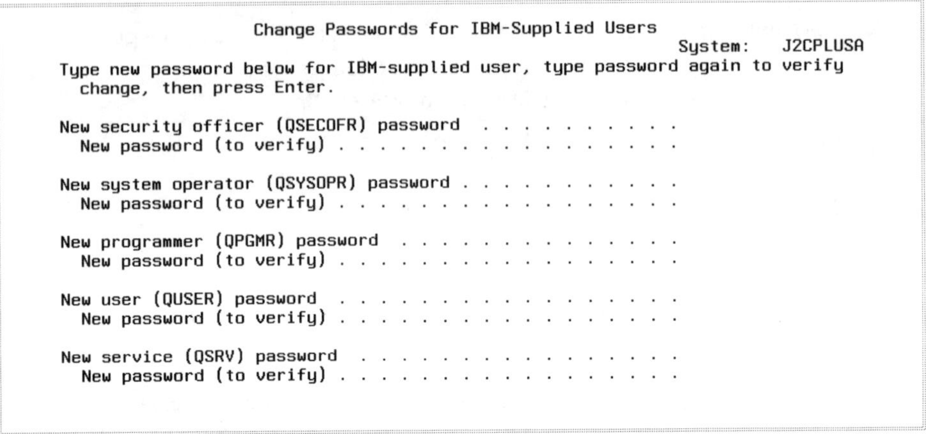

```
                        Change Passwords for IBM-Supplied Users
                                                          System:   J2CPLUSA
   Type new password below for IBM-supplied user, type password again to verify
     change, then press Enter.

   New security officer (QSECOFR) password  . . . . . . . . . .
     New password (to verify) . . . . . . . . . . . . . . . . .

   New system operator (QSYSOPR) password . . . . . . . . . . .
     New password (to verify) . . . . . . . . . . . . . . . . .

   New programmer (QPGMR) password  . . . . . . . . . . . . . .
     New password (to verify) . . . . . . . . . . . . . . . . .

   New user (QUSER) password  . . . . . . . . . . . . . . . . .
     New password (to verify) . . . . . . . . . . . . . . . . .

   New service (QSRV) password  . . . . . . . . . . . . . . . .
     New password (to verify) . . . . . . . . . . . . . . . . .
```

Figure 5-1: Screen from SETUP menu to change IBM-supplied passwords.

Change those values again whenever you have a key AS/400 person (who may know the passwords) terminate his or her association with the organization.

5.2 Managing User Profiles

There are six user-profile commands:

- CRTUSRPRF — Create user profile.
- CHGUSRPRF — Change user profile.
- DLTUSRPRF — Delete user profile.
- DSPUSRPRF — Display user profile.
- RSTUSRPRF — Restore user profile.
- RTVUSRPRF — Retrieve user profile information (CL programs only).

A seventh user profile, the WRKUSRPRF command, gets you to any of these except RTVUSRPRF, and it's handier to use.

The user profile information is pretty standard across all the commands. The CRTUSRPRF gives you an idea of what goes into a profile. Figures 5-2 through 5-5 show the four screens it takes to collect all profile information. The newer (with Version 4) parameters are indicated with boldface type.

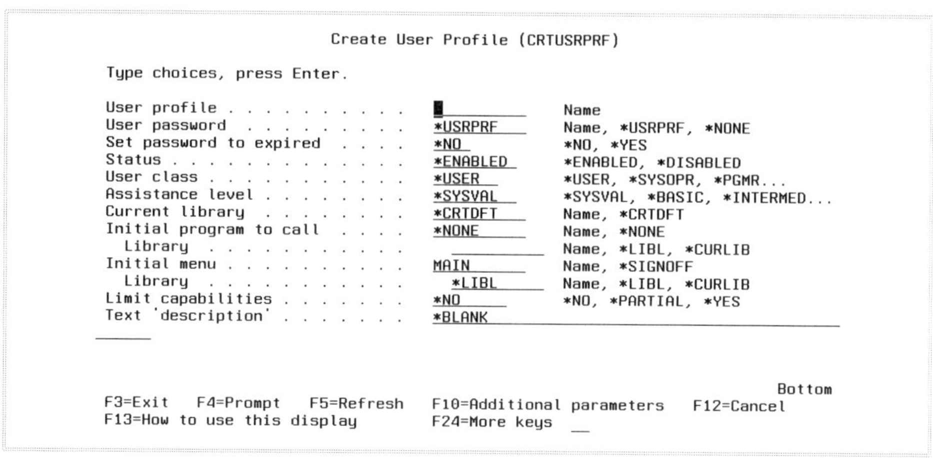

```
                          Create User Profile (CRTUSRPRF)

 Type choices, press Enter.

 User profile . . . . . . . . . .   _________   Name
 User password  . . . . . . . . .   *USRPRF     Name, *USRPRF, *NONE
 Set password to expired  . . . .   *NO         *NO, *YES
 Status . . . . . . . . . . . . .   *ENABLED    *ENABLED, *DISABLED
 User class . . . . . . . . . . .   *USER       *USER, *SYSOPR, *PGMR...
 Assistance level . . . . . . . .   *SYSVAL     *SYSVAL, *BASIC, *INTERMED...
 Current library  . . . . . . . .   *CRTDFT     Name, *CRTDFT
 Initial program to call  . . . .   *NONE       Name, *NONE
   Library  . . . . . . . . . . .   _________   Name, *LIBL, *CURLIB
 Initial menu . . . . . . . . . .   MAIN        Name, *SIGNOFF
   Library  . . . . . . . . . . .     *LIBL     Name, *LIBL, *CURLIB
 Limit capabilities . . . . . . .   *NO         *NO, *PARTIAL, *YES
 Text 'description' . . . . . . .   *BLANK


                                                                      Bottom
 F3=Exit   F4=Prompt   F5=Refresh   F10=Additional parameters   F12=Cancel
 F13=How to use this display        F24=More keys
```

Figure 5-2: Prompted version of command CRTUSRPRF.

All of the parameters are fully described in *OS/400 Security-Reference V4R3*. Here's a short description of each parameter in the Figures 5-2 through 5-5.

- User Profile (USRPRF). Up to 10 characters in length, the user profile name can contain any letter, number, or #, $, _, or @. Although a user profile cannot start with a number, you can create one that contains all numbers but starts with the letter Q. The user then can sign on with just the numbers. Example: user profile Q12345 can be used as 12345. In real life, try not to exceed eight characters in length. Don't use special characters; the user profile name doesn't have to be cryptic. Use a standard that means something (a user's initials and department code are popular choices).

- User Password (PASSWORD). A password is only required when the system security level is greater than 10. Passwords can have up to 10 characters. There are many system values that affect password constructions. For more information, see chapter 6.

- Set Password to Expired (PWDEXP). The security officer or security administrator can use this (PWDEXP(*YES)) to force the user to change her or his password the next time she or he signs on.

- Status (STATUS). The profile may be allowed to sign on (STATUS (*ENABLED)) or not be allowed to sign on (STATUS(*DISABLED)). The system may disable a profile if the user exceeds the maximum number of unsuccessful sign-on attempts. Or the security officer or system administrator may make a profile disabled.

Changing the STATUS from *DISABLED to *ENABLED can only be done by a security officer or system administrator and will allow the user to sign on again.

- Class (USRCLS). Controls the menu options the user sees on AS/400 menus. Possible values for this parameter are: *SECOFR, *SECADM, *PGMR, *SYSOPR, and *USER. *USER is the default value. Note the following:

  - ✔ This value alone does not determine to which commands the user has access.

  - ✔ This parameter can implicitly assign special authorities to a user.

- Assistance Level (ASTLVL). Three possible values:

  - ✔ *BASIC is best for new or occasional users. AS/400 Operational Assistant is used to provide messaging and help to users.

  - ✔ *INTERMED is the default value. Provides complete information and capabilities to users. All options are available and displayed.

  - ✔ *ADVANCED is only for very experienced users. All options are available, but possible options might not be displayed in order to make room for more information.

Refer to chapter 6, Security (section 6.2 System Values) for more information on assistance levels.

- Initial Program to Call (INLPGM). This is a two-variable, library/file parameter. It is used to automatically invoke a program when the user signs on. When it is used, it is almost always for users rather than for developers, operators, security officers, or system administrators.

- Initial Menu (INLMNU). This is a two-variable, library/file parameter. If an INLPGM is not specified, this is almost always MAIN (meaning the AS/400 Main Menu is displayed when the user signs on). MAIN is the default.

- Limit Capabilities (LMTCPB). Limit capabilities restricts the user's capacity to execute commands from a command line. Possible values are *NO (the default), *PARTIAL, and *YES. Note: limit capabilities has no affect on the commands within CL programs that the user executes.

- Text (TEXT). The text parameter contains up to 50 characters. Use this wisely. Spell out the user's name and perhaps his or her phone extension or LAN connection address. Decide early on whether to use "last-name-first" to facilitate alphabetic searching of user profiles.

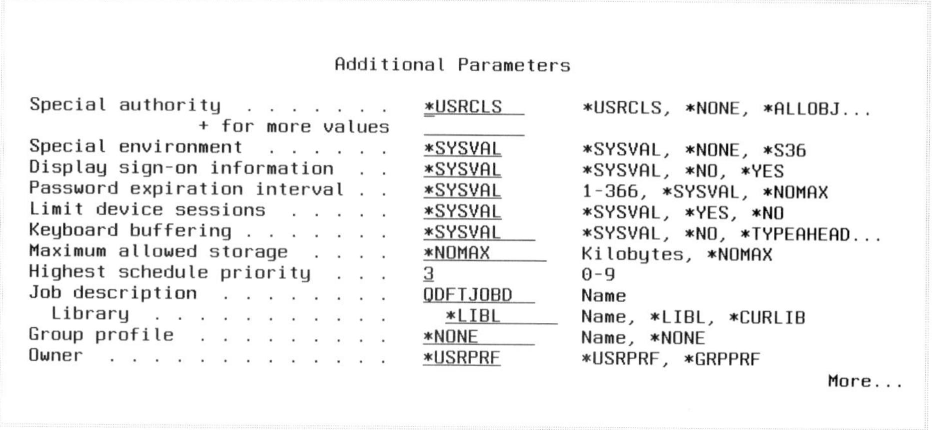

```
                          Additional Parameters

Special authority . . . . . . .   *USRCLS       *USRCLS, *NONE, *ALLOBJ...
              + for more values
Special environment . . . . . .   *SYSVAL       *SYSVAL, *NONE, *S36
Display sign-on information  . .  *SYSVAL       *SYSVAL, *NO, *YES
Password expiration interval . .  *SYSVAL       1-366, *SYSVAL, *NOMAX
Limit device sessions . . . . .   *SYSVAL       *SYSVAL, *YES, *NO
Keyboard buffering . . . . . . .  *SYSVAL       *SYSVAL, *NO, *TYPEAHEAD...
Maximum allowed storage . . . .   *NOMAX        Kilobytes, *NOMAX
Highest schedule priority . . .   3             0-9
Job description . . . . . . . .   QDFTJOBD      Name
  Library . . . . . . . . . . .     *LIBL       Name, *LIBL, *CURLIB
Group profile . . . . . . . . .   *NONE         Name, *NONE
Owner . . . . . . . . . . . . .   *USRPRF       *USRPRF, *GRPPRF
                                                                   More...
```

Figure 5-3: Prompted version of command CRTUSRPRF (additional parameters).

- Special Authority (SPCAUT). This parameter has up to ten 10-character values. See section 5.2.2.1 Special Authorities.
- Special Environment (SPCENT). This parameter specifies whether the user can run in a System/36 environment.
- Display Sign-On Information (DSPSGNINF). Determines whether sign on information is displayed when the user signs on. Sign on information is a brief display of the last date/time the user signed onto the system. Note: When a password is within days of expiring, it will display regardless of this value.
- Password Expiration Interval (PWDEXPITV). This parameter establishes how many days the password can be used before the system makes the user change it. Many shops leave this at the default, *SYSVAL, which relies on the number of days specified in the QPWDEXPITV system value. Don't use the *NOMAX value because the user will never have to change his or her password. Valid values are from 1 through 366 days. Keep the following tip in mind:

> **TIP:** Set the password change date to a shorter interval for all user profiles that have *SERVICE, *SAVSYS, and *ALLOBJ special authorities. Refer to section 5.2.2.1 Special Authorities for more information.

- Limit Device Sessions (LMTDEVSSN). This parameter prevents a user from signing onto the system from more than one device at one time. Note: This does not prevent the user from starting multiple sessions from the same workstation or from using the System Request Attention key to start another session. Keep the following tip in mind:

> ***TIP:*** Set this parameter to 1. Users should be discouraged from sharing their profiles or walking away from an active workstation and signing on at another.

- Keyboard Buffering (KBDBUF). This parameter allows or disallows a user who types faster than the system (like when the input inhibited light is on) to have keystrokes stored. This parameter separately allows or disallows buffering of the System Request Attention key. If it is buffered, all keys are buffered and it is handled just like any other key. If it is not buffered, when it is pressed, data flows into the AS/400 immediately regardless of the status of other buffering or the input capabilities of the keyboard.

- Maximum Storage (MAXSTG). This parameter is numeric (up to 11 digits) and it specifies the amount of storage in kilobytes a user's owned objects can take in DASD. Also, this parameter is used in large shops and is placed on the profile of any user who can create and own objects. Typically, that is the development staff, but it can be power users as well. Maximum storage is nice for enabling a small staff to manage DASD utilization.

- Priority Limit (PTYLMT). This parameter limits the highest priority that the users' jobs can have. A job has three priorities and this limits them all. The three priorities are:
  - ✔ Job. The priority of the job while on the job queue.
  - ✔ Run. The priority of the job while running.
  - ✔ Output. The priority of the printed output of the job while on the output queue.

- Job Description (JOBD). This parameter allows up to 10 characters for a job description. Many shops use the system default, QDFTJOBD. When the user signs onto the system, the subsystem's workstation entry contains the job description the system will use. If that value is *USRPRF, the system will get the job description specified on this parameter. For more information, see chapter 3 and especially section 3.5.1.1 How the System Starts an Interactive Job.

◆ User Group (GRPPRF). This parameter has up to 10 characters, and it makes the user a member of a group. Note: A group user profile must already exist (see section 5.4 Group Profiles).

◆ Owner (OWNER). This parameter has up to 10 characters. If the user is a member of a group, you can specify whether any object created by the user is owned by the user profile or the group user profile. Possible values are: *USRPRF (the default) and *GRPPRF. Note: If you are using group profiles, you probably want objects owned by that group.

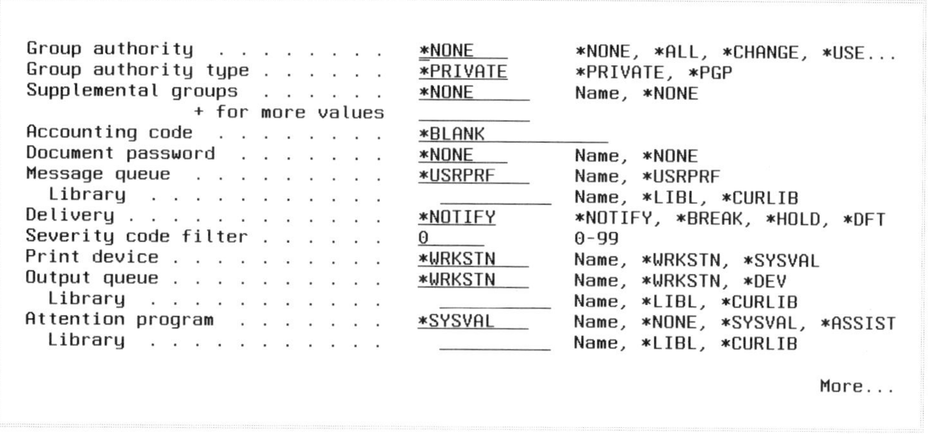

```
Group authority . . . . . . . . .   *NONE        *NONE, *ALL, *CHANGE, *USE...
Group authority type . . . . . .    *PRIVATE     *PRIVATE, *PGP
Supplemental groups . . . . . . .   *NONE        Name, *NONE
               + for more values
Accounting code . . . . . . . . .   *BLANK
Document password . . . . . . . .   *NONE        Name, *NONE
Message queue . . . . . . . . . .   *USRPRF      Name, *USRPRF
  Library . . . . . . . . . . . .                Name, *LIBL, *CURLIB
Delivery . . . . . . . . . . . . .  *NOTIFY      *NOTIFY, *BREAK, *HOLD, *DFT
Severity code filter . . . . . .    0            0-99
Print device . . . . . . . . . . .  *WRKSTN      Name, *WRKSTN, *SYSVAL
Output queue . . . . . . . . . . .  *WRKSTN      Name, *WRKSTN, *DEV
  Library . . . . . . . . . . . .                Name, *LIBL, *CURLIB
Attention program . . . . . . . .   *SYSVAL      Name, *NONE, *SYSVAL, *ASSIST
  Library . . . . . . . . . . . .                Name, *LIBL, *CURLIB

                                                                      More...
```

Figure 5-4: Prompted version of command CRTUSRPRF.

◆ Group Authority (GRPAUT). If the user profile is a member of a group user profile and the ownership was set to *USRPRF, this parameter dictates what authority is granted to other members of the same group as the creator of an object. Possible values are:

✔ *NONE—The default. No specific authority is given to the group profile.

✔ *ALL—Group members have all rights to objects created by the user.

✔ *CHANGE—Group members can change the objects.

✔ *USE—Group members can use objects created by the user.

✔ *EXCLUDE—Group members are denied access to objects created by the user.

- Group Authority Type (GRPAUTTYP). When a user creates an object, the user is the owner of that object and, if the user is a member of a group, the group shares object ownership. This parameter optionally limits granting that ownership to other group members. Refer to chapter 6 section 6.3.1 Ownership—Single and Group. Possible values are:

  - ✔ *PRIVATE—The group profile (GRPPRF) of the creating user is given private authority over the object, although the group does not become the owner of the object. The amount of authority the group has over the object is determined by the GRPAUT parameter of the creating user's profile.

  - ✔ *PGP—The group profile of the creating user becomes the primary group of the object.

- Supplemental Groups (SUPGRPPRF). User profiles can be a member of a group and, as such, receive authorities to objects created by other group members. This parameter allows you to put in up to 15 supplemental groups from which this user profile will derive authorities.

- Accounting Code (ACGCDE). Up to 15 characters can be used to specify an accounting code for the user. This supports Job Accounting, which should be active (or plan to be active) for this to make sense. For more information, see chapter 4 section 4.4 Job Accounting.

- Document Password (DOCPWD). This parameter allows the user to specify the password he or she is using to password-protect document objects.

- Message Queue (MSGQ). Up to 10 characters can be qualified with a library name. Specify the message queue for a user profile. This is where any messages from other users or programs will be placed. Most of the time, just use the default, *USRPRF, which means the message queue should be the same name as the user profile. Otherwise, specify the message queue and library to which you want messages to go. If you do specify the message queue, you should specify a unique message queue for each user.

- Delivery (DLVRY). Specifies in what way messages on the queue are delivered to the user. Possible values are:

  - ✔ *NOTIFY—The default. An alarm is sounded at the workstation and a message icon is displayed on the lower left corner of the screen. The user must use the DSPMSG (Display Message) command to see the message.

  - ✔ *BREAK—The user's workstation is interrupted by the incoming message. It goes blank and displays the message.

  - ✔ *HOLD—Messages are held in the message queue until the user requests them with the DSPMSG command.

  - ✔ *DFT—Messages requiring replies are automatically responded to with their default reply value. Informational messages are ignored.

- Severity (SEV). When DLVRY is set to *NOTIFY or *BREAK ONLY, this determines the lowest level message that is delivered to the user. The default is 00 (or all messages). You can set this to receive only more serious messages (like 30 for level 30 and above).

- Print Device (PRTDEV). Use up to 10 characters to specify the name of the printer used to print this user's output. Possible values are:

  - ✔ *WRKSTN—The default. All printed output is sent to a printer device with the same name as the workstation.

  - ✔ *SYSVAL—All printed output is sent to the system printer (as defined in the system value QPRTDEV).

  - ✔ Print Device name.

  - ✔ Output Queue (OUTQ). Up to 10 characters can be qualified with a library name to define the output queue to which the printed output for the user will go. The possible values are the same as those for the PRTDEV parameter.

  - ✔ Attention Program (ATNPGM). The attention program is activated when the user presses the attention key. The parameter is large enough to contain a library/program-name combination (20 characters).

```
 Sort sequence . . . . . . . . . .   *SYSVAL         Name, *SYSVAL, *HEX...
   Library . . . . . . . . . . . .                   Name, *LIBL, *CURLIB
 Language ID . . . . . . . . . . .   *SYSVAL         *SYSVAL...
 Country ID . . . . . . . . . . . .  *SYSVAL         *SYSVAL...
 Coded character set ID . . . . .    *SYSVAL         *SYSVAL, *HEX...
 Locale job attributes . . . . .     *SYSVAL         *SYSVAL, *NONE, *CCSID...
                 + for more values
 Locale . . . . . . . . . . . . . .  *SYSVAL

 User options . . . . . . . . . .    *NONE           *NONE, *CLKWD, *EXPERT...
                 + for more values
 User ID number . . . . . . . . .    *GEN            1-4294967294, *GEN
 Group ID number . . . . . . . . .   *NONE           1-4294967294, *NONE, *GEN
 Home directory . . . . . . . . .    *USRPRF

 Authority . . . . . . . . . . . .   *EXCLUDE        *ALL, *CHANGE, *USE, *EXCLUDE
                                                                          Bottom
```

Figure 5-5: Partial prompted version of command CRTUSRPRF.

- Sort Sequence (SRTSEQ). This parameter allows the user's data ordering to be done optionally by the sort associated with his native language or by hexadecimal.
- Language ID (LANGID). This parameter allows a user to specify a language unique to that user to be used whenever the user signs on. For a list of valid language codes, press the F4 key when the cursor is positioned on this parameter.
- Country ID (CNTRYID). This parameter allows the user to specify a country unique to the user that the system will support while that user is signed on. For a list of valid country codes, press the F4 key when the cursor is positioned on this parameter.
- Coded Character Set ID (CCSID). This parameter specifies a CCSID different from the system-wide CCSID and unique to this user. For a list of valid country codes, press the F4 key when the cursor is positioned on this parameter.
- Locale Job Attributes (SETJOBATR). This parameter accepts up to 16 10-character job attributes. This parameter specifies what job attributes are to be taken from the LOCALE parameter.
- Locale (LOCALE). This parameter specifies the path name of the locale that is assigned to the LANG environment variable for the user.
- User Options (USROPT). The user options accepts 250 10-character values. This parameter allows the user's display and some functions to be customized.
- User ID Number (UID). For users to be on a system that uses the integrated file system (IFS), that user must have a UID number. That number is used by the IFS to determine authorities. If the AS/400 is not part of an AS/400 network, use *GEN for this parameter. For networked AS/400s, you need to calculate a unique UID for each user and enter it here.

- Group ID Number (GID). User profiles that are used as part of group profiles need to have this unique number assigned. (See the preceding description of UID).
- Home Directory (HOMEDIR). This parameter is the user's initial home directory when the user signs on to access data in the IFS.
- Authority (AUT). Specifies the authority the public will have when accessing this profile.

5.2.1 User Profile Parameter Considerations

Any user who adds, changes, or deletes user profiles must have *SECADM as one of the special authorities in the user's profile.

When a password is assigned to a profile, there is no way to learn its value. Even security officers, who have all rights to everything on the system, can't learn the password.

For new users and for users who have forgotten their passwords, the procedure is as follows:

- For new users, create the user profile with any generic password.
- For forgetful users, change the user profile to any generic password.
- For both, set the parameter PWDEXP(*YES). Then tell the user the password. The next time he or she signs on, the system will force the user to change the password.

You'll see the parameter MAXSTG used a lot to limit the amount of disk space a user can have. This keeps users from building very large files and it encourages them to delete old files before they move on to new ones. Refer to chapter 6 section 6.3.1 Ownership—Single and Group.

To really restrict users to one application, INLPGM and INLMNU can be used together. Name the application the user will access as the INLPGM and name *SIGNOFF as the INLMNU. When that user signs on, he or she will only see the application's menu (or main screen). When the user exits the application, he or she is automatically signed off. Keep the following tip in mind:

> **TIP:** INLPGM = <name of application main program>
> INLMNU = *SIGNOFF

The Limit Capabilities parameter (LMTCPB) has three possible values and will limit the user's access to the following commands, based on the following values:

- *NO. The user can access all commands except where he or she is excluded by other security methods.
- *PARTIAL. The user can only use these commands:
  - ✔ CHGPRF (change profile) to change INLMNU or to change current library.
  - ✔ Any commands that the fully limited user has.
- *YES. User is limited and can only use these commands:
  - ✔ SIGNOFF—Sign off the system.
  - ✔ SNDMSG—Send a message.
  - ✔ DSPMSG—Display a message.
  - ✔ DSPJOB—Display a job.
  - ✔ DSPJOBLOG—Display the job log.
  - ✔ STRPCO—Start PC organizer.

You can use the RTVUSRPRF (Retrieve User Profile) command in a CL program to inquire about the user running the program. RTVUSRPRF can retrieve most of the user profile keywords into variables the program can use to make decisions about processing.

For PRTDEV and OUTQ parameters, most shops don't worry much about the PRTDEV, opting instead to send all printed output to one of two types of output queues. Developers and others who don't expect to print everything they generate can have a queue named the same as their user profile. When they want to print something, they move it—with the CHGSPLFA (Change Spool File Attributes) command—to a queue with an attached printer. Users who expect immediate output from their reports can get a designated output queue that normally has a printer attached.

5.2.2 Security

Two parts of the AS/400's built-in security are in the user profile: Special Authorities and Security Auditing. For more information on how special authorities fit the security picture, see chapter 4, section 4.5 Security Audit Journal, and chapter 6, Security.

5.2.2.1 Special Authorities

Most of the AS/400 authorities are granted at the object level. That's nice for most things, but it ignores the need for something special in order to have both adequate security and still allow people to do their jobs. That something special is called the *special authorities* and a user profile can have up to 10 of them. While most AS/400 security is object-based, special authorities are user-based. Here is what they do:

- *ALLOBJ: The user can do anything to any object. This is reserved for SECOFR. (Note: when the system security level is set to 10 or 20, all users have *ALLOBJ special authority.)
- *AUDIT: The user can change system values that control auditing. The user can execute the commands CHGOBJAUD and CHGUSRAUD.
- *IOSYSCFG: The user can change system configuration issues (including network and communications devices, controllers, and lines). Note that if your AS/400 supports Internet access, anyone with this special authority can configure the communication devices and the TCP/IP server. You might want to limit those with this access.
- *JOBCTL: Allows a user to manage jobs running on the system. It allows a user to change jobs to other job queues and change output to different queues. For running jobs, the user can cancel or alter them or change their priorities. For the system, the user can start/stop the entire subsystems, load the operating system, and so on. This usually is granted to system operators.
- *SAVSYS: Allows the user to perform backup/restore operations on all objects even if the user has no authority to an object. This authority is usually given to system operators.
- *SECADM: Allows a user to create and alter user profiles. Some AS/400 shops have a person dedicated to this function. Only a user with both *SECADM and *ALLOBJ authorities can grant *SECADM authority to another user.
- *SERVICE: This allows service and dump functions. These are never given to someone who is not extremely knowledgeable about the system. This authorization is more often extended to the IBM service representatives than to anyone in house.
- *SPLCTL: This allows a user to manage output queues. Users can display, move, print, release, and cancel spooled output. This is commonly granted to all users who need to be able to browse their reports directly in output queues. The problem that can come up is one user browsing other users' output—even confidential files. The solution to that is to build "restricted" output queues. Then users with *SPLCTL can browse only those output queues where they are not restricted.

One security problem special authorities take care of is the system tasks that by their nature have conflicting security needs. An example of this is a system operator who needs to save and restore files. System operators typically are excluded from access to production files (you wouldn't want one having full access to the payroll file). That would also mean that the same person wouldn't be able to save the payroll file (the user has no access rights to it) and the user especially wouldn't be able to restore it (because the restore can imply deleting an existing copy).

In this case, the special authority, *SAVSYS allows the system operator to do system level tasks like save/restore, but the user still can't read any records and certainly not change, add, or delete them.

Each of these special authorities can have two edges to them. On the one hand, certain people need the authorities to do their jobs. On the other, such authorities can grant enough power to cause a security exposure. Think through who gets what special authority before you grant it.

5.2.2.2 Security Auditing

User profiles have another, hidden, parameter not set with the CRTUSRPRF or CHGUSRPRF commands. The AUDLVL parameter concerns security auditing. It is only set with the CHGUSRAUD (Change User Audit) command. For additional information, see chapter 4, section 4.5 Security Audit Journal.

5.3 Shortcuts to Entering User Profiles

The procedures described in this chapter mean a lot of data entry for every user profile you build. In reality, many user profiles share many parameter values. If you really keyed them all in, most of that keying would be repetitious.

You can save time creating user profiles by copying existing profiles with Option 3 (COPY) on the Work with User Profiles (WRKUSRPRF) command. Let's say you have a new user, Jennie A. Jones, who works in Accounts Receivable. You probably have a standard that says use the user's initials followed by a department code. And you create a user profile named JAJAR.

For all subsequent users, your work gets easier. You can use the WRKUSRPRF'S Option 3 to copy JAJAR and create another user profile for the next user. Then just take an Option 2 (CHANGE) and make the minor changes that make the new user unique from JAJAR (probably the name and password).

One reason IBM loads the AS/400 with default user profiles is so that you have a basis in which to start. On a new AS/400, you can use WRKUSRPRF to copy QUSER into your first user profiles. However, QUSER (and the other supplied profiles) are in library QSYS. Copy them out to library QGPL and create your user profiles in QGPL. That will save you a major headache the next time you load a new version of the operating system (which likes to replace library QSYS).

For more information on IBM-supplied user profiles, refer to section 5.1.1 The New AS/400.

5.4 GROUP PROFILES

You can see how copying an existing user profile speeds things up when adding new users. The use of *group profiles* also can speed up user-profile creation. Plus, group profiles can add a level of security control.

Use group profiles when several users have the same security requirements. An example could be a group of developers, where each user can create his or her own programs and files. Without anything but user-profile security, each developer would have to grant access rights to his or her objects to all other developers. Because it's just too error prone, this method wouldn't work for very long.

If all developers belonged to the same group-user profile (PGM, for example), and object ownership was assigned to the group user profile instead of the user profiles, then any object created by one developer would be owned by the group and, therefore, would be changeable by all other developers.

The same principle applies to groups of users. This is especially important where users access common database files. Make common-group users all part of a group profile (such as AR for Accounts Receivable). Then give them all common access to each database file by granting access to each file to profile AR. Plan the group profiles before you start doing the user profiles.

Except to specify PASSWORD(*NONE), create the group profiles as regular user profiles. They don't become group profiles until you specify them on the GRPPRF parameter on a regular user profile.

In other words, create user profile PGM for developers. It will exist as just another user profile. Then create your first developer user profile and specify GRPPRF(PGM). As soon as you do, PGM becomes a group profile on your system. Keep the following tips in mind:

TIP: Create a user profile with password *NONE. Call it PGM. It is a user profile that no user can use directly.

Create a user profile for Bob the programmer called PGMBOB. On PGMBOB, specify GRPPRF(PGM). Now PGM is designated as a group profile.

User profiles that are members of a group profile inherit the group profile's authorities. Don't create a group profile with a lot of authority like *ALLOBJ or you'll inadvertently give it to all members of that group.

5.5 DELETING USER PROFILES

Use the DLTUSRPRF (Delete User Profile) or Option 4 from the WRKUSRPRF commands to delete a user profile. This is easy, but you should know that behind the scenes the system removes the user profile as owner of any objects and from any authorization lists. Objects must be owned by someone. Therefore, the system changes the ownership to QDFTUSER (one of the IBM-supplied profiles). For additional information on security, see chapter 6.

5.6 USER ROLES

Earlier, I said AS/400 users tend to clump together into like types. All the accounting users could make one type, but another way of labeling users on the AS/400 is through their role. Users have different roles within the organization or company and these roles will define how you set up user profiles and assign group profiles. Here is the typical mix of user roles on an AS/400:

- Security Officer. The system-supplied profile is QSECOFR. Sometimes referred to as "Sec-Offer," this user can do anything on the system except service functions. Service functions are better left to the IBM CE (customer engineer). The security officer has unlimited power to access objects on the system. Most AS/400 shops only have one or two security officers.

- System Administrator. No system-supplied profile is provided. The system administrator is an administrative position where someone usually is responsible for creating and maintaining user profiles.

- System Operator. The system-supplied profile is QSYSOPR. The system operator usually has authority to control jobs and do backup and restore functions.
- Programmers. The system-supplied profile is QPGMR. This user is any developer who can create programs and files and generally change records or delete files. What a programmer can do depends to a large extent on how a shop configures its AS/400 and on what libraries the programmers can access. This is a complex issue and many shops purchase CMS (Change Management Systems) to give them real sophistication in the area.
- Users. The system-supplied profile is QUSER. A user can be defined as anyone not in the computer department.

Many of the real distinctions between user types is achieved through the granting of special authorities. For additional information, see section 5.2.2.1 Special Authorities.

5.7 References

AS/400 Basic System Operation, Administration, and Problem Handling V4R3 (SC41-5206-02)

OS/400 CL Programming (SC41-5721-02)

OS/400 CL Reference (SC41-5722-02)

OS/400 Security-Reference V4R3 (SC41-5302-02)

OS/400 Security-Basic V4R1 (SC41-5301-00)

OS/400 Work Management V4R3 (SC41-5306-02)

Tips and Tools for Securing Your AS/400 V4R3 (SC41-5300-02)

6 System Values and System Security

6.1 Overview

System values are a set of parameters whose values can be retrieved system wide. These parameters and values have a great affect on how the AS/400 looks and feels. Some system values directly affect security on the AS/400. AS/400 security comes from the following places:

- System values.
- User profiles (covered in chapter 5, People).
- Each object wears a cloak of security information.
- Programs that adopt authority.

6.2 System Values

System values are global items the system needs to know. You can work with system values with these commands:

- DSPSYSVAL (Display System Value).
- CHGSYSVAL (Change System Value).
- WRKSYSVAL (Work System Value). This command combines all the system value functions; add, change, delete, and so on. Its menu provides a one-stop kind of shopping for working with system values.
- RTVSYSVAL (Retrieve System Value). This command is used within a CL program to collect a specific system value and put it into a CL variable. The CL program can then use the contents of the variable directly in its processing or pass it along to another program to use.

System values can provide default values for command keywords. For example, the CRTUSRPRF (Create User Profile) command has the ASTLVL parameter where you can specify the assistance level available to the user. Your choices are:

- *BASIC.
- *INTERMEDIATE.
- *ADVANCED.
- *SYSVAL.

If you specify the last option, the system will use the contents of system value QASTLVL, which will contain one of the first three choices. In this way, system values can speed up adding new users. If you want all or most of your users to have *INTERMEDIATE assistance levels, set the system value and don't do anything on the field when you create a new user profile; *SYSVAL is the default.

With system values, keep in mind that when you change one you could unwittingly affect many things on your AS/400. Appendix A contains a list of system values.

The following sections describe the system values (*SYSVAL) that affect security. You'll notice that there are several system values that directly control passwords. These are bypassed when a user profile's password is changed through the Change User Profile (CHGUSRPRF) command. The most commonly used value choices are noted in [brackets] at the bottom of each appropriate selection.

6.2.1 QAUDLVL—Keeping a Security Audit

System value QAUDLVL sets up a security audit. The audit can contain many parameters that tell the system what events it should record. Also, the security audit can monitor object activity, user activity, or any combination of the two. The audit records the event, who did it, when, and from what terminal. [Used or not used as the need arises.]

The audit journal is named QAUDJRN and it lives in library QSYS. You can query its contents at any time. For additional information, see chapter 4.

6.2.2 QINACTITV—Inactive Job Time-Out Interval

The QINACTITV system value sets the amount of time in minutes a job can be inactive before the system takes action and signs off the user. This might seem like a great security tool when supporting a TCP/IP connection to the Internet. However, FTP jobs are not covered under this system value. FTP jobs' inactivity intervals are set through the INACTTIMO parameter of the Change FTP Attribute (CHGFTPA) command. Refer to chapter 12 for more information.

6.2.3 INACTMSGQ—Inactive Job Message Queue

INACTMSGQ is a weird one. If you specify a message queue, a message will be sent indicating when a terminal is inactive longer than the number of minutes specified in the QINACTITV system value. A program can be written to monitor for those messages and take the appropriate action.

However, if you specify *DSCJOB instead of a message queue, the inactive job will be disconnected from the system. If you specify *ENDJOB, an inactive job will be ended.

6.2.4 QMAXSIGN—Maximum Sign-On Attempts

QMAXSIGN declares the number of times a user can unsuccessfully attempt to sign onto the AS/400 before that user profile is deactivated. Once the user ID has been deactivated, only the SECOFR or system administrator can reactivate it. [3]

6.2.5 QPWDEXPITV—Password Expiration Interval

QPWDEXPITV specifies how many days the system will allow a user to go without changing his or her password. After this interval, the user can still sign on, but the only option available is to access the change-password function. Once the password has been changed, the user can continue as usual. [Varies, but try 30 or 45.]

6.2.6 QPWDLMAJC—Limit Adjacent Characters In Password

If system value QPWDLMAJC is set to a 1, users cannot create passwords (such as 12345) that are not very secure. [0]

6.2.7 QPWDLMREP—Limit Repeated Characters In Password

If system value QPWDLMREP is set to a 1, users cannot create passwords (such as 11111) that are not very secure. [1]

6.2.8 QPWDLMTCHR—Invalid Password Characters

System value QPWDLMTCHR allows you to specify up to 10 characters that your users may never put in as a password. These can be any 10 characters (such as @, #, S, %, ^, or &), but the idea is to block special characters. [0]

6.2.9 QPWDMAXLEN—Maximum Password Length

QPWDMAXLEN specifies the maximum length of a password. It also can range from 1 to 10 characters. While this requirement might seem a little silly, the AS/400 will need this setting to match the smaller password lengths of the other machines if it is networked with other, non-AS/400 machines. [10]

6.2.10 QPWDMINLEN—Minimum Password Length

QPWDMINLEN specifies the minimum length of a password. It can range from 1 to 10 characters. The longer a password is the harder it is to guess. [6]

6.2.11 QPWDPOSDIP—Force All New Password Characters to Be Different

If system value QPWDPOSDIF is set to a 1, users cannot create new passwords with any character the same as the old password. This prevents passwords such as FRANK01, FRANK02, etc. [0]

6.2.12 QPWDRQDDGT—Force the Use of at Least One Number In a Password

System value QPWDRQDDGT, set to a 1, requires the user to build passwords that include at least one number. The number can be in any position and more than one number can be included, but there must be at least one number. [0]

6.2.13 QPWDRQDDIF—Expired Password Must Be Changed

When the maximum time for a password has expired and the user is asked to change his or her password, if SYSVAL QPWDRQDDIF is set to a 1 (instead of a 0), the new password must be different from any of the previous 32 passwords. If QPWDRQDDIF is set to a 0, the new password can be the same. [1]

6.2.14 QPWDVLDPGM—User Program to Validate Passwords

If the system doesn't give enough controls on the construction of passwords, you can specify a user-written program to validate new passwords to some other criteria. A validation program can be used to give the user additional instructions for creating a new password. [Not used.]

6.2.15 QRETSVRSEC—Retain Server Security Data

QRETSVRSEC specifies whether encrypted authentication information associated with user profiles or validation list (*VLDL) entries can be retained on the host system. (The AS/400 user profile password is not affected.) [0]

6.2.16 QSECURITY—Security Level

The first security system value is QSECURITY. It sets the security level of the whole machine. Here are the valid values for QSECURITY and a brief description of each level:

- Security Level 20 (SL20). This is a little better than SL10. The user must sign on with a valid user ID and a password. Once the user has access, however, he or she has full access—except for things reserved for SECOFR—to everything on the system.
- Security Level 30 (SL30). The user must sign on with a valid user ID and password. Users have access to objects only when the objects have been designated as useable by the individual user or by *PUBLIC (anyone). Remember, objects can be commands, files, or programs. Because there can be so many objects and so many users, designating individual access rights might seem a pain. Nevertheless, the AS/400 has some features that will speed up this task. For additional information, see section 6.3.3 Authorization Lists.

  When files are restored, there is an option on the restore command in SL30 that isn't on SL10/SL20. This is the ALLOW OBJECT DIFFERENCES option and it is defaulted to a *YES. If you are restoring a file and the file has been changed since the backup was made, if the option is still a *YES (the default), the system will complete the restore. If the option was changed to a *NO, the system will not complete the restore. [This is the security level most common with AS/400 shops.]
- Security Level 40 (SL40). The user must sign on with a valid user ID and password. Users have access to objects only when the objects have been designated as useable by the individual user or by *PUBLIC (anyone). When files are restored, the same ALLOW OBJECT DIFFERENCES option is defaulted to a *NO and must be changed if the file has been changed since the last save. This is a small thing, but it can make simple restores difficult. The biggest thing SL40 does for you that the others don't do is that it prevents applications from using "unauthorized" low-level programming techniques.
- Security Level 50 (SL50). Security Level 50 was developed for the Department of Defense and it is finding more acceptance where AS/400 systems allow open access to remote users. This level is also called C2. With the following exceptions, SL50 is the same as SL40. Users can only access objects to which they have been given explicit access. This eliminates many of the shortcuts and defaults with SL30 and SL40. Programs will blow up if they access unauthorized low-level functions. Also, programs will blow up if they access AS/400 APIs or functions and they don't pass exactly the right number of parameters. Note: This can be a problem with new releases that often add parameters to APIs. This would cause SL50 AS/400s a lot of new-release problems. With many of these functions, the number of parameters is optional.

The AS/400 used to support 10 as the lowest security level. This level didn't require passwords or even preexisting user profiles to exist—anyone could sign on with anything.

When an unknown someone signed on with an unknown user, a profile would be created for that profile. IBM dropped this level as of V4R3. Any AS/400 customer installing V4R3 on an AS/400 set to level 10 will automatically have be set to level 20.

Upon the installation, the level 10 user profiles will come over intact (their passwords will be set to the profile name). It's a good idea when going from security level 10 to 20 to set all user profile passwords to expired in order to force users to come up with their own.

6.2.17 QUSEADPAUT—Use Adopted Authority

This system value contain the name of an authorization list (refer to section 6.3.3 Authorization Lists) that names the users that can create a program that adopts authority. Optionally, this system value can contain the value *NONE, meaning that any user can create or change a program or designate a program as one that adopts authority.

6.3 Object-Level Security

Every AS/400 object carries its own list of who can do what to it. This is referred to as its *authorities*. Object-level security authorities are different from user-profile authorities. Where user-profile authorities name broad-based security powers for each user (or group of users), objects carry a list of users (or groups of users) and what functions those users can do to the object. Kind of like wearing a "kick me" sign, this naming of users can be in the following forms:

- Ownership—Every object is owned by one user profile.
- Named users & specific authorities—A list of users and what they can do to the object.
- Authorization lists—A way of listing users & specific authorities external to the object.
- Public authority—After a user profile has not been found on the object's list of users, it is considered public (*PUBLIC). The public (the unnamed users) has its own specific authority.

6.3.1 Ownership—Single and Group

The first item in an object's authority is who owns it. Ownership consists of one of the following categories:

- The person who created it.
- Previous owners' authorities (optional).
- The group user profile of the creator.
- Any other user to which ownership has been transferred.
- If the user profile has been deleted, the system changes the object's owner to the system default, QDFTOWN.

The owner automatically has all rights to the objects the owner creates. The owner can read, write, or change records as well as delete or change the object itself.

Sometimes members of a group are logically expected to share rights to an object. For an example, consider a development team where the objects any developer creates must be available to all other developers. With standard ownership by the user profile of the object creator, this would only work if, on creating an object, the developer would remember to change the object to grant authority to all the developer's workmates. Chances are the developer won't remember.

A better solution is to have the objects owned by the developers' group profile. Then all users with that same group profile have joint and equal ownership rights to the objects. Do this in the following ways (refer to chapter 5, section 5.4 Group Profiles for a detailed explanation of this):

- Set up a development group profile.
- Change or create developers' user profiles so they are members of this group (GRPPRF(<name of group profile>).
- Changer or create developers' user profiles so the objects they create are owned by the group profile (OWNER(*GRPPRF)).

In that way, one user can easily work on another user's programs or files.

You can change object ownership (with the CHGOBJOWN command) and often times will when an object moves from quality assurance (QA) into production. When you do, you have an opportunity to revoke or keep the previous owner's authorities. If you opt to keep the previous owner's authorities, you end up with an object with a single owner (the new one) and previous owners listed with the objects as having *ALL authority.

Here's a twist to object ownership. You don't want programmers changing production jobs. Therefore, when programs or files are moved from a development (or quality assurance) library into production, object ownership should be changed to some non-person owner. This would be a user profile with no password (so a real person could never sign on to the system with it). When the files or programs are checked out for maintenance, their ownership is changed back to the developers' group user profile. Object ownership can be a little complex and you might want to look at a good change-management system to do all this housekeeping for you.

In chapter 5, section 5.2.1 User Profile Parameter Considerations, refer to the paragraph regarding setting a user's maximum storage level (MAXSTG). The ownership of an object has a lot to do with what is considered a user's storage. If the user's objects are owned by the user alone, the object's size contributes to the amount of storage the user is responsible for, and it is this figure the system will attempt to limit.

If an object is owned by the group profile, its amount of storage is assigned to the group (and usually MAXSTG is set to *NOMAX for group profiles). Group ownership adds a twist to this, however, and it can throw you if you have set MAXSTG on your developers and think you can allow the team unlimited storage. All new objects are owned by the group.

When an individual creates an object, that individual owns the object through the creation process. If objects are owned by a group, ownership is transferred as soon as the object is created. This can mean that a developer creating a large object may exceed the developer's individual MAXSTG limit, even though the object is meant to be owned by the group. The way around this is to have the developer create a shell (an empty file) and then fill it after creation. Another solution is to temporarily set the developer's MAXSTG to *NOMAX until the large object is created and ownership is made under the group profile.

If the profile of the user creating the object specifies that the group profile should be the owner of the object, things are simple; after the object is created the group profile owns it. However, if the creating owner owns the object and that person is a member of a group profile, things get a little complicated.

In the case of the user owning the object (OWNER(*USRPRF)), the creating user's group profile can either:

- Be given private authority to the group. This is done by setting the parameter for group authority type (GRPAUTTYP) to *PRIVATE. When this happens:
  - ✔ The GRPAUT on the user profile determines how much authority the group gets to the object.
  - ✔ The group profile named on the GRPPRF parameter of the user profile names the group that has private authority.
- Become the primary group of the object. This is done by setting the parameter for group authority type (GRPAUTTYP) to *PGP. When this happens:
  - ✔ The GRPAUT on the user profile determines how much authority the group gets to the object.
  - ✔ The group profile named on the GRPPRF parameter of the user profile names the group that has private authority.

Because all this ownership can be confusing, three examples follow. With the first example, refer to Figure 6-1. User profile MDAWSON is set so that ownership of the objects it creates goes to *GRPPRF. MDAWSON creates a physical file, MSTFLE. Doing a Display Object Authority (DSPOBJAUT) on it results in the example shown in Figure 6-1.

```
                          Display Object Authority

Object . . . . . . . :   MSTFLE          Owner  . . . . . . . :   NEWGRP
  Library  . . . . . :     MDAWSON       Primary group  . . . :   *NONE
Object type  . . . . :   *FILE

Object secured by authorization list  . . . . . . . . . . . . :   *NONE

                         Object
User          Group      Authority
NEWGRP                   *ALL
*PUBLIC                  *CHANGE
```

Figure 6-1: File MSTFLE was created by user MDAWSON and is owned by the group, NEWGRP.

In the second example (see Figure 6-2), user profile MDAWSON is set so that ownership of the objects it creates goes to *USRPRF. Any group authority will be *CHANGE; parameter GRPAUT stores that information. Parameter GRPAUTTYP is set to *PRIVATE to give the group profile private authority. When user MDAWSON recreates the same file, MSTFLE, again displaying its authority, results in the example shown in Figure 6-2.

```
                          Display Object Authority

Object . . . . . . . :   MSTFLE          Owner  . . . . . . . :   MDAWSON
  Library  . . . . . :     MDAWSON       Primary group  . . . :   *NONE
Object type  . . . . :   *FILE

Object secured by authorization list  . . . . . . . . . . . . :   *NONE

                         Object
User          Group      Authority
MDAWSON                  *ALL
NEWGRP                   *CHANGE
*PUBLIC                  *CHANGE
```

*Figure 6-2: File MSTFLE was recreated by user MDAWSON and is owned by MDAWSON. MDAWSON'S group, NEWGRP, is listed as holding *CHANGE authority.*

If user profile MDAWSON is again changed, this time the parameter GRPAUTTYP is set to *PGP, and you see a primary group. Displaying its authority (as in Figure 6-3), shows that owner is user MDAWSON. The group NEWGRP is shown as having *CHANGE authority and also as the primary group for the object

```
                              Display Object Authority

Object . . . . . . . :   MSTFLE            Owner . . . . . . . :   MDAWSON
  Library . . . . . :     MDAWSON          Primary group . . . :   NEWGRP
Object type . . . . :   *FILE

Object secured by authorization list . . . . . . . . . . . . :   *NONE

                         Object
User        Group        Authority
MDAWSON                  *ALL
NEWGRP                   *CHANGE
*PUBLIC                  *CHANGE
```

*Figure 6-3: File MSTFLE was recreated by user MDAWSON and is owned by MDAWSON. MDAWSON'S group, NEWGRP, is listed as holding *CHANGE authority and as the primary group for the object.*

6.3.2 Named Users & Specific Authorities

There are plenty of users on a system and only one of them (or several through a group profile) can have ownership at one time. Access to others (non-owners) is granted through specific authorities.

Specific authorities are a list (attached to the object) of user profiles or group user profiles with a specific access authority for each. Although an object can only have one owner, it can have many individual specific users, and each user has access. There are four specific authorities that can be granted to an object. See Table 6-1.

Table 6-1: Specific Authorities That Can Be Granted to an Object.

Authority	Explanation
*ALL	The user can do anything with the object
*CHANGE	The user can change the object. ➢File objects—the user can clear, read, or change the records in the file. ➢Program objects and command objects—the user can use them. No matter what the object is, the user cannot delete it or change its attributes.
*USE	The user can only use the object. ➢File objects—the user can read records. ➢Program or command objects—the user can execute it. The user cannot delete it or change its attributes
*EXCLUDE	The user can do nothing with the object.

Also, keep the following tips in mind:

TIP: User profiles have special authorities; objects have specific authorities.

Special authorities define what the holder can do; specific authorities define what can be done to the holder.

Object authority is granted, revoked, or changed in a real-time mode through the following commands:

- GRTOBJAUT (Grant Object Authority).
- RVKOBJAUT (Revoke Object Authority).
- EDTOBJAUT (Edit Object Authority).
- WRKOBJ (Work with Objects, then take options for authorities).

Granting, revoking, and changing object authority is done to individual objects. Because that can be quite time-consuming, the AS/400 allows generic identification of objects on the OBJECT AUTHORITY commands. It even allows the word *ALL so that all objects (usually within a library) can be changed at once. While this method can save a lot of keying time, it should be used judiciously.

Note that when a user's specific authority is removed from an object—if the user is not the SECOFR or owner—the user's authority reverts to whatever *PUBLIC authority is set. Here are three scenarios:

- An object has these specific authorities: user TOM has *USE authority and user *PUBLIC has *USE authority. If you remove TOM from the object's authority list, user TOM still has *USE authority.
- An object has these specific authorities: user TOM has *USE authority and user *PUBLIC has *ALL authority. If you remove TOM from the object's authority list, user TOM's authority has been increased from *USE to *ALL.
- An object has these specific authorities: user TOM has *USE authority and user *PUBLIC has *EXCLUDE authority. If you remove TOM from the object's authority list, user TOM still has no authority to the object.

As a result, some AS/400 customers set public authority to *EXCLUDE on all objects.

6.3.3 Authorization Lists

While adding individual users to each object can be quite cumbersome, AS/400 objects can be secured through *authorization lists*. An authorization list is a type of object itself

(*AUTL). It contains a list of user IDs and authorizations. By attaching the authorization list to an object, you are automatically attaching the list's objects/authorities to the object.

If you have an application that has hundreds of objects and hundreds of users, you can set up one authorization list of all valid users and their authorizations. You can attach the list to each of the hundreds of objects and avoid re-keying the same set of users for each object. When you create a new object in that application, you can just attach the same authorization list and many of your security needs will be met. If a user leaves the group and is no longer eligible to access the object, you just drop that user's name from the authorization list, and that user will be off the authorization list for every object.

You can mix special authorities with authorization lists.You can even have the same users named in both places. Such practice is common in real-life but redundant. The system searches for a user's authorities for an object in the authorization list first. If it finds the user, it won't look further into the specific authorities. This can be confusing when a customer attempts to grant a user some kind of special access to an object. If that user is already named in an authorization list that the object uses, the new, keyed authority will be ignored.

The contents of authorization lists are integrated with the user profiles. If you delete a user profile, it automatically deletes from any authorization list on which it appears.

6.3.4 Public Authority

Besides ownership, specific authorities, and authorization lists, objects have *public authority*. This is the amount of authority the object will allow someone who isn't recognized in any other category. The system default is *NONE or the public has no access to the object. Public access *EXCLUDE also leaves the public with no access.

The object owner, the SECOFR, or applications such as a change-management system can change the public authority on any object. Authorities that can be granted to *PUBLIC are the same as those shown in Table 6-1. Keep the following tip in mind:

TIP: Review your authorization lists against each object's special authorities, and especially in regard to the authority *PUBLIC has. *PUBLIC is often repeated in authorization lists and object lists, with the authorization list determining the authority the *PUBLIC actually has. *PUBLIC should be mentioned once (my preference is at the object level).

6.4 OBJECT SECURITY EXAMPLE

Some simple system commands can be used to review what I've just covered. Figure 6-4 shows a sample authorization list named MCAUTLST.

```
                         Edit Authorization List

Object . . . . . . . :   MCAUTLST       Owner  . . . . . . . :   PGM
  Library  . . . . . :     QSYS         Primary group  . . . :   *NONE

Type changes to current authorities, press Enter.

              Object    List
User          Authority Mgt
PGM           *ALL       X
BWEBER        *USE       _
*PUBLIC       *EXCLUDE   _

                                                                  Bottom
F3=Exit   F5=Refresh   F6=Add new users
F11=Display detail object authorities   F12=Cancel   F24=More keys
```

Figure 6-4: The sample authorization list MCAUTLST is displayed using the EDTAUTL command.

The owner of the authorization list is PGM. PGM is not a user profile; it's a group user profile for all the users in a department. Therefore, any user in that group has all access to any object that has this authorization list on it. Notice the X (to the right of PGM) under the LIST MGT column. This symbol indicates this user (or, in this case, a group of users) can change the authorization list. Anyone not so marked may not change the list. On an authorization list, this is referred to as *list management rights*.

User BWEBER, who is a programmer, can change any records on any files that use this list, but cannot delete those files or change their descriptions. In addition, the public is excluded from any access to this file. You can investigate further and see what objects use the authorization list by pressing the F15 key. See Figure 6-5. In this case, two objects use the file, and they are both programs. No one else has access because the public is excluded in the authorization list shown in Figure 6-4.

If you want to see what security is attached to an object, you can either use the EDTOBJAUT (Edit Object Authority) or WRKOBJ (Work Object) commands. Either command will produce the screen shown in Figure 6-6. At the top right, the owner is specified as PGM. I just happen to know that PGM is a group profile name. If I didn't know that, I could use the WRKUSRPRF command to check it.

The object is secured with authorization list MCAUTLST (shown in Figure 6-4).

JJCRONEY is a user ID with use access to the program object. The public is excluded from the object. Because *PUBLIC is specified on the authorization list, this is redundant. Keep the following tip in mind:

> **TIP:** Object security is a common source of security confusion (if not problems) on AS/400s. If an object is secured with an authorization list, that list is checked first for authorities and nothing is checked later. The *PUBLIC authority the user specifies on the object has no meaning because the *PUBLIC authority specified on the authorization list has priority.

```
                    Display Authorization List Objects

Authorization list . . . . . . . . :   MCAUTLST
  Library  . . . . . . . . . . . . :     QSYS
Owner  . . . . . . . . . . . . . . :   PGM
Primary group  . . . . . . . . . . :   *NONE

                                                   Primary
Object       Library     Type       Owner          group       Text
STARTUP      MDAWSON     *PGM       PGM            *NONE       Program to start sub
ONERPGPGM    MDAWSON     *PGM       PGM            *NONE       One RPG program










                                                                          Bottom
Press Enter to continue.

F3=Exit   F12=Cancel   F17=Top   F18=Bottom
```

Figure 6-5: Results from pressing F15 (see Figure 6-4—EDTAUTL). Objects that use the authorization list MCAUTLST.

```
                         Edit Object Authority

Object . . . . . . . :   STARTUP        Owner . . . . . . . :   PGM
  Library . . . . . :     MDAWSON       Primary group . . . :   *NONE
Object type . . . . :   *PGM

Type changes to current authorities, press Enter.

  Object secured by authorization list . . . . . . . . . . . .  MCAUTLST

                          Object
User         Group        Authority
JJCRONEY                  *USE
*GROUP       PGM          *ALL
*PUBLIC                   *EXCLUDE

                                                                   Bottom
F3=Exit   F5=Refresh   F6=Add new users   F10=Grant with reference object
F11=Display detail object authorities     F12=Cancel   F24=More keys
```

Figure 6-6: Object authority from object viewpoint.

6.5 Adopted Authorities

Another way to allow access to a file is through adopted authorities. In concept, adopted authority is a little different than the others in that it affects (and resides in) executing programs only. When a program runs, it has authority and a user ID. Typically, the user who starts the program becomes the "user" of the program and that user's authority becomes the "authority" for the program while it runs.

Let's consider two users, Bob and Sue, who work in different departments in a large insurance company. Bob works in the claims department and Sue works in policies. Normally, Bob has access to claim records but not policies and Sue has access to policy records but not claim records. Because very few insurance application programs don't at least look at policy and claim records, the preceding type of arrangement could present a huge problem.

One solution would be to give access to these records to each other's department, but this particular insurance company sees that as a dilution of its security strategy.

Another solution is to have the executing programs take their authority not from the user executing them, but rather from the user profile of the developer that last created them.

A developer can get a program to adopt authority in one of two ways:

- On program creation, by specifying it on the USRPRF parameter.
- After the program has been created with the Change Program (CHGPGM) command: CHGPGM <library/program name> USEADPAUT (*YES).

When an adopt authority program executes, no matter who started it, it will adopt the authority of the developer and there shouldn't be any security problems with record accesses. There are, however, some risks and potential problems with adopting authority:

- The adopting of the developer's authority will follow and be in effect for all programs the intended program calls and all programs those programs call. This can be a problem in complex applications that allow hot keys for fast screen navigation. You could inadvertently provide a user with a back door into security the user shouldn't have. Be particularly careful in applications where a user can bring up a command line while in the program. That user will have the program developer's authority while on the command line.
- When a program that adopts authority calls another program, that call must have the library specified.
- Many shops grant their developers QSECOFR authority (by giving their user profiles special authority *ALLOBJ). Just be aware that programs in those shops that adopt authority are adopting full security officer authority.
- The authority programs adopt is not only the developer's authority to objects but all of the developer's special authorities as well.
- When a program using adopted authorities passes control to another program through the Transfer Control (TRFCTL) command (instead of the CALL command), authority adoption does not follow.
- Programs get recreated as a result of production emergencies. When these happen, don't forget to reset the program's adopted authority or you'll find the fixed programs don't work in production.
- Change management systems assign an owner to the production version of all programs. If you don't have a CMS and developers do the final production compile themselves, be careful of developers that have unequal authorities. The program might work or not work depending on the "strength" of the last developer to create it.

6.6 References

AS/400 Basic System Operation, Administration, and Problem Handling V4R3 (SC41-5206-02)

OS/400 CL Programming (SC41-5721-01)

OS/400 CL Reference (SC41-5722-02)

OS/400 Security-Reference V4R3 (SC41-5302-02)

OS/400 Security-Basic V4R1 (SC41-5301-00)

7 Backup and Recovery

7.1 Overview

Backups on the AS/400 are done with save commands (prefix SAV). Recoveries are made with restore commands (prefix RST).You can save and restore AS/400 objects for disaster protection or to move files, objects, and libraries from one system to another.

7.2 Save To...

You can save individual AS/400 objects, files, libraries, or the entire system. You can save things onto one or more diskettes, optical disks, tape reels, and cartridges. However, you may not be able to perform some saves where the media doesn't make sense. For example, if you try to save the entire system to diskettes, the AS/400 just won't let you because it would probably take about a thousand disks before it finished. The sections that follow indicate to which media each type of save can be performed.

Individual libraries or multiple files/objects also can be saved to a *save file*. All AS/400 objects that are saved are done so in a special file format that you cannot read or process directly. They are different from database files in that they have no individual fields and their contents are compressed so that multiple objects, files, and libraries can be stored within a single save file. They must be restored before you can access their contents. While most of the save media are self-explanatory, save files are not. They are special AS/400 objects with object type *SAVF.

Where media is used that must be initialized, generally speaking, it will be initialized to Save/Restore (*SAVRST) format. The exception to this might be after something is saved to a save file copied to a tape or diskette. In that case, the media could not be initialized to *SAVRST format.

Saves also can be done to other AS/400s over network connections of optical connections.

Saving objects to save files is typically faster than saving objects to tape because any write operation is faster to disk than to tape. After the save is complete and the system is restored to normal operation, the save file is stored on magnetic media with the Save Save File (SAVESAVF) command and purged from the system. The down side to save files is that they can take up quite a bit of disk space until they are archived and purged.

7.3 Backup and Recovery "Look and Feel"

New AS/400 customers sometimes feel that things are not progressing well when they first do a backup or a restore. Feelings of uncertainty are especially evident in customers who back up or recover to reel tapes where they can watch a tape drive's progress. The AS/400 backup and restore programs do some preliminary processing and post processing that makes the drive seem a little erratic.

When saving objects, files, and libraries, the backup process builds directories about the objects being saved. When each directory is complete, it is written to the save media and the objects follow. Many small objects take a long time (usually longer than a few large objects). If you view the tape progress, it advances a few inches when the process starts and then sits for several minutes before rapidly continuing. The tape might stop again for a few minutes and then continue. These "minutes" can be an hour or more (no wonder people get nervous).

Restores are similar. The tape drive will read a few inches of information and then digest it for several minutes before continuing. The same behavior happens on diskettes and tape cartridges (even save files), but there is nothing that you can watch like the older tape reels.

7.4 Save Commands

The following sections describe the AS/400 save commands and their formats.

7.4.1 SAVSYS

SAVSYS must be run with the system in a *restricted state*. In other words, all subsystems—including the controlling subsystem—are ended. Save System (SAVSYS) saves the system libraries. It will save:

- OS/400.
- Licensed internal code.
- Optionally, the system configuration. For additional information, see section 7.4.2 SAVCFG.
- System resource management objects.
- Optionally, security objects. For additional information, see section 7.4.3 SAVSECDTA.
- All PTFs. For additional information, see chapter 2.

But it won't save:

- IBM licensed programs (such as compilers).
- Any optional parts of OS/400.
- Folders.
- Libraries QGPL and QUSRSYS. Note: Although they start with a Q, the QGPL and QUSRSYS libraries are not really system libraries.
- Any user libraries.

Figure 7-1 shows the prompted version of SAVSYS.

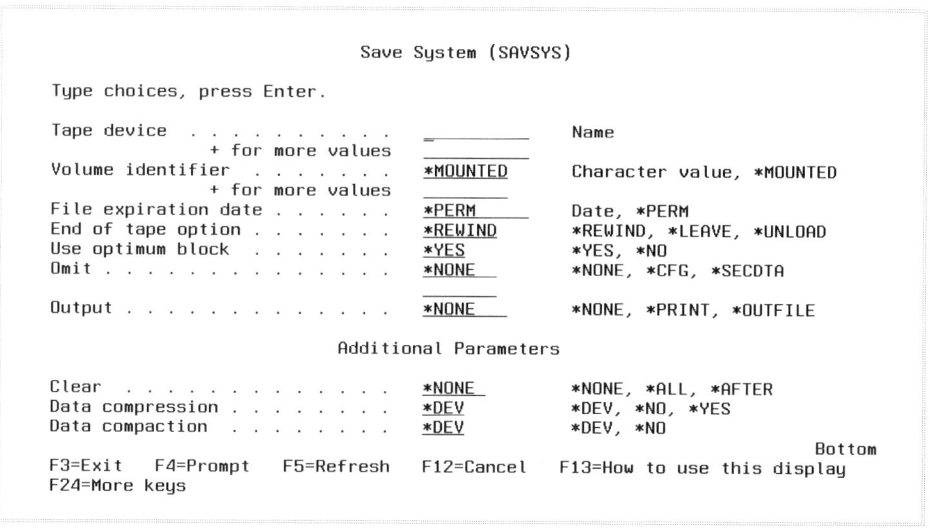
```
                           Save System (SAVSYS)

Type choices, press Enter.

Tape device . . . . . . . . . . .   _           Name
               + for more values   __________
Volume identifier . . . . . . . .   *MOUNTED    Character value, *MOUNTED
               + for more values
File expiration date . . . . . .    *PERM       Date, *PERM
End of tape option . . . . . . .    *REWIND     *REWIND, *LEAVE, *UNLOAD
Use optimum block  . . . . . . .    *YES        *YES, *NO
Omit . . . . . . . . . . . . . .    *NONE       *NONE, *CFG, *SECDTA

Output . . . . . . . . . . . . .    *NONE       *NONE, *PRINT, *OUTFILE

                         Additional Parameters

Clear  . . . . . . . . . . . . .    *NONE       *NONE, *ALL, *AFTER
Data compression . . . . . . . .    *DEV        *DEV, *NO, *YES
Data compaction  . . . . . . . .    *DEV        *DEV, *NO
                                                                  Bottom
F3=Exit   F4=Prompt   F5=Refresh   F12=Cancel   F13=How to use this display
F24=More keys
```

Figure 7-1: Prompted version of SAVSYS command.

Note the first parameter says TAPE DEVICE. You can only save the system to a tape reel or cartridge tape. If you don't know your tape device names, use the Work with Hardware Products (WRKHDWPRD) command to find it. It's probably something like TAP01.

You can start a system save quickly by naming thc tape device and pressing the Enter key. The parameter names are pretty self-explanatory, but here's a little more explanation for some of them:

- End of tape option—This tells the AS/400 what you want it to do after it completes the Save command. Your options are:
  - ✔ *REWIND—the tape is rewound but left on the drive in a ready state.
  - ✔ *LEAVE—the tape is left where it is when the save completes. This doesn't make much sense for a SAVSYS.
  - ✔ *UNLOAD—the tape is rewound completely and the drive is set off-line. The drive door might be opened for you or the cartridge might be extended into an output tray.
- Use optimum blocking—This makes for more efficient save operations. The system takes over and blocks the records to the drive in a way that is optimum for that drive. Note: This could result in making save tapes that are unreadable by other drives.
- Omit—Allows you to optionally omit saving system configurations and security data (refer to 7.4.2 SAVCFG and 7.4.3 SAVSECDTA).

7.4.2 SAVCFG

A SAVSYS takes a long time and, for the most part, it isn't necessary to do very often. The operating system is quite stable. However, you will routinely change parts of the operating system—such as device configurations, user profiles, and authorities—and you will probably want a current backup of them. Because backing up one part takes about 2 minutes, you don't want to spend hours doing a whole SAVSYS.

In order to save time, the AS/400 offers the Save Configuration (SAVCFG) command. This is similar to the SAVSYS command discussed in section 7.4.1, but it only saves device configurations. Device configurations are:

- Line descriptions.
- Controller descriptions.
- Device descriptions.
- Mode descriptions.
- Class-of-service descriptions.
- Network interface descriptions.
- Connection lists.
- Configuration lists.
- System configuration:
  - ✔ Hardware resources.
  - ✔ Token ring adapter data.

Figure 7-2 shows a prompted version of SAVCFG.

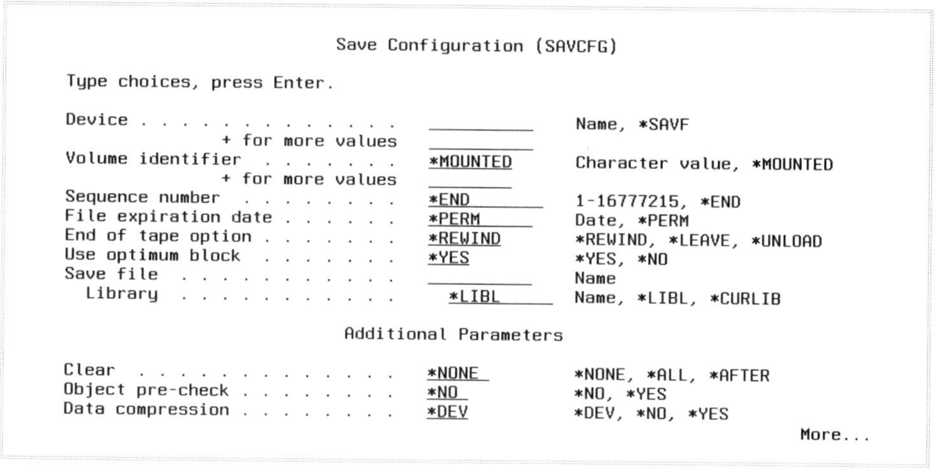

```
                    Save Configuration (SAVCFG)

Type choices, press Enter.

Device . . . . . . . . . . . . . .   __________       Name, *SAVF
               + for more values   __________
Volume identifier  . . . . . . . .   *MOUNTED         Character value, *MOUNTED
               + for more values   ________
Sequence number  . . . . . . . . .   *END             1-16777215, *END
File expiration date . . . . . . .   *PERM            Date, *PERM
End of tape option . . . . . . . .   *REWIND          *REWIND, *LEAVE, *UNLOAD
Use optimum block  . . . . . . . .   *YES             *YES, *NO
Save file  . . . . . . . . . . . .   __________       Name
  Library  . . . . . . . . . . . .     *LIBL          Name, *LIBL, *CURLIB

                      Additional Parameters

Clear  . . . . . . . . . . . . . .   *NONE            *NONE, *ALL, *AFTER
Object pre-check . . . . . . . . .   *NO              *NO, *YES
Data compression . . . . . . . . .   *DEV             *DEV, *NO, *YES
                                                                 More...
```

```
Data compaction  . . . . . . . . .   *DEV             *DEV, *NO
Output . . . . . . . . . . . . . .   *NONE            *NONE, *PRINT, *OUTFILE
File to receive output . . . . . .   __________       Name
  Library  . . . . . . . . . . . .     *LIBL          Name, *LIBL, *CURLIB
Output member options:
  Member to receive output . . . .   *FIRST           Name, *FIRST
  Replace or add records . . . . .   *REPLACE         *REPLACE, *ADD
```

Figure 7-2: Prompted version of SAVCFG *command (parts 1 and 2).*

Configuration data can be saved to:

- Tape.
- Save File.

The parameter names are fairly self-explanatory, but here's a little more explanation for some of them:

- Sequence number is the sequential number of the file on the save media. Individual saves result in files on the tape numbered sequentially from 1 to 1677215. You can place the output from this command exactly at one of these files. More likely, you just specify *END and the system will place the saved data at the end of the media. In the event you're starting with fresh media, it'll be the one and only file on the media.

- End of tape option. Refer to section 7.4.1 SAVSYS.

- Save file. If you are saving to a Save File (*SAVF), you must have specified *SAVF on the DEVICE parameter and name the save file here. Optionally, you can specify its library. Save files have to exist before you can save to one. If you must create a save file, use the Create Save File (CRTSAVF) command.
- Use optimum blocking. Refer to section 7.4.1 SAVSYS.

7.4.3 SAVSECDTA

Similar to the SAVCFG command, Save Security Data (SAVSECDTA) presumes that security data is a system component that is subject to change and, rather than require you to do a complete SAVSYS each time you add or drop a user profile, SAVSECDTA will only save system security information. The items saved are:

- User profiles.
- Private authorities to objects.
- Authorization lists.

For additional information, see chapter 6. Figure 7-3 shows a prompted version of SAVSECDTA.

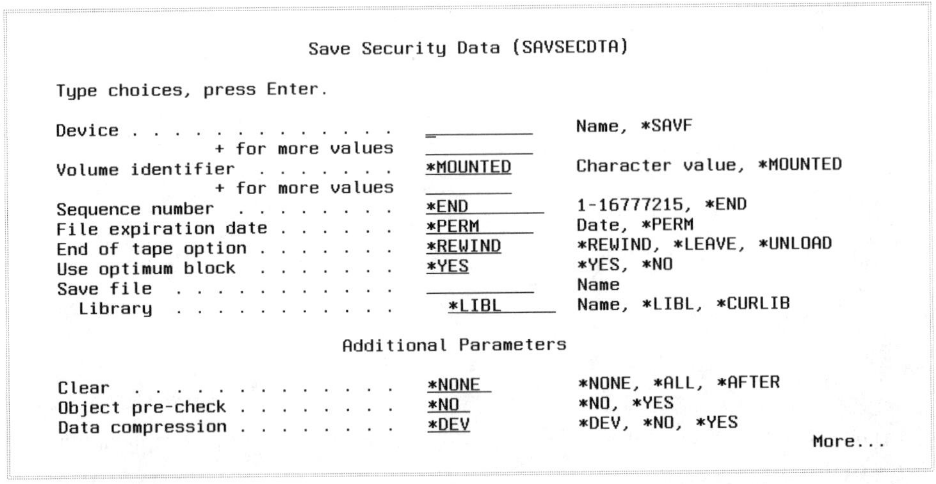

```
                        Save Security Data (SAVSECDTA)

 Type choices, press Enter.

 Device . . . . . . . . . . . . .   _________     Name, *SAVF
                + for more values   _________
 Volume identifier  . . . . . . .   *MOUNTED      Character value, *MOUNTED
                + for more values   _________
 Sequence number  . . . . . . . .   *END          1-16777215, *END
 File expiration date . . . . . .   *PERM         Date, *PERM
 End of tape option . . . . . . .   *REWIND       *REWIND, *LEAVE, *UNLOAD
 Use optimum block  . . . . . . .   *YES          *YES, *NO
 Save file  . . . . . . . . . . .   _________     Name
   Library  . . . . . . . . . . .     *LIBL       Name, *LIBL, *CURLIB

                          Additional Parameters

 Clear  . . . . . . . . . . . . .   *NONE         *NONE, *ALL, *AFTER
 Object pre-check . . . . . . . .   *NO           *NO, *YES
 Data compression . . . . . . . .   *DEV          *DEV, *NO, *YES
                                                                   More...
```

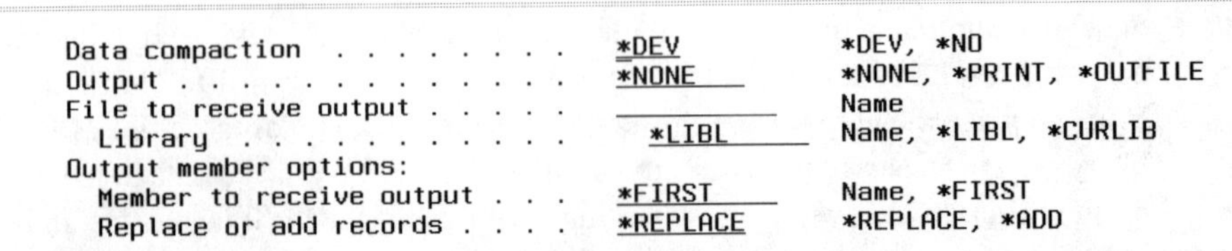

```
 Data compaction  . . . . . . . .   *DEV          *DEV, *NO
 Output . . . . . . . . . . . . .   *NONE         *NONE, *PRINT, *OUTFILE
 File to receive output . . . . .   _________     Name
   Library  . . . . . . . . . . .     *LIBL       Name, *LIBL, *CURLIB
 Output member options:
   Member to receive output . . .   *FIRST        Name, *FIRST
   Replace or add records . . . .   *REPLACE      *REPLACE, *ADD
```

Figure 7-3: Prompted version of SAVSECDTA command (parts 1 and 2).

Security data can be saved to:

- Tape.
- Save File.

The parameter names are usually self-explanatory, but here's where you'll find a little more explanation for some of them:

- Sequence number—Refer to section 7.4.2 SAVCFG.
- End of tape option—Refer to section 7.4.1 SAVSYS.
- Save file—Refer to section 7.4.2 SAVCFG.
- Use optimum blocking—Refer to section 7.4.1 SAVSYS.

7.4.4 SAVLIB

The SAVLIB command is used to save the libraries that SAVSYS didn't save and any user-created libraries. Figure 7-4 shows a prompted version of that command.

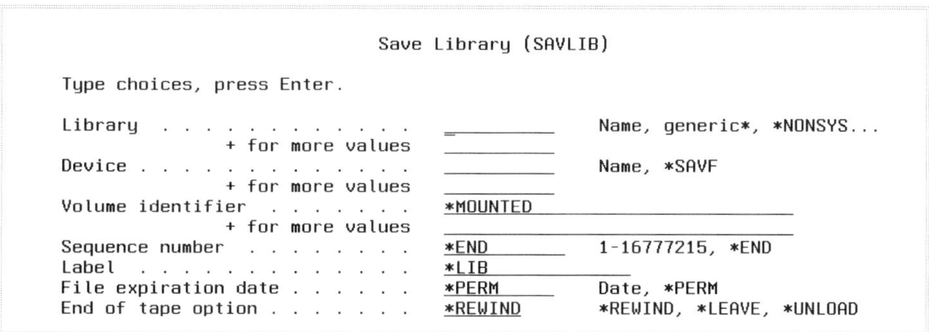
```
                         Save Library (SAVLIB)

 Type choices, press Enter.

 Library . . . . . . . . . . .   __________   Name, generic*, *NONSYS...
              + for more values  __________
 Device . . . . . . . . . . . .  __________   Name, *SAVF
              + for more values  __________
 Volume identifier . . . . . .   *MOUNTED
              + for more values
 Sequence number . . . . . . .   *END         1-16777215, *END
 Label . . . . . . . . . . . .   *LIB
 File expiration date . . . . .  *PERM        Date, *PERM
 End of tape option . . . . . .  *REWIND      *REWIND, *LEAVE, *UNLOAD
```

Figure 7-4: Prompted version of SAVLIB command.

Libraries can be saved to:

- Tape.
- Diskette.
- Save File.
- Optical media—but only if the command parameter LIB is not set to the generic values:
  - ✔ *NONSYS.
  - ✔ *ALLUSR.
  - ✔ *IBM.

For information on the save-while-active feature, refer to 7.5 Save-While-Active. The parameter names are fairly self-explanatory, but here's a little more explanation for some of them:

- The first parameter, LIB, is an important one. It's possible values are:
  - ✔ The name of up to 300 libraries to save.
  - ✔ *NONSYS:
    - ➢ Saves all non-system libraries in alphabetical order.
    - ➢ Must be run with the system in a restricted state.
  - ✔ *ALLUSR:
    - ➢ Saves including: QDSNX, QGPL, QGPL38, QPFRDATA, QRCL, QS36F, QUSER38, QUSERSYS, QUSRVXRXMX, and any other library that does not begin with a Q or #.
  - ✔ *IBM:
    - ➢ Should be run when libraries it saves are not being used.
    - ➢ Saves libraries starting with a "#" symbol.
    - ➢ Saves all Q-libraries except the ones saved by *ALLUSR.
- If you name *SAVF on the DEVICE parameter, you'll be asked to supply the save file name and library.
- Sequence number. Refer to section 7.4.2 SAVCFG.
- End of tape option. Refer to section 7.4.1 SAVSYS.

You cannot use SAVLIB to save these libraries:

- QSYS.
- QDOC.
- QSPL.
- QRPLOBJ.
- QTEMP.
- QSRV.
- QRECOVERY.

This command has an optional parameter, OMITLIB, that appears whenever one of the three generic values (*NONSYS, *ALLUSR, *IBM) are specified for the parameter LIB. With this parameter, you can exclude up to 300 specific libraries from being saved.

Although it is necessary to have the system in a restricted state only when saving with the LIB(*NONSYS) parameter, in practice the other parameters are almost as limited. Technically, you can save a library when some of its objects are in use. The ones that are active will not be saved. You really don't want a false sense of security from believing that your save tape contains all the objects from a library when it doesn't. For that reason, when backing up any library, make sure no one is using any of its objects.

Note: The way around this problem is called save-while-active. For additional information see section 7.5 Save-While-Active.

7.4.5 SAVCHGOBJ

The Save Changed Object (SAVCHGOBJ) command is used to save any object changed—such as a file with records added, changed, or deleted—since the previous save. Most shops specify *ALLUSR but you can identify specific libraries. If you use *ALLUSR, the optional OMITLIB parameter allows you to omit libraries. Figure 7-5 shows the prompted version.

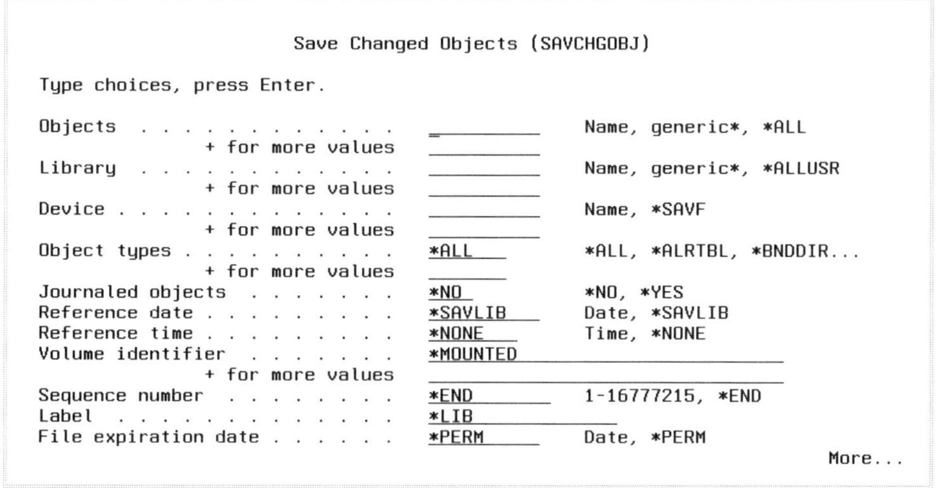

```
                    Save Changed Objects (SAVCHGOBJ)

Type choices, press Enter.

Objects . . . . . . . . . . . .   __________      Name, generic*, *ALL
               + for more values  __________
Library . . . . . . . . . . . .   __________      Name, generic*, *ALLUSR
               + for more values  __________
Device . . . . . . . . . . . . .  __________      Name, *SAVF
               + for more values  __________
Object types . . . . . . . . . .  *ALL            *ALL, *ALRTBL, *BNDDIR...
               + for more values  _______
Journaled objects  . . . . . . .  *NO             *NO, *YES
Reference date . . . . . . . . .  *SAVLIB         Date, *SAVLIB
Reference time . . . . . . . . .  *NONE           Time, *NONE
Volume identifier  . . . . . . .  *MOUNTED
               + for more values  ____________________________
Sequence number  . . . . . . . .  *END            1-16777215, *END
Label  . . . . . . . . . . . . .  *LIB
File expiration date . . . . . .  *PERM           Date, *PERM
                                                                 More...
```

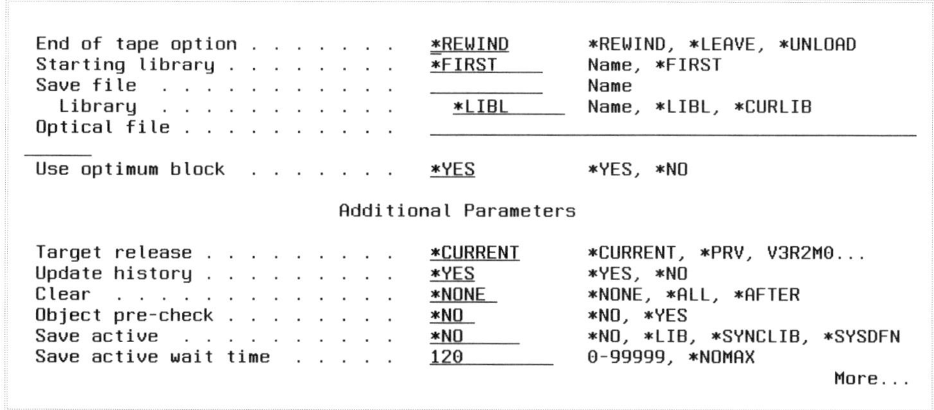

```
End of tape option . . . . . . .  *REWIND         *REWIND, *LEAVE, *UNLOAD
Starting library . . . . . . . .  *FIRST          Name, *FIRST
Save file  . . . . . . . . . . .  __________      Name
  Library  . . . . . . . . . . .    *LIBL         Name, *LIBL, *CURLIB
Optical file . . . . . . . . . .  ______________________________________

Use optimum block  . . . . . . .  *YES            *YES, *NO

                         Additional Parameters

Target release . . . . . . . . .  *CURRENT        *CURRENT, *PRV, V3R2M0...
Update history . . . . . . . . .  *YES            *YES, *NO
Clear  . . . . . . . . . . . . .  *NONE           *NONE, *ALL, *AFTER
Object pre-check . . . . . . . .  *NO             *NO, *YES
Save active  . . . . . . . . . .  *NO             *NO, *LIB, *SYNCLIB, *SYSDFN
Save active wait time  . . . . .  120             0-99999, *NOMAX
                                                                 More...
```

Figure 7-5: Prompted version of the SAVCHGOBJ command (parts 1 and 2 of 4)

```
Save active message queue . . .   *NONE          Name, *NONE, *WRKSTN
  Library . . . . . . . . . . .     *LIBL        Name, *LIBL, *CURLIB
Save access paths . . . . . . .   *NO            *NO, *YES
Save file data . . . . . . . . .  *YES           *YES, *NO
Data compression . . . . . . . .  *DEV           *DEV, *NO, *YES
Data compaction . . . . . . . .   *DEV           *DEV, *NO
Libraries to omit . . . . . . .   *NONE          Name, generic*, *NONE
               + for more values
Objects to omit:                _
  Object . . . . . . . . . . . .  *NONE          Name, generic*, *NONE, *ALL
    Library . . . . . . . . . .     *ALL         Name, generic*, *ALL
  Object type . . . . . . . . .   *ALL           *ALL, *ALRTBL, *BNDDIR...
               + for more values _
Output . . . . . . . . . . . . .  *NONE          *NONE, *PRINT, *OUTFILE
File to receive output . . . . .                 Name
  Library . . . . . . . . . . .     *LIBL        Name, *LIBL, *CURLIB
                                                                    More...
```

```
Output member options:
  Member to receive output . . .   *FIRST        Name, *FIRST
  Replace or add records . . . .   *REPLACE      *REPLACE, *ADD
Type of output information . . .   *OBJ          *OBJ, *LIB, *MBR, *ERR
```

Figure 7-5: Prompted version of the SAVCHGOBJ command (parts 3 and 4).

Changed objects can be saved to:

- Tape.
- Diskette.
- Save file.
- Optical media.

Using the save-while-active feature is possible. For more information refer to section 7.5 Save-While-Active.

The parameter names are generally self-explanatory, but here's a little more explanation for some of them:

- Journaled objects. Files currently being journaled can be saved or not. If this parameter is set to *NO, they will not be saved.
- Sequence number. Refer to section 7.4.2 SAVCFG.
- End of tape option. Refer to section 7.4.1 SAVSYS.
- Save file. Refer to section 7.4.2 SAVCFG.

- Optical file. If an optical device was named in the DEVICE parameter, this must contain the path to that device.
- Use optimum blocking. Refer to section 7.4.1 SAVSYS.
- Object to omit. Objects can be omitted from the save.

7.4.6 SAVOBJ

While not always considered part of backup or recovery, the Save Object (SAVOBJ) command nevertheless has an ancillary role. SAVOBJ will allow you to save individual objects within libraries. A good backup strategy will use the other commands, but this one fills a niche as a backup tool.

Saving something on the AS/400 isn't always done for disaster-recovery reasons. SAVOBJ is often done just because it's a convenient way of saving something or transporting a set of objects.

If you have two AS/400s linked as a networked, you should find it easy to save several objects in a save file, send the save file to the other machine, and restore the objects there. Don't attempt something like the SAVLIB (which will save a whole library as a minimum). SAVOBJ will allow you to save exactly the objects you want. Figure 7-6 shows a prompted view of the SAVOBJ command.

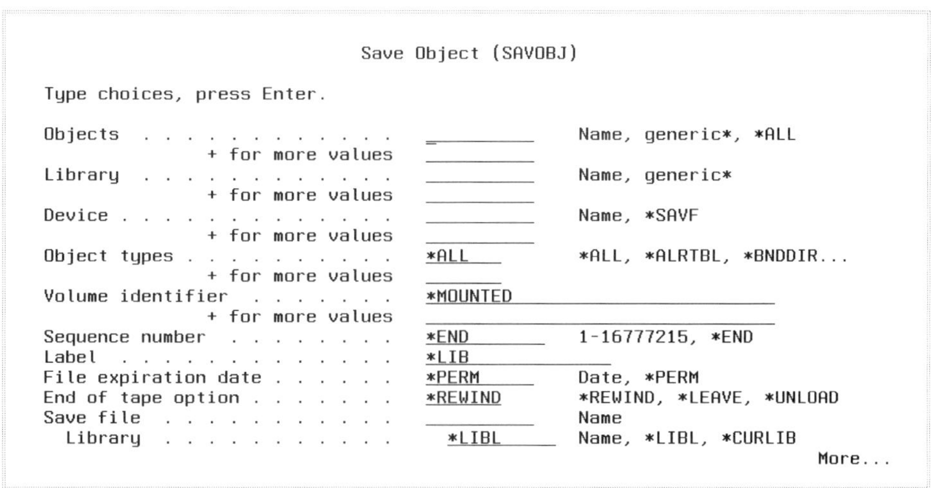
```
                        Save Object (SAVOBJ)

Type choices, press Enter.

Objects . . . . . . . . . . .   __________    Name, generic*, *ALL
              + for more values __________
Library . . . . . . . . . . .   __________    Name, generic*
              + for more values __________
Device . . . . . . . . . . . .  __________    Name, *SAVF
              + for more values __________
Object types . . . . . . . . .  *ALL          *ALL, *ALRTBL, *BNDDIR...
              + for more values ______
Volume identifier . . . . . . . *MOUNTED
              + for more values
Sequence number . . . . . . . . *END          1-16777215, *END
Label . . . . . . . . . . . . . *LIB
File expiration date . . . . .  *PERM         Date, *PERM
End of tape option . . . . . .  *REWIND       *REWIND, *LEAVE, *UNLOAD
Save file . . . . . . . . . . . __________    Name
  Library . . . . . . . . . . .   *LIBL       Name, *LIBL, *CURLIB
                                                                More...
```

Figure 7-6: Prompted version of SAVOBJ command (part 1 of 4).

```
Optical file . . . . . . . . . . .   _________________________________________

Use optimum block . . . . . . . .   *YES          *YES, *NO

                          Additional Parameters

Target release . . . . . . . . . .   *CURRENT      *CURRENT, *PRV, V3R2M0...
Update history . . . . . . . . . .   *YES          *YES, *NO
Clear  . . . . . . . . . . . . . .   *NONE         *NONE, *ALL, *AFTER
Object pre-check . . . . . . . . .   *NO           *NO, *YES
Save active  . . . . . . . . . . .   *NO           *NO, *LIB, *SYNCLIB, *SYSDFN
Save active wait time  . . . . . .   120           0-99999, *NOMAX
Save active message queue  . . . .   *NONE         Name, *NONE, *WRKSTN
  Library  . . . . . . . . . . . .     *LIBL       Name, *LIBL, *CURLIB

                                                                    More...
```

```
File member:
  File . . . . . . . . . . . . . .   *ALL          Name, *ALL
  Member . . . . . . . . . . . . .   *ALL          Name, generic*, *ALL, *NONE
               + for more values    __________
               + for more values _
Save access paths  . . . . . . . .   *NO           *NO, *YES
Save file data . . . . . . . . . .   *YES          *YES, *NO
Storage  . . . . . . . . . . . . .   *KEEP         *KEEP, *FREE
Data compression . . . . . . . . .   *DEV          *DEV, *NO, *YES
Data compaction  . . . . . . . . .   *DEV          *DEV, *NO
Libraries to omit  . . . . . . . .   *NONE         Name, generic*, *NONE
               + for more values    __________

                                                                    More...
```

```
Objects to omit:                   _
  Object . . . . . . . . . . . . .   *NONE         Name, generic*, *NONE, *ALL
    Library  . . . . . . . . . . .     *ALL        Name, generic*, *ALL
  Object type  . . . . . . . . . .   *ALL          *ALL, *ALRTBL, *BNDDIR...
               + for more values _
Output . . . . . . . . . . . . . .   *NONE         *NONE, *PRINT, *OUTFILE
File to receive output . . . . . .   __________    Name
  Library  . . . . . . . . . . . .     *LIBL       Name, *LIBL, *CURLIB
Output member options:
  Member to receive output . . . .   *FIRST        Name, *FIRST
  Replace or add records . . . . .   *REPLACE      *REPLACE, *ADD
Type of output information . . . .   *OBJ          *OBJ, *LIB, *MBR, *ERR
```

Figure 7-6: Prompted version of SAVOBJ command (parts 2 through 4).

Objects can be saved to:

- Tape.
- Diskette.
- Save file.
- Optical media.

Using the save-while-active feature is possible. For more information, refer to section 7.5 Save-While-Active.

The parameter names are fairly self-explanatory. Here's a little more explanation for some of them:

- Sequence number. Refer to section 7.4.2 SAVCFG.
- End of tape option. Refer to section 7.4.1 SAVSYS.
- Save file. Refer to section 7.4.2 SAVCFG.
- Optical file. If an optical device was named in the DEVICE parameter, this must contain the path to that device.
- Use optimum blocking. Refer to section 7.4.1 SAVSYS.
- Object to omit. Objects can be omitted from the save.

Although it might look completely functional, there are a couple of restrictions on the command's parameters that limit its use:

- If you specify more than one library, you must specify all objects (OBJ(*ALL)) within those libraries to be saved.
- If you want to save to an outfile (a *SAVF), you can only specify a single library.

7.4.7 SAVSAVFDTA

When most shops do saves to a save file, they follow up with a copy to tape. This command allows them to do a save to tape or diskette of the save file instead. While this might not make much sense at first, it does give the user a version of save files that can be restored directly from the save media.

For an example, consider a Save Library (SAVLIB) that is done to a save file. One shop might prefer to copy the resulting save file to tape and another might save the save file to tape with this command. If both shops needed to restore the library from the save file, the first would have to copy the save file from tape before they could to the restore. The second shop could restore directly from the tape.

Save a save file with the Save Save File Data (SAVSAVFDTA) command. Figure 7-7 shows a prompted version of it:

```
                      Save Save File Data (SAVSAVFDTA)

 Type choices, press Enter.

 Save file . . . . . . . . . . .   __________    Name
   Library . . . . . . . . . . .     *LIBL       Name, *LIBL, *CURLIB
 Device . . . . . . . . . . . . .  __________    Name
               + for more values   __________
 Volume identifier . . . . . . .   *MOUNTED      Character value, *MOUNTED
               + for more values   ________
 Sequence number . . . . . . . .   *END          1-9999, *END
 End of tape option . . . . . . .  *REWIND       *REWIND, *LEAVE, *UNLOAD
 Use optimum block . . . . . . .   *NO           *NO, *YES
 Clear . . . . . . . . . . . . .   *NONE         *NONE, *ALL, *AFTER

                          Additional Parameters

 File expiration date . . . . . .  *PERM         Date, *PERM
 Data compaction . . . . . . . .   *DEV          *DEV, *NO
 Output . . . . . . . . . . . . .  *NONE         *NONE, *PRINT, *OUTFILE
```

```
                      Save Save File Data (SAVSAVFDTA)

 Type choices, press Enter.

 File to receive output . . . . .  __________    Name
   Library . . . . . . . . . . .     *LIBL       Name, *LIBL, *CURLIB
 Output member options:
   Member to receive output . . .  *FIRST        Name, *FIRST
   Replace or add records . . . .  *REPLACE      *REPLACE, *ADD
```

Figure 7-7: Prompted version of SAVSAVFDTA command.

Save files can be saved to:

- Tape.
- Diskette—except for save files containing SAVCFG and SAVSEC data.

7.4.8 SAVLICPGM

The SAVLICPGM parameter saves licensed program products (LPP). The unusual thing about it is it saves them in a format that makes them restorable with the Restore Licensed Program (RSTLICPGM) command. Figure 7-8 shows a prompted view of the SAVLICPGM command.

```
                    Save Licensed Program (SAVLICPGM)

Type choices, press Enter.

Product . . . . . . . . . . . . .   _______     Character value
Device . . . . . . . . . . . . . .   _________   Name, *SAVF
               + for more values    _________
Optional part to be saved . . .     *BASE       *BASE, 1, 2, 3, 4, 5, 6, 7...
Release . . . . . . . . . . . . .   *ONLY       Character value, *ONLY
Language for licensed program  .    *PRIMARY    Character value, *PRIMARY...
Object type . . . . . . . . . . .   *ALL        *ALL, *PGM, *LNG
```

Figure 7-8: Prompted version of the SAVLICPGM command.

Objects can be saved to:

- Tape.
- Save file.

7.4.9 SAV

The SAV command allows you to save the contents of your integrated file system (IFS). To use this command, you must use the IFS file-naming conventions for files and devices. The SAV command is to the IFS what all the other save commands are to the traditional AS/400; you can save the IFS system, libraries (or directories), and objects.

I won't go into great detail here but, for example, instead of naming the tape device DEVICE(*TAP01), you would say, DEV('/QSYS.LIB/TAP01.DEVD').

Figure 7-9 shows a prompted view of the SAV command.

```
                         Save Object (SAV)

 Type choices, press Enter.

 Device . . . . . . . . . . . . . .   ______________________________

               + for more values      ______________________________

 Objects:                           _
   Name . . . . . . . . . . . . . .   '*'

   Include or omit . . . . . . . .    *INCLUDE       *INCLUDE, *OMIT
               + for more values _
 Directory subtree . . . . . . . .    *ALL           *ALL, *DIR, *NONE, *OBJ
 Save active . . . . . . . . . . .    *NO            *NO, *YES, *SYNC
 Output . . . . . . . . . . . . . .   *NONE

 Volume identifier . . . . . . . .    *MOUNTED
               + for more values      ____________________
 Label . . . . . . . . . . . . . .    *GEN
```

Figure 7-9: Prompted version of the SAV command (part 1 of 3).

```
                         Save Object (SAV)

Type choices, press Enter.

Optical file . . . . . . . . . .   ____________________________________________

Sequence number  . . . . . . . .   *END          1-9999, *END
File expiration date . . . . . .   *PERM         Date, *PERM
End of tape option . . . . . . .   *REWIND       *REWIND, *LEAVE, *UNLOAD
Use optimum block  . . . . . . .   *NO           *NO, *YES

                       Additional Parameters

System . . . . . . . . . . . . .   *LCL          *ALL, *LCL, *RMT
Time period for last change:
  Start date . . . . . . . . . .   *ALL          Date, *ALL, *LASTSAVE
  Start time . . . . . . . . . .   *ALL          Time, *ALL
  End date . . . . . . . . . . .   *ALL          Date, *ALL
  End time . . . . . . . . . . .   *ALL          Time, *ALL
Object pre-check . . . . . . . .   *NO           *NO, *YES
```

```
                         Save Object (SAV)

Type choices, press Enter.

Target release . . . . . . . . .   *CURRENT      *CURRENT, *PRV, V4R1M0...
Update history . . . . . . . . .   *NO           *NO, *YES, *SYS, *PC

Clear  . . . . . . . . . . . . .   *NONE         *NONE, *ALL, *AFTER
Data compression . . . . . . . .   *DEV          *DEV, *NO, *YES
Data compaction  . . . . . . . .   *DEV          *DEV, *NO
```

Figure 7-9: Prompted version of the SAV command (parts 2 and 3).

Objects can be saved to:

- Tape.
- Diskette.
- Save file.
- Optical media.

Using the save-while-active feature is possible. For more information, refer to 7.5 Save-While-Active.

7.5 SAVE-WHILE-ACTIVE

When save commands run, they try to grab an exclusive lock on whatever object they are saving. If they can't obtain a lock, they will not save that object. If a command can obtain a lock, it won't release it until the object is saved. By implication, then, you wait until you have a set of objects or libraries all to yourself before saving anything. This is the procedure for most shops and saves are done during off-hours. However, there are plenty of 24-hour shops where this wouldn't work.

The AS/400 has a nice feature that allows an object to be saved while it is being accessed (even updated) by users. The feature is called *save-while-active.* In the discussion of other save commands, I refrain from specifying what types of objects you are saving because typically many kinds of objects can be saved. But by implication, save-while-active refers to only database file saves.

When the system saves-while-active, it creates its own *checkpoint image* of the file being saved. At that particular point in time, the file image is captured and a save is made of the file at that point only.

Save-while-active cannot be performed if parameters STG(*FREE) or STG (*DELETE) are also specified on the save command.

7.5.1 Save-While-Active Save

Save-while-active is only available on these save commands:

- SAVLIB.
- SAVOBJ.
- SAVCHGOBJ.
- SAV.

Three parameters on each command refer to save-while-active:

- SAVACT starts/stops save-while-active and sets the synchronization level of the database files being saved. Possible values are:
  - ✔ *NO—save-while-active is not in effect. Other parameters have no affect on the command.
  - ✔ *LIB—save-while-active is in effect and the synchronization level of the files being saved are at the library level. This presumes that the files being saved all reside in the same library.
  - ✔ *SYNCLIB—save-while-active is in effect and the synchronization level of the files being saved are at the multiple library level. This presumes that the files being saved reside in different libraries.
  - ✔ *SYSDFN—save-while-active is in effect and the synchronization level of the files being saved are set by the system.

- SAVACTWAIT determines how many seconds the system will wait for a lock issue to be resolved. The default is 120 and the range is 0–99,999. If applications are stopped for the checkpoint, set this to 0.
- SAVACTMSGQ names the message queue to receive save-while-active messages.

Let's talk about the completeness of the save-while-active because saving multiple database files while they are being updated carries a unique set of problems.

The first issue is not really a problem but a consideration: No record will be saved that is partially updated (that is, with some fields updated, others not).

The second issue is that an application may, in processing a single transaction, update multiple database files. These should be checkpointed at intervals when their updates are complete (and none are waiting in buffers). For this reason, you have the control with the SAVACT parameter to specify what kind of synchronization level you'd like the system to do.

A third problem for the customer is with the application boundary. Although the system can make a pretty good guess about the synchronization level, there is no way it can determine the application boundary. This may be the same as the synchronization level or it may be higher. Only the customer, through knowledge of the application, can know for sure.

Just by turning on save-while-active, you've set some sort of synchronization level and that may be enough. If you need something further to meet an application boundary, you can either journal changes to the databases (and save the journal receiver) or come up with your own application boundary restoration method.

If the saved files are journaled, make saving the journal receiver an automatic feature as soon as the save-while-active completes. Note: you will not save the journal receiver with save-while-active on. Keep the following tips in mind:

TIP: Use SAVACT(*LIB) if all files are in one library.

Use SAVACT(*SYNCLIB) if all files are in multiple libraries and no journaling is in effect.

Use SAVACT(*SYSDFN) if all files are journaled.

Although there is a parameter that tells the system how long to wait for a lock conflict, it is possible that a lock will not be released in the allotted time. If that's the case, the save command does not save that file and moves on to the next—just as if save-while-active were not in place. Keep the following tip in mind:

> **TIP:** Don't trust the system. Double-check the results of your save even if you are doing save-while-active.

A user or a program can monitor a message queue. Create a special one with the Create Message Queue (CRTMSGQ) and name that on the SAVACTMSGQ parameter. The messages you will receive in that queue are:

- If SAVACT(*SYNCLIB), CPI3712 when the checkpoint image is completed.
- If SAVACT(*LIB) or SAVACT(*SYSDFN), CPI3710 when the checkpoint image is completed.
- If the checkpoint image does not complete normally, CPI3711 is issued for all save commands except SAV (which gets CPI3712 for an abnormal completion).

That brings up another consideration about save-while-active. Originally, it was a full save-while-active feature intended for shops where 24-hour up time was crucial. However, save-while-active took a long time to run. Many shops were willing to allow a minimum down time as a trade-off of a faster save.

For that reason, you must plan how you're going to run a save command save-while-active. If you can possibly get your users off an application for a couple minutes, the save will be cleaner and run faster. If your shop absolutely cannot endure any down time, go for save-while-active while they're up. Here's an example of how you do each:

- Some down-time:
  - ✔ Have all users sign off, stop the application.
  - ✔ Set parameter SAVACTWAIT(0) and name the message queue on the SAVACTMSGQ.
  - ✔ Start the save and monitor the message queue.
  - ✔ When a successful message hits the message queue, restart the application and let the users back on.

- No down-time:
  - ✔ Start the save, monitor the message queue.
  - ✔ If the database files were journaled, save the journal receiver.
  - ✔ Double check the job log or message queue for unsaved files.

7.5.1.1 *Save-While-Active Save Performance Considerations*

There are some things you can do to improve performance of the save-while-active feature:

- Only start the save when the system is at its lowest utilization.
- Only start the save if you have plenty of available disk space (20 percent or better).
- Move at least 1500Kb of memory into the machine pool (refer to chapter 3, section 3.3.1 Storage Pools).
- If you're saving multiple libraries, try to start individual SAVLIB jobs and have them all going to their own tape drive (if you have the drives to spare). Note: if related database files are spread across libraries, you might not be able to break up the save commands.
- Again, if you can plan your save commands, it's better to save a small number of large files than a large number of small files.

7.5.2 Save-While-Active Restore

This is the easy part; just issue the appropriate command:

- RSTOBJ.
- RSTLIB.
- RST.

If the journal receiver was saved and it is no longer on the system, restore it next. Do whatever your procedure is for bringing the restored files up to the application boundary. This could involve applying journal changes (APYJRNCHG) or removing journal changes (RMVJRNCHG). Most commonly, shops that do this are applying changes.

If journals don't do the job or only do it part way, you must have your own procedures in place to bring the files up to a boundary.

In most shops, a simple, synchronized save and restore is enough to bring the system back to its original condition. It's up to the customer to think through a save/restore plan that will work.

7.6 Things Not Saved

Not everything gets saved when you do a save. While all AS/400 objects will be technically saved, their contents are not always saved. Sometimes you can get around this and sometimes you can't. The items that will give you trouble are:

- The contents of queues.
- Two lists held within journals.
- Logical files.
- Sometimes save files (*SAVF).

You can save queues but you can't save their contents. The queues on the AS/400 are:

- Data.
- Job.
- Message.
- Output.
- User.

Except for the output queue, none of these has ever caused me a problem. For example, I wanted to save spooled output files before deleting them. When I did a SAVOBJ on the queues, all I got was the description of the queue. Big deal.

Since then I've learned to use the Copy Spool File (CPYSPLF) first. This allows me to copy a spool file to a database file, and then save the database file.

Although the contents of journal receivers (*JRNRCV) save very completely, you lose some things when you save journals (*JRN). You lose the list of journaled objects and the list of associated journal receivers.

Logical files are never saved themselves. Instead, they are saved when you save the physical file they are built over and specify on the save that you want to save the physical files' access paths.

Save files (*SAVF) are only saved when you specify SAVFDTA(*YES) on the particular save command you are executing.

7.7 RESTORES

The opposite of save (or backup) is restore. Most of the save commands covered so far have a counterpart with a prefix RST (for restore). For example, SAVLIB can be restored with a RSTLIB. Here is a list of the common restore commands:

- RST—Restores objects from the integrated file system (IFS).
- RSTLIB—Restores one or more libraries.
- RSTOBJ—Restores one or more objects from one or more libraries.
- RSTLICPGM—Restores saved licensed programs.
- Security restores:
    - ✔ RSTAUT—Restores authorizations.
    - ✔ RSTCFG—Restores configurations.
    - ✔ RSTUSRPRF—Restores user profiles.

Although the system can be restored (refer to Table 7-1), SAVSYS doesn't have a direct restore counterpart. And the restore commands have some overlap where they can be used to restore files saved with other SAV commands. Table 7-1 shows the save and restore command relationships.

Table 7-1: Save and Restore Command Relationships.

Objects/ Files/ Libraries Saved with:	Can Be Restored with:
SAVOBJ	RSTOBJ or RST
SAVLICPGM	RSTLICPGM
SAVCHGOBJ	RSTOBJ
SAVLIB	RST or
LIB(*nonsys)	RSTLIB SAVLIB(*NONSYS) or RSTLIB SAVLIB(*IBM) or RSTLIB SAVLIB(*ALLUSR) or RSTLIB SAVLIB(<library-name>)
LIB(*ALLUSR)	RSTLIB SAVLIB(*ALLUSR) or RSTLIB SAVLIB(<LIBRARY-NAME>) or
LIB(<lib-name>)	RSTLIB SAVLIB(<library-name>)

Objects/ Files/ Libraries Saved with:	Can Be Restored with:
SAVSYS	Refer to *OS/400 Backup and Recovery V4R3*, chapter 12: Restore licensed internal programs. Refer to *OS/400 Backup and Recovery V4R3*, chapter 13: Restore operating system. RSTUSRPRF or RSTAUT or RSTCFG
SAVSECDTA	RSTUSRPRF or RSTAUT or RSTCFG
SAVCFG	RSTCFG
SAV	RST

Table 7-1: Save and Restore Command Relationships (continued).

These commands are fairly simple, but RSTOBJ has two parameters you need to understand. The OPTION parameter is used to control what objects are restored. Here are the possible values for OPTION:

- *ALL—The default. All objects on the save media requested to be restored will be restored.
- *NEW—Only objects that do not exist on the system will be restored.
- *OLD—Only objects that do exist on the system will be restored.
- *FREE—Only objects that exist on the system with their storage freed will be restored.

OPTION refers to the objects on the system to which you are restoring. The default *ALL is usually what you want (all items you want restored will be restored). The other parameter, DATABASE MEMBER OPTION, refers to the objects on the media from which you are restoring. This parameter is only in effect when restoring database files. And it will cause you some grief if you're not careful. Here are its possible values:

- *MATCH—the default. Database files to be restored will only be restored if the member lists exactly match the member lists on the system. For example, if you want to restore file TRNFILE and its saved version has four members, it will only be restored if TRNFILE on the system also has four members with the same names.
- *ALL—All members of a saved file are restored.
- *NEW—Only members of a saved file that aren't members of the file on the system are restored.
- *OLD—Only members of a saved file that are also members of the file on the system are restored.

If you forget to override the default from *MATCH to something else, you will spend time wondering why your restores didn't take.

When you restore user profiles, you have two options with two commands. The restore user profile (RSTUSRPRF) actually restores user profiles. The restore authorities (RSTAUT) re-grants profile authorities.

7.8 Backup Strategy

In the event of a disaster, basically, your backups become your system. If you've lost your system, whatever isn't on the backups isn't part of your system anymore.

That's pretty extreme, though. I haven't even heard of an AS/400 going down that hard—the machine is just too reliable. On a more realistic level, you'll have to recover from applications' errors or even (gasp!) developers' errors.

Whatever the real need, you must plan for the worst and make a scenario that will meet several goals so that:

- When lightning strikes your computer center, you can back up your entire system.
- You don't back up too often and create backup down time.
- You can selectively restore any subset of the system at any time.

Within your day-to-day operations, you'll back up routinely for other, non-disaster reasons (prior to testing, for example). Some shops use save/restore commands and media to move data from one machine to another. Others plan to save large files used only in month-end processing and restore them prior to the next month end. This keeps their machine DASD utilization lower (but never low enough).

Those day-to-day operations will just take care of themselves. But the backups that support a future disaster have to be thought through for these reasons:

- Different parts of the system have different dynamics. You might only upgrade the operating system once every 18 months or so. You might put on PTFs every six months. But you have daily work that needs to be saved.
- Some backup tools take more time than others. While saving your system and your production library takes hours, saving only changed objects takes less time and saving journal receivers should require even less time.
- What time window does you company give you to do backups? Shops are "active" on the AS/400 for one, two, or three shifts, and each will have a different time available for you to back up.
- How much time does your company expect you to take restoring the system? Is an hour too much? Or is a day acceptable? Some say achieving the optimum restoration time is where you should start when developing a backup strategy.

The backup strategy you develop will strike a balance among all these factors.

The physical units available on your specific AS/400 also will affect backup strategy. What is the capacity and speed of media units (tape, diskette drives, DASD)? If *SAVF are considered, how much extra DASD is available? How much operator time is available for manual processes such as changing tapes?

Part of your routine backup strategy should be to rotate through several tapes and keep at least three generations. In the event you do have to restore objects, files, and libraries—and the tape is bad or becomes bad during the process—you at least have another tape. While the data will be somewhat obsolete, it will be better than nothing.

Use media rotation and store one or more of the rotated sets off site. This will ensure your backups survive an on-site disaster. A typical backup strategy is:

- Whenever you install a new release of the operating system, a new licensed program, or some new PTFs, back up the system.
- Monthly—save the production libraries before and after month-end processing.
- Weekly—save all production libraries. These include libraries for users and programmers as well as libraries for all applications.
- Daily—save all objects that were changed that day. Save journal receivers.

Backups take away resources from normal processing. Heavy, normal processing and backups don't get along well because each one makes the other run slow. Therefore, backups are almost always done during the night when work on the system is at its lightest. Even at 24-hour AS/400 shops, the demand on the system is lightest during evening hours. Normal system activity and the processing required to do backups conflict with each other.

7.9 Verify Your Backup Strategy

It's rare for a shop to actually lose their AS/400 to the extent that they really need to reload their systems from the backup media. However, when it does happen, a high percentage of users find that one or more important things weren't backed up. This is not a good time to discover backup problems. Check and double-check your backup strategy periodically to determine four points:

- Are the planned saves completing? Surprisingly, too many shops go for months with failed saves.
- Are you saving what you think you're saving? For example, are all user libraries really being saved? How about all libraries containing source code and all developers' libraries?
- Are the save tapes readable?
- Is the tape drive in good condition?

If you automate these checks as much as you can, make them happen soon after every backup to ensure that your strategy works. At least, be as sure as you can be without going through an actual disaster.

Don't forget to include people in your strategy. Who does what when? How long will the restore take? Supervisors like to know this stuff.

Try to schedule a surprise disaster drill on a weekend and see how everything works. Do not cause a real disaster. Just call some people in, get some tapes, and check their contents manually against what the system would lose if it had gone down.

A disaster drill is a simple concept and almost seems like a waste of time, but you'll find dumb things that you otherwise never would consider. An example is the shop that stored their tapes off-site. The off-site storage company was very security conscious. So much so that, during the Saturday drill, no one was in place (including the VP of MIS) with enough security clearance to actually receive the tapes.

7.9.1 Are Saves Complete?

So, you have a strategy and implement it with automated programs that walk the operators through the process (or even do the process automatically).

Review the job log the morning after the save was run. Just bring it up on your workstation with the Display Job Log (DSPJOBLOG) command and go to the bottom of the log. Quickly verify that the job completed normally and does not have an error code. Also, verify that the operator didn't cancel the save.

The most common exposure for incomplete saves I've seen is in small shops with night-shift operations staff. The new operators are assigned to the night shift. I've seen more than one person not recognize the message icon on the workstation and cancel the save when it requested a second tape! Even if that doesn't happen, operators are busy and aren't always alert to an abnormal termination. Perform a periodic double-check.

7.9.2 Are You Saving Everything?

When the AS/400 saves an object, it updates the date and time the object was saved. You can check this information with the Display Object Description (DSPOBJD) or Work Object (WRKOBJ) commands. The concept is that you can do a save and then check each object to verify it was actually saved. That's maximum tedium. If you have the QUSRTOOL library, you'll find two commands, CHKSAVSTS and PRTSAVSTS, that will identify any objects that have been changed since they were last saved. If you run either of these commands soon after a save, it will list the objects that weren't saved.

If you don't have the QUSRTOOL library, it's easy enough to issue the command, DSPOBJD, specifying output to a file, and then read the file with a program or query. Just have the program or query check two dates: the last save date (ODSDAT) and last changed date (ODLDAT).

The dates are both in MMDDYY format. Therefore, you will have to change them into YYMMDD for an easy check. Have the program or query report all objects with ODLDAT greater than ODSDAT. If you run it soon after a save, the list it prints will be the objects not saved.

7.9.3 Are the Tapes and Drives Okay?

The last weak link in any backup and recovery strategy is with the media or drives themselves. No one relies on tapes for everyday data processing like they used to. Tapes and drives have been relegated strictly to backup and recovery. If the recovery side of that equation is rare, you really can't be sure it will work.

7.9.3.1 Tapes and Diskettes

Verify that the tapes and diskettes you use for your saves are good. Shops reuse the same tapes and diskettes for repeated saves without taking into account that magnetic media wears thin over time. Unfortunately, drive units will write onto unreadable tapes.

You probably have a backup strategy that involves rotating sets of tapes and diskettes. Begin each set with new tapes or diskettes. As you save to them, the system will record any errors it encounters when writing to them. Individual errors aren't the problem, but lots of errors are a signal. Look for a trend. New, fresh tapes won't have many errors; older ones will have many. As errors increase, replace the entire set. Tapes are cheap. Don't mix old tapes with new tapes.

Verify tapes after the save. The tapes don't have to be on the drives to be verified. Any errors are already in the system. Start the System Service Tools (STRSST) and select Option 1 (Start a service tool). From there, select Option 1 (Error log utility), and then Option 5 (Display or print tape or diskette session statistics).

The default time period to look at errors is the previous 24 hours. Override this to the backup period. You'll get a report of each drive's read/write errors, errors corrected, as well as number of bytes written to tapes. This report can be printed and stored with the backup tape set.

7.9.3.2 Tape Drives and Diskette Drives

Again, there is a potential problem with tape drives when you only use them to create save tapes. If you have more than one tape drive and you use tapes frequently, or if you process tapes periodically from other sites, your drives are constantly being validated. Therefore, you're probably all right in this department. However, if you only have one drive that's only used to create save tapes, you might have a huge, unrecognized exposure.

Think about the kind of disasters from which you might have to recover. Isn't it possible you won't have access to the same drive that created your backup tapes? If a drive gets out of adjustment, it often can read the tapes it creates but no other drive can read them. Periodically, verify your drives by taking the tapes they create and have them read on other drives.

While you're at it, borrow tapes created on other drives and read them on your primary drive. This protects you not only from out-of-adjustment drives, but also from having a drive that suddenly decides to eat tapes when you are restoring from a disaster.

7.10 Backup and Recover Timesavers

Just assume that you'll never have enough time for the backups you need to do. Here are some things that'll speed things up. For more items specific to save-while-active, refer to section 7.5.1.1 Save-While-Active Save Performance Considerations.

Some save commands require that the system first be in a restricted state. But any backup or recovery command can run faster if the system is in a restricted state. For maximum system up time for the users, objects can be backed up with the save-while-active function. While granting maximum up time to those users, this produces the slowest backups. A compromise solution is to end the application updating the files to be saved, start the save with save-while-active on, monitor its message queue, and restart the application when it is finished making the checkpoint image. This produces some (although a minimum) down time to the users but a much faster save.

When saving many libraries, it will go faster if you can use a single SAVLIB command for all of them (rather than one SAVLIB for each library). Saving only changed objects daily with the SAVCHGOBJ command is faster than saving entire libraries.

Don't forget your restore requirements when planning your backup strategy. Saving access paths will definitely lengthen the backup process, but it will also shorten the restore. Actually, in most cases, saving access paths will enhance the restore function many times more than it degrades the backup function.

Note: To successfully save/restore logical files, the physical file save must have ACCPTH(*YES) specified on both the save and restore commands. The logical file must be built with MAINT(*IMMED) or MAINT(*DELAY). To check logical files' MAINT value, use the display file description (DSPFD) command. To change logical files, use the change logical file (CHGLF) command.

If the person doing the backups has special authority *SAVSYS or *ALLOBJ in his or her user profile, security checking on each object will be bypassed and the save operation will be faster. For more information on special authorities, see chapter 5 and chapter 6.

Data compression can reduce the amount of media required to save objects, files, or libraries, but it will slow down the backup. There are three data compression choices:

- Software data compression done by the CPU. Slows the backups down the most.
- Hardware data compression performed by the AS/400 adapter (with the attachment feature). Faster save times.

- Hardware data compacting performed by the 3480/3490 and 3590 tape units. The faster and more elaborate the data compression algorithm the shorter the save times.

7.11 References

OS/400 Backup and Recovery V4R3 (SC41-5304-02)

OS/400 CL Reference V4R3 (SC41-5722-02)

8 JOURNALING

8.1 OVERVIEW

Journaling is a facility that extends the AS/400 recovery capabilities beyond what can be obtained through backup or restore commands (see chapter 7). The best you can hope for from an adequate backup strategy that doesn't include journaling is a crashed system restored to the last save (which is probably the prior evening). Combine journaling with the same backup strategy and a system can be restored to its condition at the moment the system was lost.

Journaling can be useful in non-disaster scenarios. For example, consider the nightly batch process that ran with the wrong date supplied. If its files were journaled, you could reverse every update the program made to the files with a single command. If a data-entry operator made some gross error, with a simple command you could remove all the updating he or she did to any files.

Journaling comes into play indirectly as well. It enables files to be backed up while in use. Also, journaling makes commitment control possible.

Additionally, consider journal receivers as a huge repository of transactional data. You can programmatically access and use its records for whatever you like. This is a common, though advanced, AS/400 technique.

The two main ingredients in journaling are objects called a *journal* (object type *JRN) and a *journal receiver* (object type *JRNRCV). The journal contains the logic for capturing and storing receiver records. Another way to say it is that the journal contains all the information about what is journaled, but no real data. The journal places the data into the journal receiver.

Journaling is usually done to all database files within a library, but it is not done to all libraries.

8.2 JOURNAL RECEIVER

The journal receiver is the central repository for transactions (update events) made against the database files the journal (another object) is journaling.

The journal receiver is an interesting object in itself when compared to database files. Database files are always in a current state. For example, one record's CUSNUM field may be equal to 123456 and the AMTDUE field is equal to 100.00. A program can change either or both of those fields. Anytime you look at the record, its fields are in a current but static condition. A journal receiver on the other hand has every transaction that made changes to the database file. If you want to know not what the database fields are equal to but how they got that way, you can reconstruct it from the data in the receiver.

That's complex enough, but add to it that the journal receiver contains all updating transactions for all files it is journaling—plus a whole bunch of system information—and you start to get an idea of how powerful these can be.

The journal receiver gets filled like bags of potato chips at a potato chip factory. The journal is the machine filling the bags. The chips are database records. One bag moves along a conveyor belt and stops under the journal. The journal drops chips in the bag until it is full or something tells it to stop, and then the bag moves on and is replaced with another empty bag.

Changes to several physical files can be written to one receiver. However, changes for one physical file can be written to only one journal at a time.

Keeping records for all database files makes the journal's records a little more complex than standard database records. They contain their own fields related to journaling, but the records they collect are held in a single large, undefined, field. If you want to decipher the contents of a database record held in a journal receiver, you have to know its field definitions from its data description specifications (DDS).

Journal records show the updating activity to each record by storing the after-image of that record. Optionally, you can have the journal store the record's before-image as well. In addition to file updating activities, journal receivers also contain much file- and system-related information. For example, every time a file is opened or closed a journal receiver record will be created. Or, if the system gets IPLed, a record will be created.

You should change journal receivers as they fill up. Receivers have their own maximum size that you can't change, but you can set a percentage of that size called the *threshold*. When the receiver gets to the threshold point, the system will change receivers for you. Even if the journal receiver doesn't reach its threshold percentage, it should be changed once a day. Journals and receivers have names, but many shops just identify the journal as JOURNAL and the receiver as RECEIVXXXX (the XXXX is a sequential number to give the receivers' unique names). The following is a list of the information the receiver can contain:

- Record add, change, or delete information:
  - ✔ The before-image (optional).
  - ✔ The after-image.
  - ✔ File information—every time a file is:
  - ✔ Opened.
  - ✔ Closed.
  - ✔ Saved.
  - ✔ Restored.
  - ✔ Renamed.
  - ✔ Moved.
- File access path information.
- File member information—every time a file member is:
  - ✔ Cleared.
  - ✔ Added.
  - ✔ Removed.
- System information—every time the system is:
  - ✔ IPLed.
  - ✔ To perform dynamic tuning (per the QPFRADJ system value) for every change the system makes.
- Improvised information. Programmers can write their own records to the journal receiver. For example, users might want to record account balances or programmers may want to place records that define application boundaries.

Each entry in the journal receiver is sequentially numbered. When a physical file is journaled, adds, changes, or deletes made to that physical file through logical files are journaled as changes to the physical file. For example, consider a physical file, SWXP010, with an attached logical file named SWXP010L1. Changes are made to the physical file directly and indirectly through the logical file. If SWXP010 is journaled, all changes to that file are journaled. Even changes that are done through the logical file are recorded as changes to the physical file.

Optionally, you can journal access paths. That option means the physical file's key as well as all logical files (which, to the AS/400, are just access paths of the physical file) are included. Always take that option. While it will increase the amount of data journaled, it will greatly reduce the recovery time if you must rebuild that data.

By the way, I said journaling is an extension of the AS/400's backup and recovery features. Many AS/400 shops think journaling is too slow and instead use RAID-5 or data mirroring for their backup and recovery protection. However, those methods relate to data corruption at the system level. Journaling is the only method that focuses on corrupted data at the file, program, and user levels.

From working around computers, you know there is a cost associated with everything. With journaling, you will have high DASD use and a little slower response time. Weigh the cost against what you need journaled. The temptation at first is to journal all the files in a production library. After all, you need all the production files, right? Well, that's why you need a backup strategy (chapter 7) and a journaling strategy.

When you consider the hundreds or thousands of files that your production system relies on, think about which ones are really dynamic (those that change every day). Most applications, even large ones, have only a handful of files that are changed every day. Most of your production files can be saved weekly. For those that get changed infrequently, you might be covered just by a nightly Save Changed Objects (SAVCHGOBJ).

Make no mistake, the job of coming up with backup and journaling strategies that produce up-to-the-minute data protection and yet require the least computer time to perform is no small balancing act.

8.3 Setting Up Journaling

Setting up journaling and maintaining it routinely is really very simple. Actually, you'll soon learn that as complex and powerful as journaling is, actually doing it is fairly easy. We'll start with setting up journaling on your system. Here's all you'll do:

- Create a journal receiver (CRTJRNRCV).
- Create a journal (CRTJRN).
- Start journaling of the physical files (STRJRNPF).
- Start journaling of the access paths (STRJRNAP).

8.3.1 Create a Journal Receiver (CRTJRNRCV)

Figure 8-1 shows the prompted version of the CRTJRNRCV command.

```
                    Create Journal Receiver (CRTJRNRCV)

Type choices, press Enter.

Journal receiver . . . . . . . .   _________    Name
  Library  . . . . . . . . . . .     *CURLIB    Name, *CURLIB
Auxiliary storage pool ID  . . .   *LIBASP      1-16, *LIBASP
Journal receiver threshold . . .   *NONE        1-1919999, *NONE
Text 'description' . . . . . . .   *BLANK

                         Additional Parameters

Preferred storage unit . . . . .   *ANY         1-255, *ANY
Authority  . . . . . . . . . . .   *LIBCRTAUT   Name, *LIBCRTAUT, *CHANGE...

                                                                  Bottom
F3=Exit   F4=Prompt   F5=Refresh   F12=Cancel   F13=How to use this display
F24=More keys
```

Figure 8-1: Prompted version of CRTJRNRCV command.

The option AUXILIARY STORAGE POOL ID allows you to specify a user ASP where your journal receivers will live. In this figure, it will just reside in the same ASP the library is in.

Option JOURNAL RECEIVER THRESHOLD specifies the threshold level of the receiver. Although this is optional, it should be set and, if MNGRCV(*SYSTEM) is set on the CRTJRN command (see section 8.3.2. Create a Journal (CRTJRN)), this must be set to a value greater than or equal to 5,000. The system will send a message when the receiver becomes this size. The message will either go to the system operator message queue (QSYSOPR) or to a special message queue. You specify this on the CRTJRN command (section 8.3.2 Create a Journal (CRTJRN)).

The threshold level should be set so that it is rarely encountered between receiver changes. However, if something unusual happens on the system that causes an abnormal number of entries to go to the receiver, the threshold message alerts you to it. Note that in alerting you to an exceeded threshold, the system is actually alerting you to another abnormal situation that requires your attention. Journal receivers will continue to accept journal entries way past their threshold point, but you need to determine why the system is generating so many file updates.

If you want dual journal receivers on one journal, create them both on this step by using the command twice.

8.3.1.1 Naming Journal Objects

Part of your journaling strategy should be how you name your journal objects. There is no need to get exotic. Unless you keep more than one journal and receiver set going, use the name JOURNAL and call the receiver RECEIV0001. That way they are easy to remember and, when you programmatically change receivers late at night, the system will calculate a new name for the receiver (RECEIV0002, then RECEIV0003, and so on).

8.3.2 Create a Journal (CRTJRN)

After you have at least one journal receiver, create the journal itself with the CRTJRN (Create Journal) command. Figure 8-2 shows a sample of it in formatted form.

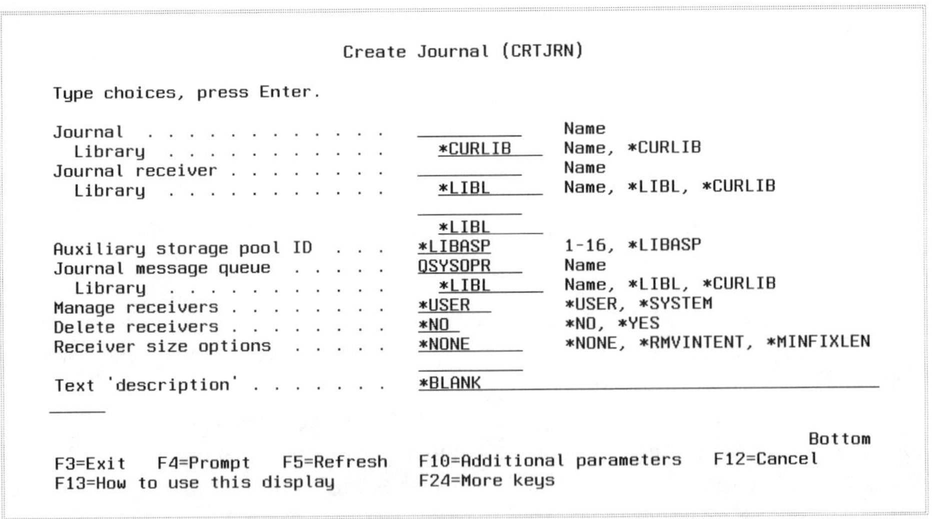

Figure 8-2: Prompted version of CRTJRN command.

Note the space for specifying dual journal receivers and specifying an ASP number. If you use single receivers (like most AS/400 shops), you only specify the initial receiver. Don't worry about the next receiver after the initial one. The system will take care of that for you. Because you specify upon journal creation what receiver(s) it is to use, you will have created the receivers first. That's why you create journal receivers prior to creating journals.

Set the parameter MNGRCV to *SYSTEM. This automates much of the journal receiver maintenance for you.

8.3.3 Start Journaling (STRJRNPF & STRJRNAP)

After the journal and receiver(s) are created, you're ready to start journaling. There are two commands to start journaling. The start journal physical file (STRJRNPF) command starts journaling your physical files and the start journal access path (STRJRNAP) command starts journaling your access paths.

Journaling access paths is optional but you should consider it. Although it is expensive as far as disk space goes, it will greatly reduce the time it takes to rebuild a system.

STRJRNPF starts journaling on one or more specified files in a library. Although files in several different libraries can be journaled together, the common practice is to journal all files in a particular library. Figure 8-3 shows a prompted version of the STRJRNPF command.

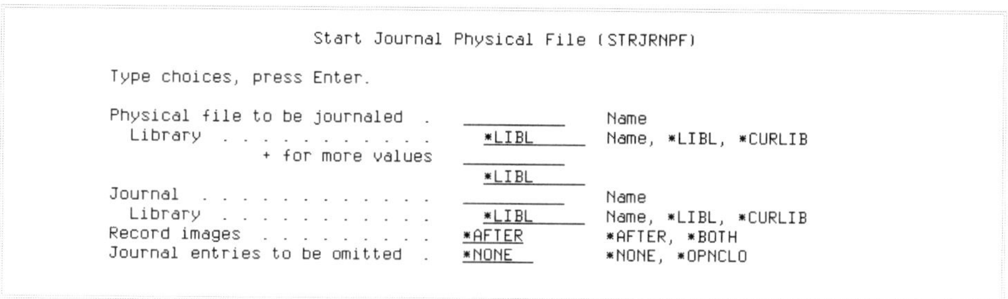

```
                    Start Journal Physical File (STRJRNPF)

Type choices, press Enter.

Physical file to be journaled .   __________    Name
  Library . . . . . . . . . . .     *LIBL       Name, *LIBL, *CURLIB
              + for more values   __________
                                    *LIBL
Journal . . . . . . . . . . . .   __________    Name
  Library . . . . . . . . . . .     *LIBL       Name, *LIBL, *CURLIB
Record images . . . . . . . . .   *AFTER        *AFTER, *BOTH
Journal entries to be omitted .   *NONE         *NONE, *OPNCLO
```

Figure 8-3: Prompted version of the STRJRNPF command.

Two STRJRNPF options will dramatically affect how much data is journaled and the resulting size of your journal receivers. They are OMTJRNE(*OPNCLO) and IMAGES(*BOTH).

OMTJRNE(*OPNCLO) omits JOURNALING when each file is opened and closed (potentially, a great many entries). IMAGES(*BOTH) journals the before-images as well as the after-images. This method provides great recovery, but it doubles the amount of DASD space your receivers will take. If you save before-images, you can recover deleted records, and that's kind of a nice feature.

Access paths are the key paths for physical and logical files. Recreating all the access paths during recovery can take quite a while. Journaling access paths will reduce this time and hasten recovery after a system crash. The system is faster at recovering an access path from the journal than it is at rebuilding the same path from scratch.

If you want to journal an access path, keep in mind that you cannot do it unless the related physical files are also journaled. Always start journaling in this order: STRJRNPF followed by STRJRNAP. Figure 8-4 shows a prompted version of the STRJRNAP (Start Journal Access Path) command.

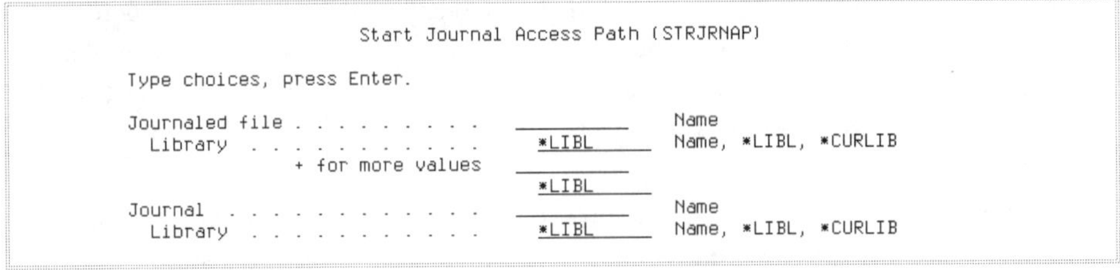

```
                    Start Journal Access Path (STRJRNAP)

 Type choices, press Enter.

 Journaled file . . . . . . . . .   __________   Name
   Library  . . . . . . . . . . .     *LIBL      Name, *LIBL, *CURLIB
              + for more values     __________
                                      *LIBL
 Journal  . . . . . . . . . . . .   __________   Name
   Library  . . . . . . . . . . .     *LIBL      Name, *LIBL, *CURLIB
```

Figure 8-4: Prompted version of the STRJRNAP command.

After you've entered one or both of these commands, journaling is in effect.

8.3.4 Save the Journaled Files (SAVOBJ)

Immediately save the files that you have started journaling. This is a crucial step; without it, the journaling you do might be useless.

You have to save your files after you start journaling (and anytime you add a new member to a journaled file) because the file being journaled is embedded on the file's file description. If you use the display file description (DSPFD) command on a journaled and a non-journaled file, you'll see that the journaled file has attached journal information.

If you have to use journaling to recover a damaged or lost file, you'll restore the file from the last good backup. Then restore the journal receiver in effect at that time and start applying journal entries forward until the file's data is brought up to the time it was lost.

The fly in the ointment is that your can't apply journal entries to a file that wasn't journaled. So, if you restore a file from a save that was done before journaling started, the file's description says it is not being journaled and you'll never get journal entries into that file. (Well, you will if you're advanced enough to write your own program to read and apply the entries, but that's a very, very advanced technique.)

This piece of data is called the *journal identifier* and is associated with each member of the file (not the file as a whole). If you are journaling a multiple-member file, make sure you do this save every time you add a new member.

At this point, journaling is happening. I will leave you with this last task, however. Check one last time that the files you started journaling on are actually being journaled. I would look at each file's description (using the DSPFD command) and the journal's description of what files it is journaling. Check the files that the journal thinks it has with the Work with Journal Attributes (WRKJRNA) command:

```
WRKJRNA JRN(<library/journal name>)
```

You can direct this command's output to a printer (OUTPUT(*PRINT)) if you expect a large list of files.

I recall too many shops where no one knew that some files were missing until they needed the data in the receivers. Be particularly careful of adding new files to an application and including them in the journaling mix. The STRJRNPF will not always fail with a nice error message; sometimes it just goes on even though the application didn't take. If this happens, see if the new file is in a different library or ASP as the rest of the files.

8.4 Maintaining Journals

After you've set up and have things running, you only have to do daily (if there is a problem, sometimes more frequently) maintenance. If you set the MNGRCV parameter to *SYSTEM when you created the journal, the system will automatically change your journal receivers whenever they are full.

In the dark days before this parameter was available, it was possible to have a CL program start automatically to change receivers, and then save and delete the journal receivers. This still isn't a bad idea. If the CL program starts at midnight every night, you would be assured of having a saved receiver(s) for that particular day.

I like setting MNGRCV(*SYSTEM) on the journal, but I still do my nightly automatic thing. That way, I maintain a daily set of receiver(s) and I have some assurance that—if the receivers really start to fill up—the system will change them for me if no one is there. The steps to maintain journals are:

- Change receivers periodically (once a day or when their threshold is reached).
- Save the filled receivers.
- Optionally, delete the filled receivers from the system.

8.4.1 Change Receivers

There are three times when you want to change receivers:

- On a regular (preferably daily) basis.
- When the receiver exceeds its threshold and the journal's MNGRCV parameter is not set to *SYSTEM.
- When you want to either reset your receiver's sequence number to 1 or change its threshold limit.

The command is Change Receivers (CHGJRN). Figure 8-5 shows the prompted form.

```
                          Change Journal (CHGJRN)

Type choices, press Enter.

Journal  . . . . . . . . . . . .  journal       Name
  Library  . . . . . . . . . . .    *LIBL       Name, *LIBL, *CURLIB
Journal receiver:
  Journal receiver . . . . . . .  *gen          Name, *SAME, *GEN
    Library  . . . . . . . . . .                Name, *LIBL, *CURLIB
  Journal receiver . . . . . . .                Name, *GEN
    Library  . . . . . . . . . .                Name, *LIBL, *CURLIB
Sequence option  . . . . . . . .  *CONT         *RESET, *CONT
Journal message queue  . . . . .  *SAME         Name, *SAME
  Library  . . . . . . . . . . .                Name, *LIBL, *CURLIB
Manage receivers . . . . . . . .  *SAME         *SAME, *USER, *SYSTEM
Delete receivers . . . . . . . .  *SAME         *SAME, *NO, *YES
Receiver size options  . . . . .  *SAME         *SAME, *NONE, *RMVINTENT...

Journal state  . . . . . . . . .  *SAME         *SAME, *ACTIVE, *INACTIVE
```

Figure 8-5: Prompted version of the CHGJRN command.

The command shown in Figure 8-5 looks more complex than it is. Most of the time you'll just specify the journal name and the generate (*GEN) keyword on the parameter JOURNAL RECEIVER. Presumably, you named your receivers so that they have a trailing four digits. If so, the system will generate the next receiver name for you.

The command to change receivers can be given at any time (even while journaling is active). The old journal receiver will be detached, the new receiver will be attached, and journaling will just continue.

The only other thing you need to watch is the journal entry sequence numbers. They start with 1 and continue on. When you change journal receivers, if you don't change the SEQUENCE OPTION parameter from *CONT (continue) to 1, the sequence numbers for the next receiver will just continue from the last number in the old receiver.

This is not a problem until the number reaches 2,147,483,136. If it gets that high, journaling will stop on your system. When the number reaches 2,147,000,000, the system operator will get a warning message to reset the sequence numbers.

If the journal was created with MNGRCV(*SYSTEM), this sequence number is reset to 1 every time the system is re-IPLed. It's another reason to let the system manage things.

This sequence number thing isn't any big deal. Even large systems take a long time to collect the maximum number of sequence numbers.

8.4.2 Saving Receivers

As soon as you can, after you've detached your old receivers, save them. You can use the save commands:

- SAVLIB.
- SAVOBJ.
- SAVCHGOBJ.

Just remember that the receiver's object type is *JRNRCV.

You can save receivers currently attached to journals, but the saved version will be a partial version.

When journal receivers are saved, they can be optionally saved with storage freed. The option and keyword is STG(*FREE). As soon as the save is complete, the storage taken up by the receiver's data (but not its description) is freed (the records are cleared). The (*FREE) option cannot be used on currently attached journal receivers.

8.4.3 Deleting Receivers

You can delete a journal receiver with the DLTJRNRCV command. However, it's a good idea to have a backup of each journal receiver before deleting it. You cannot delete a journal receiver while a journal is using it.

As of V4R2, a user program (more than likely a vendor program) could attach to an exit point to this command and make the application believe the journal was in use when, in fact, the program (and not the system) was still using it.

Because of the importance of receiver chains (refer to section 8.4.3.1 Receiver Chains), receivers can only be deleted in the order in which they were attached to the journal. The exception to this is when you have a damaged receiver. You can delete a damaged receiver at any time after you detach it from the journal. Or you can delete a receiver anytime if you are using dual receivers on a journal and its mate still exists on the system.

Although the system will allow it, it is a very bad idea to delete a journal receiver that hasn't been saved first. The system will issue error message CPF7025 to warn you if a receiver has not been saved. You can get through by taking an I (IGNORE) response.

The DLTJRNRCV has a parameter to override some of its internal protections. That parameter is DLTOPT (Delete Option). It has three valid values:

- *IGNEXITPGM ignores any messages from an attached user program that the receiver is in use.
- *IGNTGTRCV ignores the target system. This is used when deleting a journal receiver used in remote journaling. The value disables the system verification that the receiver has a full copy on a remote system prior to being removed.
- *IGNINQMSG ignores the warning message CPF7025 mentioned above. The system assumes you wanted to respond to it with I (IGNORE) and just continues processing.

8.4.3.1 Receiver Chains

Except for the first receiver you attached to a journal when you started journaling, every receiver has a predecessor. Also, every receiver—except for the current one—has a next receiver. These entries are made when receivers are attached and detached to journals. When you start using a receiver to recover data, make sure the complete chain is online. In that way, when the system applies changes, it will go from the starting receiver right through the other ones.

For example, consider a shop that changes receivers every day and loses a database file on Thursday. That shop would restore the last saved version of the file. Let's presume it was made on Sunday and that the journal receiver in effect on Sunday was RECEIV0010.

If you were doing the restore, you would start applying journal entries with the RECEIV0010 receiver. Before you start applying changes, RECEIV0010 must be on the system as well as RECEIV0011 through RECEIV0014. The system will walk through consecutive receivers until it gets current.

On the other hand, if you were restoring receivers and couldn't find RECEIV0011, you would have a problem. Not only would you have lost the changes for Tuesday, but the system couldn't apply changes after RECEIV0010 (at least not automatically—you could re-request the apply starting with RECEIV0012 after RECEIV0010 completes). Keep the following tip in mind:

> **TIP:** Good journal management includes good physical handling of the saved receivers and journals.

That missing RECEIV0011 is one example of what is referred to as a *broken chain*. Another broken chain can occur when a receiver is backed up while it is still attached to the journal. While this is theoretically possible, actually what happens is that the receiver is only partially saved and, therefore, does not complete the restore. Aside from broken chains, other causes of journal chain problems are:

- Restoring a receiver from another system.
- Restoring a receiver that has not had its storage freed by a save operation.
- Saving or freeing a receiver and then trying to use it without restoring it.

8.5 Miscellaneous Journaling Functions

There are journaling functions you just don't do very often and aren't really categorized nicely anywhere else. They are:

- End journaling.
- Deleting journals (not to be confused with deleting receivers mentioned in section 8.4.3 Deleting Receivers).

8.5.1 End Journaling

You rarely end journaling; it essentially goes on and on. If you do need to end journaling for any reason, use the End Journal Physical File (ENDJRNPF) and the End Journal Access Path (ENDJRNAP) commands.

Because you can't journal access paths if the associated physical files aren't journaled, you also can't end journaling on physical files if their access paths are still being journaled. The sequence for ending journaling is ENDJRNAP followed by ENDJRNPF. Figure 8-6 shows the prompted format of the ENDJRNAP command and Figure 8-7 shows the prompted version of the ENDJRNPF command.

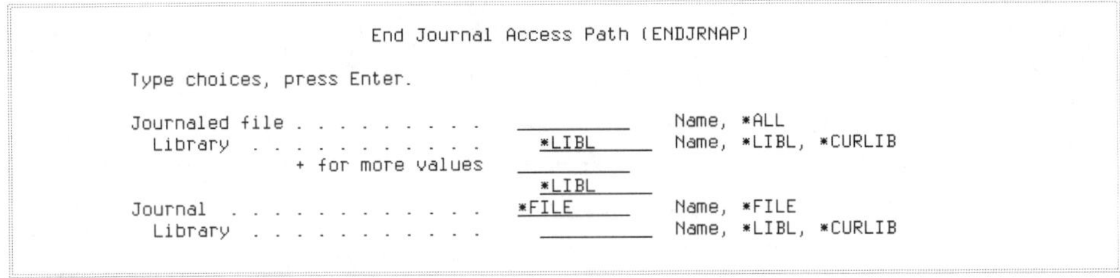

```
                    End Journal Access Path (ENDJRNAP)

Type choices, press Enter.

Journaled file . . . . . . . . .  __________    Name, *ALL
  Library  . . . . . . . . . . .    *LIBL       Name, *LIBL, *CURLIB
             + for more values    __________
                                    *LIBL
Journal  . . . . . . . . . . . .  *FILE         Name, *FILE
  Library  . . . . . . . . . . .    __________  Name, *LIBL, *CURLIB
```

Figure 8-6: Prompted version of the ENDJRNAP command.

```
                  End Journaling PF Changes (ENDJRNPF)

Type choices, press Enter.

Journaled physical file  . . . .  __________    Name, *ALL
  Library  . . . . . . . . . . .    *LIBL       Name, *LIBL, *CURLIB
             + for more values    __________
                                    *LIBL
Journal  . . . . . . . . . . . .  *FILE         Name, *FILE
  Library  . . . . . . . . . . .    __________  Name, *LIBL, *CURLIB
```

Figure 8-7: Prompted version of the ENDJRNPF command.

8.5.2 Deleting Journals

When the rare moment comes that you have to delete a journal, you do so with the Delete Journal (DLTJRN) command. You cannot delete a journal while it is journaling files. To get an active journal and its receivers off your system, here's the sequence:

- End journaling of all logical files with the ENDJRNAP (End Journal Access Path) command.
- End journaling of all files associated with the journal using the ENDJRNPF (End Journal Physical File) command.
- If commitment control is active and the journal is associated with it, end it with the ENDCMTCTL (End Commitment Control) command.
- Save/delete the journal using a save command and DLTJRN (Delete Journal) command.
- Save/delete the journal receiver using a save command and the DLTJRNRCV (Delete Journal Receiver) command.

8.6 Using Journals

Eventually every customer needs to use the journal information that's been collected forever. When this happens, the customers who set up journaling correctly always have the same reaction: "Journaling?"

The AS/400 handles journaling so smoothly that most shops forget all about it. Even if they remember having it, they certainly don't remember how to restore and apply journal entries.

8.6.1 Restoring Journals and Receivers

It's hard to say what a customer would need to restore prior to applying journal entries. If everything is there, they don't have to restore anything. If the customer is recovering from a bad system, everything will have to be restored. Just in case, this section will cover the worst cast where everything has been saved and needs to be restored.

Journals, receivers, and database files must be restored in order. If these items all resided on one library and were saved with a SAVLIB (Save Library) or RSTLIB (Restore Library), there is no problem. The system will ensure that all elements are restored in order.

If the objects were in different libraries (typically database files and journals in one library, receivers in another), the system cannot determine the order no matter what commands saved them. If the system cannot determine the correct order, it is the customer's responsibility. Restore these items in this order:

1. Journals.
2. Physical files.
3. Logical files.
4. Journal receivers (newest to oldest).

Needless to say this can be a painful process. Many shops just don't deal with it. They lump all elements into one library and let the system sort them out.

That may be fine for them, but they pay a performance penalty the whole time journaling goes on. By distributing receivers to other libraries/ASPs, the long-term system degradation due to journaling is reduced. The cost is on the restore. The customer must take on the responsibility of restoring all elements in their proper order.

8.6.2 Applying and Removing Journal Entries

Two ways of using journaled changes to fix corrupted files are:

- Applying journal entries (sometimes referred to as "going forward").
- Removing journal entries (sometimes referred to as "going backward").

If you want to remove journaled changes, you must have been journaling both before-images and after-images on the physical file.

If a database file gets corrupted in the system sense (something like a disk going bad), whatever is on the disk will not be useable. You must restore your last good version of the file, ensure that the receiver chain is present, and then apply changes from that last date forward.

However, if a database file was corrupted in a non-system way, you could use a little different method. For example, a file can be damaged because of a programming bug (it's unusual, but it happens). Say, in this instance, the database file is not damaged in the system sense, but several thousand records are bad. Because you know specifically what program and during what time period those records were corrupted, you don't have to go back to old versions of the file. You can just remove the changes made to the file by the bad program. In this case you would start at the current time and remove journal entries (going backward) until the start of the bad program.

8.6.2.1 Applying Journal Changes

Journal changes are applied from a start date forward. The implication is that a file restore must have taken place in order for you to end up with an old version of the file and more current journal entries. Here's what you do:

- Restore the latest uncorrupted version of the file.
- Restore all the journal receivers that were used from the date/time of that save and are currently not on the system or were saved with their storage freed. Do this restore in order from the newest (today) back to the oldest (the date of the save).
- Ensure that you have exclusive use of the database file and the receivers (use the Allocate Object (ALCOBJ) command)
- Apply the Journaled Changes (APYJRNCHG). Specify the journal receiver from which the system should start applying. This journal receiver should be the one that was in effect when the database file was saved. Note: you can also specify the starting time within the receiver that the system should start applying changes. You might even have to find a starting sequence number and specify that as a starting place.

Figure 8-8 shows the prompted version of the APYJRNCHG command.

```
                    Apply Journaled Changes (APYJRNCHG)

 Type choices, press Enter.

 Journal  . . . . . . . . . . . . .   __________     Name
   Library  . . . . . . . . . . . .     *LIBL____    Name, *LIBL, *CURLIB
 Journaled physical file:             _
   Journaled physical file  . . . .   __________     Name, *ALL
     Library  . . . . . . . . . . .     *LIBL____    Name, *LIBL, *CURLIB
   Member . . . . . . . . . . . . .   *FIRST____     Name, *FIRST, *ALL
                + for more values _
 Range of journal receivers:
   Starting journal receiver  . .     *LASTSAVE_     Name, *LASTSAVE, *CURRENT
     Library  . . . . . . . . . . .     __________   Name, *LIBL, *CURLIB
   Ending journal receiver  . . .     __________     Name, *CURRENT
     Library  . . . . . . . . . . .     __________   Name, *LIBL, *CURLIB
 Starting sequence number . . . .     *LASTSAVE__    Number, *LASTSAVE, *FIRST
 Ending sequence number . . . . .     *LASTRST___    Number, *LASTRST, *LAST

                                                                    More...
```

```
 Ending date and time:
   Ending date  . . . . . . . . . .   ________       Date
   Ending time  . . . . . . . . . .   ________       Time
 Fully qualified job name . . . .     __________     Name
   User . . . . . . . . . . . . . .     __________   Name
   Number . . . . . . . . . . . . .     ______       000000-999999
 Fully qualified job name . . . .     __________     Name
   User . . . . . . . . . . . . . .     __________   Name
   Number . . . . . . . . . . . . .     ______       000000-999999
 Commitment boundary  . . . . . .     *NO_           *NO, *YES
```

Figure 8-8: Prompted version of the APYJRNCHG command (parts 1 and 2).

This command requests the qualified journal name that is the source of journal entries. The next set of parameters wants to know to which file it should apply journals. You can specify a file, or multiple files, or the generic *ALL.

The next parameter, RANGE OF JOURNAL RECEIVERS, is where you specify the receiver to start. You could tell the system where the receiver should end. However, common practice is to start with the first journal receiver after the last save of the file and continue through the receiver chain until applying the current receiver's changes.

If you want to restore just the changes within a range of entry sequence numbers, you can specify the start and end numbers in the STARTING SEQUENCE NUMBER and ENDING SEQUENCE NUMBER parameters. If you don't know these numbers, you can find them by using the Display Journal (DSPJRN) command. For additional information, see the IBM manual *OS/400 Backup and Recovery V4R3.*

If you don't want to apply all journal changes from all receivers, you probably want to apply journal changes for a specific time period. You can specify any date and time range.

If you know the specific job user or job number to apply changes from, you can specify them. If your files are updated with programs that use commitment control, you have the option of adhering to those boundaries or not. If you are recovering from a system crash and you use commitment control, you probably will want to adhere to those boundaries. When the system applies journaled changes, it applies them in order from oldest to current. For additional information, see the IBM manual *OS/400 Backup and Recovery V4R3.*

8.6.2.2 Removing Journal Changes

Depending on your journaling skill and strategy and the nature of the problem you're trying to recover from, it might be easier to remove journaled changes than try to restore the file and apply lots of changes. There are three advantages to removing journal changes rather than applying journal changes:

- You don't have to reload your last saved version of the damaged file.
- Generally, you don't have to reload receivers; the current one is usually sufficient.
- The remove uses considerably fewer records and goes faster.

There are details in removing journal entries that you must be concerned about that aren't a concern when you apply journal changes:

- You must have been journaling before-images and after-images of changed records.
- When you specify where the system should stop removing journaled changes, you cannot specify a certain time (such as 7:30 A.M.). You must specify the sequence number. That's an extra step. You have to use the display journal (DSPJRN) command to determine what sequence number was in effect at 7:30 A.M.
- The current receiver is generally far enough back in the sequence, but you should check to see if the current receiver goes back to the time where you want to stop removing entries. If it doesn't go back far enough (in the example, receivers were changed sometime between 7:30 A.M. and the current time), make sure the previous receiver is on the system.
- You cannot use this command to rebuild a database file damaged from a system problem. The command works on files corrupted by a bad program or a crazed user.

Figure 8-9 shows the prompted Remove Journal Changes (RMVJRNCHG) command.

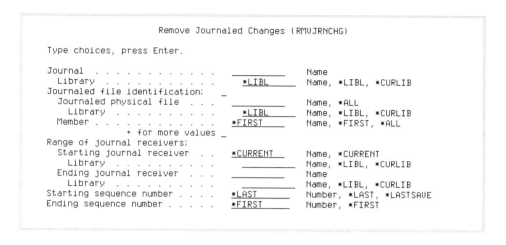

```
                     Remove Journaled Changes (RMVJRNCHG)

 Type choices, press Enter.

 Journal  . . . . . . . . . . .   __________    Name
   Library  . . . . . . . . . .     *LIBL____   Name, *LIBL, *CURLIB
 Journaled file identification:   _
   Journaled physical file  . .   __________    Name, *ALL
     Library  . . . . . . . . .     *LIBL____   Name, *LIBL, *CURLIB
   Member . . . . . . . . . . .   *FIRST____    Name, *FIRST, *ALL
                + for more values _
 Range of journal receivers:
   Starting journal receiver  .   *CURRENT__    Name, *CURRENT
     Library  . . . . . . . . .     __________  Name, *LIBL, *CURLIB
   Ending journal receiver  . .   __________    Name
     Library  . . . . . . . . .     __________  Name, *LIBL, *CURLIB
 Starting sequence number . . .   *LAST______   Number, *LAST, *LASTSAVE
 Ending sequence number . . . .   *FIRST_____   Number, *FIRST
```

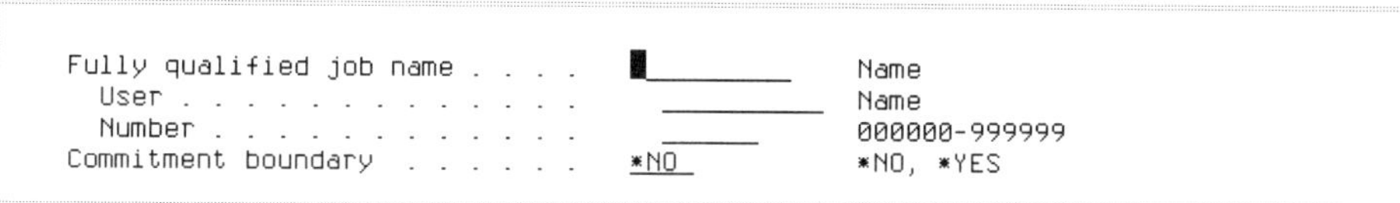

```
 Fully qualified job name . . . .  __________   Name
   User . . . . . . . . . . . . .   __________  Name
   Number . . . . . . . . . . . .   ______      000000-999999
 Commitment boundary  . . . . . .  *NO_         *NO, *YES
```

Figure 8-9: Prompted version of the RMVJRNCHG command (parts 1 and 2).

Specify a value for parameter STARTING JOURNAL RECEIVER of *CURRENT (as opposed to *LASTSAV). The sequence numbers are from the *LAST to *FIRST. Note that if you change nothing, the system will apply all changes in the current receiver only. When the system removes journaled changes, it removes them in order from current to oldest.

8.7 Journaling Performance Considerations

The bad news is that journaling costs in terms of DASD utilization and system performance. The good news is that the system helps speed up journaling activities and there are some things the customer can do.

The system will save before-images and after-images and write them to DASD in one operation rather than two. It will also analyze the write arms within the receiver ASP and try to use the fastest ten. It will also distribute the workload evenly over these ten so, as soon as one is busy, it'll use the next, then the next, and so on.

The customer, however, can do three things to make journaling less expensive on the performance side:

- Isolate journal receivers into their own user ASP.
- Record blocking is fine:
  - ✔ For files whose records are processed sequentially, set record blocking (record blocking = 32Kb / record size) and specify SEQONLY(*YES).
    - ➢ For files whose records are to be written to disk, do not specify the force-write ratio (FRCRATIO).

8.8 Journaling Strategy

There are many parts to journaling strategy. Unlike saves (except saves to a save file), journaling uses a lot of disk space. One strategy consideration will be that your journaling will use minimal disk space. One way of conserving disk space is to limit what you journal. You might not bother journaling access paths, for example. However, the recovery from that journal would take a very long time while a recovery from a more complete journal would take a lot less time. Suddenly, you have disk space versus recovery time.

Another issue is what pieces of your recovery will be on save media and what will be from the journals. Another factor is the time/space/recovery-time balancing issue.

Here's the quick way to develop your own journal strategy. Decide first what kind of recovery you expect: fast and functional or slow and limited. Then determine how much information you need to journal (system, file, access paths, before-images) to achieve that recovery goal. Once you've decided that, determine where to place the files you want journaled, the journal, and the receiver. There are several options for object placement:

- Everything goes into the same library and the same ASP. While this is the simplest and most common method of journaling, its not the most efficient.
- Files and journal in one library and receivers in another but both in the same ASP. A little better for performance and managing backup and recovery.
- Files and journal in the system ASP; receivers in a library user ASP, preferably one with its own input/output bus. Provides best performance and maximum protection of journal entries.
- Journal receivers in a non-library user ASP, files in the system ASP, and journal in either the system ASP or the same non-library user ASP as the journal recievers.

For additional information about user ASPs, see chapter 3, section 3.5 DASD and User Auxiliary Storage Pools.

At the end of the day, no matter where you place your files, journal, and receivers, run a CL program that will:

- Change journal receivers.
- Save the library with the SAVLIB command.
- Or save changed objects with the SAVCHGOBJ command, excluding journaled files and attached receivers.
- Save the old receivers and then delete them. If you have the disk space, try to leave the last several receivers on the system.

8.8.1 Duality

You can elect to journal one library's files to one journal or receiver and another set of library files to another journal or receiver. This could make journal management easier for you.

Sometimes, in crucial situations where you are worried that one journal receiver might get damaged along with the database file, you can attach two journal receivers to the same journal. Then all file updates are journaled to both receivers at once. If the system loses one journal receiver, the system will continue to write to the other. If you do this, you really should keep each receiver in its own ASP. The protection is better and the DASD load is shared more evenly.

8.9 Journaling to a Remote AS/400

New with V4R2 is the capability to *remote journal.* The functionality will probably grow in future releases but, at this time, it's a good beginning.

I'd like to get the negative stuff out of the way first. Here (at this time) are the things remote journaling won't do for you:

- Remote journaling with V4R2 does not mean that your journaling activity can be offloaded to another AS/400. You still have to have local journaling for remote journaling to work.

- It doesn't mean that a remote database can be kept synched with a local database because both platforms are sharing the same journal and receiver. Data synchronization can happen, but it must have a hot backup application on the remote platform. A *hot application* is a program that continually receives and applies journal receiver entries. Currently, the customer would have to write an application or purchase one from a third party (there are a couple available).
- Remote journaling won't improve performance while journaling. If anything, it will degrade performance to some degree.

With that out of the way, here is what remote journaling will do for you:

- It provides journal replication under the MI (machine interface) layer. Therefore, theoretically, the time it takes to do the replication should be as fast as it can get.
- By replicating journals and journal receivers on another platform, you get better data protection from a hardware failure.
- If you do implement a hot backup application and start with a mirror image of your local database on the remote system, you could maintain a real-time mirror image of an AS/400's database. With that you could:
    - ✔ Have an AS/400 and database separate from your production platform and dedicate it to development, ad hoc queries, or any similar activities that you don't want going on your production machine.
    - ✔ Have a hot-site disaster backup machine. If a physically separate AS/400 contains a real-time database, and the physical phone lines are in place, a customer who loses the primary platform could cut over and be up on the backup platform in a matter of minutes.

Remote journaling consists of a local AS/400, with a local database being updated by a local application, and those update activities being journaled. Through that local journal, a remote journal and receiver are created and activated on a remote AS/400. The local database may or may not exist on the remote AS/400 (the focus at this time is primarily on the journaling). All entries that go into the local journal are automatically sent to the remote platform and inserted into the remote journal receiver. Remote journals can be configured in two ways:

- Broadcast. This is the simplest way. The journal on machine A is replicated on machine B.
- Cascade. The journal on machine A is replicated on machine B, from machine B to machine C, and so on, to a maximum of 255 AS/400s replicating the same journal. Note, though, the name and nature of *cascade*. Journal entries must flow from machine A to machine B and from machine B to machine C. Journal entries cannot flow from machine A directly to both machine B and C.

Although remote journals and their receivers are merely journals and receivers, there are some differences. Here are some considerations about them:

- Remote journals can only receive entries from a local journal. They cannot directly journal database files on their AS/400. Nor can an application running on the remote platform force an entry into them.

- Some of the characteristics of the remote journals and receivers cannot be set or changed directly. They can only be set or changed by altering those same characteristics on the local journals/receivers.

- All AS/400s meant to support remote journaling (the source and target platforms) must be on V4R2 or later.

- Once a remote journal is added to a local journal, local receivers cannot be deleted if all entries have not been updated to the remote journal. Yes, the local journal does know the current status of the remote journal at all times.

- Because of built-in delays (different sizes or work loads of the two platforms, communication delays, etc.) an important consideration of remote journaling is the synchronization of the two journal receivers.

  - ✔ The remote journal can never be ahead of the local journal.

  - ✔ The remote journal can be at the same status as the local journal. That is, both receivers contain the same entries, and there are no unposted entries in the queue for the remote journal. This condition is referred to as *caught-up*.

  - ✔ The remote journal has fewer entries than the local journal. The missing entries either haven't gotten to the remote system yet or are in a posting queue, waiting to be placed in the remote receivers. This can simply happen when the local journal is journaling, but the remote has just been activated. While this condition exists, it is known as *catch-up*.

- Remote journals have the same directories and receiver chains as the local journals however:

  - ✔ A remote journal does not have an attached receiver until it is activated. (A local journal can have an attached receiver even when it is not journaling anything.)

  - ✔ If a remote journal is in catch-up mode, it can have a receiver attached to it that is different than the local journal's receiver.

  - ✔ A remote journal in caught-up mode will have the same receiver attached as the local journal's receiver.

- Journal management functions are also replicated across platforms. When the local platform changes a receiver or resets the sequence number, those changes take place automatically on the remote platform.
- Use careful monitoring of remote journals. If a change on the remote system fails, remote journaling might just end. Monitor by watching for messages on both the journal message queue and the system operator's message queue (QSYSOPR).
- Most of the commands to work with remote journals are APIs. Refer to the IBM manual *OS/400 Journal & Commit APIs V4R3* for more information.

8.9.1 Setting Up Remote Journaling

Here are the steps to setting up and starting remote journaling:

- Ensure all libraries are on the remote system. That means the database libraries the local journals and receivers reside in on the local platform must be duplicated on the remote system. The exception to this is if *redirection* is used. Redirection allows the journals and receivers to exist in different libraries on the two systems.
- Ensure the user profile that manages journaling on the local system exists (and has the same aurhorities) on the remote system.
- Does the journal name already exist on the remote system? If it does not, it will be created. If it does, it will be used if possible. There are three conditions that exist, any one of which will prevent the name from being used:
  - ✔ The name is not the name of a remote journal.
  - ✔ The name is of a remote journal, but one that was not previously associated with the local journal.
  - ✔ The type of journal doesn't match the type required.
- Start communication and verify that it is up at both ends. Here are the three communications protocols supported by remote journaling and their drivers that must be active on both the local and remote systems:
  - ✔ OptiConnect/400—this must have subsystem QSOC active.
  - ✔ SNA.
  - ✔ Vary on line/controller/device.
  - ✔ Subsystem QCMN must be active.
  - ✔ TCP/IP—STRTCP and DDM servers must be active.

- Create the relational database (RDB) entry (refer to 8.9.1.2 RDB Entries). This entry names the remote AS/400 and specifies the communications protocol that will be used.
- From the local platform, add remote journal with the Add Remote Journal (ADDRMTJRN) command. Make the journal STATUS (*INACTIVE).
- From the local platform, activate remote journaling with the Change Remote Journal (CHGRMTJRN) command. On this command, specify the starting point. This specification can be in the form:
    - ✔ *ATTACHED—the starting point is the starting point of the receiver currently attached to the remote journal. If no receiver is attached, journaling will just start.
    - ✔ *SRCSYS—journal entries on the remote system will start with the earliest entries in the earliest journal receivers currently attached to the local system. Note: this can require a long time in catch-up mode.
    - ✔ <libr/local rcvr>—specify the library and name of the local journal receiver from which to start taking entries to the remote system.
- Optionally, if you have a hot backup application start it on the remote system.

Remote journaling can be activated or inactivated at any time at the local level with the Change Journal (CHGJRN) command.

To remove a remote journal, first inactivate it and then use the Remove Remote Journal (RMVRMTJRN) command. Add it back again with the Add Remote Journal (ADDRMTJRN) command.

When activating remote journaling in a cascade situation, make sure all downstream platforms' remote journaling are first inactivated. Then activate the systems sequentially, starting from the local and moving outward, following the journal entries.

8.9.1.1 Asynchronous Versus Synchronous Remote Journaling

When remote journaling is activated, the system has the option of activating it asynchronously or synchronously. Both deserve careful consideration.

In an asynchronous update mode, the journal entries bound for the remote journal are sent off in that direction and control immediately returns to the application. Just assume the entry made it to the remote journal. This is the fastest method of remote journaling. On a large, active file, an asynchronous update might be the only way to go.

In a synchronous update mode, the journal entries bound for the remote journal are sent off in that direction and the local application waits until it receives notice of a successful receipt of the entry. This method has a very high reliability and security, but it has a huge cost in application wait time. Users might find their interactive response time unacceptable. On the other hand, in normal use, remote journals with synchronous update rarely have catch-up to do. Because they are always caught-up, the local and remote platforms are always in perfect synch.

These two update modes also affect how the remote journal statuses appear. For the most part, when you display their status, their update mode (or just mode) will either be *SYNC or *ASYNC. When the remote journal's mode is changed, it'll just change. However, if it was *ASYNC and is changing to *SYNC, its status may become *SYNCPEND until all pending entries are posted. Although there is a *ASYNCPEND, it is rarely seen. When changing from *SYNC to *ASYNC, generally presume there are no pending entries (because of the nature of *SYNC) and the change just happens.

When a remote journal's status is set to inactive and it is updating asynchronously, the user will often see a status of *INACTPEND in between *ACTIVE and *INACTIVE.

8.9.1.2 RDB Entries

Relational database (RDB) entries are one of those things IBM gives you just to test your sense of humor. It makes better sense if you think of it as "remote database." It's reason for being is to allow you to specify the name of the relational database your applications will be addressing. That's nice. However, every AS/400 comes with one—and only one—relational database, and you can't *not* use it.

The RDB names a relational database on another AS/400 that your applications will access. To simplify this concept even further, when you name the remote relational database, just name it the same name as the remote AS/400 named on the network.

Forget for now what RDB stands for and think of it as meaning the name of a remote AS/400 whose files you would like to access.

Every AS/400 has exactly one RDB *directory*. When you are working with a database shared between a local and remote AS/400, you must create an RDB *directory entry*. Do so with the Add Relational Database Directory Entry (addrdbdire) command. Figure 8-10 contains a sample of the ADDRDBDIRE command.

```
                    Add RDB Directory Entry (ADDRDBDIRE)

Type choices, press Enter.

Relational database . . . . . .   _________________________
Remote location:
  Name or address . . . . . . .   ____________________________________________
__________________________________________________________________________________
__________________________________________________________________________________
_______________________________________________________
  Type . . . . . . . . . . . . .  *SNA            *SNA, *IP
Text . . . . . . . . . . . . . .  *BLANK______________________________________
______
```

Figure 8-10: Prompted version of ADDRDBDIRE command.

The ADDRDBDIRE command has three parameters. One of those parameters is a text field and the other two are:

- RDB names the AS/400 for which the directory entry is being made.
- RMTLOCNAME names the other AS/400 for which the directory entry is being made.

Each AS/400 on the network (or, for remote journaling, both the local and remote AS/400s) must have RDB directory entries for the other. Here's an example of the RDB directory entries for machine A and machine B. Assume machine A is our local and machine B is remote:

- On machine A:
  - ✔ ADDRDBDIRE RDB(MACHA) RMTLOCNAME(*LOCAL) TEXT('.....')
  - ✔ ADDRDBDIRE RDB(MACHB) RMTLOCNAME(MACHB) TEXT('.....')
- On machine B:
  - ✔ ADDRDBDIRE RDB(MACHB) RMTLOCNAME(*LOCAL) TEXT('.....')
  - ✔ ADDRDBDIRE RDB(MACHA) RMTLOCNAME(MACHA) TEXT('.....')

If you don't know the name of the attached AS/400, use the Display Network Attributes (DSPNETA) command.

The RDB entry does double duty; it also is where the communications protocol is specified for remote journaling.

8.9.2 Remote Journaling Performance Considerations

Remote journaling will cost you in performance. There's no nice way to put it. However, here are some things you can do to ameliorate the impact:

- Isolate the remote journal to its own communication hardware and protocol. Don't use the communications link for other functions.
- Use the fastest communications protocol available. If possible, use the OptiConnect/400 bus transport.
- Select asynchronous update mode (it's many time faster than synchronous). However, the local and remote databases are not always in sync with this method. That might be unacceptable for some customers' needs.
- Reduce the amount of information journaled. Do this at the local journal level. Journal only after-images and do not journal file open and close events.
- The RDB entry at the time of remote journal activation determines the communication protocol in use. If you change the RDB entry, you must stop and restart remote journaling for the change to go into effect.
- The more receivers you have (in a cascade) the longer each file update is going to take. This is simple: three receivers will take three times longer to process every database update than one receiver will.
- Add memory to *BASE to increase performance on either the local or remote platform.

8.10 References

AS/400 Basic System Operation, Administration, and Problem Handling V4R3 (SC41-5206-02)

OS/400 Distributed Database Programming V4R2 (SC41-5703-00)

OS/400 Backup and Recovery V4R3 (SC41-5304-02)

OS/400 CL Programming (SC41-5721-01)

OS/400 CL Reference (SC41-5722-02)

OS/400 Journal & Commit APIs V4R3 (SC41-5882-02)

9 PERFORMANCE

9.1 OVERVIEW

Nothing gets users angrier than waiting on a computer. When the performance of your AS/400 isn't up to par, users will make your life miserable. More importantly, access and performance generally becomes the basis by which people judge the quality of the AS/400 and your shop's service. There's hardly an area that presses more hot buttons than performance.

9.2 AS/400—PERFORMANCE COMPONENTS

References to AS/400 performance implies any or all of six major areas:

- Emergencies. The performance just degrades for some reason.
- Tuning. Is the AS/400 optimally set up for your job mix?
- Monitoring. The ongoing capture of performance data.
- Analysis. Periodic reporting from captured performance data.
- Capacity planning. Measuring where you are and where you will be on the AS/400.
- Stress tests and individual program and application measurements.

All these areas come together eventually. A properly tuned AS/400 will encounter fewer emergencies. Adequate monitoring and reporting will avoid waking up one day to find the AS/400 out of capacity. Finally, testing applications for resource impact before they go into production will avoid performance emergencies.

The AS/400 has come a long way in the area of automating some of these functions. This has been an evolving area of the AS/400. As recently as just a few years ago, the automation could hurt your system more than help it. Starting with V3R7, however, the automated performance tools of the AS/400 deserve serious consideration.

As you bring up your AS/400, use the Work with System Values (WRKSYSVAL) command to set two system values:

- QDYNPTYSCD—set to 1 to turn on dynamic priority scheduling.
- QPFRADJ—set to 1, 2, or 3 to turn on performance adjustment. This manages pool memory allocations for you automatically while the AS/400 is processing.

Dynamic priority scheduling prevents a single program from gobbling up all the system resources. The classic case here is the user (or programmer) starting a large, complex interactive query. You can count on that job taking 40 percent or more of a CPU. Dynamic priority scheduling senses what is happening and knocks the job's priority back, allowing other jobs to get some system resources.

In a similar vein, dynamic priority scheduling also is sensitive to jobs that have been waiting for a period of time without receiving any system resources; these get a boost in priority. The two approaches combine to make a powerful tool that takes CPU resources away from hogging programs and gives them to languishing programs.

Although these tools are very good, you still need some manual skills for a couple of reasons. Although dynamic priority scheduling does a terrific job, it is quick to reset changed priorities that have been dropped. This is good because the earlier versions of priority-adjusting tuners changed priorities and left them there. The result was often a topsy-turvy system with interactive users having very low priorities and batch jobs having very high priorities.

However, if you really have a system-hogging program, you might want to go in and change its runtime priority so that it will stay low throughout its run. When you are running month-end or you have the computer to yourself and you want certain crucial-path programs to be hogs so they'll get done, you don't want dynamic priority scheduling in effect.

New with V4R3 is the system value QDYNPTYADJ that allows a dynamic priority adjustment. This is unique to the AS/400e servers. It allows the few interactive jobs attached to the server to either keep their priorities intact (value '0') or be changed with the rest of the system (value '1'). Of course, this system value is only in effect if QDYNPTYSCD is set to '1'.

You might not want performance adjustment changing your memory sizes. Like the dynamic priority scheduling tool, performance adjustment has been improved greatly. However, sometimes you will have set your own memory pools and simply don't want them changed. In that case, turn them off.

One thing a new AS/400 customer will want to do is set system value QPFRADJ to 1 (set memory sizes at IPL time), start the machine, and then see to what sizes the AS/400 thought the pools should be set. Or try setting the system value to 2 and run the machine for a while. Then check the memory pool sizes in the middle of the day when things are busy. You might even want to accept the system values at this point, turn off the system value, and set the pools sizes within the subsystem descriptions (refer to chapter 3).

By the way, AS/400 priorities are expressed in numbers from 00 through 99. The *higher* the number the *lower* the priority (or the less important the program is). This potentially is very confusing; be aware. If you read that a priority number is lowered, then interpret that to mean the importance was raised. If you read about a priority number being raised, interpret that to mean the importance was lowered.

Most reported performance problems have to do with interactive jobs. After all, it's the users at the workstations who get the most "tuned" to system fluctuations. To begin with, set up your interactive subsystem wisely. Give it plenty of memory and don't allow any single subsystem to support more than 200-300 workstations at one time. Through the use of workstation names and generic workstation entries (WSEs) on the subsystem, keep these limited to that number.

The default name for an interactive subsystem, and the one most used, is QINTER. If you need a second subsystem, just name it QINTER2 to make it unique. A common practice in such large shops is to split interactive workstations into subsystems by department. That way, if one department needs more horsepower than another, it's easy to raise all priorities for that department's workstations.

9.2.1 Emergencies

Computers spoil people. The satisfaction of quick response times decays too soon after any upgrade. After that, there's an underlying feeling that the computer is slow. That feeling gets prodded every once in a while when an errant program suddenly gobbles up too much of the computer's resources and it really does experience a sharp increase in response time.

It is now common practice to have all AS/400 workstations attached to a LAN rather than directly into the AS/400. Too often, response-time emergencies are caused by a problem on the LAN. While this book deals with the AS/400, I mention LAN performance problems in this chapter because they are part of the big picture of providing good user service. I don't go into any depth regarding LANs because they are often things apart from the AS/400.

Sometimes users' response-time complaints are due to simple transmission time across a busy or large LAN. The AS/400 could be working fine, but communication is being bogged down on the LAN. Unfortunately, AS/400 performance tools don't address this activity because it takes place outside the AS/400. You might want to incorporate a LAN management system to determine the amount of ongoing transmission delays.

If you are supporting users through browsers over TCP/IP, expect transmission time to be very long. Verify that the AS/400 is tuned as well as it can be. You might be able to improve performance by simply starting other servers (refer to chapter 12).

Quite often, AS/400 performance emergencies are transitory, but you really can't make that assumption. You have to look into the system on the chance that the initial symptom (slow response time) isn't going to suddenly escalate into an overflowed ASP (auxiliary storage pool) or a locked CPU. Keep the following tip in mind:

TIP: Although anyone on your MIS staff can look into a performance problem, I prefer to have one person do the investigation on the system console. The console is set to run at a very high priority (10) so it's better able than other workstations to grab system resources from a runaway program. Also, many people executing the same system commands will further bog the system down.

The primary command to isolate an emergency is Work With Active Jobs (WRKACTJOB). Figure 9-1 shows an example of the screen from that command.

With my first pass at an emergency, I am most interested in two areas. First, I want to know the overall CPU percentage in the upper left corner. Second, I want to know the CPU percentage down the middle of the screen. Those areas are highlighted in Figure 9-1.

The CPU percentage will often be around 99.9 percent (perhaps even over 100 percent, which is indicated by the symbol ++++). Check the percentage figure first. Primarily, this gives you a quick look at the overall health of the system. The CPU can be high for three reasons:

- The programs are that complex (and not doing much disk I/O or user interfacing).
- Page faulting is causing lots of extra disk I/O.
- Overall load on the system (number of jobs) is too high.

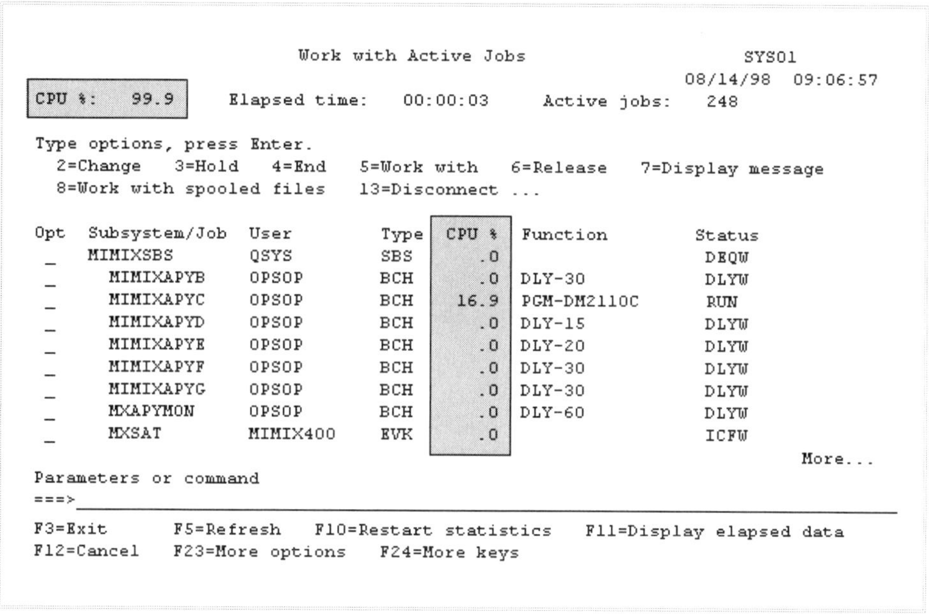

Figure 9-1: Display screen for the Work With Active Jobs (WRKACTJOB) command.

Although IBM recommends that CPU usage percentage be kept below a maximum of between 70 percent (for single processor systems) to 81 percent (for a four-way processor), in real life, if you're looking at a performance problem, your CPU percent is already pegged. In fact, most AS/400s run CPU usage in the 90-percent range all the time.

That's the reality. If your AS/400 is there, don't feel alone but do keep this in mind: Any CPU utilization running over 90 percent is getting hammered from excessive seize/lock conflicts.

If the percentage is high, continue looking for a problem. If you see 75 percent indicated, it might be a good indication that you have lost a device on the LAN. For example, if a gateway goes down and strands its users, the users will still have their screens up and will be getting tired of waiting. The AS/400 is happily cruising because it just lost 100 or so users. Having a response-time problem and seeing a low CPU percentage, I would immediately dispatch someone to look at the LAN.

One caveat to keep in mind is that, if your AS/400 is out of capacity, no amount of tuning will help. Read on, though; if you do everything you can and document the system, your own data can make the case for an AS/400 upgrade.

9.2.1.1 *Work with Active Jobs*

After checking the overall CPU percentage, I want to quickly know who is taking up the largest individual CPU percentage (and find out who made the overall so high). A nice feature of the Work With Active Jobs command is that you can review all the jobs in the order of CPU percent usage. Do this by placing the cursor onto the CPU percentage column, and press the F16 (Shift + F4) key. Figure 9-2 shows a sample.

```
                         Work with Active Jobs                          SYS01
                                                                08/14/98  09:14:03
CPU %:    99.6     Elapsed time:    00:07:09      Active jobs:   249

Type options, press Enter.
  2=Change    3=Hold    4=End    5=Work with    6=Release    7=Display message
  8=Work with spooled files      13=Disconnect ...


Opt  Subsystem/Job  User         Type  CPU %  Function          Status
 _     SQLEXEC      PGMABC       INT    35.5  CMD-EXECUTE        RUN
 _     BRM_MAINT    OPC          BCH    23.2  PGM-RBT164         RUN
 _     ESFR176      PGMDEF       BCH    11.4  PGM-RBT096         RUN
 _     ROSE05V1     PGMDEF       BCH    10.9  PGM-RBT096         RUN
 _     SQLEXEC      USRRGC       BCH     7.1  CMD-EXECUTE        RUN
 _     MIMIXAPYC    OPSOP        BCH     5.6  PGM-DM2110C        RUN
 _     XTRA0202     QUSER        EVK     3.3                     ICFW
 _     SQLEXEC      PGMXYZ       BCH     3.1  CMD-EXECUTE        RUN
 _     SERVICE      QSVCDRCTR    BCH     3.0  PGM-ANCONTROL      RUN
                                                                        More...
Parameters or command
===> ____________________________________________________________________________

F3=Exit        F5=Refresh     F10=Restart statistics    F11=Display elapsed data
F12=Cancel     F23=More options     F24=More keys
```

Figure 9-2: Display screen for Work with Active Jobs command after the display has been sorted by using the cursor and the F16 key.

There are some jobs that don't run all the time, but when they do run they take a lot of resources until they are complete. In the example shown in the Figure 9-2, if you use BRMS (Backup and Recovery Media Services), a job called BRM_MAINT, runs periodically and takes a lot of CPU. You wouldn't do anything in this case. You might not even have BRMS on your machine. The point is that packaged software and some system programs can take a lot of horsepower to run.

Figure 9-2 reveals that user PGMABC is running a structured query language (SQL) and taking 35 percent of the CPU. When a program or a user is killing the system, it will appear at the top with a CPU percentage of 30 percent or higher—after you've sorted with the cursor and F16 key.

Once I've identified a problem program like this, I put it on hold by putting a 3 on the OPTION line to the left of the job. The command options are highlighted in Figure 9-2.

After holding the job, entering a 5 on the OPTION line will show what program it is running and what files it is updating. Also, it will display any system messages the job has encountered. I would note the job program, any open files, and any messages. Next, I would call the user or programmer responsible (preferably the programmer) to confer. While this is going on, the emergency is fading away because the offending program is being held.

If the job's user or programmer confirms that the job must run, it can be released from hold by entering a 6 on the OPTION line. In addition, the SQL's priority can be reduced to give other users a chance to complete their work.

In addition to CPU percentage, you can view the impact of the jobs on the system by monitoring how much disk I/O each is doing. You can do this with the F11 key. Figure 9-3 shows the same set of jobs from Figure 9-2 after F11 has been pressed.

```
                        Work with Active Jobs                          SYS01
                                                            08/14/98  09:14:03
CPU %:    99.6      Elapsed time:    00:07:09     Active jobs:    249

Type options, press Enter.
  2=Change    3=Hold    4=End    5=Work with    6=Release    7=Display message
  8=Work with spooled files     13=Disconnect ...
                                                    --------Elapsed---------
Opt  Subsystem/Job  Type  Pool  Pty       CPU  Int       Rsp  AuxIO   CPU %
 _     SQLEXEC      INT      4   20    3120.9                   238    35.5
 _     BRM_MAINT    BCH      4   40     892.9                  3540    23.2
 _     ESFR176      BCH      4   50     718.9                  5268    11.4
 _     ROSE05V1     BCH      4   50    2097.9                    77    10.9
 _     SQLEXEC      BCH     10   50     345.3                  3312     7.1
 _     MIMIXAPYC    BCH      9   25    9162.1                  5593     5.6
 _     XTRA0202     EVK      5   19      29.3                   112     3.3
 _     SQLEXEC      BCH      4   50      88.0                 21386     3.1
 _     SERVICE      BCH      2   51     221.3                     0     3.0
                                                                       More...
Parameters or command
===> _____________________________________________________________________
F3=Exit        F5=Refresh         F10=Restart statistics    F11=Display status
```

Figure 9-3: Display screen for Work with Active Jobs command after the F11 key has been pressed.

In most shops, interactive queries and SQLs are discouraged. Programmers should use good judgment and only submit SQLs and interactive queries when they are very small or when the system is lightly loaded. Neither pattern applies in the preceding example. If the programmer really needs the SQL to run, I would lower its priority to a 50. The normal priority for a batch job is 50 and that is where this SQL should run.

To change a priority, use the screen displayed in Figure 9-3. Put a 2 (change) on the OPTION line and press Enter. You'll get the screen shown in Figure 9-4.

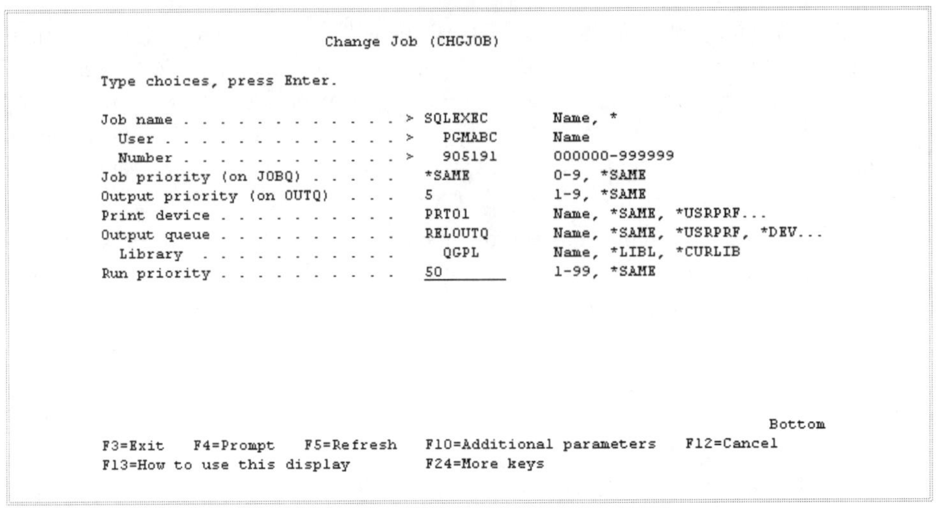

```
                          Change Job (CHGJOB)

Type choices, press Enter.

Job name . . . . . . . . . . . . > SQLEXEC        Name, *
  User . . . . . . . . . . . . . >   PGMABC       Name
  Number . . . . . . . . . . . . >   905191       000000-999999
Job priority (on JOBQ) . . . . .   *SAME          0-9, *SAME
Output priority (on OUTQ)  . . .   5              1-9, *SAME
Print device . . . . . . . . . .   PRT01          Name, *SAME, *USRPRF...
Output queue . . . . . . . . . .   RELOUTQ        Name, *SAME, *USRPRF, *DEV...
  Library  . . . . . . . . . . .     QGPL         Name, *LIBL, *CURLIB
Run priority . . . . . . . . . .   50             1-99, *SAME

                                                                        Bottom
F3=Exit   F4=Prompt   F5=Refresh   F10=Additional parameters   F12=Cancel
F13=How to use this display        F24=More keys
```

Figure 9-4: The screen to change a job's priority. Just overwrite the value in the RUN PRIORITY parameter.

Changing the job's priority is as simple as putting the 50 (its new priority) on the last parameter, RUN PRIORITY. After you change a priority like that, give the job 10 to 20 minutes to give up its hold on the system. Built-in delays are one reason why you want to react quickly to these situations.

This example has a clear offender, an interactive SQL, which is probably causing a response-time problem. If changing the SQL's priority does not return the system to normal or if that job hadn't been there, I would focus on the third and fourth jobs in the list shown in Figure 9-2.

Although each job is taking only about 11 percent and 10 percent, together they are taking 22.3 percent, and they both belong to the same user. Cases like these—two programs fired off by the same user—often will require the same resources and will be in constant conflict for those resources. An example is two queries running, looking for different things, but running against the same file. Conflicts cause sieze/lock waits and degrade the system. The solution could be to hold one of the programs until the other finishes.

Sometimes you won't find any jobs taking high CPU percentages and you have to look elsewhere. The next items to look for are unusually low (powerful) priorities where they shouldn't be. Like the CPU percentages, you can position the cursor on the priority column and press the F16 key for a quick sort. Figure 9-5 shows a sample of sorted priorities.

```
                          Work with Active Jobs                         SYS01
                                                               08/14/98  09:37:20
CPU %:    99.8     Elapsed time:    00:30:26     Active jobs:   251

Type options, press Enter.
  2=Change   3=Hold   4=End   5=Work with   6=Release   7=Display message
  8=Work with spooled files   13=Disconnect ...
                                                 --------Elapsed---------
Opt  Subsystem/Job  Type  Pool  Pty      CPU  Int     Rsp  AuxIO  CPU %
 _      MONJRN      BCH     2   10        .1                   0     .0
 _      MONSYSSTS   BCH     2   10      30.1                   2     .0
 _      MONTAPSTSD  BCH     2   10      40.6                  18     .0
 _      QBRMRCY     BCH     2   10        .5                   0     .0
 _      QSYSSCD     BCH     2   10       1.0                   0     .0
 _      QMLMAIN     PJ      2   11      68.1                   0     .0
 _      QMLRS232    PJ      2   11      35.0                   0     .0
 _      QMLTRACE    PJ      2   11     165.2                   0     .0
 _      RBCMANAGER  BCH     2   11     568.8                  37     .0
                                                                      More...
Parameters or command
===>
F3=Exit      F5=Refresh        F10=Restart statistics    F11=Display status
F12=Cancel   F23=More options  F24=More keys
```

Figure 9-5: Display screen for Work Active Jobs command after using the cursor position and the F16 key to sort by priorities.

You should know what jobs have legitimate high priorities. Scan this list for examples of high priorities that don't belong. Be particularly alert for high-priority users or programmers with special authority for job control in their user profile. These folks might have given themselves extra priority to boost their jobs through the system. For additional information, see chapter 5.

If you can't find any jobs taking large CPU percentages or priorities (and you have determined the LAN is not the problem), look deeper into the system using the command Work With System Activity (WRKSYSACT).

This screen refreshes itself every 5 seconds and that's the default. You can override it. If you're investigating a performance problem, you probably should make it 20 seconds. Otherwise, the frequency of refreshing this command might cause more degradation to the system you're trying to fix. Thanks to the constant refresh, you can monitor transitory problems. Another benefit from this screen is that it will show system tasks and their CPU percentages (which don't normally appear on the WRKACTJOB display). System tasks will have the user identification label "SYS" (notice the second column, "USER").

Figure 9-6 shows an example of that command's display.

```
                         Work with System Activity                   SYS01
                                                         08/14/98 07:38:31

Automatic refresh in seconds  . . . . . . . . . . . . . . . . . :       5
Elapsed time . . . . :   00:00:05         Overall CPU util . . : 99.9
                                        CPU 1 util . . . . . :       99.9
                                        CPU 2 util . . . . . :       99.9

 Type options, press Enter.
   1=Monitor job    5=Work with job
                                                        Total   Total
     Job or                                      CPU     Sync   Async     PAG       EAO
Opt  Task         User         Number   Pty    Util      I/O     I/O    Fault      Excp
 _   QBRMNET      QPGMR        161530    30    30.6      827     452       68         0
 _   HAL25V6      PGMDEF       161609    50    15.3       48     154        0         7
 _   SQLEXEC      PGMABC       161585    50    13.9        2     219        0         0
 _   ESFR176      PGMDEF       161460    50     9.6       70      16        0         0
 _   TSFR680      OPC          161604    50     8.7       32      32        0         0
 _   ROSEO5V1     PGMDEF       161255    50     8.6        0     222        0         0
 _   ISLWES4      PGMGHI       161495    20     1.2        7       1        2         0
 _   SERVICE      QSVCDRCTR    161488    51      .3        0       0        0         0

F3=Exit    F10=Update list     F11=View 2    F12=Cancel
F19=End automatic refresh     F24=More keys
```

Figure 9-6: Work with system activity.

Any AS/400 job can have two components: a user component and a system component. The user component is what WRKACTJOB displays. System components don't appear there because they have a very high priority and are very transitory (lasting less than a second). However, you can start a system-intensive job where the system component is long and consumes the CPU. The user component on WRKACTJOB will show a very low CPU percentage usage because it isn't doing anything. The system component of the job will be using 40 percent of your CPU and you won't see it.

A prime example of such transparent problems occurs with a large library save during the day. The user portion of the SAVLIB job will show 0-3 percent CPU utilization, yet the system will be pegged. If you look at the system with the WRKSYSACT command, you'll see USER SYS (the system portion) taking 40 percent of the CPU. And, talk about abnormally high priorities, USER SYS's task will run at a priority of 1! It takes some creativity (but not much) to associate such a SYS task with a user job. The solution is twofold:

- Cancel the user job (the system task will go with it).
- Institute a rule that the user job (like a large Save Library) won't be started during the production day unless an unusual situation exists.

9.2.1.2 Emergency Aftermath

The recovery period following an emergency has the potential to cause worse damage than the original event. Changing almost anything in the system, at a time when the system is getting hit hard, can really cause it to flop. When you change a runaway job's priority to 55 in order to minimize its impact, the first thing the system seems to do is start running at about 150 percent. Depending on how deep the program was into the system, sometimes even a simple hold will be delayed for 30 or more minutes. New priorities always require time to take effect. Meanwhile, the system performance degrades further. All you can do during this time is wait. And tell your users to take a break.

Earlier, I mentioned the potential for a LAN problem. The way LANs go down (and come back up) on an AS/400 can cause a performance "emergency" totally out of your control. As an example, consider the sudden failure of a gateway or a bridge that supports 100 workstations. Probably, the only way anyone knows there is a problem is that 100 users are stuck on a single screen.

When the AS/400 fails to see the failed hardware device, it will disconnect all its users. This can be a major problem on the AS/400 with 100-plus sessions dumping logs to disk and cleaning up after themselves. Would you be surprised to know that good old user SYS does this dumping and cleaning and anything that user SYS does runs at a very high priority?

Then another problem happens when the device is replaced or fixed and all 100 users are told (usually through an overhead announcement) to sign back on again. Even on a powerful AS/400, you're going to see performance die for 15 to 45 minutes as it handles 100 new sign-ons, and there is nothing you can do about it. In particularly large shops, you'll see the help desk used to selectively bring up groups of users at a time. Keep the following tip in mind:

TIP: Another problem with LANs and AS/400s is that LANs tend to be a little flaky. Rather than have workstations dropping on and off all the time, many customers customize their AS/400s slightly to accommodate that instability. They modify system value QDSCJOBITV (Disconnect Job Interval) to keep LAN-connected interactive jobs active until 10 or 15 minutes of no communications has elapsed.

Quite often, the aftermath of any performance emergency, even those internal to the AS/400, not the LAN-based ones, is so severe that many shops just cross their fingers and hope any response-time degradation is transitory. That strategy works about half the time.

Every AS/400 shop needs to develop emergency guidelines. Depending on your job mix and LAN usage, your emergency procedures should include the following:

- First indications of problems (calls from users, monitoring programs, etc.).
- Initial steps to identify the type of problem:
  - ✔ Who takes what action. Assign one person, usually someone with ready access to the system console.
  - ✔ What to look for.
  - ✔ Specific things to do.
- Problem identification:
  - ✔ Action taken:
    - ➢ Hold programs.
    - ➢ Contact developers.
    - ➢ Change job priorities.
    - ➢ Cancel jobs.
    - ➢ Get hardware back up.
  - ✔ Who must be notified:
    - ➢ LAN administration.
    - ➢ Programming.
    - ➢ Management.
- Recovery:
  - ✔ What is the status of the AS/400?
    - ➢ Is the AS/400 suffering from heavy user disconnections?
    - ➢ Have all job changes taken effect?
    - ➢ Have high-hitting jobs released their holds on the system?
  - ✔ Are users to sign off and then sign on or just be patient?

9.2.2 Performance Tuning

While an emergency can happen to any AS/400, getting your AS/400 into tune and keeping it there generally will allow your shop to have fewer emergencies. The art of performance tuning an AS/400 is almost a lost art. No one really bothers anymore and that's too bad. Most AS/400s being considered for upgrade really only need a good tune-up.

There really aren't too many specific tasks to tuning, but there is a definite lack of what's right for any particular system. The problem is that the AS/400 gets tuned to support a job mix. As the mix changes, the tuning requirements change. And guess what? Because the mix is always changing, customers try to strike a happy medium. Defining what that happy medium is remaines the challenge.

A lightly loaded AS/400 always runs well and looks relatively healthy. Don't waste your time doing performance tuning during those times. Always monitor AS/400s during the busiest time for any job mix. Take note of what I'm saying here. The busiest time for a set of interactive jobs tends to be from 10:00 A.M. to 2:00 P.M. (excluding lunch hour). The busiest time for a batch job mix is generally during nightly processing. Some 24-hour shops are even more complex. For example, the job mix might not completely change from interactive to batch, but the emphasis on either could change.

There are two performance tuning tasks: monitoring and modifying. Monitoring tasks should be done during the busy, stressful times mentioned in the previous paragraph. Modifying system parameters—such as changing memory or activity levels—should be done, if possible, during less busy times. Because monitoring is boring, consider writing a program to do it.

9.2.3 Monitoring Tasks

So what values do you monitor to check the health of an AS/400? Well, it's not the CPU percentage alone. That's like diagnosing a mechanical problem with a car by measuring how fast its engine is running: "It's running very fast, we need another car." Not true. Like car engines, computer CPUs sometimes are supposed to run fast and sometimes idle. Don't overreact the first time you see a CPU percentage of 99.9 percent. The AS/400 might have a serious problem, but the percentage alone doesn't tell you that. The two AS/400 monitoring issues of concern are:

- Wait-to-ineligible ratio.
- Non-database faults:
  - ✔ Non-machine pool.
  - ✔ Machine pool.
  - ✔ All pools.

9.2.3.1 Wait-to-Ineligible Ratio

The wait-to-ineligible ratio is the primary factor you want to monitor. Here's what that means. Jobs have three run states.

- Active—currently running.
- Wait—waiting for something.
  - ✔ A disk access, which could be a page retrieval or some record retrieval.
  - ✔ A user's response to a screen.
- Ineligible—the job is ready to run, and just waiting for the system to allocate resources to it.

From these three states, IBM defines six transition states (or the act of a job going from one state to another). Three of the six are significant and the most significant is the wait-to-ineligible:

- Active-to-wait.
- Active-to-ineligible.
- Wait-to-ineligible.
- Ineligible-to-active.
- Wait-to-active.
- Ineligible-to-wait.

The AS/400 uses transition state numbers as ratios to each other. Such a ratio would be the number of one type of transition to the number of another type of transition as measured within a period (like a minute). Transition ratios are used to define what you want to see in a healthy system. Valid ratios are available for each AS/400 model and each version of the operating system. The ratios are found in appendix A of the IBM Redbook, *AS/400 Performance Management.*

Keep in mind that the text and examples in this chapter all use acceptable values for an AS/400, but the samples shown might not be anything like yours. Follow the discussion but don't take any of my values for your AS/400. Before you start tuning, check the manual for your AS/400's values. In the text that follows, I use actual numbers from one AS/400 model, but I leave blank spaces for you to fill in the appropriate values for your AS/400. For example, when I say that an appropriate wait-to-ineligible ratio is 10 (____), assume 10 is just for discussion, but write your own wait-to-ineligible ratio from the work management manual.

For this example, the primary transition ratio is the wait-to-ineligible to active-to-wait. Expect the ratio to be around 10 (___) percent. In other words, 10 (___) percent of the jobs that went from active to wait are unable to become active right away again when they are done waiting due to system resources being committed to other jobs.

To understand why the preceding 10 (___) percent is a good situation, consider what happens when no jobs wait to run. When there are no jobs ineligible, it is an indication that not too much is running on the system or that you have an overtuned system.

In other words, so many system resources are allocated that no jobs ever have to become ineligible. That's great for individual jobs and it's usually the way customers new to the AS/400 tune their machines. Nevertheless, with an overtuned system, you will discover that random jobs just degrade for no reason. The monitoring command for these ratios is Work With System Status (WRKSYSSTS). Figure 9-7 shows a sample.

```
                             Work with System Status                    TEST400
                                                              08/14/98  07:39:53
 % CPU used . . . . . . . :          1.2    Auxiliary storage:
 Elapsed time . . . . . . :     00:00:01      System ASP . . . . . . :     14.55 G
 Jobs in system . . . . . :          211      % system ASP used  . . :     40.0559
 % addresses used:                            Total  . . . . . . . . :     14.55 G
   Permanent  . . . . . . :         .007      Current unprotect used :      375 M
   Temporary  . . . . . . :         .009      Maximum unprotect  . . :      409 M

 Type changes (if allowed), press Enter.

 System     Pool    Reserved    Max    -----DB-----  ---Non-DB---
  Pool    Size (K)  Size (K)  Active   Fault  Pages  Fault  Pages
    1     _ 39312     22872    +++++      .0     .0     .0     .0
    2       60940         0    ___18      .0     .0     .0     .0
    3     ___1308         0    ____1      .0     .0     .0     .0
    4     __29512         0    ____6      .0     .0    5.7    6.5

                                                                          Bottom
 Command
 ===> ___________________________________________________________________________
 F3=Exit   F4=Prompt              F5=Refresh   F9=Retrieve   F10=Restart
 F11=Display transition data      F12=Cancel   F24=More keys
```

Figure 9-7: Work with system status.

To transition monitoring, focus on two columns: ACTIVE-TO-WAIT and WAIT-TO-INELIGIBLE. You want to see WAIT-TO-INELIGIBLE at approximately 10 (___) percent or less (but not equal to 0 percent) of the ACTIVE-TO-WAIT value.

As a result of monitoring these columns, the next step is to *modify* information. The only way you can make the WAIT-TO-INELIGIBLE column change up or down is to change the MAX ACT figure. You lower the figure in increments of 2, until the WAIT-TO-INELIGIBLE number drops to almost 0, and then increase the figure by 2 one time.

You also can change POOL SIZES from this screen by positioning the cursor on the appropriate pool size field and type in the new figure.

9.2.3.2 Non-Database Faults (Non-Machine Pool)

Although it is not obvious, Figure 9-7 actually shows three types of memory pools:

- System pool 1. This is called the *machine pool.* It is always present on any functioning AS/400 and it is where the system does its system tasks.
- System pool 2. This is called the *base pool*. Because it is often written as *BASE, it may be referred to as "star-base." This is the repository for all memory not otherwise assigned to system pool 1 or system pools 3-16.
- System pool 3 through 16. These are optional (you don't have to have any) and they are the *user-defined pools.*

Non-database faults are another crucial point to monitor for appropriate system tuning. User pools are what this section is about. Database faults can be application issues, but non-database faults are a way of saying that there isn't enough memory to adequately support the program.

Monitor the non-database (NON-DB) fault value on the screen as shown in Figure 9-7. Make the fault rate change by changing the POOL SIZE value. Raising the pool size makes more memory available and lowers the non-database faulting rate.

These pools should have non-database faults of between 10 (___) and 20 (___) pages per minute. Actually, don't worry too much about the ones that are below 10 (___). In the example shown in Figure 9-7, the below-10 faults are for non-interactive jobs that are lightly loaded during the day. Actually, none may be running on the system from which this example was taken. In this case, the fault rate for non-interactive jobs would be low. If a pool supporting interactive jobs needed some extra memory, however, you could get it from one of these batch pools.

Pool 7 in Figure 9-7 is an interactive pool and has a fairly high non-database fault rate of 44. You should adjust this value by increasing its pool size. For specific information, see section 9.2.4 What to Modify.

9.2.3.3 Non-Database Faults (Machine Pool)

Pool 1, the machine pool, should have a non-database fault rate between 3 (___) and 5 (___) pages per minute. And you can adjust the memory assigned to pool 1 until you get that rate.

9.2.3.4 Non-Database Faults (All Pools)

Another activity to monitor is the total of all non-database faults for all pools (including the machine pool). The value for this specific AS/400 should be between 180 (___) and 300 (___).

If the value isn't between 180 (___) and 300 (___), it could mean that one or more pools are seriously out of tune. If all pools are tuned as good as you can get them or there are no further steps you can take (such as no inactive pools from which to draw memory), your AS/400 could be out of capacity and in need of an upgrade.

9.2.3.5 When to Monitor

If the AS/400 is lightly loaded, you'll get zeros for your key monitoring points. If you make adjustments based on those values, your AS/400 will not function when any serious workload hits it. Always monitor when the AS/400 is getting hammered.

Take several monitor samples and don't worry about reacting to every little thing. On the best-tuned AS/400s, you will get periods where the monitored values are not good. What you want is a trend where you can say they're acceptable most of the time. Remember, you can tune any AS/400 for any job mix, but job mixes change. So tune yours for its most representative mix.

Approach performance monitoring like stock brokers advise you to approach investing. Establish a long-term goal and try to reach that without flipping out over every little glitch. As with investing in the stock market, if you check performance hourly or daily, you'll go crazy. Look only at the big picture. Don't seriously consider every individual monitoring sample until several of them indicate a trend.

9.2.4 What to Modify

Again refer to Figure 9-7; its second and fourth left-side columns represent the things you can change:

- Pool size.
- Max Active.

The preceding are both poorly named columns. Read them this way:

- Memory.
- Activity level.

9.2.4.1 Memory

Pool size or memory is the amount of memory a set of jobs has available to play in. You will see a memory pool for all interactive jobs and one for all batch jobs. The more memory a set of jobs has the faster they will run. But this could be at the expense of other jobs.

Notice from the display shown in Figure 9-7 that you cannot modify the memory for pool 2 (*BASE). The memory in it is all the system memory not used in any other pool. For additional information on memory storage pools, see chapter 3.

When you decrease the memory in any pool, the extra amount of memory you don't need anymore goes into pool 2. When you increase the memory in any pool, the amount you need comes from pool 2.

When you want to modify the system to take memory from one storage pool that isn't using it and put it in another that needs it, you do so by:

- Decreasing the first pool's memory.
- Increasing the second pool's memory.

To set the storage pools' memory initially, set QPFRADJ to 1 and IPL the AS/400. For more information, refer to the IBM manual *OS/400 Work Management V4R3,* section 14, Subsystems.

9.2.4.2 Activity Level

Activity level is hard to explain. Primarily because it is called MAX ACT on the WRKSYSSTS display, people confuse it with MAXACT jobs on the subsystem description and job-queue descriptions. First, those MAXACTS refer to how many jobs can be running at any one time.

The MAX ACT on the WRKSYSSTS display is really the activity level and is quite different. The activity level doesn't affect how many jobs can run at one time. It affects how many jobs can be active at one time. Remember the three job states mentioned in section 9.2.3.1, Wait-to-Ineligible Ratio?

When a job returns from a wait state, it has two states it can go to:

1. Active if there are system resources for it.
2. Ineligible if there are none.

Whether the job can become active again or have to wait for another job to go into a wait is determined by the activity level (or MAX ACT) setting for the storage pool.

You could have a storage pool with MAXACT jobs at 6, but an activity level of 3. Theoretically, you set it that way because you know that the six jobs running will have a certain amount of waiting activities every minute. If you ever set the activity level to 6 for six active jobs, no job would ever go ineligible when it returned from a wait (it would just go active again). But this kind of overtuning comes at some cost. Usually, some job somewhere suddenly goes belly-up because there are no resources for it. Jobs can be active and go straight to ineligible. The effect is a kind of drive-by faulting.

You don't want this to happen to an otherwise healthy job. You want the job to run until it normally goes to wait. Then your job would be allowed to start. How do you know that level of detail about any of your jobs? You don't. That's why you use the ratios as a guideline.

Monitoring and modifying this area has a look and feel that is very different from batch and interactive pools. Interactive pools go into waits when they display a screen to a user. In computer-use time, those waits are small eternities.

You could have a storage pool supporting 100 interactive users, with an activity level of only 6, because you expect most of them to be waiting on screens anyway. Batch programs do a lot of waiting, but only for the system to get something for them. These waits are very fast; the time is minimal. Therefore, you will have a batch storage pool with the activity level around 50 percent of the maximum active jobs.

Adjust activity levels in sets of 2 at a time and wait until you can monitor before you make another adjustment. If you're new to the AS/400, the IBM manual, *OS/400 Work Management V4R3*, has the recommended initial values for activity-level settings.

Don't underestimate the importance of a good activity level setting. Too low a setting will degrade performance as much as too high a setting. Find the optimum setting range in the manual and adhere to it.

9.2.4.3 When to Modify

When you change either the memory level or the activity level, your system must go through a fairly intensive rearranging of the jobs in those pools. This can get intensive when you are taking memory from one or more pools and putting it into one or more other pools. When you make these changes, you can watch your CPU activity light go steady for anywhere from several seconds to several minutes. For this reason, don't make modifications when your system is heavily loaded.

If you change an activity level in response to a performance emergency, don't expect dramatic changes to happen right away. It can take several minutes for the system to settle in and realize the benefits of a better activity level.

9.2.5 Performance Tuning Summary

Performance tuning must be an ongoing activity. It's not a real good task to start doing when your system is crashing. Remember the rules:

- Monitor when the system is at its busiest (for the job mix).
- Modify when the system is at its lightest.
- When reassigning memory among pools, do so in the following order:
  - ✔ Decrease memory in all pools.
  - ✔ Increase memory in all pools.

Also, remember that monitoring is an ongoing process, and that it is a fairly boring task. Consider writing a program to monitor your system at known busy times and just collect data that you can scan periodically. Then make modifications when the time is right. If you're good about making performance tuning an ongoing activity, you'll never be backed into a corner where your system is limping along with a tuning problem and you must make a change in the middle of a busy period.

9.2.6 Performance Monitoring and Analysis

Under the umbrella of Performance Tools/400, the AS/400 has some powerful data collecting and reporting tools:

- Performance Data Monitor will collect and report performance data. Start it with the Start Performance Monitor (STRPFRMON) command.
- Automatic data collection also can be started with the Add Performance Collection (ADDPFRCOL) command.
- Performance trend analysis can be done automatically every month with the Automated Performance Management Tool. Start this with the Analyze Performance Data (ANZPFRDTA) command. Because this is a CPU hog, run it during off-hours.
- The Performance Tools Advisor will provide an overall analysis of the performance settings within your AS/400. Optionally, the Advisor will ask if you want it to implement its recommendations. If you answer affirmative, it will make the changes. Note: Set QPFRADJ to 0 to run this program. Keep the following tip in mind:

TIP: Try this. Set QPFRADJ to 2 or 3 to have the AS/400 self-tune itself. Later run it off and run Performance Tools Advisor and see how the AS/400 scores its own attempts at tuning.

- Print Transaction (PRTTNSRPT) will help locate "hot spots" of jobs you suspect are causing performance problems. To run this command, Performance Monitor (STRPFRMON) must have been started with the parameter TRACE(*ALL).

If you aren't fully comfortable with the AS/400 tuning automatically, use it once and use its settings as guidelines. Then set your system up according to those guidelines, capture performance data, and periodically run an analysis report or two.

You'll be using Print Transaction to locate stubborn performance problems. For example, the users might complain that the system runs terribly for a period of 15 minutes to half an hour some mornings (but not all mornings). Maybe you have checked with Work with System Status (WRKSYSSTS) and Work Active Jobs (WRKACTJOB) and haven't found anything wrong. Print Transaction will focus you on a particular job. Once armed with a suspect, try the last (and my favorite) AS/400 performance tool, Performance Explorer.

Performance Explorer asks you for a set of programs or jobs to analyze and prints a report that'll tell you everything about them in incredible detail. It's educational, too. I've learned a lot about what the system runs to run my programs. Try it by naming one of your own programs (even if it's not a bad performer). Then print the reports and you'll see all the system level modules and programs the AS/400 calls to execute that program. It's quite enlightening and I've used it to help me refine my programming techniques.

When CPU usage goes over 90 percent, seize/lock conditions increase and degrade performance. If you have slow periods during the day, try running the Print Transaction report. Limit the time of the seize/locks to greater than 50 milliseconds and use the time of day (TOD) to limit the analysis to a time of day. You'll get a report isolating the seize/locks that occurred when the CPU percentage hits the roof. From the report on isolated seize/locks, you can get a list of the programs that were hurt most or caused the most trouble (it's kind of a chicken and the egg thing) during the period.

The key to monitoring and analysis is to do it all the time. This product writes thousands of records to hundreds of files. There is more information here than you could ever want. IBM has a subscription service that takes this data monthly and produces more reports than you could ever use.

Simplify this process by collecting the data and doing your own analysis and you can eliminate a lot of confusing detail. When I do this, I only analyze the things I mentioned in this chapter. You should review the files and information and decide what you need to collect for your shop.

Try focusing on one file, QAPMJOBS, in library QPFRDATA. Use the display file field definitions (DSPFFD) to see what its fields capture even it has too much data. Write a program or programs to sift it down to something reasonable.

In all the performance monitor files, every day's transactions are captured in unique *members* within the files. By the end of the month, this file and all its members are in the gigabyte range. That's why I like to extract that data into summary files in a form that is meaningful and reduced enough that I can keep it online for a while.

I like to have this summary data handy for trend analysis. Also, I will review individual programs or applications to see if their hit on the system is reasonable or not. When a new application goes live, this collected data can be compared to new data to see if the change has caused an application to suddenly adversely impact the system. Here's the sifting process I use:

- Many members to one (or one per month).
- Many, many job types are monitored. I only extract the interactive and batch jobs because they are the only ones I have control over.
- I don't collect for non-working days.
- Only the QPFRDTA/QAPMJOBS file.

Within the records I do collect, I only include:

- Response time—interactive programs only. The response time is the amount of time the system takes to process a transaction. An example of response time is the amount of time elapsed from when the user presses the Enter key until a screen is returned. However, you lose the time the transaction spends in the network.
- CPU utilization—batch and interactive. The amount of CPU seconds used.
- CPU percent utilization—batch and interactive. The percentage of CPU used by both batch and interactive jobs.
- Number of transactions—interactive programs only. The number of times the Enter key was pressed.
- Cost per transaction—interactive programs only. My own measurement. Pure CPU seconds can be misleading because a program can legitimately take a lot of CPU

seconds. Also, transactions can be misleading because lots of transactions with little processing behind them don't impact the system. I divide the CPU used by the number of transactions in order to come up with a cost (in CPU seconds) per transaction. This is much more meaningful for uncovering problem applications.

- Asynchronous Database I/O—batch and interactive. Asynchronous DASD I/O is good I/O because it is something that programs don't have to wait for. For example, when reading records sequentially, if they were read from disk in blocks, the program doesn't wait for the next record when it comes from the input buffer.
- Synchronous DASD I/O—batch and interactive. These are not so good I/O because the programs have to wait. Random record reads and screen displays are examples of valid synchronous DASD I/Os.
- Wait for asynchronous Database I/O—batch and interactive. These are very bad I/O because—although the program shouldn't have to wait—it does. An example would be a program that is sequentially reading records. The system expects the records to be blocked and expects not to have to wait. If it does wait, you get that information here. In the blocked records example, a program legitimately has to wait whenever the buffer is exhausted and the system has to get another set of records from the disk. So some activity in here is acceptable. However, if the program had a problem and the system had to wait on every record, this count would go way up, and you would know to take a look at it.

I extract these to a spreadsheet and graph them to review each day of the previous month. Monthly graphs are kept together to create visual long-term trends. These trending graphs track a year or more history of:

- Average response time per job.
- Average number of jobs per day.
- Total number of interactive jobs.
- Average number of transactions per interactive job.
- Average CPU utilization per interactive job.
- Total number of interactive transactions.
- Total CPU used by interactive jobs.

9.2.7 Capacity Planning

The AS/400 comes with a built-in capacity-planning product called BEST/1. Unfortunately, I've never had it tell me anything other than "buy more hardware."

That is not to say the conclusion is invalid. Most people don't run it when they have lots of capacity. Therefore, the conclusion is probably valid. Given just that conclusion, I would have to do a lot of support work before I would use it alone to make a board-level recommendation for a major upgrade.

Look at capacity planning as the ultimate culmination of the other techniques covered in this chapter. Performance activities and measuring must ultimately result in capacity planning information. You must be able to provide evidence that you've done all you reasonably can accomplish. You must have a track record of:

- Performance tuning. Have you done all you can?
  - ✔ What have you monitored?
  - ✔ What have you modified?
  - ✔ Why can't you keep on modifying?
- You've kept monthly graphs of the key items the AS/400 uses. Over time, these graphs should reflect a trend to higher:
  - ✔ Response times.
  - ✔ CPU utilization.
  - ✔ DASD utilization.
- Your staff handles emergencies as efficiently as anyone. At some point, you need to be able to demonstrate:
  - ✔ Your performance-related emergencies have grown in number.
  - ✔ Your performance-related emergencies have grown in frequency.
  - ✔ The emergencies are caused by:
    - ➢ Growth in applications on the system.
    - ➢ Growth in the number of users on the system.
    - ➢ Growth in transaction levels.

If you really have all the preceding, capacity issues are easy to spot and easy to document. That data works very nicely to support BEST/1 findings.

When considering a model upgrade, you'll be interested in the amount of power gain the different AS/400 models have. There are two measurements of this: RPR and the newer CPW.

Relative Performance Rating (RPR) has been the old standard and was based on how many times faster any particular configuration is than the original, smallest AS/400 (a model B10). The testing standard was based on an IBM-developed method called *RAMP-C*. The problem with this is that the transactions pumped through were too simple. As disk I/O got better and AS/400 memory got big enough that entire files could be cached, the measurement became meaningless.

The more sophisticated replacement is Commercial Processing Workload (CPW). CPW uses order-entry transactions that access and update many database files. Where RPR counted transactions completed when the CPU usage percentage was at 70 percent, CPW disregards CPU percentage. Instead, CPW counts the number of transactions the system can complete while delivering 90 percent of those transactions at less than a 5-second response time. This measurement (and its more complex transaction structure) guarantees a more realistic measurement guideline.

9.3 PERFORMANCE TIPS

Here are some miscellaneous things you can do to improve how your applications run.

Use the Set Object Access (SETOBJACC) command to pre-load entire files into their own dedicated storage pool for certain kinds of processing. I like to use this for crucial batch programs that are run off-hours. Assign a lot of memory to a storage pool, load a physical file or logical file into it, and then kick off the job. It'll run very fast. On the subsystem description, assign the normal system pool 2 (*BASE), one user pool for the program and other files, then one or more pools dedicated to the largest and busiest of the files the program will access. Before using the SETOBJACC command:

- Set system value QPFRADJ to 0 (turn it off).
- Issue the CLRPOOL command to clear the pool.

Keep in mind that most applications are disk-bound (not CPU-bound). Keeping that in mind, remember that disk-intensive operations cost you dearly. These operations are journaling, commitment control, and (to a lesser extent), RAID-5 and mirroring. The trade-off is database security for speed. RAID-5 and mirroring have gotten fast over the years; I don't worry about them anymore. But journaling and commitment control will still make their sting felt. If you need either or both, go for it, but don't fall into the trap that many do and just turn on journaling for a whole library. Think and plan through your journaling/commitment control strategy.

Disk accessing technology has gotten much better over the years. Actually, the improvement in fast-access and controller-based caching has been exponential. When looking at the big picture (your applications and the AS/400), keep in mind that, as the DASD block is removed, the CPU becomes the next blockage. In other words, as you replace older DASD with new, watch your CPU usage percent increase.

Implementing ILE HLL (High Level Languages) properly will significantly enhance the performance of an AS/400. Especially in applications that rely on much calling of external programs, ILE allows those programs to be *bound modules* of a single program. If you're an ILE shop, however, keep *activation groups* to a minimum or you'll start to lose some of those gains.

9.3.1 The AS/400 Server

If you have an AS/400 set up and sold as a server, it is tuned to favor batch processing. Leave it as a server! The temptation is to look at the hardware packed in one of those servers and how fast it runs and think it would be a nice platform for some interactive workstations.

Two things I'll promise you: One, the few workstations you attach will run terribly. Two, if you attach more than a few of them (enough to make the interactive CPU percentage go up to 10 percent of the machine), nothing will run well—neither batch nor interactive. Plan to limit the access to the server machine to the minimum interactive. IBM recommends less than 2 percent of the interactive CPU percentage.

Sometimes the definition of what is an interactive job is in doubt. If an interactive job just collects input parameters and then starts a batch-reporting job, that job might or might not be interactive (depending on how it was started). If you suspect applications problems on an AS/400 server, use the Work with Active Job (WRKACTJOB) command and look in the Type column. Interactive jobs will be identified with an INT; all others are non-interactive jobs.

In addition, the system will do dynamic prioritizing on a server AS/400, but you might want to limit it to only adjusting the priorities of batch jobs. This is assuming that the one or two interactive jobs running on the system could be crucial to its being. If you are running dynamic prioritizing, and don't want interactive jobs' priorities changed, set system value QDYNPTYADJ to '0'. If you do want interactive jobs' priorities changed, set it to '1'.

9.4 References

AS/400 Basic System Operation, Administration, and Problem Handling V4R3 (SC41-5206-02)

AS/400 Performance Management V3R6/V3R7 (SG24-4735-00) (Redbook).

OS/400 Work Management V4R3 (SC41-5306-02)

AS/400 Performance Explorer Tip & Techniques (SG24-4781-00)

10 Communications: SNA, APPC, and APPN

10.1 Overview

In the beginning (of the AS/400), there was only asynchronous and 5250 (also referred to as *twin-ax* because of the unique cabling it required) communications support.

Today, we snicker at the old 5250 protocol because we forget that 5250 was years ahead of its time. When the rest of the computer world was limping along with ASCII asynchronous line-at-a-time input, the AS/400 was dazzling everyone with the unheard-of 1 megabit/second speed (the others were 9600 bits per second) and screen-at-a-time transmission. For years the AS/400 had a user interface that blew away everything else.

IBM was smart to allow 5250 to be eclipsed by the rest of the world, and then open the AS/400 to the emerging protocols. Today the AS/400 offers native support to all the existing protocols.

The AS/400 owes its roots to 5250 and its host-to-host architectures, advanced peer-to-peer communications (APPC), and advanced peer-to-peer networking (APPN). AS/400 customers do support 5250 directly. Emulation products are used to "GUI-ize" 5250 green screens. And when you connect AS/400 hosts, you are still using APPC or APPN.

This chapter explores 5250, APPC, and APPN. Chapter 11 specifically addresses six industry-wide protocols that the AS/400 supports.

When the AS/400 supports a new protocol, it generally does so in an emulation mode. After a year or so and some acceptance by AS/400 customers, generally the protocol support is offered as native. It gets confusing about what is emulated and what is native or even what those terms mean to the customer.

Here's a rule I use to help me keep everything straight. If IBM merely supports a protocol, it will probably run under APPC or APPN. If IBM offers *native support* for a protocol, it will run on its own—not under APPC/APPN.

The whole subject of communications on any platform is very complex. This handbook describes the high points. If you get overwhelmed (and you probably will), remember that just by relying on IBM-supplied defaults and automatic configuration, you can do a pretty fair job of bringing up a network. If you're interested in more detail on any of the specific areas, refer to the IBM manuals referenced in this chapter.

10.2 Systems Network Architecture

Systems Network Architecture (SNA) is at the highest level of IBM communication. SNA isn't as simple as a protocol. SNA is a collection of descriptions of logical structures, protocols, and instruction sequences that handle all parts of IBM communications.

SNA is omnipresent over all IBM platforms, but relatively unknown in the LAN world. An exception is the servers designed specifically for SNA communications.

10.2.1 Advanced Peer-to-Peer Communications

Under SNA is the *advanced peer-to-peer communications* (APPC) that handles AS/400 communications. Another way to put it is that APPC uses what it needs of SNA to support AS/400 communications. For readers so inclined, it does so as an implementation of SNA logical unit 6.2 and node type 2.1 architectures.

A key thing to remember about APPC is that it is a peer-to-peer architecture. You can have one platform act as the master to the other hosts if you want to, but that's not required. Multiple hosts can exist as equal partners on the network. You can write programs on any one system that starts, controls, and ends jobs on any other system.

One other key point to remember is that APPC isn't a protocol; it supports protocols.

10.2.2 APPC Functions

Most AS/400 customer contact with APPC is through the following functions it offers. For all the functions, you must have APPC or APPN in effect to use them.

- Distributed data management (DDM). Allows a program or user on one system to access database files on another system. See section 10.8.1 Distributed Data Management.
- SNA distribution services (SNADS). Allows electronic mail and files to be sent to another system. See section 10.8.3 SNA Distribution Services.
- Display station pass-through. Allows a user signed onto one AS/400 to pass through it into another AS/400 and sign on there as a "local" workstation. See section 10.8.4 Display Station Pass-Through.
- OptiConnect/400. This is a combination hardware and software that provides very high-speed communications between host AS/400s. See section 10.8.2 OptiConnect/400.

- Electronic Customer Support (ECS). Allows a customer to access question-and-answer, problem-solving databases at IBM. Also, a customer can use ECS to order OS releases and PTFs. PTFs also can be delivered via ECS. See section 10.8.5 Electronic Customer Support.
- SNA pass-through. Allows SNA data to be passed between applications.
- File transfer support. Moves file members from one system to another.
- CA/400. Provides system access and functions to an attached personal computer.
- Alert support. When a problem or impending problem is detected by the system, it alerts the operator.
- CICS/400. Allows developers to write programs to process workstation transactions.

Refer to Section 10.7 Using APPC/APPN Functions for more detailed discussion of all these topics.

10.2.3 Programming for APPC

If you write programs that use communication links, they will use APPC interfaces. You must have APPC or APPN in effect to use the APPC communications interfaces available to your programs:

- Interprogram communications function (ICF):
  - ✔ Make ICF calls through DDS.
  - ✔ Can be used in RPG, COBOL, C/400, and FORTRAN.
  - ✔ Refer to the IBM manual *OS/400 APPC Programming V4R1* for more information.
- Common programming interface communications (CPI-C):
  - ✔ Make CPI-C calls through CPI communications calls.
  - ✔ Can be used in the ICF languages plus REXX.
  - ✔ Refer to the IBM manual *CPI Communication Reference* for more information.
- CICS:
  - ✔ Make CICS calls through EXEC CICS commands.
  - ✔ Can be used in COBOL programs.
  - ✔ Refer to the IBM manual *CICS/400 Administration and Operations Guide* for more information.

- Sockets:
  - ✔ Access socket commands through APIs.
  - ✔ Can be used in any HLL.
  - ✔ Refer to the IBM manual *OS/400 Sockets Programming V4R1* for more information.

10.2.4 Communication Lines Support

All your AS/400 communications lines will be under APPC. Each line can be one of the following types of communications (a line adapter for each must be installed on the AS/400):

- Distributed data interface (DDI).
- Frame-relay network (FR).
- ISDN data line control (IDLC):
  - ✔ Switched.
  - ✔ Non-switched.
- Synchronous data link (SDLC):
  - ✔ Point-to-point switched.
  - ✔ Point-to-point non-switched.
  - ✔ Multiple-point non-switched.
- X.25.
- Token ring.
- Ethernet.
- Wireless.

10.2.5 System Names in APPC/APPN

Whether you're using APPC (two AS/400s connected) or APPN (multiple AS/400s networked), you should give serious consideration to meaningful system names.

If your connected AS/400s are within one local facility, you could make their departments or buildings the prefix to the system names. If you are supporting multiple AS/400s scattered around the city, make their streets or areas the name prefix. If you have

AS/400s around the country, make their cities the name prefix. Follow each prefix with a rotating number. Here are examples of three AS/400s each:

- Local facility:
  - ✔ ACTRCV01
  - ✔ ORDENT01
  - ✔ ORDENT02
- Local city:
  - ✔ SOUTH01
  - ✔ BEVHIL01
  - ✔ WODHIL01
- Nationwide:
  - ✔ LOSANG01
  - ✔ NEWYRK01
  - ✔ NEWYRK02

The preceding system might seem simplistic now, but location-based system names will save you hours of frustration later as you manage your APPC/APPN network.

10.3 Advanced Peer-to-Peer Networking

Advanced peer-to-peer networking (APPN) is an enhanced APPC. Whereas APPC is concerned with two AS/400s connected by a single line, APPN is concerned with multiple AS/400s, multiple lines, and even multiple APPN networks. Keep the following tip in mind:

> **TIP:** APPN offers enough added functionality that many AS/400 customers use APPN to support a simple, two-AS/400 network instead of APPC.

You could support a network solely with APPC. You would have an APPC session for each line, but the work to use it could be prohibitive. On the other hand, APPN takes on the network-support chores for you such as:

- Working with distributed directories.
- Selecting routes dynamically.
- Creating and starting remote locations automatically.
- Prioritized data routing.

APPN will control your transmissions, in complex networks, where multiple AS/400s are attached. Not all AS/400s have direct routes between them. APPN automatically will choose AS/400s (or nodes) it can use as intermediate systems to get to a target AS/400. If all systems and lines are under APPN control, no operator on the system has to worry about how a transmission will get to its destination. An APPN network can consist of any mixture of these devices:

- Personal computer.
- IBM Midrange Computers.
    - ✔ S/36.
    - ✔ S/38.
    - ✔ RISC System 6000.
- DPPX/370.
- The following mainframe hosts, providing they are running CISC or ACF/NCP with VTAM.
    - ✔ S/370.
    - ✔ S/390.
    - ✔ 30xx.
    - ✔ 43xx.
    - ✔ 9370.

In addition to the APPC functions just discussed, APPN provides:

- Distributed directory services. APPN, given a remote system name, will search the network to locate that system.
- Dynamic route selection based on user-defined rules. APPN will determine the best route to take to send a transmission to a remote system. You define the parameters it will use. For example, you can specify lowest cost or fastest route.
- Intermediate session routing. Any AS/400 can be used as an intermediate station for routing objects to a final destination.
- Automatic creation and vary on of APPN controller descriptions on token-ring or Ethernet networks. APPN dynamically determines the remote system's LAN address.
- Automatic creation and starting of remote device descriptions necessary to complete a network transmission.

10.3.1 Nodes, Control Points, and Class-of-Service

Each device on APPN is referred to as a *node*. There are basically two types of nodes:

- A *network node.* A network device running APPN and fully participating by providing intermediate-session routing, route-selection services, and distributed-directory services. These are network links between other nodes.
- An *end node* sometimes called *peripheral nodes.* An end node is a network device on the end of a network line, connected to a single network node. End nodes can also be:
    - ✔ A low-entry networking node (basically, a network device on an APPN network, but only running APPC).
    - ✔ An APPN end node (a network device on an APPN network, running APPN, but it can receive some additional automatic configuration benefits from APPN).

Although an end node is on the periphery of a network, it also can be an end node on another network.

When end nodes are attached to network nodes, the network node must be configured as a *network node server.* APPN allows you to have up to five network node servers per APPN network. They are created within the Change Network Attributes (CHGNETA) command (refer to section 10.5 Network attributes for more information). These servers provide services for the attached end nodes:

- Directory searches.
- Route calculations.
- Remote locations do not have to be configured on the end nodes; the network node servers will do that.
- The end nodes are able to inform the network server node of all their local locations. That information stays within the network server node for its use in routing transmissions.

Note that the designations of the nodes have nothing to do with the quality or type of the AS/400s. They are only configuration decisions. However, network nodes require significantly more system resources than end nodes.

When APPN is up, *control points* are established. A simple control point is the directory and route information between two nodes. Network nodes build control-point information about themselves and all attached nodes.

End node control points only contain their own information, and that comes from the control point on the attached *network server node.* Once the connection is established and this information is obtained, it becomes part of the *network topology database* that is kept on each network node (but not end nodes). Each network node always contains complete system information. It uses the information to route transmissions.

When a network link goes down, the adjacent control points reconfigure themselves and update all nodes' network topology databases (so each network node is aware that the network configuration has changed). Each network node always has a real-time network topology with which to work.

Any network node knows (from its network topology database) all the links and nodes between it and the destination node. This information is referred to as the *transmission group*. The transmission group contains:

- Communication speed.
- Security.
- Cost:
  - ✔ By connect time.
  - ✔ By the byte transmitted.
- Propagation delay (how much time will elapse between sending and receiving the transmission based on optimum conditions. This isn't always significant but it can be. For example, a transmission from San Francisco to London will have a propagation delay. If it had a choice of going via satellite or land line, the propagation delay difference between the two could be significant.

The network configurator also has some influence into the potential traffic routing through two parameters on the Change Network Attributes (CHGNETA) or Create Network Attributes (CRTNETA) command (for more information, refer to section 10.5 Network Attributes):

- The Route Addition Resistance (RAR) parameter is a number from 0 through 255 that describes how you feel about using a node for intermediate routing to other nodes. The higher the number the more resistant the network nodes will be to use that node for intermediate routing.
- Route Congestion is a parameter that allows you to set a percentage regarding a node's availability to do intermediate routing. The default is 90 percent. If a node's utilization is 90 percent or above, the network will try not to use it for intermediate routing. If it is below 90 percent, the network will use it but it will take into consideration any RAR value the customer has set.

APPN uses something called a *class-of-service* to determine the best routing (by your definition) for a transmission. The class-of-service uses the network node attributes and the transmission group (TG) characteristics together to come up with an optimum routing plan. Note that class-of-service does this for every transmission. As a result, APPN's routing is considered dynamic and therefore always optimum.

Class-of-service is created with the Create Class-Of-Service Description (CRTCOSD) command. The APPN session locates the class-of-service through the mode description specified on each session initiation. For additional information, see section 10.4.7 Create Mode Descriptions.

10.4 APPC/APPN Configuration

The user configuring for APPC or APPN must have *IOSYSCFG in his or her user profile. That's a special authority. For more information, refer to chapter 5.

Each AS/400 pair and the line between them make an APPC configuration. You can have more than one APPC configuration up at a time, but each must have a unique name. You have to configure several objects to make one APPC configuration. Here are the items and the order they must be created in:

- Location/Configuration list (for APPN only).
- Connection list (for ISDN only).
- Network interface (for ISDN or frame relay only).
- Lines:
  - ✔ SNA pass-through requires two lines (one to send and one to receive).
  - ✔ Non-SNA pass-through only requires one line.
- Controller:
  - ✔ SNA pass-through requires two controllers (one for each line).
  - ✔ Non-SNA pass-through only requires one controller.
- Device:
  - ✔ SNA pass-through requires type *SNPT.
- Mode description.

10.4.1 Creating Location/Configuration Lists (APPN only)

Location or configuration lists contain the local and remote names of all the systems APPN is to support. Not all locations need to be in a location list, but those that are have a weak spot you need to consider. Many of the parameters of the create and change commands use a default of *NETATR or network attribute. Logically enough, *NETATR takes information from the network. However, if any network attribute is changed (through the CHGNETA) after the location list is prepared, changes will not be reflected in the location list. If you use location lists and you make any changes to the network attributes, delete the location entry and re-add it.

Local and remote locations are kept on separate location lists for APPN networks. A local list contains the names of the locations defined on the local system. This sounds really complex but it isn't. Just enter the name of the local system. Figure 10-1 shows a prompted version of the Create Configuration List (CRTCFGL) command.

```
                        Create Configuration List (CRTCFGL)

 Type choices, press Enter.

 Configuration list type . . . .   __________     *APPNDIR, *APPNLCL...
 Configuration list . . . . . . .  __________     Name
 Default filter action  . . . . .  *REJECT        *ACCEPT, *REJECT
 APPN remote CFGL filter  . . . .  *ACCEPT        *ACCEPT, *NONE
 Text 'description' . . . . . . .  *BLANK

                           Additional Parameters

 APPN local location entry:       _
   Local location name  . . . . .  *PROMPT        Name, *PROMPT
   Entry 'description'  . . . . .
              + for more values _
```

Figure 10-1: Prompted version of the CRTCFGL command.

There are lots of parameters to this command but, for creating a local list, keep it simple. Enter *APPNLCL as the type of list. The list name, QAPPNLCL, is supplied by the system and is mandatory. You cannot have a location/configuration list with another name on your system. By the way, you can only have one location/configuration list on any system.

The LOCAL LOCATION NAME can be the name of your system plus the names of any other systems you would like your system to respond for. As an example, if you had two AS/400s—named PHX01 and PHX02—and PHX02 went down, you could name PHX01 and PHX02 on the real PHX01 to get PHX01 to receive messages for both systems. You can name up to 476 local names on this parameter.

Optionally, you could enter *PROMPT on this parameter. Every time APPN came up on that machine, you would have a chance to put in from 1-476 local system names. This can be a nice feature. Just keep in mind that, if you are putting in multiple local system names, you have to enter all every time APPN starts.

Give a brief description of the list on the ENTRY 'DESCRIPTION' parameter. Then enter the local system name as the APPN local location entry.

Similarly, location names remote to the local system must be defined in lists. The same command, CRTCFGL, is used but the list type must be *APPNRMT. Instead of simply entering the local system name, you must enter three things:

- Remote location name. The remote location name can be the actual name of the remote system, a generic name, or the generic *ALL. The following are valid values:
  - ✔ PHX02
  - ✔ PHX*
  - ✔ *ALL
- Network ID. The name of the network that the remote location resides on is the network identification.
- Local location name. The location name of the local AS/400. APPN links the local and remote location names to make a unique pair name.

That's about all you need for identifying remote locations. If you'll be using directory entries, you also should enter the:

- Control-point name. The name of the control point providing network functions for the remote location.
- Control-point network ID. The name of the network on which the control point resides.

If the remote location is going to provide transparent access, the password to that system must be defined on a remote location list. To do that enter the:

- Location password.
- Secure location. The secure location determines where password verification occurs. If a *YES is specified and a remote location wants to start a program on the local location, it can verify the password before starting the program. If *NO (the default) is specified, the remote location may not verify the password. The local location must verify the password.

When defining a single-session connection, you must enter the:

- Single session location. The option is *YES.
- Locally controlled location. For this local and remote pair network, is the session controlled locally? Options are *YES and *NO (with *NO being the default).
- Preestablished session. Will the session be automatically started when the node is started between the two systems? Options are *YES and *NO (with *NO being the default).
- Number of conversations. How many conversations will be allowed? Valid values are 1 through 512 (with the default being 10).

10.4.2 Creating a Connection List (ISDN Only)

The ISDN lines and controllers can refer to entries on the connection list to obtain information on managing calls sent or received across the network. First, you create the list and then you manage the entries in it. The commands to work with the list are:

- WRKCNNL — Work with Connection Lists
- CRTCNNL — Create Connection List
- CHGCNNL — Change Connection List
- DSPCNNL — Display Connection List
- DLTCNNL — Delete Connection List

The commands to work with communications list entries are:

- WRKCNNLE — Work with Connection List Entries
- ADDCNNLE — Add Connection List Entries
- CHGCNNLE — Change Connection List Entries
- RNMCNNLE — Rename Connection List Entries
- RMVCNNLE — Remove Connection List Entries

10.4.3 Creating a Network Interface Description (ISDN or Frame Relay Only)

The network interface description is an object the system will refer to when it needs information about how the AS/400 and the network should interface. The commands to work with the description are:

- WRKNWID — Work with Network Interface Description
- CRTNWIXXXX — Create Network Interface Description
- CHGNWIXXXX — Change Network Interface Description
- DSPNWID — Display Network Interface Description
- DLTNWID — Delete Network Interface Description

Some of these commands are specific to ISDN networks and some are specific to frame relay. Where the commands have *xxxx*, substitute:

- "ISDN" for ISDN.
- "FR" for frame relay.

10.4.4 Creating a Line Description

The line description will describe to the system the physical line connection and the data link protocol to be used between the AS/400 and the network. The commands to work with lines are:

- WRKLNID Work with Line Description
- CRTLINXXXX Create Line Description
- CHGLINXXXX Change Line Description

Some of these commands are particular to specific line types. Where the commands have *xxxx*, substitute:

- "DDI" for DDI.
- "ETH" for Ethernet.
- "FR" for frame relay.
- "IDLC" for IDLC.
- "SDLC" for SDLC.
- "TRN" for token ring.
- "X25" for X.25.
- "WLS" for wireless .

When you work with a line for an APPC connection, you don't have much more to do than the basic command. However, when you configure an APPN line, you can use more of the command parameters:

- Link Speed (LINKSPEED). The speed of the link. The default is *INTERFACE and it provides automatic speed setting. In most cases, just use this default. If you need to, you can specify a line speed.
- Cost Per Connect Time (COSTCNN). Cost per connect times is the relative (not the actual) cost of being connected on the line. The default *CNN bases relative cost on the type of connection. You can override this with any number from 0 through 255. The lower numbers represent lower costs.
- Cost Per Byte (COSTBYTE). Cost per byte is the relative (not the actual) cost per byte of being connected on the line. The default *CNN bases relative cost on the connection type. You can override this with any number from 0 through 255. The lower numbers represent lower costs.

- Security Used on the Line (SECURITY). Security on the line does not apply to AS/400 user identification, passwords, or object security. This parameter's possible values are:
  - ✔ *NONSECURE—No security.
  - ✔ *PKTSWTNET—Packet-switched network. Security is through packets' random routing through the network.
  - ✔ *UNDGRDCBL—Underground cable in secured conduit.
  - ✔ *SECURECND—Secured conduit; not guarded.
  - ✔ *GUARDCND—Guarded conduit; protected against physical tampering.
  - ✔ *ENCRYPTED—Data flowing on line is encrypted.
  - ✔ *MAX—Guarded conduit; protected against physical tampering and radiation tapping.
- Propagation Delay (PRPDLY). Propagation delay is the amount of time you expect a transmission to take to travel from one end of a link to another. Possible values are:
  - ✔ *MIN—Minimum delay.
  - ✔ *LAN—Less than .48 milliseconds. Specifies local area network delay.
  - ✔ *TELEPHONE—From .48 milliseconds to 49.152 milliseconds. Specifies telephone network delay.
  - ✔ *PKTSWTNET—From 49.152 milliseconds to 245.76 milliseconds. Specifies packet-switched network delay.
  - ✔ *SATELLITE—Greater than 245.76 milliseconds. Specifies satellite network delay.
  - ✔ *MAX—Maximum delay.
- User-Defined Value 1, 2, 3 (USRDFN1, USRDFN2, USRDFN3). You can specify a numeric value from 0 through 255. The default is 128. The values can be changed during operations to indicate various activities on the network.
- Automatically Create Controller (AUTOCRTCTL). Specifies whether the system is to automatically create controller descriptions when incoming calls are received. Possible values are *YES and *NO (with *NO being the default).
- Automatically Delete Controller (AUTODLTCTL). Specifies whether and for how long the APPC controller can remain idle (status VARIED ON PENDING) before the controller description is varied off and deleted. These values are the number of minutes. The default is 1440 (24 hours). However, any values from 1 to 10,000 can be used.

10.4.5 Creating a APPC/APPN Controller Description

A controller defines the network node. A lot of the controller information on a local machine is actually used more by the adjacent nodes than the one it is on.

You can start with the Work With Controller Description (WRKCTLD) command. It will take you to the Create Controller APPC (CRTCTLAPPC) command. This command, which can be used directly if you want, creates an APPC controller, and it has a parameter (APPN-CAPABLE) that allows you to turn it into an APPN controller. Figure 10-2 shows the prompted version of the WRKCTLD command.

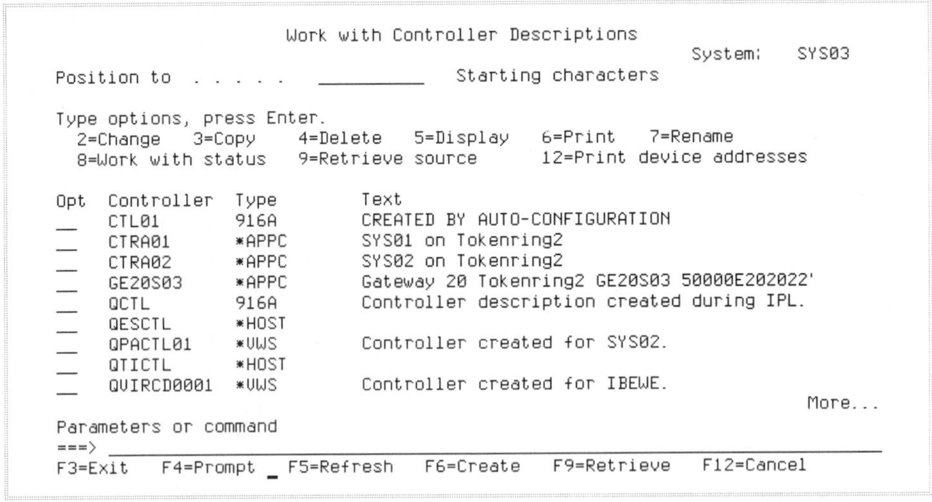

Figure 10-2: Prompted version of the WRKCTLD command.

This is the list of all the controllers on a sample system. If you press COMMAND 6, you can create a new controller description. Figure 10-3 shows the prompted version of that screen.

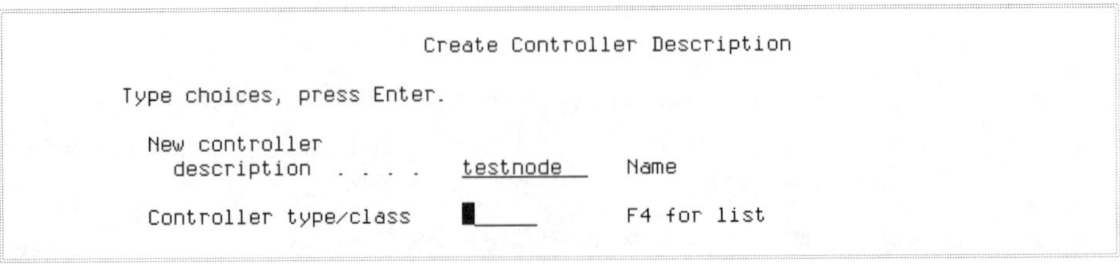

Figure 10-3: The resulting screen after pressing F6 (Create) from the WRKCTLD command.

Notice that the description starts off simply with just two parameters. Enter the controller name, in this case TESTNODE, and the type/class of the controller. If you position the cursor on this parameter and press F4, you'll get all possible values for the type/class:

- *APPC Advanced Program-To-Program Communications.
- *ASYNC Asynchronous communications.
- *BSC Binary synchronous communications.
- *FNC Finance.
- *HOST SNA host.
- *LWS Local workstation.
- *NET Network.
- *RTL Retail.
- *RWS Remote workstation.
- *TAP Tape.
- *VWS Virtual workstation.

As shown in Figure 10-3, I selected *APPC as the type of controller. When I press Enter, I get a new command, CRTCTLAPPC, with the controller name and type/class filled in, but with new, specific APPC parameters added. See Figure 10-4.

```
                    Create Ctl Desc (APPC) (CRTCTLAPPC)

Type choices, press Enter.

Controller description . . . . . > TESTNODE       Name
Link type  . . . . . . . . . . .   ______         *ANYNW, *FAX, *FR, *IDLC...
Online at IPL  . . . . . . . . .   *YES           *YES, *NO
```

Figure 10-4: Prompted version of the CRTCTLAPPC command.

If you've done this command a few times, you know you could have just invoked the command directly instead of going through WRKCTLD. This command has a couple of presentations. The first one, displayed in the Figure 10-4, requests three types of information:

- The name of the controller (already provided and it was carried over).
- The link type.
- Whether the controller will be automatically online anytime the AS/400 IPLs.

Focus now on the link type. If you put the cursor on the parameter and press F4, you'll get a list of valid link types:

- *ANYNW
- *FAX
- *FR
- *IDLC
- *ILAN
- *LAN
- *LOCAL
- *SDLC
- *TDLC
- *X25

If you are defining a controller for an ISDN link, specify either *IDLC or *X25 for the link type.

I selected the *LAN link type. When you press the Enter key, the command will expand as shown in Figure 10-5.

```
                     Create Ctl Desc (APPC) (CRTCTLAPPC)

 Type choices, press Enter.

 Controller description . . . . . > TESTNODE      Name
 Link type  . . . . . . . . . . . > *LAN          *ANYNW, *FAX, *FR, *IDLC
 Online at IPL  . . . . . . . . .   *YES          *YES, *NO
 APPN-capable . . . . . . . . . .   *YES          *YES, *NO
 Switched line list . . . . . . .   __________    Name
                + for more values   __________
 Maximum frame size . . . . . . .   *LINKTYPE     265-16393, 256, 265, 512
 Remote network identifier  . . .   *NETATR       Name, *NETATR, *NONE, *AN
 Remote control point . . . . . .   ________      Name, *ANY
 Exchange identifier  . . . . . .   ________      00000000-FFFFFFFF
 Initial connection . . . . . . .   *DIAL         *DIAL, *ANS
```

Figure 10-5: Prompted version of the CRTCTLAPPC command.

The significant parameter for this is APPN CAPABLE. The default is *YES. This is what differentiates a controller as APPC or APPN. If you leave the default and press Enter, the command will again expand as shown in Figure 10-6.

```
                    Create Ctl Desc (APPC) (CRTCTLAPPC)

Type choices, press Enter.

Controller description . . . . . > TESTNODE     Name
Link type  . . . . . . . . . . . > *LAN         *ANYNW, *FAX, *FR, *IDLC...
Online at IPL  . . . . . . . . .   *YES         *YES, *NO
APPN-capable . . . . . . . . . .   *YES         *YES, *NO
Switched line list . . . . . . .                Name
               + for more values
Maximum frame size . . . . . . .   *LINKTYPE    265-16393, 256, 265, 512...
Remote network identifier  . . .   *NETATR      Name, *NETATR, *NONE, *ANY
Remote control point . . . . . .                Name, *ANY
Exchange identifier  . . . . . .                00000000-FFFFFFFF
Initial connection . . . . . . .   *DIAL        *DIAL, *ANS
Dial initiation  . . . . . . . .   *LINKTYPE    *LINKTYPE, *IMMED, *DELAY
LAN remote adapter address . . .                000000000001-FFFFFFFFFFFF
LAN DSAP . . . . . . . . . . . .   04           04, 08, 0C, 10, 14, 18, 1C...
LAN SSAP . . . . . . . . . . . .   04           04, 08, 0C, 10, 14, 18, 1C...
APPN CP session support  . . . .   *YES         *YES, *NO
                                                                       More...
```

Figure 10-6: CRTCTLAPPC expanded for APPN information.

The last parameter in Figure 10-5, APPC CP SESSION SUPPORT, defines the node as capable of being a control point on the network. The command has now expanded to the point where it continues onto a second screen. See Figure 10-7.

```
                    Create Ctl Desc (APPC) (CRTCTLAPPC)

Type choices, press Enter.

APPN node type . . . . . . . . .   *ENDNODE     *ENDNODE, *LENNODE...
APPN/HPR capable . . . . . . . .   *YES         *YES, *NO
HPR path switching . . . . . . .   *NO          *NO, *YES
APPN transmission group number     1            1-20, *CALC
APPN minimum switched status . .   *VRYONPND    *VRYONPND, *VRYON
Autocreate device  . . . . . . .   *ALL         *ALL, *NONE
Autodelete device  . . . . . . .   1440         1-10000, *NO
User-defined 1 . . . . . . . . .   *LIND        0-255, *LIND
User-defined 2 . . . . . . . . .   *LIND        0-255, *LIND
User-defined 3 . . . . . . . . .   *LIND        0-255, *LIND
Model controller description . .   *NO          *NO, *YES
```

Figure 10-7: Second screen of the CRTCTLAPPC command.

APPN NODE TYPE is where you designate the node as an end node or a network node. For more detailed descriptions of the controller description parameters, see the IBM manual *OS/400 APPN Support V4R2*.

10.4.6 Create APPC/APPN Device Descriptions

The device description tells the networked nodes something about the logical (not the physical) connection between them. Each pair of nodes has a connection and must have a device description describing that connection.

The command, Create Device Description for APPC (CRTDEVAPPC), creates a description for an APPC device. Figure 10-8 shows a prompted version of that command.

```
                     Create Device Desc (APPC) (CRTDEVAPPC)

Type choices, press Enter.

Device description . . . . . . .    __________         Name
Remote location  . . . . . . . .    ________           Name
Online at IPL  . . . . . . . . .    *YES               *YES, *NO
Local location . . . . . . . . .    *NETATR            Name, *NETATR
Remote network identifier  . . .    *NETATR            Name, *NETATR, *NONE
Attached controller  . . . . . .    __________         Name
Mode . . . . . . . . . . . . . .    *NETATR            Name, *NETATR
               + for more values    ________
Message queue  . . . . . . . . .    QSYSOPR            Name, QSYSOPR
  Library  . . . . . . . . . . .      *LIBL            Name, *LIBL, *CURLIB
APPN-capable . . . . . . . . . .    *YES               *YES, *NO
Single session:
  Single session capable . . . .    *NO                *NO, *YES
  Number of conversations  . . .    ______             1-512
```

Figure 10-8: Prompted version of the CRTDEVAPPC command.

The parameter, Remote Location Name (RMTLOCNAME), is the name of the remote AS/400. This name can be:

- The LCLLOCNAME of the remote AS/400 (APPC only).
- A name specified in the local location list of the remote AS/400 (APPN only). For more information, refer to 10.4.1 Creating Location/Configuration Lists (APPN).
- The local location name specified on the remote AS/400's network attributes (controlled through the CHGNETA command (APPN only)).
- The local control-point name (APPN only).

The Local Location Name (LCLLOCNAME) is the name of the local AS/400. The default *NETATR tells APPC to take the local name from the network attributes. Alternatively, you can specify the local network name.

The Remote Network Identifier (RMTNETID) is the name of the remote network where the location resides. The default *NETATR tells APPC to take the name from the network attributes.

The network node servers take this information and find matches to consider a link valid. If an AS/400 is paired with several other AS/400s, there must be a device description for each pair. The network server node must detect matching remote name/remote ID and local name/local ID information on two AS/400s for the link to be recognized.

For example, SYS01 is connected to SYS02 and SYS03. Conversely, SYS02 is connected to SYS01 and SYS03 is connected to SYS01. The network server node must find a device description on SYS01 with this combination:

- SYS01 device description
  RMTLOCNAME = SYS02
  RMTNETID = SYS02s network ID
  LCLLOCNAME = SYS01
- SYS02 device description
  RMTLOCNAME = SYS01
  RMTNETID = SYS01s network ID
  LCLLOCNAME = SYS02

Only when the network server node finds this combination will it consider the connection valid.

MODE NAME (MODE) tells both ends of the network which mode to use. Unless the Single Session Location (SNGSSNLOC) is set to one, a maximum of 14 modes are allowed. If the SINGLE SESSION LOCATION is set to one, only one mode may be specified.

The USE APPN FUNCTION (APPN) specifies whether or not the device (the AS/400) will be used on an APPN network. The default is *YES but you can specify *NO.

The Single Session Location (SNGSSNLOC) command allows you to specify if the communications over the network will be limited to one session or not. Valid values are *YES (only one session will be allowed) and *NO (multiple sessions will be allowed).

For more detailed information on the other parameters, see the IBM manual *OS/400 APPN Support V4R2.*

10.4.7 Create Mode Descriptions

Mode descriptions describe the session characteristics and numbers of communications sessions that will be allowed between network nodes. When considering a mode in the device or network description, remember that a mode of the same name must exist on both local and remote AS/400s in order for a session to happen. The mode does not need to exist on an intermediate session because the communication is being routed to another network. When you have low-entry networking nodes as remote locations, their modes must exist on the network node server that services them. To help you, every AS/400 comes shipped with five predefined modes:

- BLANK. The name really is "BLANK." You can specify this name (BLANK) and APPN will look for the default mode named with eight blank characters.
- #BATCH. A mode tailored for batch communications.
- #BATCHSC. The same as #BATCH except it has security built-in for packets (*PKTSWTNET).
- #INTER. A mode tailored for interactive communications.
- #INTERSC. The same as #INTER except it has security built-in for packets (*PKTSWTNET).
- QCASERVR. A mode for use with AS/400 server functions.
- QRMTWSC. A mode tailored for use with the 5494 remote workstation controller.
- QSPWTR. A mode used for Advanced Function Printing (AFP) support.

Use one of the preceding modes. If you feel you need to create your own mode, at least display these to see how IBM has set up parameters. For a detailed description of the IBM-Supplied modes, see the IBM manual *OS/400 APPN Support V4R2*.

If you still want to create your own mode, do so with the Create Mode Description (CRTMODD) command. Figure 10-9 shows a prompted version of that command.

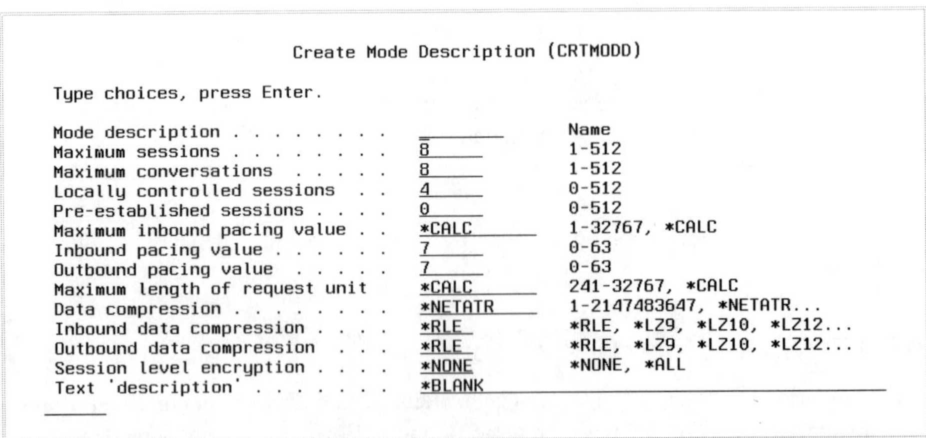

```
                    Create Mode Description (CRTMODD)

Type choices, press Enter.

Mode description . . . . . . . .   __________    Name
Maximum sessions . . . . . . . .   8             1-512
Maximum conversations  . . . . .   8             1-512
Locally controlled sessions  . .   4             0-512
Pre-established sessions . . . .   0             0-512
Maximum inbound pacing value . .   *CALC         1-32767, *CALC
Inbound pacing value . . . . . .   7             0-63
Outbound pacing value  . . . . .   7             0-63
Maximum length of request unit     *CALC         241-32767, *CALC
Data compression . . . . . . . .   *NETATR       1-2147483647, *NETATR...
Inbound data compression . . . .   *RLE          *RLE, *LZ9, *LZ10, *LZ12...
Outbound data compression  . . .   *RLE          *RLE, *LZ9, *LZ10, *LZ12...
Session level encryption . . . .   *NONE         *NONE, *ALL
Text 'description' . . . . . . .   *BLANK
```

Figure 10-9: Prompted version of the CRTMODD command (part 1 of 2).

```
                        Additional Parameters

 Class-of-service . . . . . . . .   #CONNECT      Name, #CONNECT, #BATCH...
 Authority  . . . . . . . . . . .   *LIBCRTAUT    Name, *LIBCRTAUT, *CHANGE...
```

Figure 10-9: Prompted version of the CRTMODD command (part 2 of 2).

Put the name of the mode you are creating in the Mode Description Name (MODD) parameter.

Maximum Number of Sessions (MAXSSN) specifies how many sessions can be active at one time through the mode. The maximum in this parameter is 512 and the default is 8. The value for this parameter should be equal to the number specified for the locally controlled sessions (LCLCTLSSN) parameter on the local system—plus the value specified for the remote system.

The Maximum Number of Conversations (MAXCNV) specifies how many conversations can be active at one time over this mode. The maximum is 512 and the default is 8. Conversations are temporary transmissions sent over a session while the session is active. For an APPC AS/400, the maximum total conversations for all modes cannot exceed 512.

The Locally Controlled Sessions (LCLCTLSSN) parameter specifies the minimum number of sessions this local AS/400 will establish and control. The Preestablished Sessions (PREESTSSN) parameter specifies the number of concurrent sessions that will be established automatically when the mode is started. Others can be established after the mode is started, as they are needed, so long as their number doesn't exceed the number specified in the MAXSSN parameter.

Specify the class of service of the mode in the Class of Service (COS) parameter. Possible values are:

- #CONNECT—The default.
- #BATCH.
- #INTER.
- #BATCHSC.
- #INTERSC.
- Class-of-service name.

The class-of-service is only required for APPN configurations; don't worry about it for APPC. However, if you name the class-of-service for an APPN configuration, it must already exist on the system. For more information, refer to 10.4.7.1 Create Class-of-Service Descriptions.

For more detailed information on the other parameters, refer to the IBM manual *APPN Support V4R2.*

10.4.7.1 Create Class-of-Service Descriptions

Class-of-service descriptions are used to select the nodes and groups to be included in the APPC/APPN session routes. If you have a small, two- or three-node network, don't worry too much about class of service. Just use one of the IBM-supplied descriptions. If you have a large and complex network—especially if your network is international and you must deal with multinational telephone regulations—you should analyze how you want to set up your classes of service.

Every AS/400 comes with five classes of service already configured for you by IBM. They are:

- #CONNECT—The default.
- #BATCH—A class of service for batch communications.
- #BATCHSC—The same as #BATCH except that it has a data-link security for switched packets (*PKTSWTNWK).
- #INTER—A class of service for interactive communications.
- #INTERSC—The same as #INTER except that it has data link security for switched packets (*PKTSWTNWK).

If you need to create your own classes of service, use the Create Class Of Service Description (CRTCOSD) command. With this command, you can dictate many routing rules for communicating by APPN. With these rules, APPN can save you communications dollars and maximize communications throughput.

With class of service, if you aren't using the defaults, you're probably going to want to specify all the classes of service on your networks. Through class of service, you can specify routing rules to reflect:

- Link speed.
- Cost per connect time.
- Cost per byte.
- Line performance.
- Security.

As you specify each class of service, you will indicate your preference through weighting factors. The lower the weighting factor the more desirable the factor. Each class of service has eight rows in order of weight (1 is the smallest weight and 8 is the largest). Therefore, what you specify in row 1 should be more desirable than what you specify in row 2 (which would be more desirable than what is in row 3, and so on).

When specifying link speed and security, the higher speeds should be near the bottom rows because higher is better. When specifying link costs, the higher costs should be near the higher rows because higher costs are less desirable.

You don't have to knock yourself out coming up with eight rules for every item. You can specify one or two values in the tables. However, putting those one or two in rows 1 or 2 or in rows 7 or 8 will weight the overall result when that decision table is compared to others.

Use the Create Class Of Service Description (CRTCOSD) command to create a class of service. Figure 10-10 shows a prompted version of the command.

```
                     Create Class-of-Service Desc (CRTCOSD)

 Type choices, press Enter.

 Class-of-service description . .   __________    Name
 Transmission priority  . . . . .   *MED          *LOW, *MED, *HIGH
```

```
                     Create Class-of-Service Desc (CRTCOSD)

 Type choices, press Enter.

 Row 1 for lines:
   Line row weight  . . . . . . . .   30            0-255
   Minimum link speed . . . . . . .   4M            *MIN, 1200, 2400, 4800...
   Maximum link speed . . . . . . .   *MAX          *MIN, 1200, 2400, 4800...
   Minimum cost/connect time  . . .   0             0-255
   Maximum cost/connect time  . . .   0             0-255
   Minimum cost/byte  . . . . . . .   0             0-255
   Maximum cost/byte  . . . . . . .   0             0-255
   Minimum security for line  . . .   *NONSECURE    *NONSECURE, *PKTSWTNET...
   Maximum security for line  . . .   *MAX          *NONSECURE, *PKTSWTNET...
   Minimum propagation delay  . . .   *MIN          *MIN, *LAN, *TELEPHONE...
   Maximum propagation delay  . . .   *LAN          *MIN, *LAN, *TELEPHONE...
   Minimum user-defined 1 . . . . .   0             0-255
   Maximum user-defined 1 . . . . .   255           0-255
   Minimum user-defined 2 . . . . .   0             0-255
```

Figure 10-10: Prompted version of the CRTCOSD command (parts 1 and 2 of 5).

```
                Create Class-of-Service Desc (CRTCOSD)

Type choices, press Enter.

  Maximum user-defined 2 . . . .   255          0-255
  Minimum user-defined 3 . . . .   0            0-255
  Maximum user-defined 3 . . . .   255          0-255
Row 1 for nodes:
  Node row weight  . . . . . . .   5            0-255
  Min route addition resistance    0            0-255
  Max route addition resistance    31           0-255
  Minimum congestion for node  .   *LOW         *LOW, *HIGH
  Maximum congestion for node  .   *LOW         *LOW, *HIGH
```

```
                Create Class-of-Service Desc (CRTCOSD)

Type choices, press Enter.

Row 8 for lines:
  Line row weight  . . . . . . .   240          0-255
  Minimum link speed . . . . . .   *MIN         *MIN, 1200, 2400, 4800...
  Maximum link speed . . . . . .   *MAX         *MIN, 1200, 2400, 4800...
  Minimum cost/connect time  . .   0            0-255
  Maximum cost/connect time  . .   255          0-255
  Minimum cost/byte  . . . . . .   0            0-255
  Maximum cost/byte  . . . . . .   255          0-255
  Minimum security for line  . .   *NONSECURE   *NONSECURE, *PKTSWTNET...
  Maximum security for line  . .   *MAX         *NONSECURE, *PKTSWTNET...
  Minimum propagation delay  . .   *MIN         *MIN, *LAN, *TELEPHONE...
  Maximum propagation delay  . .   *MAX         *MIN, *LAN, *TELEPHONE...
  Minimum user-defined 1 . . . .   0            0-255
  Maximum user-defined 1 . . . .   255          0-255
  Minimum user-defined 2 . . . .   0            0-255
```

```
                Create Class-of-Service Desc (CRTCOSD)

Type choices, press Enter.

  Maximum user-defined 2 . . . .   255          0-255
  Minimum user-defined 3 . . . .   0            0-255
  Maximum user-defined 3 . . . .   255          0-255
Row 8 for nodes:
  Node row weight  . . . . . . .   150          0-255
  Min route addition resistance    0            0-255
  Max route addition resistance    255          0-255
  Minimum congestion for node  .   *LOW         *LOW, *HIGH
  Maximum congestion for node  .   *HIGH        *HIGH, *LOW
Text 'description' . . . . . . .   *BLANK

                      Additional Parameters

Authority  . . . . . . . . . . .   *LIBCRTAUT   Name, *LIBCRTAUT, *CHANGE...
```

Figure 10-10: Prompted version of the CRTCOSD command (parts 3 through 5).

Name your class of service on the Class-Of-Service Description Name (COSD) parameter. On the Transmission Priority (TMSPY) parameter, specify the priority any transmission under this class of service will have. Possible values are:

- *LOW.
- *MED—The default.
- *HIGH.

Things get interesting on the Row N for Lines (ROW1LINE through ROW8LINE) parameters. You don't see the table you're building. Instead, you only use these parameters to enter data into the table. When you put in values for multiple rows, you must specify them in ascending sequence: row 1 first, row 8 last. Most rows have minimum and maximum values. When they do have values, the minimum value you enter cannot be greater than the maximum value. Additionally, the maximum values cannot be less than the minimum value.

10.5 Network Attributes

AS/400s come with IBM-supplied values for AS/400 network attributes. Most of the time these defaults are adequate, but you ought to know what they are. Take a look at them with the Display Network Attributes (DSPNETA) command.

If you feel you need to make a change in any of them, use the Change Network Attributes (CHGNETA) command. Unfortunately, you can't both display and change from the same command. The CHGNETA command just shows *SAME for all the network attributes (hiding the current values). Therefore, you must use DSPNETA to get an idea of what you're changing.

New with Version 3 is the base level of High-Performance Routing (HPR). This is an enhancement to APPN to improve data routing performance and reliability over high-speed links such as (but not limited to) Opticonnect/400.

New with Version 4 is the HPR Tower RTP (rapid transport protocol) function. This is another speed enhancement. For a node to support HPR Tower RTP, at least one other node must have the same RTP support.

HPR takes intermediate node traffic switching down below the MI layer. Beyond that, it uses its own routing algorithms and can accomplish the same switching with less storage and processing requirements than traditional APPN.

Controlling network attributes is something you do with both APPC and APPN networks. There are only four parameters you can change on APPC-only networks:

- Local network ID (LCLNETID).
- Local control-point name (LCLCPNAME).
- Default local location name (LCLLOCNAME).
- Default mode name (DFTMODE).

On APPN networks, you can also use the CHGNETA command to change:

- Local Network ID (LCLNETID). IBM supplies APPN for this value, but you should change it to a network ID of your own. Later, if you end up with a large APPN network, management and configuration will be easier. It's a good idea to create a name here that is unique in the world and not just unique to the organization. IBM maintains a registry of such names. Connect your IBM branch about how to contact IBM's SNA Network Registry.

- LOCAL CONTROL-POINT NAME. IBM supplies S*nnnnnnn* where *nnnnnnn* is the serial number of your machine. You can override this value but its not necessary. Make note of this name. When you later configure the connected AS/400's (the remote one's) controller description, you must enter this name as the remote control-point name (RMTCPNAME).

- DEFAULT LOCAL LOCATION NAME. IBM supplies S*nnnnnnn* where *nnnnnnn* is the serial number of your machine. This is adequate; just leave it intact.

- DEFAULT MODE. The IBM default is a mode called BLANK. This mode is also supplied by IBM. If you want to specify your own default mode, you must have defined it already with the Create Mode (CRTMOD) command.

- APPN NODE TYPE. The APPN node specifies whether the local system (the one you're working on) is an end node (*ENDNODE) or a network node (*NETNODE). This must agree with the APPN NODE TYPE parameter of the CRTCTLAPPC command you use to create the APPC/APPN controller.

- MAXIMUM NUMBER OF INTERMEDIATE SESSIONS ALLOWED. Only used for APPN network nodes, intermediate sessions determine the congestion level for your node. Intermediate sessions are APPN sessions that have started to receive or resend network traffic not addressed to the local AS/400. The valid values for this parameter are 0-9999. The IBM-supplied default is 200. When the number of intermediate sessions reaches 90 percent of the number in this parameter, APPN considers the node congested and starts routing traffic around it until its number of intermediate sessions falls below 80 percent of this value.

- Route Addition Resistance (RAR). Only used for APPN network nodes, a RAR is a relative number, between 0 and 255, indicating how desirable the node is as a intermediate traffic handler. The default from IBM is 128. Increase the number on a node and it becomes less desirable. Decrease the number on a node and it is more desirable.

- NETWORK NODE SERVICE PROVIDER LIST. Only used for end nodes, the list contains the names of up to five network node servers. Each name is a combination network ID and control-point name of each network node server. IBM supplies *LCLNETID and *ANY. These generic values give the most flexibility and, unless you're really into control, these should suffice.

- Allow HPR Transport Tower Support (ALWHPRTWR) specifies the network attribute that allows the use of HPR transport tower support for APPN session traffic. Possible values are *YES or *NO.

- HPR Path Switch Timers (HPRPTHTMR) specifies the amount of time in minutes to allow for a path switch attempt of an RTP connection. Four categories of priorities can be specified to control the time allowed:

  - ✔ Element 1: Network Priority. Possible values are:

    - ➢ TRANSMISSION PRIORITY. Default value of 1 minute.

    - ➢ *NONE. No path switch is allowed.

    - ➢ NETWORK-PRIORITY. Specify the amount of minutes for the system to attempt to switch paths in an RTP connection that has network transmission priority. Valid values range from 1 through 10,000.

  - ✔ Element 2: High Priority. Possible values are:

    - ➢ TRANSMISSION PRIORITY. Default value of 2 minutes.

    - ➢ *NONE. No path switch is allowed.

    - ➢ HIGH-PRIORITY. Specify the amount of minutes for the system to attempt to switch paths in an RTP connection that has high priority. Valid values range from 1 through 10,000.

  - ✔ Element 3: Medium Priority. Possible values are:

    - ➢ *NONE. No path switch is allowed.

    - ➢ MEDIUM-PRIORITY: Specify the amount of minutes for the system to attempt to switch paths in an RTP connection that has medium priority. Valid values range from 1 through 10,000.

- ✔ Element 4: Low Priority. Possible values are:
  - ➢ *NONE. No path switch is allowed.
  - ➢ LOW-PRIORITY: Specify the amount of minutes for the system to attempt to switch paths in an RTP connection that has low priority. Valid values range from 1 through 10,000.

There are a couple considerations before changing any APPN values.

- ◆ Any APPN controllers (which are controller descriptions with APPN(*YES)) must be varied off before making changes.
- ◆ The values for parameters LOCAL NETWORK ID, LOCAL CONTROL-POINT NAME, and DEFAULT LOCAL LOCATION NAME cannot be changed to any values that cause a combined name similar to one used on a location list for any remote AS/400.

10.6 CL Commands for Communications

There are lots of CL commands for controlling communications, but CL's construction makes them easy to remember:

- ◆ Lines:
  - ✔ Can be created or changed with the CRT or CHG prefix attached to the noun LIN (CHGLIN..., CRTLIN...).
  - ✔ Both commands must have a suffix of one of the following:
    - ➢ DDI (DDI)
    - ➢ ETH (Ethernet)
    - ➢ FR (Frame Relay)
    - ➢ IDLC (IDLC)
    - ➢ NET (Network)
    - ➢ SDLC (SDLC)
    - ➢ TDLC (TDLC)
    - ➢ TRN (Token-ring Network)
    - ➢ X25 (X.25)

- Controllers:
  - ✔ Can be created or changed with the CRT or CHG prefix attached to the noun CTL (CHGCTL..., CRTCTL...).
  - ✔ Both commands must have a suffix of one of the following:
    - ➢ APPC (for APPC or APPN)
    - ➢ HOST
- Device descriptions:
- Can be created or changed with the CRT or CHG prefix attached to the noun DEV (CHGDEV..., CRTDEV...)
  - ✔ Both commands must have a suffix of one of the following:
    - ➢ DDI (DDI)
    - ➢ ETH (Ethernet)
    - ➢ FR (Frame Relay)
    - ➢ IDLC (IDLC)
    - ➢ NET (Network).
    - ➢ SDLC (SDLC)
    - ➢ TDLC (TDLC)
    - ➢ TRN (Token-ring Network)
    - ➢ X25 (X.25)
- Mode descriptions:
  - ✔ Can be created or changed with the CRT or CHG prefix attached to the noun MOD (CHGMOD, CRTMODD).
- Class-of-service (COS) descriptions:
  - ✔ Can be created or changed with the CRT or CHG prefix attached to the abbreviation COS (CHGCOSD, CRTCOSD).

10.7 Using APPC/APPN

After all that configuration effort, using the APPC/APPN network is simple. You will:

- Vary the configuration on and off.
- Control modes.

For those unfamiliar with IBM terminology, read "vary" as "turn." To vary a device on is to turn the device on. While it's already on as far as power goes, the vary command turns it on logically or makes it start doing its thing.

The Vary Configuration (VRYCFG) command works on all those communications devices that go with a network. Figure 10-11 has a prompted version of the command.

```
                    Vary Configuration (VRYCFG)

Type choices, press Enter.

Configuration object . . . . . .   __________    Name
               + for more values   __________
Type . . . . . . . . . . . . . .   *NWI____      *NWS, *NWI, *LIN, *CTL...
Status . . . . . . . . . . . . .   *ON_______    *ON, *OFF, *RESET...
```

Figure 10-11: Prompted version of the VRYCFG command. Used to start/stop APPC and APPN networks.

The STATUS (STATUS) parameter actually turns the network on and off. The values *YES and *NO signify an on or off operation.

Specify the name of the object you are varying with the CFGOBJ parameter.

Specify the type of object that is being varied on or off on the CFGTYPE parameter. The five possible values for the CFGTYPE parameter are:

- *NWS (network server).
- *NWI (network interface).
- *LIN (line).
- *CTL (controller).
- *DEV (device).

There are a lot of objects that make up an APPC/APPN network. You don't have to vary them all on or off individually. You can specify RANGE(*NET) to automatically vary on all objects downstream from the one description you specified. When starting the network, just do this specifying *NWS or *NWI for the CFGTYPE parameter and all devices connected to the CFGOBJ will be varied on or off together.

After the APPC/APPN configuration is varied on, a mode must be started. Modes are specified on the device descriptions (refer to section 10.4.6 Create Device Descriptions and section 10.4.7 Create Mode Descriptions). There can be many modes for one configuration. Once the mode is started, individual sessions can be established between locations. Modes get started in four ways:

- For device descriptions automatically created by APPN, a mode is started when a request to start a session is received.
- For device descriptions created with APPN(*YES), a mode is started when a request to start a session is received.
- For device descriptions manually created with APPN(*NO), a mode is started when the device description is varied on.
- You can start a mode with the Start Mode (STRMOD) command.

Once a mode is started (with the command or automatically), you can end it with the End Mode (ENDMOD) command. You can check on any mode with the Display Mode Status (DSPMODSTS) command.

Occasionally, sessions will fail to be established. You can look at the number of sessions on a mode as well as its maximum number of sessions value. You can use the Change Sessions Maximum (CHGSSNMAX) command to increase the number of sessions that may be active over an individual mode.

10.8 Using APPC Functions

Section 10.2.2 introduced 10 of the more significant interconnectivity functions you get with APPC. Remember, APPN is an extension of APPC. Although these functions are part of APPC, APPN networks share them as well. The following sections provide a more in-depth discussion of each.

10.8.1 Distributed Data Management

Distributed data management (DDM) is a way for a program or user on one system to access database files on another system. Through DDM, you can also submit a command from a local machine to do something to a file on a remote machine.

DDM is for accessing the file's records to read, add, change, and delete them. Although it can be used to move files from one system to another, you are better off using SNADS to move files. See section 10.8.3, SNA Distribution Services. The five commands to work with DDM files are:

- WRKDDMF — Work with DDM Files (an easy way to get to the other DDM commands).
- CRTDDMF — Create DDM File.
- CHGDDMF — Change DDM File.
- DSPDDMF — Display DDM File.
- DLTF — Delete DDM File.

The prompted versions of the commands (except DLTF) are similar. I will go through the CRTDDMF to explain the parameters. Figure 10-12 shows the prompted version:

```
                         Create DDM File (CRTDDMF)

 Type choices, press Enter.

 DDM file . . . . . . . . . . . .   _________    Name
   Library  . . . . . . . . . . .     *CURLIB    Name, *CURLIB
 Remote file:
   File . . . . . . . . . . . . .   _________    Name, *NONSTD
     Library  . . . . . . . . . .   _________    Name, *LIBL, *CURLIB
   Nonstandard file 'name'  . . .   ____________________________________
 ________________________________________________________________________
 ________________________________________________________________________
 ____________________________________________________

 Remote location  . . . . . . . .   _________    Name
 Text 'description' . . . . . . .   *BLANK
```

```
                         Create DDM File (CRTDDMF)

 Type choices, press Enter.


                           Additional Parameters

 Device:
   APPC device description  . . .   *LOC         Name, *LOC
 Local location . . . . . . . . .   *LOC         Name, *LOC, *NETATR
 Mode . . . . . . . . . . . . . .   *NETATR      Name, *NETATR
 Remote network identifier  . . .   *LOC         Name, *LOC, *NETATR, *NONE
 Access method:
   Remote file attribute  . . . .   *RMTFILE     *RMTFILE, *COMBINED...
   Local access method  . . . . .   _________    *BOTH, *RANDOM, *SEQUENTIAL
 Share open data path . . . . . .   *NO          *NO, *YES
 Protected conversation . . . . .   *NO          *NO, *YES
 Record format level check  . . .   *RMTFILE     *RMTFILE, *NO
 Authority  . . . . . . . . . . .   *LIBCRTAUT   Name, *LIBCRTAUT, *ALL...
 Replace file . . . . . . . . . .   *YES         *YES, *NO
                                                                   Bottom
```

Figure 10-12: Prompted version of the CRTDDM command (parts 1 and 2).

It is a common but not necessary practice to create a special library on the source computer for DDM files. If you do this, name the library something like DDMLIB.

The DDM FILE parameter is the local name you will use to refer to the file. That doesn't have to be the real name of the file. The REMOTE FILE parameter is the library and name of the file on the remote system. If you just want to access an AS/400 file, enter its file and library name on this parameter. If you want to access an S/38 or S/36 file or just one member of an AS/400 file, enter *NONSTD as the remote file name and the name of the remote file (enclosed in single apostrophes) on the NONSTANDARD FILE "NAME" parameter.

For example, the System/38's naming convention would require a library and file name in this form: 'MASTFILE.LIBR-NAME'.

The REMOTE LOCATION NAME parameter is the name of the remote system on which the file resides.

The additional parameter screen has a couple of interesting items in it. The device, location, and mode are APPC related and are usually left to *LOC (or the values used when APPC is set up). The RECORD FORMAT LEVEL CHECK parameter allows you to continue level checking the remote file. A value of *NO will disable level checking. You can use this to give yourself more latitude on level checks when accessing DDM files.

DDM files are extremely simple. Once you've created a DDM file, you can start using it right away. Think of DDM files as files on your system. Not only are they easily accessible by application programs, you can run almost any database file-related CL command against them, and you can use them as outfiles to CL commands.

The command to submit other commands to a remote system is the Submit Remote Command (SBMRMTCMD). It is similar to the Submit Job (SBMJOB) command in that it contains a command embedded within itself. This command can be an OS/400 command, your own command, or a CALL to start a program running.

For more information, refer to the IBM manual *Distributed Data Management V4R1.*

10.8.2 OptiConnect/400

OptiConnect/400 is a high-speed, high-availability optical bus between two or more AS/400s. It is a combination of hardware (referred to as OptiConnect), software support from APPC (referred to as OptiConnect/400), and APIs.

The addition of special APIs for the product is nice because not only is the optical bus extremely fast, savvy developers and business partners can write programs to access records or move entire files by using them. And APIs run under the MI level, yielding even faster throughput.

OptiConnect/400 is only currently available for high-end AS/400s. OptiConnect does not replace DDM (refer to section above) or SNADS (refer to 10.8.3 SNA Distribution Services), it enhances their performance. It also provides a fast path for remote backup and recovery and remote journaling.

We've been talking about two systems as local and remote. In OptiConnect/400 parlance, these become *hub* and *satellite*. An OptiConnect network can consist of one hub and up to 13 satellites.

OptiConnect comes with its own library (QSOC), subsystem description (QSOC), "pre-startable" management job, and job description. The customer doesn't have to create any of this.

To start OptiConnect, use the Start Subsystem (STRSBS) command:

```
STRSBS QSOC/QSOC
```

To end OptiConnect, use the End Subsystem (ENDSBS) command:

```
ENDSBS QSOC/QSOC *IMMED
```

OptiConnect comes with its own commands:

- Verify Optical Connection (VFYOPTCNN) verifies the optical connection. The results of this verify end up in a job log. Run the command from any command line, and then use the Display Job Log (DSPJOBLOG) when it completes.
- Work with Opticonnect Activity (WRKOPCACT) checks the OptiConnect activity on the systems (the hub and all satellites).

Don't forget that these commands come with the product; they're found in the QSOC LIBRARY.

OptiConnect/400 can be configured in two ways:

- For standard configuration, just specify the keyword, QYCTSOC on the DEVICE DESCRIPTION parameter on the DDM file when it is created (CRTDDM) or changed (CHGDDM). Refer to 10.8.1 Distributed Data Management. This method works fine except it doesn't support two-phase commit and SNADS won't work this way.
- Using an *OPC controller and device requires a special controller and the device must be created for OptiConnect/400. It does support two-phase commit and SNADS can be brought up over OptiConnect.

To create the *OPC controller, use the same Create Controller (CRTCTLAPPC) previously discussed. Figure 10-13 contains a prompted example of that command.

```
                    Create Ctl Desc (APPC) (CRTCTLAPPC)

Type choices, press Enter.

Controller description . . . . . > OPTICTL       Name
Link type  . . . . . . . . . . . > *OPC          *ANYNW, *FAX, *FR, *IDLC...
Remote System Name . . . . . . .   rmtsys        Character value
Data link role . . . . . . . . .   *NEG          *NEG, *PRI, *SEC
```

Figure 10-13: Example of CRTCTLAPPC for an OptiConnect controller.

Create a controller on each system, the hub, and all satellites. The DATA LINK ROLE parameter must be *PRI (primary) for the hub and *SEC (secondary) for the satellites.

The DSAP value can be 04, 08, 0C, 10, 14, 78, or 7C, but they must be the same on paired systems' controllers.

Next, create devices on both systems. Use the Create Device Description (CRTDEVD) command. A sample is shown in Figure 10-14.

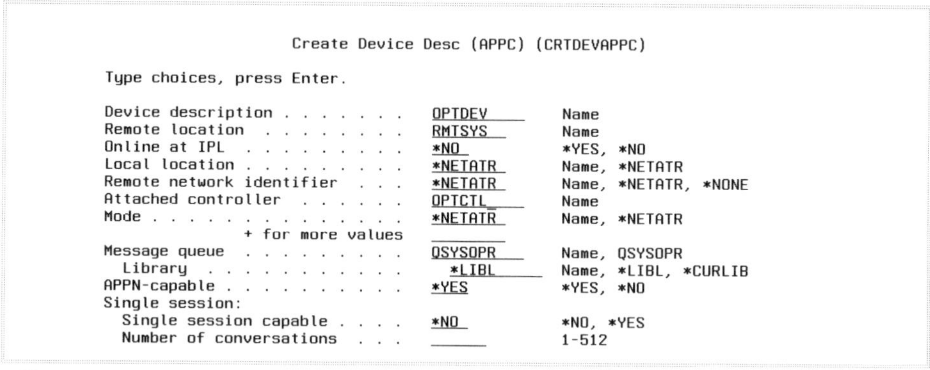

```
                    Create Device Desc (APPC) (CRTDEVAPPC)

Type choices, press Enter.

Device description . . . . . . .   OPTDEV        Name
Remote location  . . . . . . . .   RMTSYS        Name
Online at IPL  . . . . . . . . .   *NO           *YES, *NO
Local location . . . . . . . . .   *NETATR       Name, *NETATR
Remote network identifier  . . .   *NETATR       Name, *NETATR, *NONE
Attached controller  . . . . . .   OPTCTL        Name
Mode . . . . . . . . . . . . . .   *NETATR       Name, *NETATR
               + for more values
Message queue  . . . . . . . . .   QSYSOPR       Name, QSYSOPR
  Library  . . . . . . . . . . .     *LIBL       Name, *LIBL, *CURLIB
APPN-capable . . . . . . . . . .   *YES          *YES, *NO
Single session:
  Single session capable . . . .   *NO           *NO, *YES
  Number of conversations  . . .                 1-512
```

Figure 10-14: An example of an OptiConnect device created with the CRTDEVD command.

Note that both the APPN and ONLINE AT IPL parameters must be set to NO. After the controller and device are created on both systems, start OptiConnect by varying on the controller and specifying RANGE(*NET). Here's an example:

```
VRYCFG CFGOBJ(<controller name>) CFGTYPE(*CTL) STATUS(*ON)
```

For more information, refer to the IBM manual *OptiConnect for OS/400.*

10.8.3 SNA Distribution Services

Systems Network Architecture Distribution Services (SNADS) is a method to distribute objects to other systems. It can distribute documents, files, input streams, and messages. Along with distribution (sending and receiving objects), SNADS also performs the routing of those objects. The objects to be distributed can be done so immediately or held until a later time. Think of SNADS as an application program that runs on both the local and remote AS/400s that are connected with APPC or APPN.

The SNADS program features are dependent on the APPC device's description. In addition, you need three system objects on each system to make SNADS work. Fortunately, every AS/400 comes loaded with one of each of these objects, and they are all named QSNADS:

- QSNADS subsystem. The subsystem comes with an autostart job entry of QZDSTART. For more information on autostart jobs, see chapter 3, Configure Your System.
- QSNADS job queue.
- QSNADS user ID.

Along with the three system objects, you'll need three SNADS objects:

- System Distribution Directory:
  - ✔ User ID/Address. The user identification and address are used as a pair to create a unique name. The address is the name of the remote system. This combined pair will make a match on the System Distribution Directory of the remote system.
  - ✔ System Name/Group. The system name is the name of the remote system. The system name and group are used as a pair to create a unique name. Group is optional and can be left off. This pair is used to make a match on the System Distribution Routing Table.

- System Distribution Routing Table:
  - ✔ System Name/Group. The system name is the name of the remote system. The system name and group are used as a pair to create a unique name. Group is optional and can be left off. This pair is used to make a match on the System Distribution Queue.
- System Distribution Queue. The following four items are used together to locate an APPC device configuration:
  - ✔ Remote location name.
  - ✔ Mode.
  - ✔ Remote network ID.
  - ✔ Local location name. Note: this is the first time in these three items where the local system is specified.

The SYSTEM DISTRIBUTION DIRECTORY must be in place both on the local and remote AS/400s. The requesting user's identification and address is sent with the objects being transmitted and the remote machine uses that to find a match in its own system distribution directory. From that match, it assigns a local (to it) user ID. That user ID is a valid user on the remote system who will receive the object.

Note that, if two machines can both send and receive each other's objects, each directory must contain two entries for each user ID:

1. User ID/local system name.
2. User ID/remote system name.

One entry will be used when the machine is sending and the other when it is receiving.

The remote location name of the SYSTEM DISTRIBUTION QUEUE is used to find a matching APPC DEVICE DESCRIPTION on the local AS/400. That, in turn, is used by APPC to find the correct remote AS/400. Therefore, the APPC device description must exist on both the local and remote systems.

When a SNADS application receives an object, it doesn't presume that object is for its AS/400. SNADS first tries to match the object's destination user ID/address to one in its own system distribution directory. If the address is for another AS/400 it is communicating with, SNADS merely forwards the object on. If it finds a match, and the local user ID has a local address, it completes the transaction by receiving the object for the user. The CLs to work with these SNADS items are:

- System Distribution Directory:
  - ✔ WRKDIR—Work with directory.
- System Distribution Routing Table:
  - ✔ ADDDSTRTE—Adds an entry.
  - ✔ CHGDSTRTE—Changes an entry.
  - ✔ RMVDSTRTE—Removes an entry.
- System Distribution Queue:
  - ✔ ADDDSTQ—Adds an entry.
  - ✔ CHGDSTQ—Changes an entry.
  - ✔ HLDDSTQ—Holds the distribution queue.
  - ✔ INZDSTQ—Initializes the distribution queue, optionally deleting entries.
  - ✔ RLSDSTQ—Releases the distribution queue.
  - ✔ RMVDSTQ—Removes an entry.
  - ✔ SNDDSTQ—Sends an entry.
  - ✔ WRKDSTQ—Work with distribution queues or entries. Allows you to check the status of distribution.
- All items:
  - ✔ CFGDSTSRV—Adds, changes, removes, and displays distribution queue or routing-table entries. This command has one parameter, OPTION, that controls its navigation. Possible values are:
    - ➢ *SELECT causes a menu to display.
    - ➢ 1—Bypass the menu and work on distribution queues.
    - ➢ 2—Bypass the menu and work on the routing table.
    - ➢ 3—Bypass the menu and work on the secondary system name table.
  - ✔ DSPDSTSRV—Displays the distribution queues and routing tables.

SNADS is basically an application of several programs. Four of these are called Router, Sender, Receiver, and Arriver.

- Router. The program name for router is QROUTR. Only one router program is used in a SNADS subsystem. Router should be an autostart job so it will start when the subsystem starts. If the router fails, SNADS communication is impossible and error CPC8803 is sent to the operator. The router performs three tasks:
  - ✔ Delivers objects.
  - ✔ Forwards objects to other users on other systems.
  - ✔ Redirects objects to users who may have once been on the local system but who have moved.
- Sender. This program sends objects from the distribution queue to the remote system. It can send objects immediately or schedule them for later, it recognizes objects' delivery priorities, and it will attempt to re-try a delivery that failed for any reason. While the program name varies, it assumes the RMTLOCNAME specified on the distribution queue. Sender jobs are active as long as the SNADS subsystem is active. If you suspect problems, check it with the Work with Distribution Queues (WRKDSTQ) command.
- Receiver. This program receives incoming objects. The program name is determined by the device you use to connect to the remote system. This job starts as soon as you start the APPC/APPN conversation and stays up until you end that conversation or an error occurs.
- Arriver. This program delivers mail intended for users on the local system.

10.8.3.1 Setting Up SNADS

Here are the steps for bringing up SNADS on your system:

- Have APPC or APPN active.
- Make sure the IBM-supplied subsystem, QCMN, is active. It has one communications entry and SNADS will use it.
- Start the QSNADS subsystem. This is another supplied by IBM.
- If you're going to use SNADS to distribute mail, start the mail server framework with the STRMSF command.

- With the Configure Distribution Services (CFGDSTSRV) command:
  - ✔ Define the distribution queue(s). Use parameter OPTION(1). A distribution queue that you name must exist. If one does not, add one with the Add Distribution Queue (ADDDSTQ) command.
  - ✔ Define the routing table. Use parameter OPTION(2). A routing table that you name must exist. If one does not exist, add one with the Add Distribution Routing Entry (ADDDSTRTE) command.
- With the Work With Directory (WRKDIR) command, enroll network users in the system distribution directory.
- With the Work With Distribution Lists (WRKDSTL) command, set up distribution lists.
- Save the SNADS configuration. Saving the configuration now will make it easy to restore later.

When working with your configuration directory, you can be more flexible with user IDs by specifying *ANY. Any transmission bound for that AS/400 will be received and routed. You can combine *ANY with legitimate user IDs. Include it at the bottom of the distribution directory for incoming objects or mail for anyone (such as visitors from other locations) not on the list. For more information, refer to the IBM manual *SNA Distribution Services V4R1.*

10.8.3.2 Routing SNADS over OptiConnect

Refer to sections 10.8.2 OptiConnect/400 and to section 10.8.3.1 Setting up SNADS. To get SNADS to run over OptiConnect, configure the OptiConnect/400 controller and device and configure SNADS. Then you must:

- Add a Directory Entry (ADDDIRE):

```
ADDDIRE  USRID(<address of remote system>/*ANY)  +
         USRD(description) +
         SYSNAME(<name of remote system>)
```

- Add a Distribution Queue (ADDDSTQ):

```
ADDDSTQ DSTQ(<name of queue>) +
  RMTLOCNAME(<name-must be same name from APPC dev desc>) +
  DSTQTYPE(*SNADS) +
  MODE(*NETATR)  +
  RMTNETID(*NONE) +
  LCLLOCNAME(<name-must be same name from APPC dev desc>)
```

◆ Add a Distribution Routing Entry (ADDDSTRTE):

```
ADDDSTRTE SYSNAME(<name of system>) +
          FAST(<fast data queue name>) +
          STATUS(<status data queue name>) +
          DATAHIGH(<datahigh data queue name>) +
          DATALOW(<datalow data queue name>)
```

10.8.4 Display Station Pass-Through

Display station pass-through is a method of signing onto a remote AS/400 through a workstation connected to a local AS/400. Though this sounds like access to multiple AS/400s via a network, it really isn't. In this case, the workstation itself has no direct connection to the remote AS/400. Nevertheless, the two AS/400s are connected. To make the pass-through happen, the user must be signed on to the local AS/400 at the time.

Display station pass-through gets really interesting when you have an APPN network with lots of AS/400s with routing entries. With pass-through, you can sign onto any remote AS/400 from your local AS/400. Depending on the number of sessions allowed at one time on your workstation, you can even pass through to many remote AS/400s at one time.

Remember one important capacity point with display station pass-through: Every pass-through takes up one session.

Start the display station pass-through function with the Start Pass-Through (STRPASTHR) command. Figure 10-15 shows the prompted form.

```
                      Start Pass-Through (STRPASTHR)

Type choices, press Enter.

Remote location . . . . . . . .   ________      Name, *CNNDEV
APPC device . . . . . . . . . .   *LOC______    Name, *LOC
             + for more values    __________
Virtual controller . . . . . . .  *NONE_____    Name, *NONE
Virtual display device . . . . .  *NONE_____    Name, *NONE
             + for more values    __________
Mode . . . . . . . . . . . . . .  *NETATR__     Name, *NETATR
Local location . . . . . . . . .  *LOC_____     Name, *LOC, *NETATR
Remote network identifier . . .   *LOC_____     Name, *LOC, *NETATR, *NONE
System request program . . . . .  *SRQMNU___    Name, *SRQMNU
  Library . . . . . . . . . . .     __________  Name, *LIBL, *CURLIB

                       Additional Parameters

User profile . . . . . . . . . .  *NONE_____    Name, *NONE, *CURRENT
User password . . . . . . . . .   *NONE_____    Name, *NONE
```

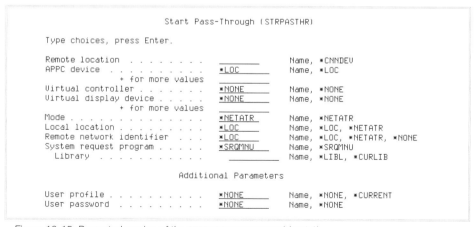

Figure 10-15: Prompted version of the STRPASTHR command (part 1).

```
                    Start Pass-Through (STRPASTHR)

Type choices, press Enter.

Initial program to call . . . .   *RMTUSRPRF     Name, *RMTUSRPRF, *NONE
Initial menu . . . . . . . . . .   *RMTUSRPRF     Name, *RMTUSRPRF, *SIGNOFF
Current library . . . . . . . .   *RMTUSRPRF     Name, *RMTUSRPRF
Display option . . . . . . . . .   *YES           Character value, *YES, *NO
```

Figure 10-15: Prompted version of the STRPASTHR command (part 2).

Most of the time, you just need to specify the remote AS/400 name on the RMTLOCNAME parameter. This will suffice in every case unless you're running APPN and supporting multiple APPN networks. In that case, you also need to specify the network ID on the remote network identifier (RMTNETID) parameter.

What constitutes a system name can be confusing. In this case, it is the local name of the remote system. As such, the system name can be one of these three choices:

- As defined on the remote system's APPN configuration list (as a local location).
- The local location name of the remote system.
- Local control point name (APPN only).

If you're not certain about the system name, use one of the following commands at the remote system to determine what location names are valid:

- Work with Configuration List (WRKCFGL).
- Display Network Attributes (DSPNETA).
- Display APPN Information (DSPAPPNINF).

Most of the time, you'll just use the remote system's name and your own user ID/password. The next thing you'll see is a logon menu from the remote system. Sign on and continue as if it were your primary machine. If you want to go back to the other AS/400, you must issue the Transfer Pass-Through (TRFPASTHR) command or use one of these command keys:

- While on the target AS/400:
  - ✔ System Request, option 10.
  - ✔ System Request, option 13.
  - ✔ System Request, option 14.

- While on the source AS/400:
  - ✔ System Request menu, F3.
  - ✔ System Request, option 15.

When you're through, terminate the session with the End Pass-Through (ENDPASTHR) command.

10.8.4.1 Configuring Display Station Pass-Through

The controller and device configurations you did for APPC/APPN are enough for display station pass-through. But there two areas you should think about:

- Whether to have the remote system configure its controller automatically or configure it manually.
- Whether to allow remote sign-on capability.

10.8.4.2 Automatic or Manual Configuration

Although the remote system has its own physical devices and controllers for its communications, it needs a logical configuration in order to support communication. The remote system can be set to configure devices automatically or the customer can do them manually.

If automatic configuration is desired, these devices and controllers so configured are referred to as *virtual devices*. They will be controlled by the QAUTOVRT system value (which can contain any number between 0 and 9999). If QAUTOVRT is set to any non-zero number, autoconfig is on until the system has configured as many devices as is specified in the system value. To get started, use the Change System Value (CHGSYSVAL) command to set QAUTOVRT to 10.

If you are relying on autoconfig (you haven't configured any devices or controllers) and either QAUTOVRT is set to 0 or it has already configured the number of devices specified on the system value, display station pass-through will fail.

Even a 10-device limit isn't as limiting as it might seem. Autoconfigured devices stay on the system until they are deleted.

By the way, consider this for security purposes. When the system automatically creates devices, the user who is signing on becomes their owner.

Controllers can support many devices and automatic configuration will create one controller for every 250 devices. It will not create a second controller until it needs to attach device 251.

This might seem like a lot of devices on a controller, but everything is virtual. Therefore, it's really no big deal. However, from a management perspective, 250 devices on one controller doesn't help you when you have system problems. The main reason for manually configuring controllers and devices is that you can group smaller numbers of devices to individual controllers.

If QAUTOVRT is set to 0, automatic configuration for virtual devices is turned off and all controllers and devices must already exist on the target system before pass-through can occur.

Create device and controller descriptions manually with the Create Device Description (CRTDEVD) and Create Controller Description (VIRTUAL WORKSTATION) (CRTCTLVWS) commands. Creating device descriptions is covered in section 10.4.6 Create Device Descriptions. Figure 10-16 shows the prompted version of the CRTCTLVWS command.

```
                    Create Ctl Desc (Virtual WS) (CRTCTLVWS)

 Type choices, press Enter.

 Controller description . . . . .   _________     Name
 Online at IPL  . . . . . . . . .   *YES          *YES, *NO
 Text 'description' . . . . . . .   *BLANK

                           Additional Parameters

 Attached devices . . . . . . . .   _________     Name
                + for more values   _________
 Authority  . . . . . . . . . . .   *LIBCRTAUT    Name, *LIBCRTAUT, *CHANGE...
```

Figure 10-16: Prompted version of the CRTCTLVWS command.

Devices must be created before controllers are created.

Virtual controllers and devices on the remote system must match physical devices on the local system. If a like device is not available, an alternate virtual device can be used, but the VRTDEV parameter must have been specified on the STRPASTHR command. For a chart of matching displays and acceptable alternatives, see the IBM manual *OS/400 Remote Work Station Support V4R1.*

10.8.4.3 User Profile Configuration

User profiles must exist on the remote system for users who are passing through. Use the Create User Profile (CRTUSRPRF) command to create the pass-through profiles.

When you initially set up display-station pass-through, relax security temporarily so that you can work out connection issues without getting confused by those issues. But when you are live with pass-through, seriously consider security. A user entering a system from another AS/400 is not "local" and should probably (but not necessarily) have limited access.

The automatic creation of controllers and devices is a weak point in security for display station pass-through. When an unknown user attempts to sign-on to the remote system, the system will create the devices for that unknown user. There is a system value, QMAXSIGN, that is supposed to limit the number of failed sign-on attempts. It does very well for controllers and devices that are manually configured (and no automatic configuration is allowed). However, all that it does with automatic configuration is to set the newly configured controller/device to inactive after the number of failed sign-on attempts. Then the system will automatically create new controllers/devices.

There are two things about display station pass-through that somewhat ameliorate this issue:

- The incoming user was at least a valid user on another, connected, AS/400. While it might not be that big of a problem, it bears thinking about.
- The Create Line Description commands now have a parameter, AUTODELETE CONTROLLER (it follows the AUTOCREATE CONTROLLER parameter) where you can specify after how many idle minutes the system is to automatically delete the controller.

Beyond that, there is another issue to consider. When a user starts a pass-through, you must decide if that user will be presented with a sign-on screen or if the pass-through will be transparent (automatic sign on). If a program (or menu option) automatically starts pass-through for its own use, you could allow it automatic sign-on capability. Also, you should specify that it automatically signs off when its job ends.

If you want a sign-on screen to appear, use the Change System Value (CHGSYSVAL) command to change system value QRMTSIGN to *FRCSIGNON. Set it to *SAMEPRF when you want automatic sign-on to occur. It's easier if you use *FRCSIGNON when setting up a pass-through. Change it after you're confident of the connection.

With system value QRMTSIGN set to *SAMEPRF (transparent sign-on), the system will take the user profile and password from the parameters of the STRPASTHR command. Even with automatic sign-on, the user will see system messages as the pass-through is accomplished. You can suppress those from the user's screen by specifying PASTHRSCN(*NO) on the STRPASTHR command.

For more information on display station pass-through, refer to the IBM manual, *OS/400 Remote Work Station Support V4R1.*

10.8.5 Electronic Customer Support

Electronic Customer Support (ECS) comes with every AS/400. The ECS feature allows you to contact IBM directly and inquire about current PTFs, log problems, and even order PTFs or operating system upgrades. Also, when your AS/400's internal self-diagnostics sense a problem developing, your AS/400 will use the ECS line to initiate a service call to IBM. Or you can contact IBM for question/answer support through this connection.

You receive an ECS modem with your AS/400 and you should have connected an outside phone line to it when you installed your machine. The ECS lines, controllers, and devices are already configured for you. Most customers just use the equipment as delivered. The lines and controllers IBM defined for your ECS are:

- For non-service related issues (problems, PTFs, OS/400, and product information):
  - ✔ Line—QTILINE.
  - ✔ Controller—QTICTL.
  - ✔ Device—QTIDA.
- For IBM service:
  - ✔ Line—QESLINE.
  - ✔ Controller—QESCTL.
  - ✔ Device—QESPAP.

You'll almost never need to change any of the preceding items, but if you do change something use one of the following commands:

- Work with Line Description (WRKLIND).
- Work with Controller Description (WRKCTLD).
- Work with Device Description (WRKDEVD).

Although it's never happened yet, you might have to change the phone number for the IBM Service Department. If so, type either call QESPHONE or call QTIPHONE on any command and press Enter. You'll be presented with a screen to change the phone number.

The AS/400 contains contact information about products, service, and PTFs. You will need to keep this contact information updated. To do so, go to the AS/400 main menu and take Option 7 (DEFINE OR CHANGE THE SYSTEM), and then take Option 4 (WORK WITH SUPPORT CONTACT INFORMATION). You'll have an opportunity to change one of six contact areas:

- Q & A database.
- Local service.
- IBM product.
- Technical information exchange.
- Upgrade order.
- Service providers.

If you need more information on the ECS, refer to the IBM manuals *OS/400 Communication Configuration V4R1* and *AS/400 System Operations V3R6*.

10.9 References

APPN Support V4R2 (SC41-5407-02)

AS/400 System Operation V3R6 (SC41-4203-00)

Distributed Data Management (SC41-5307-00)

OptiConnect for OS/400 V4R2 (SC41-5414-00)

OS/400 APPC Programming V4R1 (SC41-5443-00)

OS/400 Communication Management V4R2 (SC41-5406-01)

OS/400 Communications Configuration V4R1 (SC41-5401-00)

Remote Work Station Support V4R1 (SC41-5402-00)

SNA Distribution Services V4R1 (SC41-5410-00)

SNA Upline Facility Programming V4R1 (SC41-5446-00)

11 COMMUNICATIONS: LANS

11.1 OVERVIEW

Although SNA, APPC, and APPN provide the basis for all AS/400 connectivity and provide functionality that other platforms only dream about, the actual communication connection is usually done through industry-standard protocols.

This chapter walks you through the LAN "stack" similar to how it is implemented on the AS/400. This chapter also covers the physical network layer's protocols. Chapter 12 covers the Internet/intranet layers that use TCP/IP and other functions of TCP/IP.

The focus of the following sections is on supporting basic 5250 workstations on one or more AS/400s via APPC. Supporting an in-house LAN or LANs can be accomplished with the information in this chapter. For information on going out over the Internet ("going public" in a way) see chapters 10, 11, and 12.

The protocols in this chapter explain how AS/400 access is provided using personal computers, local area networks, and, in the case of Frame-Relay and ATM, wide-area networks (WANs). This chapter details how AS/400s and LANs connect.

Initially, networking referred to connecting a handful of PCs in a department. Now, networking means having up to thousands of workstations all coming together for sharing of resources, data, and general communication. Also, AS/400s commonly were the central focus of a network. Today, your AS/400 can be one of several computers sharing network duties.

Even the term *network* has expanded from connecting a handful of PCs to linking several networks. Each separate network is called a *network segment* of the larger network. Yes, things have gotten complicated.

Networks are linked by common nodes that can route data packets from one network to other. These common connecting nodes are referred to as:

- IP routers (or simply as routers).
- Gateways.
- Bridges.

A *router* isn't anything magical; it's a dedicated PC that connects two or more networks and routes packets from one to the other. The connected networks can have the same or different protocols. For example, an Ethernet network can connect with a token-ring network through a router.

The term *gateway* is often used in place of router. The terminology is pretty much interchangeable, but there are important distinctions. While both do data routing and transferring, the device called a *gateway* often offers specialized functions. For example, in the AS/400 arena, gateways are available that convert green screens on the fly into HTML Internet-friendly screens. These gateways help make the AS/400 Internet-ready without converting any application coding. Other gateways specialize in providing a *firewall* or an extra layer of security dedicated to securing Internet-bound data.

A *bridge* can also connect networks. Again, a bridge is pretty much the same as a router except a bridge uses physical addresses instead of IP addresses. A bridge does not have an assigned IP address like an IP router. A bridge is transparent in the TCP/IP network. A set of bridged networks (or segments) appear and act as if they are a single physical network.

A network physically connected to an AS/400 is a *local network* for that system. A network a system can reach only after passing through one or more IP routers is a *remote network* to the AS/400. On the other hand, consider two networks connected by a node (each of which has an AS/400). One AS/400's local network is the other's remote network and vice versa.

11.2 Protocols

The LAN protocols the AS/400 supports are:

- Token ring.
- Ethernet.
    - ✔ IEEE 802.3.
    - ✔ Version 2.
- Wireless (not really a protocol, runs over Ethernet).
- DDI.
- Frame-relay.
- ATM (asynchronous transfer mode).

Wireless communications actually uses Ethernet's frame protocol. However, it is mentioned in this chapter because of its growing popularity. In addition, wireless communications requires some additional steps for configuration.

Of the listed protocols, Ethernet Version 2 is the most "native." It has a single layer, the medium access control (MAC), between the hardware and the network. The other six have two layers:

- MAC is the layer closest to the hardware. It provides the adapter address. Sometimes this address is simply referred to as the MAC address. The MAC layer does frame transmission and reception, recognition, and error detection.
- The logical link control (LLC) provides logical connection, disconnection, flow control, and error handling.

11.3 AS/400 LAN OVERVIEW

Protocol support for the AS/400 LAN falls into two broad categories:

- Acknowledged—provides better error handling capability, but must run under SNA. Most AS/400 communications are acknowledged.
- Unacknowledged—provide data transfer without SNA, but error handling is minimal.

The LAN devices attached to an AS/400 are logically switched. That's a little confusing at first because a dial-up remote device is considered switched. In this case, *switched* simply means that a workstation can connect to the AS/400 and expect that a communication session will be started for it, then disconnect (the session will be ended), and again reconnect.

Connecting any device to a LAN requires a LAN adapter card. Introducing an AS/400 to a LAN is no exception. To connect to a LAN, the AS/400 needs one or more adapter cards, and each of those cards supports a specific number of SNA connections.

AS/400 support of PC LANs can be treated with one of two strategies. With the first option, the AS/400 supports all devices directly. This requires a device configuration for each personal computer. Configuring each PC can be a pain, but the nice part is that LAN support is under the AS/400 umbrella. The other option is to separate the PC LAN from the AS/400 with a gateway.

Using a gateway can be advantageous in a large shop where the AS/400 staff doesn't do LAN work and the LAN staff doesn't do AS/400 tasks. Set up your AS/400(s) on a small network with the AS/400(s) and a few gateways as nodes. Each gateway will support its own section of a much larger LAN.

Bridges connect dissimilar LANs. If you have this situation, be especially aware of addressing issues. Ethernet addresses are slightly different from token-ring and DDI addresses. Dissimilar addresses can be corrupted passing through a bridge. For more information about this configuration, see appendix D in the IBM manual *OS/400 LAN, Frame-Relay and ATM Support V4R2.*

One thing you'll see over and over when configuring LAN objects is the *resource name.* This term indicates a concatenation of the adapter and port of that adapter the object will use. Use the WRKHDWRSC *CMN command to find the input/output adapter (IOA) you'll use, and then the port number. Concatenate the port number onto the IOA name and you'll have a resource name. For example, if the IOA name is LIN01, and you'll be using the second port on the adapter, your resource name is LIN012.

11.3.1 LAN Addresses

Every device on the LAN, including any AS/400s, requires a LAN adapter card. The adapter address, or MAC address, can be found on that card. While the MAC address is a 6-byte address, it is more frequently known by the 12 hexadecimal characters that make up the 6 bytes. Although many AS/400 customers think of the MAC address as a 12-character address, it has only 6 bytes. While the technically correct name for this is the MAC address, most AS/400 customers refer to it as the *adapter address.*

Every AS/400 adapter comes out of the factory with a unique address called the *preset address.* You can assign your own additional address when you configure the line description. You don't have to, but it's a good idea for later LAN maintenance. If the adapter card has to be replaced, and the network relies on the preset address only, someone will have to assign the old preset address as the additional address anyway. On the other hand, if the customer relied on an additional address from the start, the customer only has to invoke the same additional address on the new adapter.

A frame-relay network adapter does not come with a preset address. If you are configuring a bridged frame-relay environment (see section 11.8 Frame Relay) that will connect to a remote token-ring, Ethernet, or DDI LAN through a network processor, you must assign an adapter address for each line description you create.

When working with LAN devices, you will often need to know adapter addresses. To quickly find them for all devices on a varied-on line, use the Display Line Description (DSPLIND) command.

Another set of addresses associated with adapters are *service access points* (SAPs) that come in pairs: the source SAP (SSAP) and the destination SAP (DSAP). LAN communication flows from a SSAP address on one device to a DSAP address on another device. SSAP and DSAP addresses must be the same for a communication direction and destination to be established. The AS/400 will provide default SAP addresses and most customers just accept them.

If you like to define your own SAP addresses, you can define up to 24 SSAPs per token-ring or Ethernet adapter. Acknowledged services require that the addresses you use have SAP addresses in the range of hex 04 to hex 9C. The ones you specify must end in a 0, 4, 8, or C. If you are using TCP/IP, use hex AA as a SAP. Unacknowledged services can use any address from hex 02 through hex FE (as long as it is divisible by 2).

11.3.2 General Notes on Configuring LANs

Before you attempt any configurations commands, make sure you are doing so with a user profile that has *IOSYSCFG special authority. Many of the configuration commands are restricted from anyone without this authority.

I'll walk you through configuring the line descriptions and controller descriptions on each LAN type. In reality, many shops let the AS/400 do most of the work by accepting the default values and using autoconfiguration. Other shops worry about security with autoconfiguration.

For the customer completely new to AS/400s and LANs, I suggest bringing up a LAN using autoconfiguration, then check all those autoconfigured devices to see what the AS/400 used for parameter values. That'll give you an idea of what works. Then, if the customer wants more security, the customer can delete the autoconfigured devices and manually create new ones.

The only thing the customer must create is the line description (CRTLIND). Optionally, the AS/400 will automatically configure the controller and device descriptions.

The command parameters of CRTLIND that turn on automatic configuration are APPC Controllers Created Automatically (AUTOCRTCTL(*YES)) and Create Device Descriptions (AUTOCRTDEV(*YES)). These parameters are on the CRTLIND and the Change Line Description (CHGLIND), but you won't see them when you display the line description (DSPLIND).

With automatic configuration on, when a workstation attempts to connect and a controller or device doesn't exist, the system will create one even if only the (AUTOCRTCTL(*YES)) was specified (that's only the controller). If the device doesn't exist, the system will create one also.

To accommodate logically switched devices, the description for the LAN controller on an AS/400 always has the Initial Connection (INLCNN) parameter set to *DIAL. The setting is to *DIAL even if *APPN automatically creates your controller descriptions. This parameter has more to do with when polling occurs than when anything is physically dialed.

Another parameter, Dial Initiation (DIALINIT), can be set to *IMMED to initiate polling as soon as the controller is varied on. Or it can be set to *DELAY to delay polling until the first program attempts to access the link. A better suggestion is to just use the default *LINKTYPE.

A parameter that really should be left alone is the Data Link Role (ROLE). Its default is negotiable (*NEG) and that's the best setting for all but the most sophisticated shops. The *NEG value allows the AS/400 to determine what stations are primary and secondary for communications.

11.4 Token Ring

A token-ring LAN supports the IEEE 802.5 standard. It uses a token to pass data. Using a ring topology—tokens go around the ring and pass through every workstation—each workstation either passes the token on (if it isn't the addressee) or receives it.

Several workstations on a token ring can be attached to a concentrator called a *multistation access unit (*MAU). IBM's 8228 MAU supports seven workstations. A token-ring LAN supports two transmission speeds: 4 megabytes per second (Mbps) and 16 Mbps. A token-ring LAN uses shielded-twisted pair (STP) cabling.

Although token ring was a giant step forward in speed for the AS/400 (it was the first to break past the 1Mbps of 5250), computing demands have also made it too slow. There is a work-around, however, and that is to use a concentrator in place of the MAU. IBM's 8272 Controller works just find. This device creates a star topology, receives all tokens, and routes them directly to their destination.

Okay, it's not a ring and some say it's not even tokens anymore. But, although speeds stay the same, performance is dramatically higher and the network gets a higher bandwidth.

When a token ring relies on a MAU, it is considered a half-duplex token ring. When it relies on the controller, it is considered a full-duplex token ring.

11.4.1 Token-Ring Adapter Addressing

The token-ring adapter address is a 6-byte or 48-bit address. Read it like it's transmitted: from bit0/byte0 to bit7/byte5. There are two of these addresses—the destination address and the source address—on a token. Figure 11-1 shows the destination address. Note that three bits are reserved.

Byte 0							
0	1	2	3	4	5	6	7
IG	UL						
Byte 1							
0	1	2	3	4	5	6	7
FAI							
Byte 2							
0	1	2	3	4	5	6	7
Byte 5							
0	1	2	3	4	5	6	7

Figure 11-1: Token-ring destination address.

- IG—Individual/group:
  - ✔ The 0 means the address is an individual address or one associated with a particular station on the network.
  - ✔ The 1 means the address is a group address or that it is destined for more than one destination.
- UL—Universal/local:
  - ✔ The 0 means the address is universally administered.
  - ✔ The 1 means the address is locally administered.
- FAI—Only refers to locally administered group addresses:
  - ✔ The 0 means the locally administered address is a functional address.
  - ✔ The 1 means the locally administered address is a group address.

Figure 11-2 shows the token-ring source address (two bits reserved).

Byte 0							
0	1	2	3	4	5	6	7
U	UL						
Byte 1							
0	1	2	3	4	5	6	7
Byte 2							
0	1	2	3	4	5	6	7
Byte 5							
0	1	2	3	4	5	6	7

Figure 11-2: Token-ring source address.

- U:
  - ✔ The 0 means routing information is not present in the frame.
  - ✔ The 1 means routing information is present in the frame.
- UL—Universal/local:
  - ✔ The 0 means the address is universally administered.
  - ✔ The 1 means the address is locally administered.

These bits must be considered when assigning or working with token-ring addresses because their use limits the range of numbers available for addressing.

- Bit0/byte0 has two implications:
  - ✔ Destination addresses:
    - ➢ Individual adapter addresses can be 000000000000 through 7FFFFFFFFFFF.
    - ➢ Group addresses can be 800000000000 through FFFFFFFFFFFF.
  - ✔ Source addresses:
    - ➢ Routing information present. The range of token-ring addresses will be 800000000000 through FFFFFFFFFFFF.
    - ➢ No routing information present, token-ring addresses will be in the range 000000000000 through 7FFFFFFFFFFF.
- Bit1/byte0. If the address (destination or source) is locally administered, the range is limited to 400000000000 through 7FFFFFFFFFFF.
  - ✔ If the address is locally administered, bit0/byte1 further limits the address.
    - ➢ Group address. The adapter's address range is limited to the range 400080000000 through 7FFFFFFFFFFF.
    - ➢ Functional address. The adapter's address range is limited to the range C00000000000 through C00040000000. There are some dedicated functional addresses and some that can be user defined.

Heterogeneous LANs using bridges must pay particular attention to token-ring addressing. If this description fits your shop, see section 2.1.2 of the IBM manual *AS/400 LAN, Frame-Relay, and ATM Support V4R2.*

11.4.2 Token-Ring Considerations

A token-ring network requires a token-ring adapter card on each device (AS/400 and workstations) and every device's adapter card must connect to a MAU or concentrator. There are two factors to plan for before starting to configure your token-ring network:

- Speed.
- Maximum frame size.

Token-ring networks have the option to run at two speeds: 4 Mbps or 16 Mbps. Once you've chosen a speed, all token-ring adapter cards must be set to the same speed.

Token-ring data is stored in the token as a *frame*. A frame can be from 265 through 16,393 bytes, and this is called the *frame size*. The larger the frame size, the more efficiently data can be moved. There are four areas where the frame size is determined:

- The Maximum Frame Size (MAXFRAME) parameter on the Create Token-Ring Line Description (CRTLINTRN) command.
- The maximum frame size (MAXFRAME) parameter on the Create Token-Ring Controller Description (CRTCTLTRN) command.

The system may override your selected frame size at any time with the smallest of the large frame sizes any individual adapter can handle. If most of your adapters can handle a 16,393-byte frame size (and that is what you specified on one of the MAXFRAME parameter fields), but one adapter can only handle a 4096 frame size, you will get the 4096 size frame.

If a token-ring network passes its frames across a bridge, you must take that into consideration in your frame-size calculation. If you define a frame size too large for the bridge, that frame will be discarded when the network tries to send it through the bridge. Unfortunately, the network doesn't automatically incorporate the bridge frame size in its calculations. You must do that calculation for it. Just ensure that your bridge size is at least as large as the smallest of one of the three frame sizes listed in the preceding description.

11.4.3 Configuring a Token-Ring Network

Before configuring a token-ring network, four decisions need to be made:

- Resource name. For a discussion of how to determine the resource name, see section 11.1, LAN Overview. This is the second parameter of the CRTLINTRN command.
- Adapter address. The adapter address you'll use must have 12 characters and start with 40000.
- Speed. For additional information about the speed of the network, see section 11.4.2, Token-Ring Considerations.
- Frame size. For additional information about frame sizes, see section 11.4.2, Token-Ring Considerations.

After determining the preceding four items, do the following commands in sequence:

- Create Line Description (CRTLINTRN).
- Create Controller Description (CRTCTLAPPC)—optional.
- Create Device Description (CRTDEVAPPC)—optional.

11.4.3.1 Create Line Description (Token Ring) (CRTLINTRN)

Figure 11-3 shows the screens to create line descriptions for a token-ring network.

```
                    Create Line Desc (Token-Ring) (CRTLINTRN)

 Type choices, press Enter.

 Line description . . . . . . . . > TOKENRING1    Name
 Resource name  . . . . . . . . . > IPCSNOTE00    Name, *NWID, *NWSD
 NWI type . . . . . . . . . . . . > *FR           *FR, *ATM
 Online at IPL  . . . . . . . . .   *YES          *YES, *NO
 Vary on wait . . . . . . . . . .   *NOWAIT       *NOWAIT, 15-180 seconds
 Maximum controllers  . . . . . .   40            1-256
 Line speed . . . . . . . . . . . > 16M           4M, 16M, *NWI
 Duplex . . . . . . . . . . . . .   *HALF         Character value, *HALF, *FULL
 Maximum frame size . . . . . . . > 16393         265-16393, 265, 521, 1033...
 Local adapter address  . . . . . > 40000A010111  400000000000-7FFFFFFFFFFF...
 Exchange identifier  . . . . . .   *SYSGEN       05600000-056FFFFF, *SYSGEN
 SSAP list:
   Source service access point  .   *SYSGEN       02-FE, *SYSGEN
   SSAP maximum frame . . . . . .   _________     *MAXFRAME, 265-16393
   SSAP type  . . . . . . . . . .   _______       *CALC, *NONSNA, *SNA, *HPR
                + for more values
```

```
                    Create Line Desc (Token-Ring) (CRTLINTRN)

 Type choices, press Enter.

 Text 'description' . . . . . . . > 'TOKEN RING 1 LINE DESCRIPTION'


                             Additional Parameters

 Network controller . . . . . . .   __________    Name
 Activate LAN manager . . . . . .   *YES          *YES, *NO
 TRLAN manager logging level  . .   *OFF          *OFF, *MIN, *MED, *MAX
 TRLAN manager mode . . . . . . .   *OBSERVING    *OBSERVING, *CONTROLLING
 Log configuration changes  . . .   *LOG          *LOG, *NOLOG
 Token-ring inform of beacon  . .   *YES          *YES, *NO
 Functional address . . . . . . .   *NONE         *NONE, C00000000001...
                + for more values   ___________
 Early token release  . . . . . .   *LINESPEED    *YES, *NO, *LINESPEED
 Error threshold level  . . . . .   *OFF          *OFF, *MIN, *MED, *MAX
 Link speed . . . . . . . . . . . > 16M           *MIN, 1200, 2400, 4800...
```

```
                    Create Line Desc (Token-Ring) (CRTLINTRN)

 Type choices, press Enter.

 Cost/connect time  . . . . . . .   0             0-255
 Cost/byte  . . . . . . . . . . .   0             0-255
 Security for line  . . . . . . .   *NONSECURE    *NONSECURE, *PKTSWTNET...
 Propagation delay  . . . . . . .   *LAN          *MIN, *LAN, *TELEPHONE...
 User-defined 1 . . . . . . . . .   128           0-255
 User-defined 2 . . . . . . . . .   128           0-255
 User-defined 3 . . . . . . . . .   128           0-255
 Autocreate controller  . . . . . > *YES          *YES, *NO
 Autodelete controller  . . . . .   1440          1-10000 (minutes), *NONE
 Recovery limits:
   Count limit  . . . . . . . . .   2             0-99, *SYSVAL
   Time interval  . . . . . . . .   5             0-120 minutes
 Authority  . . . . . . . . . . .   *LIBCRTAUT    Name, *LIBCRTAUT, *CHANGE...
```

Figure 11-3: CREATE LINE DESCRIPTION for token-ring network (parts 1, 2, and 3).

The entries marked with a > are the entries I made. Before V3R7, the resource name used to be something like LIN012 (refer to 11.3 AS/400 LAN Overview). After V4R1, the resource name must be the adapter name.

The duplex parameter refers to the hardware making the token ring connection. The traditional 8228 MAU makes a half-duplex token ring while an 8272 controller makes a full-duplex token ring.

The autodelete controller parameter allows the system to automatically delete any automatically created controller after it has been idle for so many minutes. The default, 1440 minutes, is 24 hours. This is a nice feature and should be used anytime controllers are automatically created.

11.4.3.2 Create Controller Description for APPC (CRTCTLAPPC) (Optional)

If you specify the AUTOCREATE CONTROLLER parameter on the line description as *YES, you will not have to do this step at all. When you attempt to establish a communication session, the line will create the controller for you.

By specifying AUTOCREATE DEVICE(*YES), the system also will automatically create your device description for you.

Note the relationship of the autocreates. The first object created was the line description and it had the option of specifying that the controller (the next item to create) could be created automatically for you. The controller is the second object to be created and it has the optional parameter to autocreate a device. But if a user requested that the controller be autocreated, the user would never get into the CREATE CONTROLLER command to specify that the device should also be autocreated. The rule is this, if the controller is to be autocreated, the device is also autocreated.

If the option to autocreate the controller is not selected when the line is created, the controller has to be created. For an AS/400-to-AS/400 network, you will use CRTCTLAPPC. See Figure 11-4.

```
                    Create Ctl Desc (APPC) (CRTCTLAPPC)

Type choices, press Enter.

Controller description . . . . . > TRAS400       Name
Link type  . . . . . . . . . . . > *LAN          *ANYNW, *FAX, *FR, *IDLC...
Online at IPL  . . . . . . . . .   *YES          *YES, *NO
APPN-capable . . . . . . . . . .   *YES          *YES, *NO
Switched line list . . . . . . . > TOKENRING1    Name
               + for more values
Maximum frame size . . . . . . .   *LINKTYPE     265-16393, 256, 265, 512...
Remote network identifier  . . .   *NETATR       Name, *NETATR, *NONE, *ANY
Remote control point . . . . . .   LANAPPN       Name, *ANY
Exchange identifier  . . . . . .                 00000000-FFFFFFFF
Initial connection . . . . . . .   *DIAL         *DIAL, *ANS
Dial initiation  . . . . . . . .   *LINKTYPE     *LINKTYPE, *IMMED, *DELAY
LAN remote adapter address . . . > 40000A020222  000000000001-FFFFFFFFFFFF
LAN DSAP . . . . . . . . . . . .   04            04, 08, 0C, 10, 14, 18, 1C..
LAN SSAP . . . . . . . . . . . . > 08            04, 08, 0C, 10, 14, 18, 1C..
APPN CP session support  . . . .   *YES          *YES, *NO
                                                                        More..
```

```
                    Create Ctl Desc (APPC) (CRTCTLAPPC)

Type choices, press Enter.

APPN node type . . . . . . . . .   *ENDNODE      *ENDNODE, *LENNODE...
APPN/HPR capable . . . . . . . .   *YES          *YES, *NO
HPR path switching . . . . . . .   *NO           *NO, *YES
APPN transmission group number     1             1-20, *CALC
APPN minimum switched status . .   *VRYONPND     *VRYONPND, *VRYON
Autocreate device  . . . . . . .   *ALL          *ALL, *NONE
Autodelete device  . . . . . . .   1440          1-10000, *NO
User-defined 1 . . . . . . . . .   *LIND         0-255, *LIND
User-defined 2 . . . . . . . . .   *LIND         0-255, *LIND
User-defined 3 . . . . . . . . .   *LIND         0-255, *LIND
Model controller description . .   *NO           *NO, *YES
```

Figure 11-4: CREATE CONTROLLER DESCRIPTION for AS/400-AS/400 token-ring network (parts 1 and 2).

The remote-control point, LAN DSAP, and LAN SSAP parameters must agree between the local and remote AS/400s' controllers. Don't make the mistake of making them agree between controller and line—lines agree with lines, controllers with controllers.

Also, by "agree," I mean that the DSAP on the local machine must be the same as the SSAP on connected machine and the SSAP on one must be the same as the DSAP on the connected machine. If you are in doubt of the value of any of these, use the Display Network Attribute (DSPNETA) command on the remote machine to check them. The ADAPTER ADDRESS is the address of the adapter on the remote AS/400.

For an AS/400-to-PC network, you will use CRTCTLAPPC. See Figure 11-5.

```
                    Create Ctl Desc (APPC) (CRTCTLAPPC)

Type choices, press Enter.

Controller description . . . . . CTLD          > TRLAN01
Link type  . . . . . . . . . . . LINKTYPE      > *LAN
Online at IPL  . . . . . . . . . ONLINE          *YES
APPN-capable . . . . . . . . . . APPN            *YES
Switched line list . . . . . . . SWTLINLST     > TOKENRING1
                       + for more values
Maximum frame size . . . . . . . MAXFRAME        *LINKTYPE
Remote network identifier  . . . RMTNETID        *NETATR
Remote control point . . . . . . RMTCPNAME     > GE01S01
Exchange identifier  . . . . . . EXCHID
Initial connection . . . . . . . INLCNN          *DIAL
Dial initiation  . . . . . . . . DIALINIT        *LINKTYPE
LAN remote adapter address . . . ADPTADR       > 10004A00512B
LAN DSAP . . . . . . . . . . . . DSAP            04
LAN SSAP . . . . . . . . . . . . SSAP            04
APPN CP session support  . . . . CPSSN         > *NO
```

```
                    Create Ctl Desc (APPC) (CRTCTLAPPC)

Type choices, press Enter.

APPN node type . . . . . . . . .   *ENDNODE      *ENDNODE, *LENNODE...
APPN/HPR capable . . . . . . . .   *YES          *YES, *NO
HPR path switching . . . . . . .   *NO           *NO, *YES
APPN transmission group number     1             1-20, *CALC
APPN minimum switched status . .   *VRYONPND     *VRYONPND, *VRYON
Autocreate device  . . . . . . .   *ALL          *ALL, *NONE
Autodelete device  . . . . . . .   1440          1-10000, *NO
User-defined 1 . . . . . . . . .   *LIND         0-255, *LIND
User-defined 2 . . . . . . . . .   *LIND         0-255, *LIND
User-defined 3 . . . . . . . . .   *LIND         0-255, *LIND
Model controller description . .   *NO           *NO, *YES
```

Figure 11-5: CREATE CONTROLLER DESCRIPTION for AS/400-PC token-ring network (parts 1 and 2).

The remote-control point is the name assigned to the remote PC. You should have a naming convention for this to make device status checks easy. For example, you could name every device something starting with the letters PC. Then, when you run Work With Configuration Status (WRKCFGSTS), you could specify the generic name PC* and isolate devices to just personal computers. You could go one step further and follow the PC label with some kind of designation for the department or location. An example would be the phone extension where the device is located.

The adapter address parameter is the manufacturer's address of the adapter on the PC.

11.4.3.3 Create Device Description for APPC (CRTDEVAPPC) (Optional)

Figure 11-6 shows the screen to create a device description for a token-ring network.

```
                   Create Device Desc (APPC) (CRTDEVAPPC)

 Type choices, press Enter.

 Device description . . . . . . . > TR400HOST      Name
 Remote location  . . . . . . . . > TEST4001       Name
 Online at IPL  . . . . . . . . .   *YES           *YES, *NO
 Local location . . . . . . . . . > TEST4002       Name, *NETATR
 Remote network identifier  . . .   *NETATR        Name, *NETATR, *NONE
 Attached controller  . . . . . . > TRAS400        Name
 Mode . . . . . . . . . . . . . . > BLANK          Name, *NETATR
               + for more values    ________
 Message queue  . . . . . . . . .   QSYSOPR        Name, QSYSOPR
   Library  . . . . . . . . . . .     *LIBL        Name, *LIBL, *CURLIB
 APPN-capable . . . . . . . . . .   *YES           *YES, *NO
 Single session:
   Single session capable . . . .   *NO            *NO, *YES
   Number of conversations  . . .   ______         1-512
 Text 'description' . . . . . . .   APPC Device for TEST4001
```

Figure 11-6: CREATE DEVICE DESCRIPTION for a token-ring network.

If you specified the AUTOCREATE DEVICE parameter as *ALL when you created the controller description (Figure 11-5), the system creates the device description for you, and you can skip this step.

If you specify AUTOCREATE CONTROLLER(*YES) on the line description and the line description creates the controller description for you, it creates it with AUTOCREATE DEVICE(*ALL) and you can still skip this step. The parameters I changed, as shown in Figure 11-6, are marked with a > symbol.

11.4.4 Token-Ring LAN CL Commands

To work with the token-ring LAN adapters, use the WRKHDWRSC command with *TRN as the second parameter. Figure 11-7 shows how it looks.

```
                  Work with Hardware Resources (WRKHDWRSC)

 Type choices, press Enter.

 Type . . . . . . . . . . . . . . > *LAN           *CMN, *CSA, *LAN, *LWS...
 Line type  . . . . . . . . . . . > *TRN           *ALL, *DDI, *TRN
```

Figure 11-7: The WRKHDWRSC command for token-ring adapters.

Pressing the Enter key gives you the screen shown in Figure 11-8.

```
                         Work with LAN Adapter Information
                                                               System:    SYS01

 Type options, press Enter.
   1=Add entry    2=Change    4=Remove entry    7=Rename


                                      Line
 Opt   Address          Name          Type   Description
  _    ____________
  _    50000E919111    GE91S01       *TRN   E/400 Gateway 91
  _    40000A010111    TOKENRING1    *TRN   SYS01 -- Token Ring 1
  _    40000A020211    TOKENRING2    *TRN   SYS02 -- Token Ring 2
  _    50000E909011    GE90S01       *TRN   E/400 Gateway 90
  _    50000E171711    GE17S02       *TRN   E/400 Gateway 17
  _    50000E131311    GE13S02       *TRN   E/400 Gateway 13
  _    50000E111111    GE11S02       *TRN   E/400 Gateway 11
  _    50000E010122    GE01S01       *TRN   E/400 Gateway 01

                                                                        Bottom
```

Figure 11-8: Formatted version of the WRKHDWRSC command used for token-ring adapters.

This screen displays information about an adapter. The user can then remove, add, or change an adapter. Although this is a somewhat limited command for working with adapters, it's great for the user that hasn't memorized all the adapters.

If the specific adapter is known, a more potent alternative is the Work with LAN Adapter (WRKLANADPT) command. Figure 11-9 shows the prompted version of the WRKLANADPT command.

```
                         Work With LAN Adapters (WRKLANADPT)

 Type choices, press Enter.

 Line description . . . . . . . . . > TOKENRING1     Name
 Output . . . . . . . . . . . . . .   *              *, *PRINT
```

Figure 11-9: The WRKLANADPT command setup.

When you press the Enter key from the screen shown on Figure 11-9, you get detailed information about line TOKENRING1 (as shown in Figure 11-10).

```
                          Work with LAN Adapters
                                                    System:    SYS01
  Line description . . . . . . . . :    TOKENRING1
  Line type  . . . . . . . . . . . :    *TRN

Type options, press Enter.
  1=Add entry   2=Change   4=Remove entry   5=Display profile   6=Print
  7=Rename

Opt  Address       Name                     Status   Description

 _   40000A010111  TOKENRING1               Active   SYS01 -- Token Ring 1
 _   0002BA0200A6  D2BA0200A6               Active
 _   40000A020211  TOKENRING2               Active   SYS02 -- Token Ring 2
 _   50000E131311  GE13S02                  Active   E/400 Gateway 13
 _   50000E010122  GE01S01                  Active   E/400 Gateway 01
 _   0000F61B9EE0  D0F61B9EE0               Active
 _   50000E919111  GE91S01                  Active   E/400 Gateway 91
```

Figure 11-10: The WRKLANADPP command for adapter TOKENRING1.

From this screen, you can do several things. Put a 5 on the option line to the left of adapter TOKENRING1 and you can get a description of the LAN adapter profile as shown in Figure 11-11.

```
                          Display Adapter Profile
                                                    System:    SYS01
Product ID . . . . . . . . . . . . . :    000000000000000000000000000000000000
Licensed internal code . . . . . . . :    F0F0F0F8F4F4F0F4F940
Group address  . . . . . . . . . . . :    C00080000000
Adapter address  . . . . . . . . . . :    40000A010111
Adapter name . . . . . . . . . . . . :    TOKENRING1
Adapter description  . . . . . . . . :    SYS01 -- Token Ring 1

NAUN address . . . . . . . . . . . . :    0002BA0200A6
NAUN name  . . . . . . . . . . . . . :    D2BA0200A6
NAUN description . . . . . . . . . . :



                                              Functional
Function                                      Address
Ring Error Monitor                            C00000000008
Configuration Report Server                   C00000000010
```

Figure 11-11: The LAN adapter profile for TOKENRING1.

This displays the LAN adapter information as well as the next LAN adapter from it on the network (in the NAUN ADDRESS parameter). This can help you troubleshoot a token-ring problem by identifying the next adapter for you to check.

Note that the line and the adapter are both named TOKENRING1. This is common practice and it helps the user quickly locate all the pieces of a communication point.

If you press the F10 key from Figure 11-11, you'll get the status of the adapter as shown in Figure 11-12.

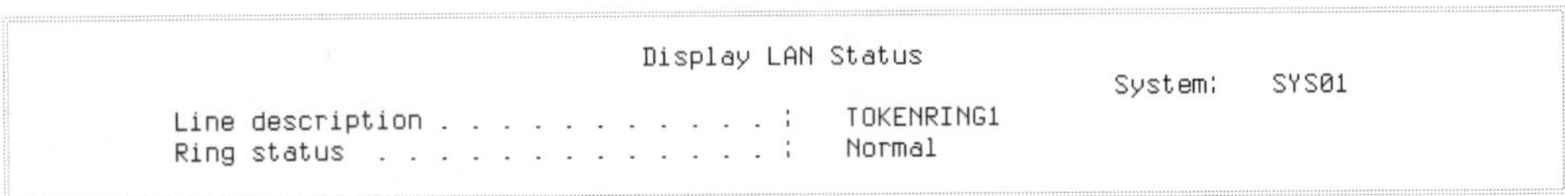

Figure 11-12: Status of adapter TOKENRING1.

You can see that the adapter's status is NORMAL.

11.5 ETHERNET

An Ethernet LAN supports one of two standards: Ethernet Version 2 and the IEEE 802.3 standard. You're better off using the IEEE 802.3 standard on the AS/400 because it is acknowledged; Version 2 is unacknowledged. Unacknowledged service is faster but error checking is minimal. Using Ethernet with reduced error checking is risky.

Ethernet uses the Carrier Sense Multiple Access with Collision Detection (CSMA/CD) protocol. Basically, when a station has something to transmit, it checks to see if the line is busy. If the line is not busy, the station transmits and monitors the line while transmitting (in case another station also transmits). If one station does transmit, that causes a collision and both stations first will stop transmitting, then wait some random amount of time, and then try again.

Standard Ethernet uses a bus topology whereby cable is laid and individual nodes are dropped along its path. That method works for small networks but ultimately leads to problems in large networks. A solution is to connect Ethernet nodes to a central switch in a star topology. IBM's switch is the 8271 Ethernet Switch. Generically, this device is referred to as a *switching hub.* Similar to the introduction of star topology in token-ring networks, this results in a non-traditional network, but one that is faster and more reliable.

Today, large Ethernet LANs reduce their errors (and increase throughput) by isolating network segments. Straight buses are isolated by the use of *repeating hubs* while star topologies are isolated by the use of several switching hubs.

Ethernet networks can be tricky because they really don't have much traffic management capability. Therefore, a lot of transmissions on the line cause many collisions to occur and performance can rapidly decay. Part of setting up and maintaining an efficient Ethernet network is knowing exactly what transmission level is acceptable and what the level will be on your line. Note: transmission activity level is independent of the number of workstations on the line.

The traditional Ethernet transmits data at 10 Mbps and the fast Ethernet transmits data at 100 Mbps. An Ethernet network uses a coaxial cable. AS/400s connect to Ethernet networks through an Ethernet controller card on the AS/400, a *transceiver* that is attached to or built into the network coaxial cable, and a cable to connect the controller card and transceiver. The controller must come from IBM, but the plug, cable, transceiver, and coaxial cable can come from any vendor.

11.5.1 Ethernet Adapter Addressing

The Ethernet adapter address is a 6-byte or 48-bit address. Read the bytes in the same order they are transmitted—from bit0/byte0 to bit7/byte5. Figure 11-13 is a sample address. Note that two bits are reserved.

- UL—Universal/local:
  - ✔ The 0 means the address is universally administered.
  - ✔ The 1 means the address is locally administered.
- IG—Individual/group:
  - ✔ The 0 means the address is an individual address or one associated with a particular station on the network.
  - ✔ The 1 means the address is a group address or that it is destined for more than one destination.

The range of valid adapter addresses are Hex 000000000000 through hex FFFFFFFFFFFF. However, the implications of these two bits on possible valid addresses are:

- If bit7/byte0 = 0, then Byte 0 must be an even number.
- If bit6/byte0 = 1, then Byte 0 must be in the range hex 020000000000 through hex FEFFFFFFFFFF and the second digit must be 2, 6, A, or E.

Heterogeneous LANs using bridges must pay particular attention to Ethernet addressing. If this description fits your shop, see section 2.1.2 of the IBM manual *AS/400 LAN, Frame-Relay, and ATM Support V4R2.*

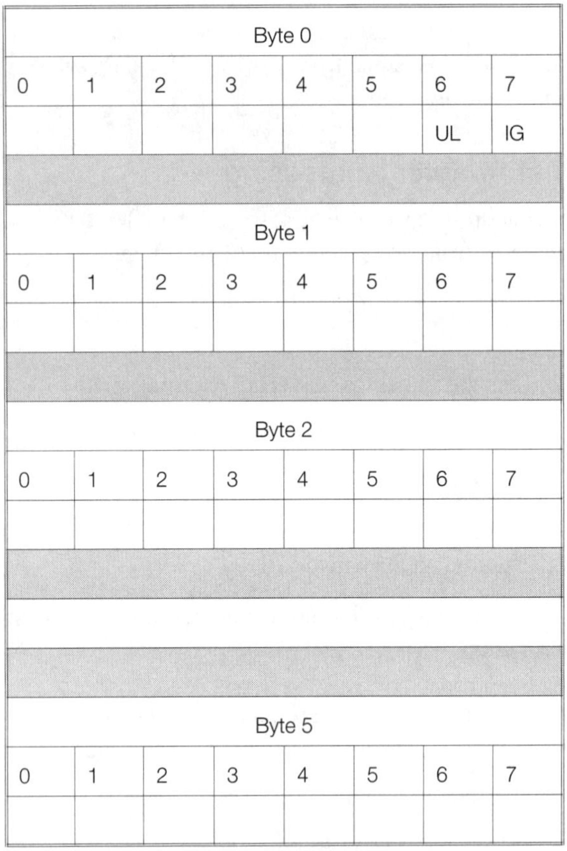

Byte 0							
0	1	2	3	4	5	6	7
						UL	IG
Byte 1							
0	1	2	3	4	5	6	7
Byte 2							
0	1	2	3	4	5	6	7
Byte 5							
0	1	2	3	4	5	6	7

Figure 11-13: Ethernet adapter address.

11.5.2 Ethernet Configuration

Ethernet line descriptions default to a maximum frame size of somewhere around 1500 (computed by the AS/400). The range is narrow (from 1493 to 1500). That is the maximum frame size. The minimum size—including addressing bytes and one byte of data—is 20. Optionally, the user can suggest a maximum frame size in two places:

- On the line description, at the SSAP parameter.
- On the controller description.

When Ethernet connects, the frame size will be the smallest of these values:

- Default line description maximum frame size (around 1500—you cannot specify this on the line description).

- SSAP MAXFRAME parameter value.
- Controller MAXFRAME parameter value.

If an Ethernet network passes its frames across a bridge, you must take the maximum frame size of the bridge into consideration in your frame-size calculation. If you define a frame size too large, that frame will be discarded when the network tries to send it through the bridge. Unfortunately, the network doesn't automatically incorporate the bridge frame size in its calculations. You must do the calculation. Make certain your bridge size is at least as large as the smallest of one of the three frame sizes listed earlier.

After determining the preceding four items, do the following commands in sequence:

- Create Line Description (CRTLINTRN).
- Create Controller Description (CRTCTLAPPC)—optional.
- Create Device Description (CRTDEVAPPC)—optional.

11.5.2.1 Create Line Description (Ethernet) (CRTLINETH)

Create a line description for an Ethernet LAN with the Create Line Description—Ethernet (CRTLINETH) command. Figure 11-14 shows a prompted version of that command.

```
                     Create Line Desc (Ethernet) (CRTLINETH)

 Type choices, press Enter.

 Line description . . . . . . . . > ETHLINE1      Name
 Resource name  . . . . . . . . . > LIN121        Name, *NWID, *NWSD
 Online at IPL  . . . . . . . . .   *YES          *YES, *NO
 Vary on wait . . . . . . . . . .   *NOWAIT       *NOWAIT, 15-180 seconds
 Local adapter address  . . . . .   020055010111  020000000000-7EFFFFFFFFFF...
 Exchange identifier  . . . . . .   *SYSGEN       05600000-056FFFFF, *SYSGEN
 Ethernet standard  . . . . . . .   *ALL          *ETHV2, *IEEE8023, *ALL
 Line speed . . . . . . . . . . .   10M           Character value, 10M, 100M...
 Duplex . . . . . . . . . . . . .   *HALF         Character value, *HALF...
 SSAP list:
   Source service access point  .   04            02-FE, *SYSGEN
   SSAP maximum frame . . . . . .   *MAXFRAME     *MAXFRAME, 265-1496, 265...
   SSAP type  . . . . . . . . . .   *CALC         *CALC, *NONSNA, *SNA, *HPR
                + for more values _
 Text 'description' . . . . . . .   Ethernet Line 1 Description_
```

Figure 11-14: CREATE LINE DESCRIPTION for AS/400 Ethernet network.

Note the local adapter address because any remote nodes will have to use this address to communicate to this node. In this case, I made up an address, but I could have used the adapter's preset address.

The Ethernet Standard (ETHSTD) parameter determines what type of Ethernet is to be supported and, by implication, what the maximum frame size will be. The ETHSTD parameter cannot be changed after the line description has been created. Possible values for ETHSTD and their possible maximum frame sizes are:

- *ALL (the default)—Either Ethernet version will be supported. Maximum frame size will match the version.
- *IEEE8023—Ethernet version IEEE 802.3. Maximum frame size 1496.
- *ETHV2—Ethernet version 2. Maximum frame size:
  - ✔ SNA support—1493.
  - ✔ Non-SNA support—1500.

There is a LINE SPEED parameter on the command that determines whether the line will use Ethernet at 10Mbps or 100Mbps.

The DUPLEX parameter determines whether the data on the Ethernet line will be sent half-duplex or full-duplex. Half duplex means that only one line is used and the network can either send or receive at any time. Full duplex requires two lines and a controller, and means that the network can send or receive simultaneously.

If AUTOCREATE CONTROLLER(*YES) is specified on the last screen, any controllers the system needs but doesn't have will be created automatically when a communication event starts. If this parameter contains *YES and the device that should be attached to the controller also doesn't exist, that too will be automatically created.

11.5.2.2 Create Controller Description for APPC (CRTCTLAPPC) (Optional)

This step is optional. It is only necessary if the controller does not exist and AUTOCREATE CONTROLLER on the create line description command was set to *NO.

Figure 11-15 shows a prompted version of the Create Controller Description APPC (CRTCTLAPPC) command.

```
                    Create Ctl Desc (APPC) (CRTCTLAPPC)

Type choices, press Enter.

Controller description . . . . . > APPCETH1      Name
Link type  . . . . . . . . . . . > *LAN          *ANYNW, *FAX, *FR, *IDLC...
Online at IPL  . . . . . . . . .   *YES          *YES, *NO
APPN-capable . . . . . . . . . . > *NO           *YES, *NO
Controller type  . . . . . . . .   *BLANK        *BLANK, *FBSS, 3174, 3274...
Switched line list . . . . . . . > ETHLINE1      Name
               + for more values
Maximum frame size . . . . . . .   *LINKTYPE     265-16393, 256, 265, 512...
Remote network identifier  . . .   *NETATR       Name, *NETATR, *NONE, *ANY
Remote control point . . . . . .                 Name, *ANY
Exchange identifier  . . . . . .                 00000000-FFFFFFFF
Initial connection . . . . . . .   *DIAL         *DIAL, *ANS
Dial initiation  . . . . . . . .   *LINKTYPE     *LINKTYPE, *IMMED, *DELAY
LAN remote adapter address . . . > 020055010222  000000000001-FFFFFFFFFFFF
LAN DSAP . . . . . . . . . . . .   04            04, 08, 0C, 10, 14, 18, 1C...
LAN SSAP . . . . . . . . . . . . > 08            04, 08, 0C, 10, 14, 18, 1C...
                                                                     More...
```

```
HPR path switching . . . . . . .   *NO           *NO, *YES
Autocreate device  . . . . . . .   *ALL          *ALL, *NONE
Text 'description' . . . . . . . > 'Ethernet controller APPCETH1-line ETHLINE1'
```

Figure 11-15: CREATE CONTROLLER DESCRIPTION for AS/400 Ethernet network (parts 1 and 2).

Note that the switched-line list is the name of the line you created in Figure 11-14. The line must exist before it is used on the CRTCTLAPPC command. More than one line can be listed here (just put a '+' on the + FOR MORE VALUES parameter), but they all must exist before they can be listed.

The LAN REMOTE ADAPTER ADDRESS must be the address of the remote adapter (not the local). The AUTOCREATE DEVICE (*ALL) parameter and value on the second screen tells the AS/400 to go ahead and automatically create a device description when one doesn't exist when a communications event starts. If the controller is set up this way, you can skip the next step.

11.5.2.3 Create Device Description for APPC (CRTDEVAPPC) (Optional)

This step is optional. It is only necessary when the device doesn't exist and the AUTOCREATE DEVICE and AUTOCREATE CONTROLLER parameters were specified as *NO on previous commands.

Figure 11-16 shows a prompted version of the Create Device Description APPC (CRTDEVAPPC) command.

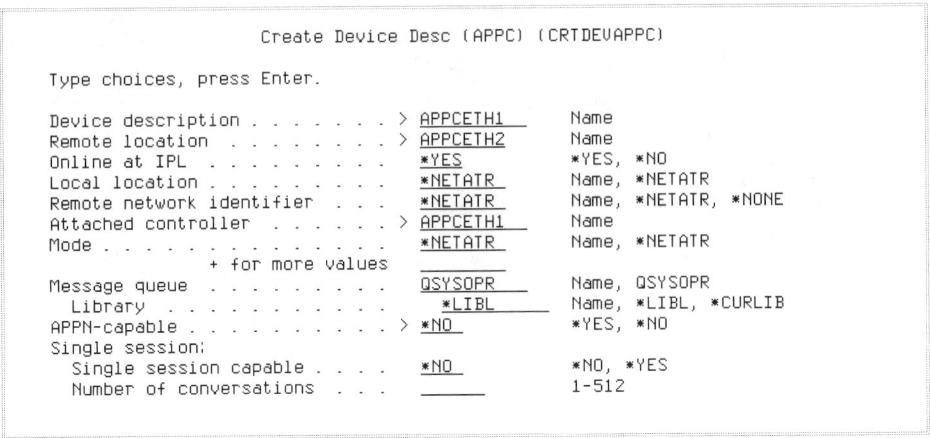
```
                    Create Device Desc (APPC) (CRTDEVAPPC)

Type choices, press Enter.

Device description . . . . . . . > APPCETH1      Name
Remote location  . . . . . . . . > APPCETH2      Name
Online at IPL  . . . . . . . . .   *YES          *YES, *NO
Local location . . . . . . . . .   *NETATR       Name, *NETATR
Remote network identifier  . . .   *NETATR       Name, *NETATR, *NONE
Attached controller  . . . . . . > APPCETH1      Name
Mode . . . . . . . . . . . . . .   *NETATR       Name, *NETATR
               + for more values
Message queue  . . . . . . . . .   QSYSOPR       Name, QSYSOPR
  Library  . . . . . . . . . . .     *LIBL       Name, *LIBL, *CURLIB
APPN-capable . . . . . . . . . . > *NO           *YES, *NO
Single session:
  Single session capable . . . .   *NO           *NO, *YES
  Number of conversations  . . .                 1-512
```

Figure 11-16: CREATE DEVICE DESCRIPTION for Ethernet connection.

The ATTACHED CONTROLLER parameter must be an Ethernet controller that already exists. If you are following this sequence, it is the name of the controller created in section 11.5.2.2.

11.6 WIRELESS

Wireless communication with the AS/400 supports mobile and stationary communication devices that connect to the AS/400 using RF (radio frequency) rather than cabling. Wireless is found mostly in the retail and warehousing industries where users routinely work with handheld computing devices called *portable transaction computers* (PTCs). Wireless communications with the AS/400 can support PTCs, bar code readers, and stationary desktop computers.

Wireless communications' networks are defined as being single- or multiple-cell networks. A *cell* is the sphere of sensitivity surrounding an antenna. A single-cell network has one antenna mounted on one *access point.* Wireless devices (each with its own antenna) access the AS/400 through that access point.

A multiple-cell network has several access points. The access points are generally connected to each other so they can share communication responsibilities as mobile PTCs move from one sphere to another. Access points can themselves connect to the AS/400 through RF. Multiple-cell networks allow users more consistent coverage while mobile.

Hardware requirements to wireless LANs on the AS/400 include:

- An IBM 2668 Wireless LAN adapter on the AS/400. This adapter card has a co-axial connector for an antenna and an RS-485 port to connect cabled access points. Both can be used simultaneously.
- A 266A Virtual Workstation Controller built into the 2480 adaptor. Remember this because, as the wireless network is configured, the line configures to the 2480 adapter and the controller configures to the 266A Virtual Workstation Controller. Trust me, remember these two pieces of hardware.
- An IBM 2480 Model RS Access Point for each access point. It communicates to PTCs through an antenna, of course, but it can communicate to the AS/400 either through RF or through an RS-485 cable.

Wireless isn't a communications protocol; it's merely another way of connecting a LAN. Think of it as a cableless Ethernet. Wireless LAN speeds are either 1 Mbps or 2 Mbps. Either is okay, but the same speed must be set consistently across all network devices.

11.6.1 Wireless Adapter Addressing

Wireless adapter addressing is identical to Ethernet addressing. For more information, refer to section 11.5.1 Ethernet Adapter Addressing. However, wireless addressing has some additional complexity. The 2668 Wireless LAN Adapter has two 6-byte hexadecimal addresses in it. Also, the 266A Virtual Work Station Controller incorporated on the adapter carries two addresses. These addresses and where they are located are:

- Adapter Address—located on the 2668 Wireless LAN Adapter. Specified on the ADPTADR parameter on the Create Line Description (Wireless) (CRTLINWLS) command.
- Hop ID—located on the 2668 Wireless LAN Adapter. This is the access point address. It is specified on the HOPID parameter on the Add Extended Wireless Line Member (ADDEWLM) command.
- Destination ID—located on the 266A Virtual Workstation Controller. This is the local destination ID (transport address) that the PTC will connect to at emulation startup time. This is the TXPADR parameter on the Add Extended Wireless Line Member (ADDEWCM) command.
- Transport Port—located on the 266A Virtual Workstation Controller. This is the local destination ID (transport address) that the PTC will connect to at emulation startup time. This is the TXPPORT parameter on the Add Extended Wireless Line Member (ADDEWCM) command.

Valid address ranges for the four addresses are:

- Adapter address—020000000000 through FEFFFFFFFFFF. Where the second character from the left must be 2, 6, A, or E.
- Hop ID—020000000000 through FEFFFFFFFFFF. Where the second character from the left must be 2, 6, A, or E.
- Destination ID—4001 through 4FFE and this value must match the destination ID specified for the PTC or Bar Code device.
- Transport port—0 through 15.

11.6.2 Wireless Configuration

When configuring wireless devices, the configuration commands are similar to other configuration commands. In fact, the line/controller/device are the same as Ethernet. Therefore, in addition to the material presented here, be familiar with section 11.5.2 Ethernet Configuration

Wireless devices require more information to configure and this is entered through *extended commands.* However, that's not enough; the extended information is stored as source in a file member and retrieved and downloaded when a remote device or the line is varied on. (*Varying on* a line and device is how communications is established on the AS/400.) To configure a wireless network, follow these steps in this order:

- Create Line Description (Wireless) (CRTLINWLS).
- Add Extended Wireless Line Member (ADDEWLM).
- Create Controller Description (Local Work Station) (CRTCTLLWS).
- Add Extended Wireless Controller Member (ADDEWCM).
- Add Extended Wireless Controller PTC Entry (ADDEWCPTCE)—for PTC devices, but not for bar coding devices.
- Add Extended Wireless Controller Bar Code Entry (ADDEWCBCDE)—for bar coding devices only.

While that seems like a lot more than the line, controller, and device you are used to configuring, it really isn't. Remember, you need more data to configure wireless networks. Therefore, first create a line description (CRTLINWLS), then add wireless-specific information to it (ADDEWLM), and store that information as source in a file member.

The controller is next. Create the controller (CRTCTLLWS), add wireless-specific data to its member (ADDEWCM), and store that information as source in a file. Next, add a little more information about the devices the controller will have to support. You add that data with either the ADDEWCPTCE or ADDEWCBCDE commands.

If you specify INZPGM(QZXCINZ) as the initialization program on both the CRTLINWLS and CRTCTLWLS commands, that program will automatically call the ADDEWLM and ADDEWCM commands after the create commands. But it won't call either the ADDEWCPTCE or the ADDEWCBCDE commands because it doesn't know whether your devices will be PTC or bar code.

Both the line and controller descriptions require a resource name (parameter RSRCNAME). There are two resource names on the system to use and many customers mix these up. Use the Work with Hardware Resources (WRKHDWRSC) command to determine the correct resource names, but use the command as follows:

- Line description resource name—WRKHDWRSC *CMN. The resource name will be in the form LIN*XXX* where *XXX* are three numeric digits. The resource name you want will be the one associated with the 2668 Wireless Connection.

- Controller description resource name—WRKHDWRSC *LWS. The resource name will be in the form CTL*XX* where *XX* are two numeric digits. The resource name will be the one associated with the 266A Virtual Controller.

When configuring a wireless network, all the configuration data (normal and enhanced) is stored in two files:

- QGPL/QEWLSRC—contains line configuration data.

- QGPL/QEWCSRC—contains controller configuration data.

The person configuring the network can put each network segment's configuration data in unique file members in these files. All configuration data (the normal and the enhanced data) gets into these files. When the line is varied on, the data from QEWLSRC is sent to the line and the data from QEWCSRC goes to the controller.

I've been ignoring creating device description. After doing the line and controller and all enhanced configuring, the system has more than enough to automatically configure the devices. This configuration happens when the communications is established.

For anyone who really wants to, the devices can be created manually with the Create Device Description (CRTDEVD) command. These devices are created with the TYPE 3476 and a DEVICE CLASS as *LCL.

11.6.2.1 Create Line Description (Wireless) (CRTLINEWLS)

Here is a sample of configuring a wireless network. First, create the line description (CRTLINWLS). Figure 11-17 has a sample of that command.

```
                    Create Line Desc (Wireless) (CRTLINWLS)

 Type choices, press Enter.

 Line description . . . . . . . . > WLSLIN       Name
 Resource name  . . . . . . . . . > LIN011       Name
 Online at IPL  . . . . . . . . .   *YES         *YES, *NO
 Vary on wait . . . . . . . . . .   *NOWAIT      *NOWAIT, 15-180 seconds
 Local adapter address  . . . . .   *ADPT        020000000000-FEFFFFFFFFFF...
 Exchange identifier  . . . . . .   *SYSGEN      05600000-056FFFFF, *SYSGEN
 Ethernet standard  . . . . . . .   *ALL         *ETHV2, *IEEE8023, *ALL
 SSAP list:                         _
   Source service access point  .   *SYSGEN      02-FE, *SYSGEN
   SSAP maximum frame . . . . . .   ________     *MAXFRAME, 265-1496, 265...
   SSAP type  . . . . . . . . . .   _______      *CALC, *NONSNA, *SNA
               + for more values _
 Initialization source file . . . > QEWLSRC      Name, *NONE
   Library  . . . . . . . . . . . >   QGPL       Name, *LIBL, *CURLIB
 Initialization source member . . > WLS001       Name, *NONE
```

```
                    Create Line Desc (Wireless) (CRTLINWLS)

 Type choices, press Enter.

 Initialization program . . . . . > QZXCINZ      Name, *NONE
   Library  . . . . . . . . . . .     *LIBL      Name, *LIBL, *CURLIB
 Text 'description' . . . . . . . > 'Create Line Description for wireless networ
k'
```

Figure 11-17: Prompted version of the Create Line Description (Wireless) (CRTLINWLS) command.

The screen, shown in Figure 11-17, is defining a line named WLSLIN that is attached to resource name LIN011. The resource name was obtained by using the WRKHDWRSC *CMN command and seeing what resource was attached to the 2668 wireless adapter.

At the bottom of the screen, you can see the initialization source file specified as QGPL/QEWLSRC, and this configuration is to be stored in member WLS001 of that file.

The second screen of the command shows the initialization program QZXCINZ named. This program is invoked when the user presses the Enter key. It, in turn, invokes the related command, ADDEWLM. A sample of that is shown in Figure 11-18.

```
                  Add Wireless Line Member (ADDEWLM)

Type choices, press Enter.

Initialization source member . . > WSL001          Name

                         Additional Parameters

Initialization source file . . . > QEWLSRC         Name, QEWLSRC
  Library . . . . . . . . . . . >   QGPL           Name, *LIBL, *CURLIB
Adapter configuration . . . . .    *ALL            *ALL, *RADIO, *WIRED
Hop identifier . . . . . . . . .   *ADPT           020000000000-FEFFFFFFFFFF...
Root cell . . . . . . . . . . .    *YES            *YES, *NO
Frequency . . . . . . . . . . .    1               1, 2, 3, 4, 5
Data rate . . . . . . . . . . .    2M              2M, 1M
Radio system identifier . . . .    000002          000002-FFFFFE
Text 'description' . . . . . . . > 'Automatically called ADDEWLM'
```

Figure 11-18: Command ADDEWLM automatically called by the program named on the command in Figure 11-17.

This command came up with the initialize source member, file, and library already filled in. The rest of the parameters were all right. In this simple example, the AS/400 only had one adapter so the HOP IDENTIFIER didn't have to be changed. As a result, the default *ADPT was sufficient.

- Pressing the Enter key (see the screen shown in Figure 11-18) creates the line description. Actually, it copies the line configuration data into file QGPL/QEWLSRC, member WLS001.

11.6.2.2 Create Controller Description (Wireless) (CRTCTLLWS)

After the line, configure the controller. Figure 11-19 contains a sample of the Create Controller Description (Wireless) (CRTCTLLWS) command.

```
                  Create Ctl Desc (Local WS) (CRTCTLLWS)

Type choices, press Enter.

Controller description . . . . . > WLSCTL          Name
Controller type . . . . . . . . > 266A            2637, 2638, 2661, 6040...
Controller model . . . . . . . . > 1               1, 0001
Resource name . . . . . . . . . > CTL11           Name
Online at IPL . . . . . . . . .    *YES            *YES, *NO
Initialization source file . . . > QEWCSRC         Name, *NONE
  Library . . . . . . . . . . . >   QGPL           Name, *LIBL, *CURLIB
Initialization source member . . > WLS001          Name, *NONE
Initialization program . . . . . > QZXCINZ         Name, *NONE
  Library . . . . . . . . . . .      *LIBL         Name, *LIBL, *CURLIB
Text 'description' . . . . . . . > 'Create controller for wireless network'
```

Figure 11-19: Prompted version of the Create Controller Description (CRTCTLLWS) command.

This screen creates a wireless controller named WLSCTL, type 266A. Resource name CTL11 was obtained through WRKHDWRSC *LWS and seeing what resource was attached to the 266A Virtual Workstation Controller.

The initialization source file, library, and member are specified as QGPL/QEWCSRC, member WLS001. Because they are members of different physical files, note that the member can be named the same as the member in the line description.

Finally, initialization program QZXCINZ is named and it calls the related command, Add Extended Wireless Controller Member (ADDEWCM). Refer to Figure 11-20 for a sample of that command.

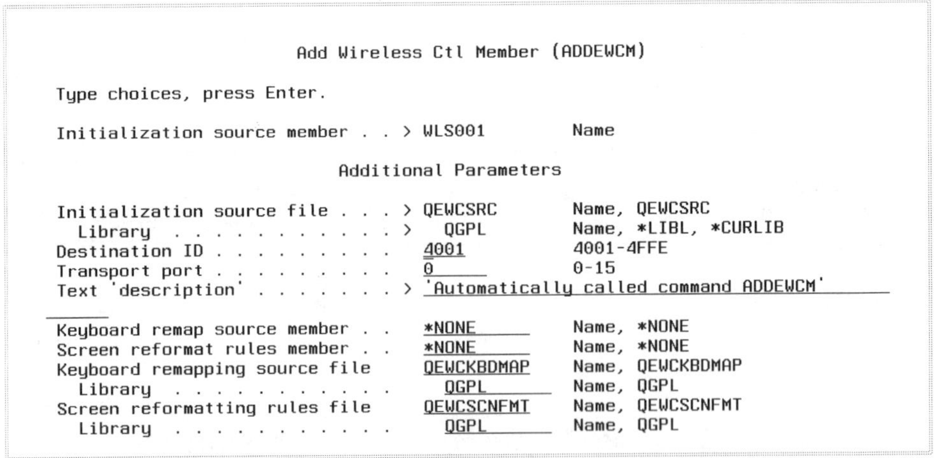

```
                      Add Wireless Ctl Member (ADDEWCM)

 Type choices, press Enter.

 Initialization source member . . > WLS001        Name

                          Additional Parameters

 Initialization source file . . . > QEWCSRC       Name, QEWCSRC
   Library  . . . . . . . . . . . >   QGPL        Name, *LIBL, *CURLIB
 Destination ID . . . . . . . . .   4001          4001-4FFE
 Transport port . . . . . . . . .   0             0-15
 Text 'description' . . . . . . . > 'Automatically called command ADDEWCM'

 Keyboard remap source member . .   *NONE         Name, *NONE
 Screen reformat rules member . .   *NONE         Name, *NONE
 Keyboard remapping source file     QEWCKBDMAP    Name, QEWCKBDMAP
   Library  . . . . . . . . . . .     QGPL        Name, QGPL
 Screen reformatting rules file     QEWCSCNFMT    Name, QEWCSCNFMT
   Library  . . . . . . . . . . .     QGPL        Name, QGPL
```

Figure 11-20: Prompted version of the ADDEWCM command.

In this case, like the previous, I just accepted the defaults. Complete the controller configuration with either the Add Extended Wireless Controller PTC Entry (ADDEWCPTCE) or the Add Extended Wireless Controller Bar Code Entry (ADDEWCBCDE). Neither of these commands will start automatically. The configurator must start them on the command line.

Figure 11-21 has a prompted version of the Add Extended Wireless Controller PTC Entry (ADDEWCPTCE) command.

```
                     Add EWC PTC Entry (ADDEWCPTCE)

Type choices, press Enter.

PTC group . . . . . . . . . . . PTCGRP       > PTC001
Initialization source member  . . INZMBR       > WLS001

                        Additional Parameters

Initialization source file . . . INZFILE        QEWCSRC
  Library . . . . . . . . . . .                   *LIBL
PTC ID range:                    PTCRANGE
  Begin ID . . . . . . . . . . .                 0001
  End ID . . . . . . . . . . . .                 1022
Intensity . . . . . . . . . . . INTENSITY      *NORMAL
Status line . . . . . . . . . . STSLINE        *YES
Cursor type . . . . . . . . . . CSRTYPE        *UNDERLINE
Inactivity timer . . . . . . . . INACTTMR       *DEV
Backlight timer . . . . . . . . BCKLTTMR       *DEV
Backlight key . . . . . . . . . BCKLTKEY       *ON
```

```
                     Add EWC PTC Entry (ADDEWCPTCE)

Type choices, press Enter.

Bypass exit . . . . . . . . . . BYPASSEXIT      *YES
Automatic run . . . . . . . . . AUTORUN         *YES
Printer . . . . . . . . . . . . PRINTER         *SYSTEM
Wand type . . . . . . . . . . . WANDTYPE        *NONE
Wand pecking rate . . . . . . . PECKRATE        *DEV
Laser read timer . . . . . . . . LASERTMR        *DEV
Barcode function keys . . . . . BCDFKEY         *OFF
Auto Enter . . . . . . . . . . . AUTOENTER       *OFF
Cursor location . . . . . . . . CSRLOC          *HOLD
Short scan . . . . . . . . . . . SHORTSCAN       *YES
Scan end of file . . . . . . . . SCANEOF         *YES
Fast poll interval . . . . . . . POLL          > 125
Fast poll delay . . . . . . . . POLLDLY       > 0
Fast poll decay . . . . . . . . POLLDECAY     > 2
Slow poll interval . . . . . . . SLOWPOLL      > 200
```

```
                     Add EWC PTC Entry (ADDEWCPTCE)

Type choices, press Enter.

Destination hop:                 DESTHOP       _
  Destination ID . . . . . . . .                *NONE
  Frequency . . . . . . . . . .
  Data rate . . . . . . . . . .
  Radio system identifier . . .
                        + for more values _
Barcode group . . . . . . . . . BCDGRP          *NONE
                        + for more values
Text 'description' . . . . . . . TEXT          > 'Enhanced Controller configurat
ion data for PTC'
Enable keyboard remapping . . . ENBKBDMAP       *NO
Enable screen reformatting . . . ENBSCNFMT       *NO
Device name prefix . . . . . . . DEVPFX          QWLS
```

Figure 11-21: Prompted version of the ADDEWCPTCE command. (parts 1 through 3)

The PTC devices (but not the bar code readers) have some interesting polling parameters. There are four of them at the bottom of the second screen shown in Figure 11-21. In the example, I entered the default values to make the explanation clearer. The four parameters refer to polling sequences.

Polling is a piece of LAN protocol where the one device just makes sure another is still there. It's an "Are you there?" query issued in regular periods of time. If the receiving device doesn't answer, it may be taken off line as inactive.

Both the AS/400 and each PTC unit poll each other. Sometimes it's the AS/400 polling the PTC and sometimes the PTC polls the AS/400. They both need to know the other is there. The poll-related parameters refer to the PTC polling of the AS/400 and are intended to exert enough control to conserve battery power. Here's a description of the four poll parameters:

- POLL sets the fast poll interval for the PTC. The default, 125ms, means that the PTC will poll the host every 125 milliseconds.
- POLLDLY is the amount of time polling is suspended following the start of a transmission in either direction (to the host or from the host).
- POLLDECAY is the number of PTC polls before the poll rate is cut in half. Polling proceeds rapidly at first, at the rate specified in the POLL parameter, then halves its rate. If the fast poll was 125ms, after two such polls (the default is 2), the new rate could be every 250ms.
- SLOWPOLL is the slowest rate that polling will occur. SLOWPOLL is the slowest rate the poll can get to through poll decay.

Figure 11-22 has a prompted version of the Add Extended Wireless Controller Bar Code Entry (ADDEWCBCDE) command.

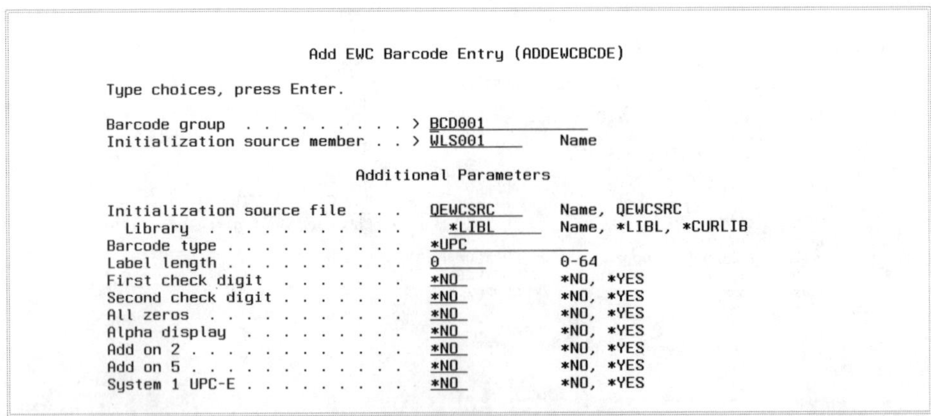
```
                      Add EWC Barcode Entry (ADDEWCBCDE)

 Type choices, press Enter.

 Barcode group  . . . . . . . . . > BCD001
 Initialization source member . . > WLS001        Name

                             Additional Parameters

 Initialization source file . . .   QEWCSRC       Name, QEWCSRC
   Library  . . . . . . . . . . .     *LIBL       Name, *LIBL, *CURLIB
 Barcode type . . . . . . . . . .   *UPC
 Label length . . . . . . . . . .   0             0-64
 First check digit  . . . . . . .   *NO           *NO, *YES
 Second check digit . . . . . . .   *NO           *NO, *YES
 All zeros  . . . . . . . . . . .   *NO           *NO, *YES
 Alpha display  . . . . . . . . .   *NO           *NO, *YES
 Add on 2 . . . . . . . . . . . .   *NO           *NO, *YES
 Add on 5 . . . . . . . . . . . .   *NO           *NO, *YES
 System 1 UPC-E . . . . . . . . .   *NO           *NO, *YES
```

Figure 11-22: Prompted version of the ADDEWCBCDE command (part 1 of 2)

```
                    Add EWC Barcode Entry (ADDEWCBCDE)

Type choices, press Enter.

System 0 UPC-E . . . . . . . . .   *NO          *NO, *YES
UPC-E  . . . . . . . . . . . . .   *NO          *NO, *YES
EAN 13 . . . . . . . . . . . . .   *NO          *NO, *YES
Extended Character Set . . . . .   *NO          *NO, *YES
Add on . . . . . . . . . . . . .   *BIDIRECTIONAL
Drop begin . . . . . . . . . . .   0            0-64
Drop end . . . . . . . . . . . .   0            0-64
Text 'description' . . . . . . . > 'Sample bar code device controller configura
tion'
```

Figure 11-22: Prompted version of the ADDEWCBCDE command (part 2 of 2)

When the customer varies on the line, the sequence of events should start that ends up with the remote devices communicating with the AS/400. Normally, you allow device descriptions to be created automatically by the system. Nevertheless, Figure 11-23 contains a sample of the command, Create Display Device Description (CRTDEVDSP).

```
                  Create Device Desc (Display) (CRTDEVDSP)

Type choices, press Enter.

Device description . . . . . . . > WLSDEV1        Name
Device class . . . . . . . . . . > *LCL           *LCL, *RMT, *VRT, *SNPT
Device type  . . . . . . . . . . > 3476           3101, 3151, 3161, 3162...
Device model . . . . . . . . . . > 1              0, 1, 2, 3, 4, 5, 12, 23...
Port number  . . . . . . . . . . > 0              0-17
Switch setting . . . . . . . . .                  0, 1, 2, 3, 4, 5, 6
Online at IPL  . . . . . . . . .   *YES           *YES, *NO
Attached controller  . . . . . . > WLSCTL         Name
Keyboard language type . . . . .   *SYSVAL        *SYSVAL, AGB, AGI, ALI...
Allow blinking cursor  . . . . .   *YES           *YES, *NO
Text 'description' . . . . . . . > 'Sample Wireless device'
```

Figure 11-23: Prompted version of the CRTDEVDSP command.

11.7 Distributed Data Interface

Distributed data interface (DDI) is a LAN that supports the ANSI X3T9.5 standard. DDI devices are attached on two counter-rotating rings that run at 100 Mbps. One ring is designated the primary ring and is active most of the time. The other, the secondary ring, can maintain the network if a device becomes inactive.

On the AS/400, you'll usually see DDI referred to as FDDI (fiber-optic DDI) or SDDI (shielded twisted-pair DDI). It is very common to use DDI to connect multiple AS/400s for superior file-transfer speeds. DDI networks consider all devices as members of one of two classes:

- Class A. Devices attached to both rings.
- Class B. Devices attached to only one ring or attached to the ring through a concentrator.

DDI is normally used to connect two or more AS/400s over a high-speed network. As such, all you need are the ring media (the cables) and the appropriate adapters in the AS/400s. Unless you're connecting LAN devices to your DDI ring, you don't need other hardware, as you do with other protocols.

You also can connect personal computers to your DDI ring, but you have to use a concentrator (IBM's is the 8240 FDDI Concentrator). One side of this concentrator attaches to the DDI rings. The concentrator contains one or more (up to a maximum of six) *device attachment* (*DA*) *cards*. These cards connect to the personal computers. You purchase DA cards for fiber optic or copper connections. Each DA card can support up to four devices.

The DDI adapter uses the same 48-bit adapter address as the token-ring adapters. Frame size considerations are the same as those for token-ring frame sizes. On a DDI network, valid frame sizes range from 265 through 4444 (with the default being 4105).

Sometimes DDI networking people refer to frame sizes in *symbols* (with two symbols representing one byte). Therefore, a DDI network supporting a frame size of 8210 symbols is, in other words, the same way as saying it supports a 4105-byte frame size.

11.7.1 DDI Configuration

To configure a DDI network over two AS/400s, create these objects in the following sequence.

- Create Line Description (CRTLINDDI).
- Create Controller Description (CRTCTLAPPC)—Optional.

11.7.1.1 Create Line Description (DDI) (CRTLINDDI)

Create the DDI line with the Create Line Description (Dds) (CRTLINDDI) command. Figure 11-24 has a sample of it.

```
                    Create Line Desc (DDI) (CRTLINDDI)

 Type choices, press Enter.

 Line description . . . . . . . . > DDILIN1       Name
 Resource name  . . . . . . . . . > LIN441        Name, *NWID
 Online at IPL  . . . . . . . . .   *YES          *YES, *NO
 Vary on wait . . . . . . . . . .   *NOWAIT       *NOWAIT, 15-180 seconds
 Maximum controllers  . . . . . .   40            1-256
 Maximum frame size . . . . . . . > 4105          265-4444
 Logging level  . . . . . . . . .   *OFF          *OFF, *ERRORS, *ALL
 Local manager mode . . . . . . .   *OBSERVING    *OBSERVING, *NONE
 Local adapter address  . . . . . > 400050010111  400000000000-7FFFFFFFFFFF...
 Exchange identifier  . . . . . .   *SYSGEN       05600000-056FFFFF, *SYSGEN
 SSAP list:                       _
   Source service access point  .   *SYSGEN       02-FE, *SYSGEN
   SSAP maximum frame . . . . . .   _________     265-4444, *MAXFRAME
   SSAP type  . . . . . . . . . .   _______       *CALC, *NONSNA, *SNA
              + for more values _
```

```
                    Create Line Desc (DDI) (CRTLINDDI)

 Type choices, press Enter.

 Text 'description' . . . . . . .   *BLANK
______

                          Additional Parameters

 Network controller . . . . . . .   __________    Name
 Group address  . . . . . . . . .   *NONE         800000000000-FFFFFFFFFFFE...
              + for more values     ____________
 Token rotation time  . . . . . .   *CALC         4-167, *CALC
 Link speed . . . . . . . . . . .   *MAX          *MIN, 1200, 2400, 4800...
 Cost/connect time  . . . . . . .   0             0-255
 Cost/byte  . . . . . . . . . . .   0             0-255
 Security for line  . . . . . . .   *NONSECURE    *NONSECURE, *PKTSWTNET...
 Propagation delay  . . . . . . .   *LAN          *PKTSWTNET, *LAN, *MIN...
 User-defined 1 . . . . . . . . .   128           0-255
 User-defined 2 . . . . . . . . .   128           0-255
```

```
                    Create Line Desc (DDI) (CRTLINDDI)

 Type choices, press Enter.

 User-defined 3 . . . . . . . . .   128           0-255
 Autocreate controller  . . . . .   *NO           *YES, *NO
 Autodelete controller  . . . . .   1440          1-10000 (minutes), *NONE
 Recovery limits:
   Count limit  . . . . . . . . .   2             0-99, *SYSVAL
   Time interval  . . . . . . . .   5             0-120 minutes
 Authority  . . . . . . . . . . .   *LIBCRTAUT    Name, *LIBCRTAUT, *CHANGE...
```

Figure 11-24: CREATE LINE DESCRIPTION for DDI network (parts 1, 2, and 3).

The token rotation time parameter sets the amount of time in milliseconds that the token will take to circumvent the ring. The sending system will continue to send packets of data until this time limit is reached. One possible value for this parameter is *CALC, and that is the one most customers use. When the DDI circuit become active, the system will calculate the rotation time based on the equipment attached.

This command also has (on the third screen) AUTOCREATE CONTROLLER and AUTODELETE CONTROLLER parameters that are similar to token ring and Ethernet lines.

11.7.1.2 Create Controller Description (CRTCTLAPPC)

Create the controller description with the Create Controller Description (CRTCTLAPPC) command. Figure 11-25 contains a sample of that command.

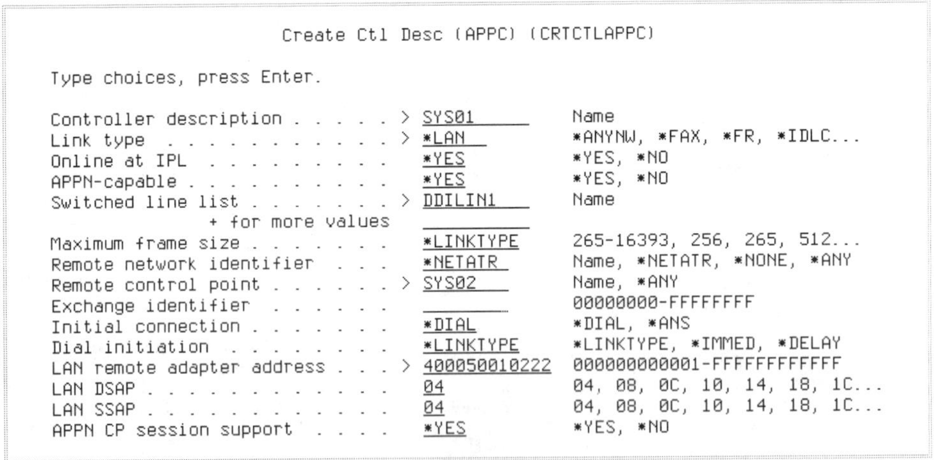

```
                    Create Ctl Desc (APPC) (CRTCTLAPPC)

Type choices, press Enter.

Controller description . . . . . > SYS01          Name
Link type  . . . . . . . . . . . > *LAN           *ANYNW, *FAX, *FR, *IDLC...
Online at IPL  . . . . . . . . .   *YES           *YES, *NO
APPN-capable . . . . . . . . . .   *YES           *YES, *NO
Switched line list . . . . . . . > DDILIN1        Name
               + for more values
Maximum frame size . . . . . . .   *LINKTYPE      265-16393, 256, 265, 512...
Remote network identifier  . . .   *NETATR        Name, *NETATR, *NONE, *ANY
Remote control point . . . . . . > SYS02          Name, *ANY
Exchange identifier  . . . . . .                  00000000-FFFFFFFF
Initial connection . . . . . . .   *DIAL          *DIAL, *ANS
Dial initiation  . . . . . . . .   *LINKTYPE      *LINKTYPE, *IMMED, *DELAY
LAN remote adapter address . . . > 400050010222   000000000001-FFFFFFFFFFFF
LAN DSAP . . . . . . . . . . . .   04             04, 08, 0C, 10, 14, 18, 1C...
LAN SSAP . . . . . . . . . . . .   04             04, 08, 0C, 10, 14, 18, 1C...
APPN CP session support  . . . .   *YES           *YES, *NO
```

Figure 11-25: CREATE CONTROLLER DESCRIPTION for DDI network.

Create the controller only if one doesn't exist and if AUTOCREATE CONTROLLER was set to *NO on the Create Line Description command.

That's it for configuring a DDI network. There is no need to configure a device because the computer is the device. DDI is primarily for host-to-host communications.

11.8 FRAME-RELAY

Frame-relay is a packet-switching protocol that is similar to X.25, but much faster (up to 2 Mbps). Frame-relay uses established data-communications networks, like phone and cable companies, outside the organization. You connect to such networks by becoming a subscriber. Built-in reliability is such an accepted part of established data-communications networks that frame-relay doesn't provide as much error handling as the other protocols.

Frame-relay is very expensive for in-house LANs or even across the same city. It is generally used to connect two LANs (or two AS/400s) across very large distances. It is the protocol of choice for wide-area network (WAN) support.

A frame-relay LAN can be configured as direct or bridged. A *direct frame-relay* is typically two or more AS/400s connected over a frame-relay network and running APPC or APPN. A direct frame-relay can also connect to remote systems supporting the IP or IPX direct format.

A *bridged frame-relay* network is similar except that the remote device is a remote bridge (such as the IBM 6611 Network Processor) to a LAN. Another AS/400 can be on the remote LAN, but it is not necessary. Through a bridged frame-relay network, an AS/400 can communicate with workstations on a remote LAN as efficiently as if they were locally attached. The AS/400 itself can act as a bridge on the frame-relay network.

The frame-relay physical pieces are more complex than those used by the other protocols. The AS/400 is referred to as *terminal equipment* (TE) on a frame-relay network. A network node on a frame-relay network (much like an intermediate node in APPN) is referred to as a *frame handler* (FH). TEs are connected to FHs through a device that is really two bundled devices. The bundled devices are a *data service unit* (DSU) and a *channel service unit* (CSU). Together they are referred to as a *DSU/CSU.*

All together, you'll have an AS/400 (the TE) connected by some physical wiring into a DSU/CSU. The DSU/CSU connects to an FH and the FH then connects to the frame-relay network. At other points on the frame-relay network, other FHs come off and connect to other TEs through DSU/CSUs.

Although you need at least the cabling and FH on both ends of the frame-relay network, each end also can be an *SNA-direct connection* or bridged. An SNA-direct connection allows SNA systems to connect directly to the FH. Otherwise, token ring, Ethernet, and DDI all connect to an FH by a bridge.

You can connect two AS/400s using frame-relay without going through a frame-relay network. The result is much like connecting two PC communication ports by directly using a modem eliminator rather than a modem. In this case, you can use the high-speed benefits of a frame-relay without the expense of joining the network. Just configure one AS/400's network interface description as LMIMODE(*FH) and the others as LMIMODE(*TE).

Drilling down into the physical stuff a little more, the AS/400 requires an adapter. The adapter can be any of the following:

- 2666 High Speed Communications Input/Output Processor (IOP).
- 2629-2699 High Speed Communications Input/Output Processor.
- 2809-2721 High Speed Communications Input/Output Processor.
- 2629-2699 LAN/WAN/Workstation IOP—Two-line WAN IOA (input-output adapter).
- 2809-2721 PCI LAN/WAN/Workstation IOP—PCI Two-line WAN IOA.

These adapters support any of four *physical interfaces* (or cable connectors). The possible physical interfaces, their cable connectors, and parameter values (see the following section on CRTNWIFR) are listed in Table 11-1.

Table 11-1: Physical Interfaces.

Physical Interface	Cable Connector Parameter Value	Interface
EIA RS-449	ISO4902 (37-pin)	*RS449V36
CCITT V.36	ISO4902 (37-pin)	*RS449V36
CCITT X.21	ISO4903 (15-pin)	*X21
CCITT V.35	ISO2593	*V35

The cable types and adapter combinations dictate the cable lengths, clocking speed, and maximum speed available over the network. For more information on these relationships, refer to section 5.1.1 of the IBM manual *OS/400 LAN, Frame-Relay, and ATM Support V4R2.*

11.8.1 Frame-Relay Addressing

A single physical cable between nodes can support up to 256 virtual circuits. A virtual circuit between two nodes is referred to as a *permanent virtual circuit* (PVC) and is identified by a *data link connection identifier* (DLCI). The DLCI number can be between 1 and 1018 (although you can only have 256 of them on one physical cable). The frame-relay network provider assigned DCLI numbers at subscription time.

You must have the DLCI number when you configure either the line or network interface description. If you specify it on the line, you'll put it in on the NWIDLCI parameter. If you specify the DLCI number on the network interface description, you'll have to specify both the DLCI number and the line description name.

Unlike the other adapters in this chapter, frame-relay communications adapters do not come with preset addresses. This address is not required for SNA direct connections.

The Remote Adapter Address (ADPTADR) parameter on the controller description must match the adapter address of the remote system.

11.8.2 Frame-Relay Configuration

To set up a frame-relay connection, you must create the following objects in sequence. In the example that follows, I've include samples of setting up a two-AS/400, frame-relay network. With my example, one AS/400 is in Phoenix as the local machine and one is in New York as the remote machine.

11.8.2.1 Create Network Interface Description

Use the Create Network Interface Description (Frame-Relay) (CRTNWIFR) command as shown in Figure 11-26.

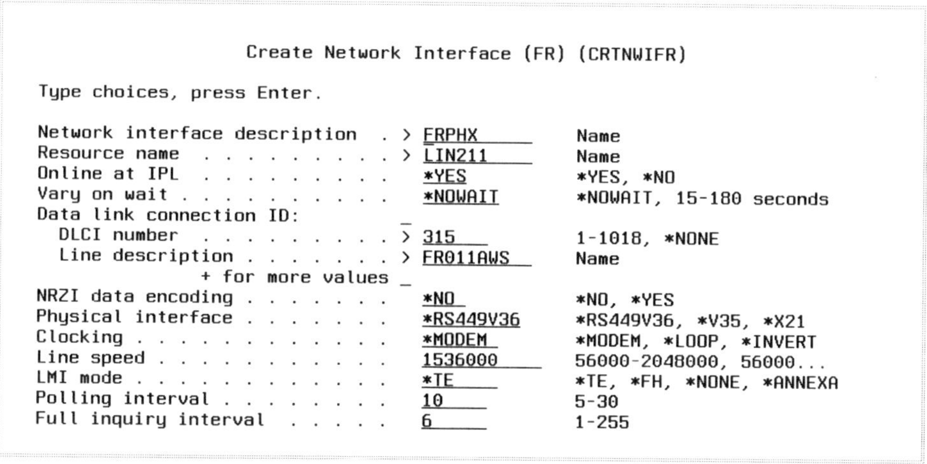

```
                     Create Network Interface (FR) (CRTNWIFR)

 Type choices, press Enter.

 Network interface description  . > FRPHX          Name
 Resource name  . . . . . . . . . > LIN211         Name
 Online at IPL  . . . . . . . . .   *YES           *YES, *NO
 Vary on wait . . . . . . . . . .   *NOWAIT        *NOWAIT, 15-180 seconds
 Data link connection ID:           _
   DLCI number  . . . . . . . . . > 315            1-1018, *NONE
   Line description . . . . . . . > FR011AWS       Name
              + for more values   _
 NRZI data encoding . . . . . . .   *NO            *NO, *YES
 Physical interface . . . . . . .   *RS449V36      *RS449V36, *V35, *X21
 Clocking . . . . . . . . . . . .   *MODEM         *MODEM, *LOOP, *INVERT
 Line speed . . . . . . . . . . .   1536000        56000-2048000, 56000...
 LMI mode . . . . . . . . . . . .   *TE            *TE, *FH, *NONE, *ANNEXA
 Polling interval . . . . . . . .   10             5-30
 Full inquiry interval  . . . . .   6              1-255
```

Figure 11-26: CREATE NETWORK INTERFACE DESCRIPTION for the frame-relay AS/400 located in Phoenix. The remote AS/400 is in New York.

Note that the PHYSICAL INTERFACE and LINE SPEED parameters are supplied by the frame-relay network provider (the phone or cable company). When a system connects using frame-relay, it is not like a direct connection. The frame-relay network allows a mismatch of things like line speeds between the nodes.

This example shows how to create the local end (in this case, Phoenix). On the remote end (New York), change all instances of PHX to NEWYORK (or whatever your naming standards are).

11.8.2.2 Create Line Description

Frame-relay lines can be created directly with the CREATE LINE DESCRIPTION (FRAME-RELAY) command. See Figure 11-27 for an example. Alternatively, frame-relay lines can be created as a bridged line description for the following topologies:

- Token Ring: Create Line Description (Token Ring) (CRTLINTRN). For a bridged token-ring connection, you must connect to a controller created with the LINKTYPE(*LAN) parameter.
- Ethernet: Create Line Description (Ethernet) (CRTLINETH). For a bridged Ethernet connection, you must connect to a controller created with the LINKTYPE(*LAN) parameter.
- DDI: Create Line Description (DDI) (CRTLINDDI). For a bridged DDI connection, you must connect to a controller created with the LINKTYPE(*LAN) parameter.

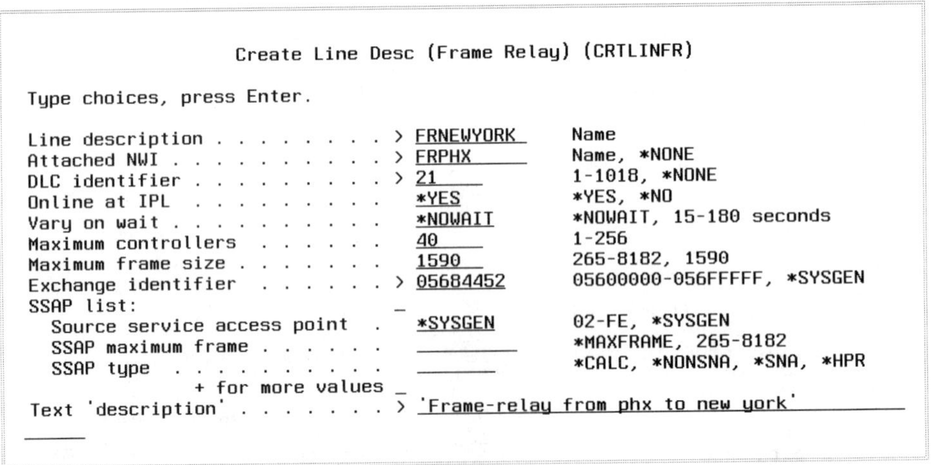

```
                     Create Line Desc (Frame Relay) (CRTLINFR)

 Type choices, press Enter.

 Line description . . . . . . . . . > FRNEWYORK      Name
 Attached NWI . . . . . . . . . . . > FRPHX          Name, *NONE
 DLC identifier . . . . . . . . . . > 21             1-1018, *NONE
 Online at IPL  . . . . . . . . . .   *YES           *YES, *NO
 Vary on wait . . . . . . . . . . .   *NOWAIT        *NOWAIT, 15-180 seconds
 Maximum controllers  . . . . . . .   40             1-256
 Maximum frame size . . . . . . . .   1590           265-8182, 1590
 Exchange identifier  . . . . . . . > 05684452       05600000-056FFFFF, *SYSGEN
 SSAP list:                           _
   Source service access point  .     *SYSGEN        02-FE, *SYSGEN
   SSAP maximum frame . . . . . .                    *MAXFRAME, 265-8182
   SSAP type  . . . . . . . . . .                    *CALC, *NONSNA, *SNA, *HPR
                + for more values _
 Text 'description' . . . . . . . . > 'Frame-relay from phx to new york'
```

Figure 11-27: CREATE LINE DESCRIPTION for frame-relay AS/400 located in Phoenix. The remote AS/400 is in New York.

Remember that the DLCI parameter comes from the frame-relay network provider. Also, for information on calculating the maximum frame size (MAXFRAME), refer to sections 11.4.2 Token Ring Considerations and 11.5.2 Ethernet Configuration.

This example shows how to create the local end (in this case, Phoenix). On the remote end (New York), change all instances of PHX to NEWYORK (or whatever your naming standards are). Also, change the DCL IDENTIFIER to the address assigned to the remote's line from the frame-relay service provider.

11.8.2.3 Create Controller Description

Frame-relay controllers are created with the Create Controller Description (APPC) (CRTCTLAPPC) command. See Figure 11-28 for an example.

```
                      Create Ctl Desc (APPC) (CRTCTLAPPC)

 Type choices, press Enter.

 Controller description . . . . . > FRNEWYORK      Name
 Link type  . . . . . . . . . . . > *FR            *ANYNW, *FAX, *FR, *IDLC.
 Online at IPL  . . . . . . . . .   *YES           *YES, *NO
 APPN-capable . . . . . . . . . .   *YES           *YES, *NO
 Switched line list . . . . . . . > FRNEWYORK      Name
                + for more values
 Maximum frame size . . . . . . .   *LINKTYPE      265-16393, 256, 265, 512.
 Remote network identifier  . . .   *NETATR        Name, *NETATR, *NONE, *AN
 Remote control point . . . . . . > NEWYORK        Name, *ANY
 Exchange identifier  . . . . . . > 05622844       00000000-FFFFFFFF
 Initial connection . . . . . . .   *DIAL          *DIAL, *ANS
```

Figure 11-28: CREATE CONTROLLER DESCRIPTION for frame-relay AS/400 located in Phoenix. The remote AS/400 is in New York.

Specify APPN-CAPABLE(*YES). The LINKTYPE parameter is set at *FR (frame-relay). If this frame-relay connects using a bridge to a token-ring, Ethernet, or DDI network, specify LINKTYPE(*LAN).

This example shows how to create the local end (in this case, Phoenix). On the remote end (New York), change all instances of PHX to NEWYORK (or whatever your naming standards are).

11.8.2.4 Device Description

Use the Create Device Description (CRTDEVAPPC) command. See Figure 11-29.

```
                      Create Device Desc (APPC) (CRTDEVAPPC)

 Type choices, press Enter.

 Device description . . . . . . . > FRNEWYORK      Name
 Remote location  . . . . . . . . > NEWYORK        Name
 Online at IPL  . . . . . . . . .   *YES           *YES, *NO
 Local location . . . . . . . . .   *NETATR        Name, *NETATR
 Remote network identifier  . . .   *NETATR        Name, *NETATR, *NONE
 Attached controller  . . . . . . > FRNEWYORK      Name
 Mode . . . . . . . . . . . . . .   *NETATR        Name, *NETATR
                + for more values
 Message queue  . . . . . . . . .   QSYSOPR        Name, QSYSOPR
   Library  . . . . . . . . . . .     *LIBL        Name, *LIBL, *CURLIB
 APPN-capable . . . . . . . . . .   *YES           *YES, *NO
 Single session:
   Single session capable . . . .   *NO            *NO, *YES
   Number of conversations  . . .                  1-512
 Text 'description' . . . . . . . > 'FR connection in Phoenix for remote in New
```

Figure 11-29: CREATE DEVICE DESCRIPTION for frame-relay AS/400 located in Phoenix. The remote AS/400 is in New York.

The device description parameter is the name of the remote system (in this example, FRNEWYORK), the remote location name is the name of the remote system, and the attached controller is the name of the remote system's controller.

This example shows how to create the local end (in this case, Phoenix). On the remote end (New York), change all instances of PHX to NEWYORK (or whatever your naming standards are).

When you configure objects for frame-relay, you must be concerned with the maximum frame size. The frame-relay network provider provides a "frame size" referred to as the "N203 number." The number can be between 262 and 8192 bytes for everything except bridged DDI and Ethernet. Most commonly, the number is 1600 bytes. Bridged DDI can be between 262 and 4488 and bridged Ethernet can be between 262 and 1522.

When you configure your network, you subtract routing information from this number to come up with a good number for the maximum frame size. The number you subtract is dependent on the connection type and protocol. Table 11-2 lists guidelines (presuming you take the maximum frame size for each protocol).

Table 11-2: Frame-Size Guidelines.

	Size of Routing Data	Maximum Frame Size
Direct:		
SNA	10	8182
IP	2	8190
IPX	2	8190
HPR	6	8196
Bridged:		
Token Ring	44	8148
DDI	44	4444
Ethernet IEEE 802.3:	26	1496
Ethernet V2 SNA:	22	1493
Ethernet V2 Non-SNA	26	1500

You can specify the maximum frame size in three places during your configuration:

- Line description MAXFRAME parameter.
- Line description SSAP has a maximum frame-size parameter.
- Controller description MAXFRAME parameter.

11.9 AS/400 LAN CL COMMANDS

After a LAN is configured, no matter what it's protocol is, there are several CL commands common to all protocols to help. The overall most powerful one is the Work With Configuration Status (WRKCFGSTS) command. It allows the customer to work with adapters, lines, controllers, or devices. It will display their attributes, vary them on and off, display the mode or connection status, and hold or release a device. Figure 11-30 shows a sample of that command set up to work with the line, controller, and devices for all token-ring LANs (but it could be used for Ethernet, DDI, and frame-relay).

```
                 Work with Configuration Status (WRKCFGSTS)

 Type choices, press Enter.

 Type . . . . . . . . . . . . . . > *LIN          *NWS, *NWI, *LIN, *CTL, *DEV
 Configuration description  . . . > *TRLAN        Name, generic*, *ALL, *CMN...
 Output . . . . . . . . . . . . .   *              *, *PRINT
 Range  . . . . . . . . . . . . .   *NET           *NET, *OBJ
 Status                             *ALL           *ALL  *ACTIVE  *FAILED
```

Figure 11-30: Prompted screen for WRKCFGSTS command.

After you press Enter, the command displays all the objects related to the protocol requested (in this example, the token ring LAN). See Figure 11-31.

```
                     Work with Configuration Status                SYS02
                                                          12/05/96  07:34:18
 Position to  . . . . .   __________   Starting characters

 Type options, press Enter.
   1=Vary on   2=Vary off   5=Work with job   8=Work with description
   9=Display mode status ...

 Opt  Description        Status              -------------Job--------------
 _    TCP_IP01           ACTIVE
 _      TCP_INET         ACTIVE
 _        TCP_ITCP       ACTIVE              QTCPIP      QTCP        036772
 _    TOKENRING1         ACTIVE
 _      GE11S02          ACTIVE
 _        WDRSE          ACTIVE
 _          QPCSUPP      ACTIVE/TARGET       WDRSE       PCS         046630
 _        WSHSE          ACTIVE
 _          QPCSUPP      ACTIVE/TARGET       WSHSE       PCS         046749
                                                                       More...
 Parameters or command
 ===> ______________________________________________________________________
 F3=Exit   F4=Prompt   F12=Cancel   F23=More options   F24=More keys
```

Figure 11-31: Token ring lines, controllers, and devices from the WRKCFGSTS command.

Figure 11-31 shows the screen after you press Enter. Notice on this system that TCP/IP is running over token ring. That is reflected in the first three objects. From this screen, you can do a lot of work with the lines, controllers, and devices.

Another CL command is the Work with Hardware Resource (WRKHDWRSC) command. Figure 11-32 shows its basic form. The example requests information about communication (*CMN) resources.

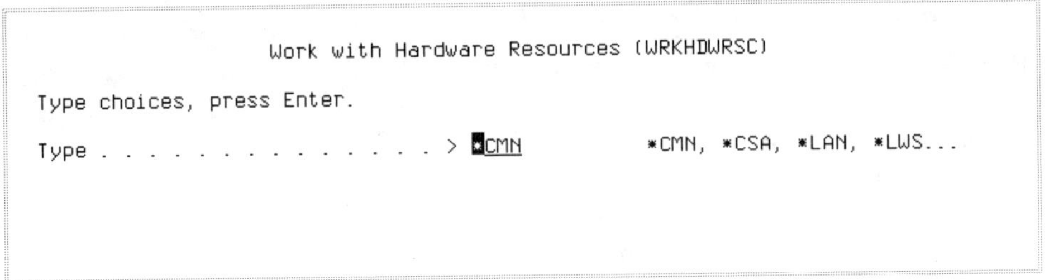

```
                     Work with Hardware Resources (WRKHDWRSC)

Type choices, press Enter.

Type . . . . . . . . . . . . . . > *CMN            *CMN, *CSA, *LAN, *LWS...
```

Figure 11-32: Formatted version of the WRKHDWRSC command.

Figure 11-33 shows the next screen after you press Enter key.

```
                       Work with Communication Resources
                                                            System:   SYS02
Type options, press Enter.
  5=Work with configuration descriptions   7=Display resource detail

Opt  Resource          Type  Status             Text
_    CMB01             9162  Operational        Combined function IOP
_      LIN01           2612  Operational        Comm Adapter
_        CMN01         2612  Operational        V.24 Port Enhanced
_      LIN02           2612  Operational        Comm Adapter
_        CMN02         2612  Operational        V.24 Port Enhanced
_    CC02              2618  Operational        Comm Processor
_      LIN04           2618  Operational        LAN Adapter
_        CMN03         2618  Operational        FDDI Port
_    CC01              2619  Operational        Combined function IOP
_      LIN03           2619  Operational        LAN Adapter
_        CMN04         2619  Operational        Token-Ring Port
_      LIN10           605A  Operational        Virtual Controller
_    CC03              2623  Operational        Comm Processor
_      LIN07           2609  Operational        Comm Adapter
_        CMN05         2609  Operational        V.24 Port Enhanced
                                                                  More...
F3=Exit   F5=Refresh   F6=Print   F12=Cancel
```

Figure 11-33: IOPs, adapters, and lines displayed by the WRKHDWRSC command.

11.10 ATM (Asynchronous Transfer Mode)

New with Version 4 is Asynchronous Transfer Mode (ATM) support on the AS/400. ATM provides data exchange between computers in the speed range of up to 155 Mbps, over a wide variety of cable types and connecters, and over distances formerly only possible with WANs.

ATM provides something new: LAN Emulation (or LANE). It can run over Ethernet (IEEE 802.3 or Version 2) or token ring lines. The AS/400 doesn't do LAN emulation; that must take place on some attached hardware such as:

- IBM 8260 Network Switch.
- IBM 2210 Multi-Protocol Switched Service (MSS).

When an ATM client station wants to transmit something to a server or another client, it doesn't have to know the ATM address of either device at transmission time. An ATM network is a switched network. That is, without a physical topology and layout scheme, every transmission must be dynamically routed or switched to its destination. APPN-based networks had predetermined nodes and lines. Even the network servers had directories of related nodes and lines.

A group of LAN workstations attached to a single LAN segment within an ATM network is referred to as a *LAN Emulation Domain (LED)*.

A client on an ATM network is referred to as a *LAN Emulation Client* (*LEC*). This can be the AS/400 (which can service many of its own workstations, devices, or sessions, providing them a single access to the ATM network), PC, or UNIX computer. When an AS/400 is used as a LEC, only one client can be attached to an IOP (Input-Output Processor), but many IOPs supporting one client each can exist (each having its own adapter address).

The ATM interoperability standards that the AS/400 supports are UNI3.0 and UNI3.1. The piece of software that carries out these standards is the Interim Local Management Interface (ILMI). These standards are very important in ATM networks because together they determine how the end nodes and switches create and manage calls and addresses.

This isn't that big a deal as long as you remember to configure the AS/400 to use the same UNI standard as the switch to which it is connecting. Do this when you create or change the ATM network interface.

In addition to the adapter cards on each node, an ATM LED has three components (all of them optional):

- ◆ LAN Emulation Configuration Server (LECS)—A LECS is a server that provides configuration to clients. This "configuration" is not the same as the configuration one deals with when configuring a physical network. The LECS provides addresses and data forwarding services. Only one can exist on a LED. It also provides some security because it can be told what stations to recognize. If the LECS is not used, all clients must know the ATM addresses of all other clients.
- ◆ LAN Emulation Server (LES)—The LES provides ATM address resolution and control services. There is only one LES per LED.
- ◆ Broadcast And Unknown Server (BUS)—Provides frame forwarding and broadcast-related services to clients.

You'll see the LECS omitted where a customer has connected two AS/400s and only wants ATM to pump data very quickly between them. There is no ATM network (only the two machines) per se. In that case, the two machines' IOP cards are just connected together physically with a crossover cable and, on the line configuration (refer to section 11.10.3.2 Line Description Parameters for ATM Lines), the ACCESS TYPE parameter is set to *DIRECT.

11.10.1 ATM Addresses

An ATM address is a 20-byte hexadecimal number. Each end node must have its own unique address. On the AS/400, this address is composed of:

- ◆ 13 byte ATM address.
- ◆ 6 byte adapter MAC address.
- ◆ 1 byte selector byte.

You should be used to dealing with MAC addresses on AS/400 LANs and on ATM networks. You still have to know the MAC addresses of the devices to which you are sending data. This address can be the manufacturer's preset address or one you assign the adapter (for more information, refer section 11.3.1 LAN Addresses).

Receiving AS/400s use the selector byte to resolve which of several sessions attached to the adapter card is to receive the transmission.

11.10.2 ATM Transmission (Typical)

The ATM protocol is enabled when the line is varied on. It becomes active when the transmission starts. The client wishing to transmit data to another client must have the receiver's 6-byte adapter address. It sends that address to the LECS for address resolution.

If the LECS cannot determine the receiving client's ATM address, the request is passed to the BUS for address resolution. Either the LECS or the BUS calculates the receiver's 20-byte ATM address and returns it to the sending LEC.

The sending LEC then bundles the full ATM address with the data and begins the transmission to the LES. The LES forwards the data to the receiver LEC.

11.10.3 ATM Configuration

To configure an ATM network, create:

- An ATM network interface.
- ATM line description parameters. These are parameters on the Ethernet (refer to 11.5.2.1 Create Line Description (Ethernet) (CRTLINETH)) or token ring (refer to 11.4.3.1 Create Line Description (Token Ring) (CRTLINTRN) line descriptions
- ATM Controller description parameters. Ethernet (refer to 11.5.2.2 Create Controller Description for APPC (CRTCTLAPPC) (Optional)) or token ring (refer to 11.4.3.2 Create Controller Description for APPC (CRTCTLAPPC) (Optional)) controller description
- ATM Device description parameters. Ethernet (refer to 11.5.2.3 Create Device Description for APPC (CRTDEVAPPC) (Optional)) or token ring (refer to Create Device Description for APPC (CRTDEVAPPC) (Optional)) device description.

11.10.3.1 Create ATM Network Interface

The ATM *network interface* defines all common attributes of the ATM interface. Each IOP has one network interface attached and one line attached. Work with network interfaces with these commands:

- Create Network Interface (CRTNWIATM).
- Change Network Interface (CHGNWIATM).
- Display Network Interface (DSPNWIATM).

While all the preceding commands are similar, Figure 11-34 contains a prompted version of the CRTNWIATM command.

```
                       Create NWI ATM (CRTNWIATM)

Type choices, press Enter.

Network interface description  . > ATM1NWI       Name
Resource name  . . . . . . . . . > CMB01         Name
Online at IPL  . . . . . . . . .   *YES          *YES, *NO
Vary on wait . . . . . . . . . .   *NOWAIT       *NOWAIT, 15-180 seconds
Network type . . . . . . . . . .   *AUTO         *AUTO, *UNI30, *UNI31...
Text 'description' . . . . . . . > 'Network Interface for ATM'

                          Additional Parameters

Maximum PMP end systems  . . . .   0             0-2048
Switched virtual connections . .   516           16-2064
Network switch timeout . . . . .   2             *NOMAX, 1-30 minutes
Physical layer options . . . . .   *NONE         *NONE, 0000-FFFF
Attached lines . . . . . . . . . > ETHLINE1      Name
               + for more values
```

Figure 11-34: Prompted version of the CRTNWIATM command.

Name the interface on the NETWORK INTERFACE DESCRIPTION parameter. The resource name is the name of the IOP to which the interface is attached. If you don't know the name of the IOP, use the command:

```
WRKHDWRSC *CMN
```

This command will display a list of communications hardware.

The NETWORK TYPE parameter is to indicate what interface standard the switch supports (so the AS/400 will be at the same support level). The valid values for this parameter are:

- UNI3.0
- UNI3.1
- *AUTO
- *PVCONLY

The most common value for this parameter is *AUTO. That one will have the system make the match.

The *PVCONLY parameter calls for a permanent virtual circuit and may be used when the LINE TYPE (on the CRTLINATM command, discussed in the next section) is set to *PVC. If CRTLINEATM's line type is set to *DIRECT, *PVCONLY must be used here.

The Switched Virtual Connections (SVC) parameter is the maximum number of connections that may be active at one time for all devices associated with this interface.

The NETWORK SWITCH TIMEOUT value determines how many minutes the system will wait for the ATM switch to respond on initial contact. The default is 2 minutes and that's fine most of the time.

Specify the name of the line that will be created in the next step on the ATTACHED LINES parameter.

Two parameters, MAXIMUM PMP END SYSTEMS and PHYSICAL LAYER OPTIONS are ignored at this time.

11.10.3.2 Line Description Parameters for ATM Lines

Line descriptions aren't created just for ATM lines. They begin life as Ethernet or token ring lines (refer to sections 11.5.2.1 Create Line Description (Ethernet) (CRTLINETH)) or token ring (refer to 11.4.3.1 Create Line Description (Token Ring) (CRTLINTRN) for more information). Only a few parameters on these descriptions make them ATM. The parameters specific to ATM lines and their possible values are:

- ATM Access Type (ACCTYPE) determines the type of access the line will have. Possible values are:

  - ✔ Switched Virtual Connections (*SVC). Access through *SVC is through a connection that is created as needed, and then deleted or dropped when no longer needed.

  - ✔ Permanent Virtual Connections (*PVC). Access through *PVC is through a connection that is always present. No call through the switch is required with *PVC. To use *PVC, you must configure all physical paths to other LECs in the ATM switch. This connection uses no LES or BUS to connect LECs.

  - ✔ Direct (*DIRECT). Access is between two AS/400s with their IOPs directly attached with a *crossover cable.* A crossover cable is like a modem eliminator cable, where the transmit from one end crosses over to become the receive on the other end, and vice versa for the receive/transmit pair.

- Emulated LAN Name (EMLLANNAME) is the name of the emulated LAN the client is to join. Use EMLLANNAME when ACCTYPE is set to *SVC. This field is sort of case-sensitive (be careful with the resulting match to the LAN name). You can use uppercase, lowercase, or mixed uppercase/lowercase characters to name the emulated LAN. However, lowercase and mixed-case names are converted to uppercase before the match is made (and the match is definitely case-sensitive). For a match with unconverted characters, put this value in quotes.
- LEC Disconnect Time Out (LECDSCTIMO). The LECDSCTIMO value specifies the number of minutes (from 1 to 30) that a LEC will stay connected to a virtual circuit after the circuit has become idle. If you expect the circuit to be idle and want the connection to stay up, specify *NOMAX here.
- LEC Frame Size (LECFRAME). The LECFRAME parameter specifies the size of the frame of data that will be used. To set the LEC frame size, first determine the frame size of the LES, and then add 20 bytes to it (for the ATM address).
- LES ATM Address (LESATMADR). If transmissions aren't to be sent to a LECS to determine ATM addressing, LESATMADR is the address of the server to which they should be sent. The full 20-byte address must be specified: 13 byte network address of the switch, 6 byte switch adapter address, and 1 selector byte address.
- Local Adapter Address (ADPTADR). The ADPTADR is the local computer's 6-byte MAC address.
- Local ATM Address (LCLATMADR). The local ATM address is the full 20-byte address of the local LEC. It must contain the 13-byte network address, 6-byte adapter address, and 1 selector byte.
- Maximum Frame Size (MAXFRAME) is the maximum frame size for this line. The MAXFRAME must be at least 20 bytes less than the LEC frame size.
- Network Interface Type (NWITYPE) must be set to *ATM.
- Use LECS Address (USELECS). If USELECS is set to *YES, the LEC contacts the LECS to obtain the ATM address of the LES. If USELECS is set to *NO, the LES ATM address must be supplied in the LES ATM Address parameter.

These are the ATM-specific parameters that may be supplied on the create or change line description (Ethernet and token ring) commands. Other parameters specific for Ethernet and token ring also must be supplied.

In addition, although they have no ATM-specific parameters, controllers and devices must be created for those lines.

11.11 References

OS/400 LAN, Frame-Relay, and ATM Support V4R2 (SC41-5404-01)

AS/400 Wireless LAN V1R1 Installation & Planning Guide (G571-0303)

OS/400 Communications Configuration V4R1 (SC41-5401-00)

OS/400 Communications Management V4R2 (SC41-5406-01)

12 Communications: TCP/IP and the Internet

12.1 Overview

While Ethernet, token ring, DDI, and the other protocols covered in chapter 11 are sufficient to connect many workstations into a single LAN, they are not enough when you want to communicate outside of the LAN. The idea of communicating outside of the local LAN is to give many computers access to each other's networks to facilitate common marketing, commerce, messaging, or whatever. Extending the computing boundaries beyond the local LAN is referred to as *inter-networking* or, more popularly, the *Internet.*

You can have a LAN (a rather large one, too) with just the information provided in chapters 10 and 11. But as soon as you venture past its boundaries into public networks, you're into the Internet and you'll use TCP/IP as your protocol. Because TCP/IP runs over a physical network already in place, TCP/IP runs over any of the protocols discussed in the preceding chapter.

Writing (and reading) about TCP/IP and the Internet takes some nonlinear thinking. This subject doesn't progress in nice A, B, then C sequence. Some of the tasks are independent of each other. For example, bringing up TCP/IP requires you to know:

- An IP address.
- A subnet mask.
- A remote *domain name* server address.

All of the preceding items are supplied by an Internet Service Provider (ISP) (and covered in section 12.5). But you should know about TCP/IP (refer to sections 12.2 through 12.4) before you try to arrange for Internet service.

To make sure where you are going, read this entire chapter before you start to bring up anything. Specifically, sections 12.2 through 12.4 explain how you can get TCP/IP and its applications up on your AS/400. Section 12.5 describes who can get you on the Internet.

12.2 TCP/IP

TCP stands for Transmission Control Protocol. IP stands for Internet Protocol. They are almost always used together and we think of TCP/IP as a single protocol. TCP/IP is a *packet-switching protocol.* Data is encapsulated into packets called *datagrams.*

Even though TCP/IP is almost always thought of as the Internet protocol, it is becoming a defacto communication standard. Years ago, computer hardware vendors would always offer their product with at least an asynchronous communication capability. That was the widest used protocol there was. Today, thanks to TCP/IP's ubiquitous acceptance, the honor goes to TCP/IP. Even if you have no intention of ever using the Internet, you might find yourself with a need to bring up TCP/IP to support some piece of hardware.

The Internet application layer (above TCP/IP) is also very functional; some AS/400 customers look at that area for quick and reliable functionality. For example, Telnet provides inexpensive, simple remote AS/400 access through, for example, a computer that doesn't have terminal emulation loaded on it.

As you get into TCP/IP, first take care of a system value. Because TCP/IP relies on virtual devices, check system value QAUTOVRT (the autoconfigure of remote devices). Check the value with the Display System Value (DSPSYSVAL) command and change it with the Change System Value (CHGSYSVAL) command. Do both at once with the Work with System Values (WRKSYSVAL) command. This system value determines how many virtual devices you'll allow your AS/400 to configure. V4R3 allows possible values of from 0 through 32,500 and *NOMAX, which says there is no limit. Keep the following tips in mind:

TIP: System value QAUTOVRT has to have a value greater than 0 or TCP/IP isn't going to work.

You're going to have some users signing onto your system through Telnet or the Internet. For any users you expect, make sure their User IDs exist and are active on the system before you begin.

12.2.1 Operations Navigator

For customers needing TCP/IP support and who are too new to the AS/400 to feel comfortable with it, IBM introduced AS/400 Operations Navigator. This product is a graphical interface into the AS/400 through Windows 95/NT clients.

With this product, customers can manage and administer their AS/400 systems through the more familiar Windows environments. Even the uninitiated can work with database administration, file systems, Internet network administration, users, and user groups. They can schedule regular system backups and display hardware and software inventory. Most important is that it provides a familiar interface to bringing up TCP/IP.

In order to use Operations Navigator, you must have Client Access installed on your Windows 95/NT PC and have an AS/400 connection from that PC.

To access Operations Navigator, the client first needs either Windows NT or Windows 95 installed on a PC. Then an AS/400 connection must be established. After that, the Operations Navigator icon will be found in the Client Access folder on the desktop. Double-click on the icon to activate it.

This is a powerful interface tool and particularly useful to anyone new to the AS/400. For more information, refer to the IBM manual, *Client Access for Windows 95/NT – Setup (SC41-3512).*

12.2.2 IP Addressing

Like other protocols discussed in this chapter, you must deal with addresses for TCP/IP nodes. Remember that TCP/IP runs over another LAN protocol. Therefore, the MAC for addressing every adapter is still there.

Because TCP/IP's purpose is to communicate with any computer network in the world, it has to have another layer of addressing. That's right. Every computer in the world, one way or the other, must have a unique address. A mathematical genius, taking a critical look at the Internet's addressing scheme, would instantly see a problem. There aren't enough bits for every computer host in the world to have a unique address.

The solution has been a combination of straight addressing from a central authority and subnets in order to give organizations the capability to concoct their own addressing scheme for hundreds of in-house hosts. This solution has also yielded an addressing scheme that gives most normal people nightmares.

12.2.2.1 IP's Basic Address

The basic TCP/IP address is a 32-bit integer expressed in terms of four hexadecimal numbers or four three-digit decimal numbers, each separated by a period. Here's how it works. A typical Internet address might be 204.145.193.104. The bits that make that up are listed in Table 12-1.

Table 12-1: Internet Address Bits.										
Bit positions' values:	**128**	**64**	**32**	**16**	**8**	**4**	**2**	**1**		
Byte 0: (Hex=X'CC')	1	1	0	0	1	1	0	0	=	204
Byte 1: (Hex=X'91')	1	0	0	1	0	0	0	1	=	145
Byte 2: (Hex=X'C1')	1	1	0	0	0	0	0	1	=	193
Byte 3: (Hex=X'68')	0	1	1	0	1	0	0	0	=	104

You can bring up a TCP/IP network between your AS/400(s) and other nodes and, if it is entirely local (never joining the actual Internet), you are free to make up your own TCP/IP addresses. Be careful, though; TCP/IP brought up with made-up IP addresses will have to be torn down and recreated if at some later date you decide to join the Internet. With all the clients and servers you could have in place, this could be a daunting job.

If you really don't believe you'll ever be on the Internet, but you want to bring up TCP/IP locally, you should use one of the reserved private addresses mentioned as follows in this section.

Internet addresses come from an organization called the InterNIC. But the InterNIC no longer deals directly with individuals (including your company). You'll get your IP address from your Internet Service Provider (ISP), (refer to section 12.5).

You have a little more flexibility with your domain name, however. Your domain name also comes from the InterNIC, but you can deal with the organization yourself without going through an ISP. If you anticipate being on the Internet at any time in the future, you can contact InterNIC and find out if the domain name you want is available for your company. For a small fee, you can register a domain name so that it will be reserved when you are ready to use it. Domain names are covered later in this chapter.

If you are interested in contacting the InterNIC about either subject, it has two e-mail addresses:

- For information about IP addresses: hostmaster@internic.net
- For domain name information: info@is.internet.net

You'll be getting your Internet access through a local ISP. For a list of ISPs, contact the InterNIC at the second address. When you get an IP address, it will be made up of 32 bits. These bits are actually carved into two addresses:

- <Network address><Host address>

The question is how many bytes for each piece? The division is a moving target. When more bytes are taken up by the network address, there are fewer bytes to hold individual host addresses. Conversely, fewer bytes for the network yield more bytes for host addressing.

This shifting demarcation determines the *class of network.* If the network address is low, the number of individual hosts that can be directly addressed is high and this is a *class A network.* On the other hand, if the network address is high, the number of hosts that can be directly addressed is low and this is a *class D network.* Table 12-2 lists the classes of service and their network/host address divisions and possible values.

Table 12-2: Classes of Service, Divisions, and Values.

Class	Range of Left Byte	Bytes for Network	Bytes for Host	Maximum Number of Hosts
A	0-126	1	3	16,777,214
B	128-191	2	2	65,534
C	192-223	3	1	254
D	224-239			Multicast

A large network would be a class A network and an example of its address would be 9.4.3.1, where 9 is the network address and 4.3.1 is the host address. A small network would be a class C network and an example of its address would be 221.5.6.233, where 221 is the network address and 5.6.233 is the host address. Class D is a *multicast network* where the first four bits of the address determine that the address is multicast and the last 28 bits determine the multicast group address. The Internet has a fifth class, E, reserved for future use. The AS/400 does not support that class at this time.

For a quick clue to identify what class an address is, refer to its left three bits:

Class A	000
Class B	100
Class C	110
Class D	111

When you get a unique Internet address from the ISP, you actually get a unique network IP address and a range of addresses for host addressing. The customer has the option of assigning addresses in the host address part of the IP address.

12.2.2.2 IP Special Addresses

Before I discuss subnet mask construction, you should know that there are two forms of *special IP addressing*:

- Any 4-bit element of the address containing all zeros means "this" host.
- Any 4-bit element of the address containing all ones means "any" host.

Because 4-bit values of 0 and 15 have special meaning, they are excluded from IP addressing. Therefore, any 4-bit element's maximum number of possible addresses is only 14.

Another special address is a network address of 127 in the left-most (network address) position, like 127.56.27.1. This indicates a loopback address for testing and must not be sent out over the network.

Finally, for those customers who really only want local TCP/IP and will never take their network out on the Internet, there are address ranges set aside for private use. They also have classes.

Class A	10.255.255.255
Class B	172.16.255.255 through 172.31.255.255
Class C	192.168.255.255 through 192.168.255.255

Remember that the decimal number 255 is special because it is an 8-bit field containing all 1s. It really means *any* address. So read the local addresses like this: "Class A private address has a 10 for its first address segment and can be followed by anything for its other three segments."

12.2.2.3 Masks

Masks are a way of referring to significant portions of the IP address through a mathematical filter. Let's apply a mask to what we know so far. The InterNIC supplies the network address and the customer supplies the host addresses. The boundary is variable so the question is, "which is which?"

The mathematical device is a *logical AND* operation. Two bit arrangements are stacked and, if either one of the operands is a 1, a 1 results. If both are 0, a 0 results. Here's a sample:

1101 (13)
1001 (9)
1101 (13)

Another way to read that is 13 ANDed with 9 yields 13. Remember 255, our "any" address? Here's how that works:

1101 1001 (217)
1111 1111 (255)
1111 1111 (255)

Read this one that 217 (or any value) ANDed with 255 yields 255. Or read it this way, any 8-bit number ANDed with 255 yields 255. Or, again, 255 is your wild card.

Once more, try ANDing with the other special IP address, 0 or "this" address:

1101 1001 (217)
0000 0000 (0)
1111 1111 (217)

Read this one that 217 (or any value) ANDed with 0 yields 217 (or the original value). Or, when a mask has a 0 bit, the original values come through.

12.2.2.4 Subnet Masks

When you establish a TCP/IP configuration, your ISP will supply both a host address and a *subnet mask*. This mask applies a series of 1s and 0s to tell the Internet communications devices how to use addresses bound for your host.

Start to build the subnet mask by assigning 1s to all the network address bits. For an example, consider a class B network (see Table 12-2). Class B networks reserve 2 bytes or 16 bits for the network portion of the IP address.

A subnet mask for a class B network would be 255.255. But you won't be finished until you've come up with the other 2 bytes of the mask. Here's a list of the network classes and the start of their subnet masks:

Class A	255
Class B	255.255
Class C	255.255.255

The problem of a finite number of addresses still exists within the host address, however. Many customers further divide the host address into two components:

<sub-network><host address>

There are no restrictions or rules on how to do this. You really don't need a sub-network address at all. Each addressable host could have a unique address, but what works for the Internet community at large also works for large companies.

One server can act as the "doorway" into the Internet, but many other servers can address their own local networks. A sub-network then could be the designation of a router or host on the network. Then the host addresses could be a set of network end nodes each host supports.

For example an internal, secured network may have 100 AS/400 servers. The customer might anticipate some growth and allocate one full byte to identifying those servers as servers on the subnet. Then, if this were a class B network, the remaining byte would be reserved for addressing the individual devices served by each AS/400. If another full byte were allocated to that, each AS/400 could service 254 devices directly.

When considering subnet and host addressing, there is no law that says you have to stick with even-byte boundaries. The IP host address portion is wide open. Typically, customers will designate the subnet portion of the host address with 1s and the actual host addresses with 0s.

Consider the class B example again. Remember, no matter what the customer decides, its subnet mask will start with 255.255. But one customer wants to describe the system as 254 servers each supporting 254 hosts. This customer will have a subnet mask of: 255.255.255.0 where each segment is:

255	network address byte 1	1111 1111
255	network address byte 2	1111 1111
255	Subnet Address—byte 3	1111.1111
0	Host addressing—byte 4	0000.0000

Another class B customer has 10 AS/400s and each supports thousands of end nodes. This customer doesn't have to stick with byte boundaries. It takes 4 bits to make a 10 (1010) so this customer might dedicate those four bits to the subnet address and the other 12 bits to host addresses. The subnet mask will look like this: 255.255.240.0 where each segment is:

255	IP network address byte 1	1111 1111
255	IP network address byte 2	1111.1111
240	Subnet address—first 4 bits of byte 3 (1111) plus Start of host addresses—second 4 bits of byte 3 (0000)	1111.0000
0	Remaining byte 4 for host Addressing	0000.0000

It is a common practice to set byte 4 of the subnet mask to either (00000000), 128 (10000000), or 240 (11110000). A subnet mask of 255.255.255.128 on a host with an IP address of 29.4.72.128 tells you two things:

- It will allow local host addresses of 29.4.72.126 through 29.4.72.254.
- If a packet came in with the address 29.4.72.132, it is destined for local host ID 4 (132 minus 128).

Internet addresses are not very intuitive. It's one thing to sweat through setting up one's own network, but it's another thing to expect customers to remember them. To make accessing Internet addresses easy, use a domain name. This is usually the company name followed by .com (for example, ibm.com). Like addresses, domain names must be unique and are administered by InterNIC or an ISP. If your company is planning to bring up an Internet site in the future, it can reserve a domain name now through InterNIC.

The Internet has name servers loaded with huge tables just to convert domain names into IP addresses. Internet-bound transmissions armed with only a domain name start by resolving the domain name to an absolute IP address before they even start.

12.2.3 TCP/IP Configuration

TCP/IP is a protocol that rides over other protocols as long as they are Ethernet, token ring, DDI, or frame relay. The first thing you need, then, are the line, controller, and device supporting one of those protocols. Configure these just as you did in the preceding chapter.

The unusual TCP/IP addresses and domain names are a factor when you add the TCP/IP protocol. This protocol is added through an interface and a couple of address and name tables names after you've got the lines up.

If you need additional information about any of these lines, refer to the appropriate section in chapter 11:

- ◆ 11.4.3.1 Create Line Description (token ring).
- ◆ 11.5.2.1 Create Line Description (Ethernet).
- ◆ 11.7.1.1 Create Line Description (DDI).
- ◆ 11.8.2.2 Create Line Description (frame-relay).

Just make sure the SSAP parameter is filled in on the line description this way:

- ◆ If the line is token-ring, Ethernet IEEE802.3, DDI, or wireless, X'AA' must be specified as an SSAP. You can add it to the SSAP on an existing line.
- ◆ If the line is Ethernet V2, *ALL, or *SYSGEN, no special SSAPs needs to be configured, the system will include X'AA' automatically.

12.2.3.5 Configure a TCP/IP Interface

The AS/400 relies on an interface to identify its direct connection to TCP/IP. For other protocols, the line description is enough, but TCP/IP also works with host addressing. Therefore, the interface connects the IP address and subnet mask with the line being used.

When you configure TCP/IP, the AS/400 automatically creates one interface record—the one that supports the loopback. Use the Configure TCP/IP (CFGTCP) command and take Option 1, WORK WITH TCP/IP INTERFACES. This command will list all existing interfaces. If you try it immediately after the line is created with SSAP = "AA", you'll see the single loopback interface (its IP address will start with '127').

Configure other TCP/IP interfaces using the Add TCP/IP Interface (ADDTCPIFC) command or Option 1 from the Configure TCP/IP (CFGTCP) command. Figure 12-1 shows a prompted version of the ADDTCPIFC command.

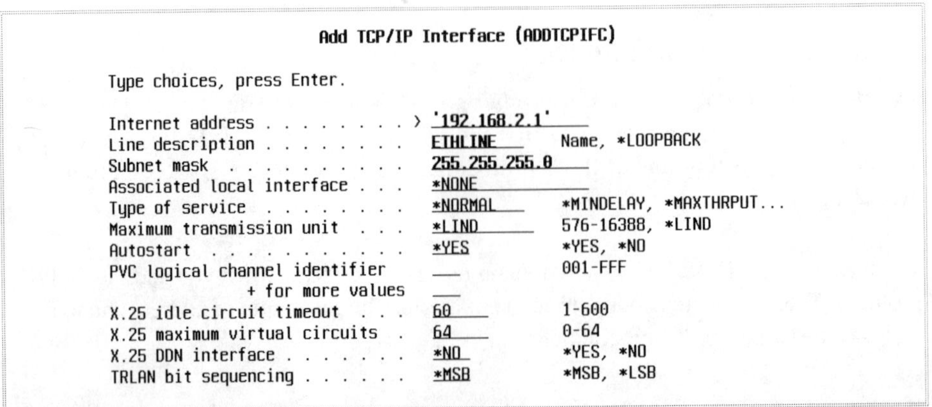

```
                    Add TCP/IP Interface (ADDTCPIFC)

Type choices, press Enter.

Internet address . . . . . . . . > '192.168.2.1'
Line description . . . . . . . .   ETHLINE       Name, *LOOPBACK
Subnet mask  . . . . . . . . . .   255.255.255.0
Associated local interface . . .   *NONE
Type of service  . . . . . . . .   *NORMAL       *MINDELAY, *MAXTHRPUT...
Maximum transmission unit  . . .   *LIND         576-16388, *LIND
Autostart  . . . . . . . . . . .   *YES          *YES, *NO
PVC logical channel identifier                   001-FFF
              + for more values
X.25 idle circuit timeout  . . .   60            1-600
X.25 maximum virtual circuits  .   64            0-64
X.25 DDN interface . . . . . . .   *NO           *YES, *NO
TRLAN bit sequencing . . . . . .   *MSB          *MSB, *LSB
```

Figure 12-1: Prompted version of command ADDTCPIFC.

Keep in mind that you are building an interface to other networks. This interface doesn't define all other hosts on the network. It should only define the address of the local AS/400.

12.2.3.6 Set TCP/IP Attributes

This step is optional and may be skipped when as you begin to learn how to use the AS/400 on the Internet. For the most part, the AS/400 defaults will work.

However, you can tailor your TCP/IP connection by setting it to use Rapid Information Protocol (RIP) for faster packet routing or you might want to set up your server to allow forwarding of datagrams not addressed to the host. Do both of these with the Change TCP Attributes (CHGTCPA) command.

12.2.3.7 Add Routing Table Entries

Routing table entries can be optional. Use them if:

- You are going to attach to the Internet.
- If you aren't on the Internet but you are supporting a very complex TCP/IP LAN.

In the first instance, the actual connection from the AS/400's LAN out to the network is through a hardware device, called an IP router, not the AS/400. Define at least a default route to this router.

Add routing table entries with the Add TCP Route (ADDTCPRTE) command. Figure 12-2 contains a prompted version of that command.

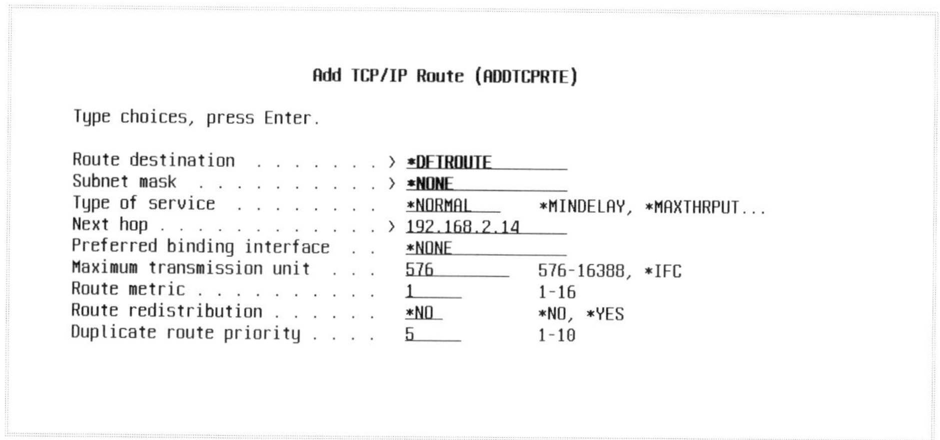

```
                     Add TCP/IP Route (ADDTCPRTE)

Type choices, press Enter.

Route destination . . . . . . . . > *DFTROUTE
Subnet mask . . . . . . . . . . . > *NONE
Type of service . . . . . . . . .   *NORMAL      *MINDELAY, *MAXTHRPUT...
Next hop . . . . . . . . . . . . . > 192.168.2.14
Preferred binding interface . . .   *NONE
Maximum transmission unit . . . .   576          576-16388, *IFC
Route metric . . . . . . . . . . .  1            1-16
Route redistribution . . . . . . .  *NO          *NO, *YES
Duplicate route priority . . . .    5            1-10
```

Figure 12-2: Prompted version of the Add TCP Route (ADDTCPRTE) command.

Note that, like the interface, the route table entry requires a subnet mask. The basic bits of information here are the route destination (the host address is the AS/400 to look for), the valid address range (determined by the subnet mask), and the destination (the next destination for the transmission). The next hop might or might not be the final destination of the transmission.

12.2.3.8 Remote Domain Name Server

The typical way of communicating to stations on the Internet is by using domain names because they are a lot simpler to remember than IP addresses. Domain name servers support huge tables that convert domain names into IP addresses.

The AS/400 is more functional than most computers in that it has its own domain name server. But in reality, that server isn't enough because it only holds the domain names for the local AS/400 hosts. Domain-to-address translation is fastest on this server, but most of the communications could be destined for hosts on the Internet and the AS/400 would have no knowledge of them.

Think of domain name servers as first a local one that resides on your AS/400 and provides very fast address translation for the local LAN nodes. The other is a remote domain name server on the Internet that contains foreign domain names and IP addresses.

One of the services a good ISP provides is a remote domain name server. Subscribers to that ISP are provided with the server's IP address.

When you configure your AS/400 for Internet access, give it this address so it'll know where to resolve remote domain names. Do so with the Configure TCP/IP (CFGTCP) command and take Option 13, CHANGE REMOTE NAME SERVER, from its menu screen.

Enter the ISP-supplied IP address for its domain name server on the SERVER ADDRESS parameter.

12.2.3.9 Add Host Table Entries

Similar to the domain name servers and remote name servers that connect domains with IP addresses, you must specify an IP address-to-host name connection for the local AS/400 nodes. This is the host (not the domain) name. This connection is made through the AS/400's Host Table Entries.

Add new entries with the add TCP/IP Host Table Entry (ADDTCPHTE) command or Option 10 from the Configure TCP/IP (CFGTCP) command. See Figure 12-3 for a prompted version of the ADDTCPHTE command.

```
                    Add TCP/IP Host Table Entry (ADDTCPHTE)

 Type choices, press Enter.

 Internet address . . . . . . . . > '192.168.2.1'
 Host names:
   Name . . . . . . . . . . . . . . > TEST400.BIGCOMPANY.COM



   Name . . . . . . . . . . . . . . > TEST400



                + for more values _
 Text 'description' . . . . . . .   'Two host names for one IP address'
```

Figure 12-3: Add TCP/IP Host Table Entry (ADDTCPHTE).

Up to four local host names can be associated with each IP address. When a TCP/IP line description is created, it automatically creates a loopback interface; it also automatically creates two local host names with that loopback address. Those names are LOOPBACK and LOCALHOST.

Because you can define up to four local host names, it is common practice to give the host name in a couple of versions. If your host name is TEST400 and its domain is BIGCOMPANY.COM, define (as in Figure 12-3) two host names for its address:

- TEST400.BIGCOMPANY.COM
- TEST400

After host table entries are added, they can be changed with the Change TCP/IP Host Table Entries (CHGTCPHTE) command. They can be removed with the Remove TCP/IP Host Table Entries (RMVTCPHTE) command.

12.2.3.10 Configure the Domain and Host Names

After the host name and IP address are associated as host table entries, associate the domain name with the host name. Use Option 12 from the Configure TCP/IP (CFGTCP) menu or the Change TCP Domain (CHGTCPDMN) command. See Figure 12-4.

```
                    Change TCP/IP Domain (CHGTCPDMN)

 Type choices, press Enter.

 Host name . . . . . . . . . . . .   TEST400

 Domain name . . . . . . . . . . .   TEST400.BIGCOMPANY.COM

 Host name search priority . . .     *LOCAL        *REMOTE, *LOCAL, *SAME

   Internet address . . . . . . .    '192.168.2.1'
                                     *SAME
                                     *SAME
```

Figure 12-4: Associate local domain name to local host name.

The example shown in Figure 12-4 uses the same host and domain name examples mentioned in the previous section. If a datagram comes in with a domain name that does not match the one supplied, this table will help the system resolve the unknown name to a host. The HOST NAME PRIORITY tells the system to look in the DNS first at a remote host or a local one. The Internet address parameter tells the system the REMOTE INTERNET ADDRESSES of hosts that contain DNSs it can check.

12.3 TCP/IP CL Commands

There are several CL commands to assist managing TCP/IP on the AS/400:

- TCP/IP must be started on the AS/400 before it'll do anything. To start TCP/IP:

  1. Type GO TCPADM on the command line and take Option 3.

  2. Issue the command STRTCP.

- To see if TCP/IP is running, enter on a command line:

  ```
  WRKACTJOB SBS(QSYSWRK) JOB(QT*)
  ```

  Look for job QTCPIP to be active.

- To end TCP/IP:
  1. Type GO TCPADM on the command line and take Option 4.

  2. Issue the command ENDTCP.
- Messages from a TCP/IP session go to two queues:
  1. The system operator queue (QSYSOPR). To display these messages, use the command: DSPMSG QSYSOPR.
  2. Its own queue (QTCP). To display these messages, use the command: DSPMSG QTCP.
- If you have problems and find no messages or you find nondescriptive messages, refer to the TCP/IP job log. Use the command: WRKSPLF QTCP.
- One function you'll find in all TCP/IP sites is the PING function. It is used to verify that a connection exists between two TCP/IP nodes. You can PING a remote system by system name or IP address with the commands: PING RMTSYS(TEST400).
- PING '192.168.2.1'. You can see if your PING is successful by checking messages in the job log. If you're currently online and do the PING from the command line, use the Display Job Log (DSPJOBLOG) command.
- To perform many TCP/IP network functions, use the Work with TCP/IP Status (WRKTCPSTS) command and follow the menu.
- To perform many TCP/IP configuration functions, use the Configure TCP/IP (CFGTCP) command.

12.4 TCP/IP Applications

TCP/IP is more than a communication protocol. It is that, but once the software is up on the computer it provides a suite of functionality beyond communication protocol support. These additional applications are:

- Telnet (terminal emulation).
- FTP (file transfer).
- SMTP (mail interface).
- POP server (mail interface).
- REXEC server (command execution from a client).
- LPR/LPD (send and receive print files within a network).
- SNMP (network management).
- Workstation Gateway (WSG) (automatic screen conversion into HTML).
- OS/400 TCP/IP functions (miscellaneous but neat TCP/IP stuff).

Note that there is no standard for what functions other computers' TCP/IP offer. These functions are the AS/400's only; other computers might not offer all of them.

12.4.1 Telnet

Telnet stands for Teletypewriter Network. It's about as old and simple a protocol as you can get without getting into punched cards. But it's far from obsolete and, in some ways, it's far from simple. It's a great way to communicate to any computer from any computer. The AS/400 can be a client or server in a Telnet session.

With Telnet, a workstation could have equal access to an AS/400 or a UNIX machine without investing in and loading various terminal emulation packages. For quick remote access of computers on a heterogeneous network, Telnet can't be beat. The terminal emulations Telnet provides are:

- 3270 (for mainframes).
- 5250.
- VT100.
- VT200.

Could 5250 and VT100 be included in one program? That's right. And the downfall of Telnet (at least for a lot of serious work) is that things don't always flow that smoothly. VT100 is an asynchronous ASCII protocol and 5250 is bisynchronous EBCDIC. Every key pressed in a VT100 session sends a character to the host. In contrast, in a 5250 session, nothing goes to the host until the Enter key is pressed. Also, VT100s won't support any more than 4 function keys. On the other hand, 5250 supports 24 keys.

Hats off to IBM for enhancing such a low-level application to the point that it supports the high- to low-end range of the terminals. But there must have been a lot of concessions that went into the emulation.

12.4.1.1 Configuring the AS/400 as a Telnet Client

With the AS/400 configured as a Telnet client, a user—signed onto an AS/400 through TCP/IP—can dial up another host (running TCP/IP and Telnet server) and act as a workstation on that computer.

Start a Telnet session with the Start TCP/IP Telnet (STRTCPTELN) command in one of these two formats:

- If you know and want to refer to the remote system by its domain name, type:

```
STRTCPTELN <name of remote system>
```

- If you prefer to use the actual IP address of the remote system, type:

```
STRTCPTELN *INTNETADR <IP address of remote system>
```

That's all you do to start an AS/400 as a Telnet client. With the AS/400 as a server, as soon as you sign off the remote system, Telnet ends.

12.4.1.2 Configuring the AS/400 as a Telnet Server

Ensure your AS/400 can support 5250 full-screen sessions by configuring Telnet with the Configure TCP/IP Telnet (CFGTCPTELN) command. When the CFGTCPTELN command presents a menu, take Option 1, CHANGE TELNET ATTRIBUTES. Or use the Change Telnet Attributes (CHGTELNA) command directly.

Telnet provides relatively free AS/400 access to the public. Because anyone with even an obsolete PC and modem could access your AS/400, you must think about security. Carrying a security level 30 on your system (through the value of 30 on system value QSECURITY) allows a security officer to specially grant access. Another security step to consider is to limit the security officer with the QLMTSECOFR system value. By setting QLMTSECOFR to 1, no security officer will be able to use the virtual devices configured by Telnet.

Another security issue is to be careful to set two timeout values within Telnet. Change these both with the Change Telnet Attributes (CHGTELNA) command. The parameters and what they do are:

- Telnet Inactivity Timeout Value. This value states how long a Telnet session can be inactive (the user presses no keys) before the system will sign the user off normally. "Normally" means taking the user off the system in the same way as it would if the user had requested to log off.
- Telnet Timemark Timeout Value. This value states how long a Telnet session can be active if it doesn't respond to the host's timemark. This is behind the scenes and doesn't affect the user. The AS/400 sends a TIMEMARK command to the Telnet workstation. If it doesn't receive an answer within this many seconds, it assumes the connection has broken and normally signs off the user.

Telnet devices must be known to an interactive subsystem. To check the workstations a subsystem will support, use the Display Subsystem Description (DSPSBSD) command and look at the workstation entries (WSE). To add Telnet workstations, use the Add Workstation Entries (ADDWSE) command:

```
ADDWSE SBSD(QINTER) WRKSTNTYPE(*ALL)
```

The QSYSWRK subsystem must be active. Use the Work with Active Jobs (WRKACTJOB) command and look for it. If you don't see it listed, enter on the command line:

```
STRSBS QSYSWRK
```

Be sure to create user profiles and passwords for the users who will be signing on through Telnet (if they don't already have AS/400 access).To end the Telnet session on an AS/400 Telnet server, press the Attention (ATTN) key and take option 99 End Telnet session. The AS/400 Telnet server will not end automatically when a client signs off.

12.4.2 FTP

FTP (file transfer protocol) moves files and programs from one system to another. It'll usually do the work rather quickly and is especially nice for moving large files between systems.

FTP features automatic data type conversion—from ASCII to EBCDIC or vice versa—as the need arises. It also treats files as a stream of bits and not as fields or records. For this reason, plan to unpack all packed numeric fields before using FTP.

FTP is often used to transfer data between AS/400s. Be sure to specify that no translation is to happen during the transfer and numeric data won't have to be unpacked.

Files can be sent with FTP interactively or scheduled to run in batch.

FTP sessions—consisting of starting the session, moving a file or two, and then ending the session—tend to be short. Once your are in the session, the work is done through FTP-specific commands referred to as *subcommands*. I'll go over accessing the AS/400 as an FTP client and server, and then present an overview of several of the subcommands.

In FTP, the difference between what is a client and what is a server is usually based on this simple rule: the computer making the requests is the client and the other is the server. It makes no difference where the data is actually stored.

Only DB2/400 supports files with members. Although you can copy a file from another host into an AS/400 file member, when you attempt to copy a file member to a host other than the AS/400, FTP will create a new file consisting solely of that member.

FTP is built to move file data quickly and efficiently between hosts. With the AS/400, you can send or receive only a member of a file. But in no case can you select (or omit) records from a file. You can only send all the records within the file or member.

The AS/400 supports file-naming conventions beyond its traditional library/file. When referring to files in FTP, you have the option of using the traditional form or the UNIX form (with a path of subdirectories prefixing the name). You don't have to do anything special; you can use either at will. However, be aware that the AS/400 refers to library/file.member as NAMEFMT 0 and the other as NAMEFMT 1. Here are examples of each:

```
NAMEFMT 0        library/file.member
NAMEFMT 1        /QSYS.LIB/libname.LIB/filename.FILE/mbrname.mbr
```

In the text that follows, file name formats for source and target can be mixed. In other words, to copy an AS/400-based file to a non-AS/400-based file, use NAMEFMT 0 for the source and NAMEFMT 1 for the target on the GET/PUT subcommand parameters.

Although the target parameter is optional on the GET and PUT commands, make it a point of using this to specify the target file names. If you don't, the system will attempt to name the file for you and, when going from dissimilar hosts, this can become unpredictable.

When sending a file to an AS/400, "pre-create" the file on the AS/400. Just make sure the file length is correct (use the SIZE parameter of the Create Physical File (CRTPF) command. Also, ensure the file can accommodate the records you are going to send it. I prefer to use the MAXSTG(*NOMAX) parameter of the CRTPF command.

When you enter the AS/400 through an FTP session, the initial program (INLPGM) does not get invoked. INLPGM is a program named in every user profile that starts automatically when that user signs on. Therefore, library lists might not be set like you expect.

12.4.2.1 Configuring the AS/400 as an FTP Client

Start an FTP client session from an AS/400 workstation with either the Start TCP/IP File Transfer Protocol (STRTCPFTP) command or by entering FTP on the command line. There is only one command (STRTCPFTP) involved; FTP simply is another way to invoke it. Figure 12-5 contains a prompted version of that command.

```
                              Select Product
                                                          System:    TEST400
  Position to . . . . . . .   _______        Product

  Type option, press Enter.
    1=Select

                    Product
  Opt  Product     Option    Release
   _   5769999     *BASE     V4R2M0
   _   5769SS1     *BASE     V4R2M0
   _   INFOAS4     *BASE     V3R1M0
   _   INFOAS4     *BASE     V3R2M0
   _   INFOAS4     *BASE     V3R6M0
   _   INFOAS4     *BASE     V3R7M0
   _   INFOAS4     *BASE     V4R1M0
   _   INFOAS4     *BASE     V4R1M4
   _   INFOAS4     *BASE     V4R2M0
   _   INFODSL     *BASE     V0R0M1
   _   5716CX4     *BASE     V3R6M0
                                                                     More...
  F5=Refresh   F11=Display descriptions   F12=Cancel   F19=Display trademarks
```

Figure 12-5: Prompted version of the STRTCPFTP command.

The STRTCPFTP command is similar to the STRTCPTELN command that starts a Telnet session. You can either enter the remote system's name or its IP address. If you enter its IP address, you don't have to also enter the *INTNETADR parameter as you did on the other command.

However, the STRTCPFTP command is significantly different from most other AS/400 commands because you really have to watch the value you enter for the coded character set identifier (CCSID) parameter. You see, FTP moves files from one computer to the other. It is almost always translates ASCII to EBCDIC or vice versa. The CCSID parameter on this command sets the default data type value when FTP TYPE subcommand is used.

Most normal ASCII data types will work when CCSID is set to 819. That'll work most of the time on AS/400s. If it doesn't, try 850. After typing the command and pressing the Enter key, the FTP session is started.

The session will appear a little weird because the AS/400 workstation attempts to emulate the ASCII asynchronous mode that FTP would normally run on. That is, everything is a line at a time. You'll never see a full screen like the AS/400 uses. You only have access to a command line.

If the FTP application wants to know something, it will ask a simple question and you will answer it on the command line. Both question and answer will roll up to the first available line on the screen. If no question has been asked but you want to initiate something, type the subcommand and its parameter(s) on the command line and you'll see your command roll up into the upper part of the screen and the results of your command (successful or not) follow it.

12.4.2.2 Configuring the AS/400 as an FTP Server

The good news here is that FTP server is normally automatically started when TCP is started. If for some reason TCP is up and the FTP server isn't (FTP AUTOSTART may be set to *NO within TCP), you can start it on the command line with the Start FTP Server (STRFTPSVR) command.

The FTP server only runs in the QSYSWRK subsystem. The FTP server job names within the subsystem are QTFTP*nnnnn* where *nnnnn* is the job number of the particular FTP server job.

The good thing about the AS/400 as an FTP server is that you can simultaneously support up to 20 FTP servers on the same AS/400. This is nice for a company that distributes free services along with software that is offered for sale. The company can have an FTP server that requires no logon for the free stuff. At the same time, it can have another FTP server that requires a logon for the retail stuff.

To set the number of FTP servers the AS/400 will support, use the Change FTP Attributes (CHGFTPA) command and set the NBRSVR parameter to any number from 1 through 20.

12.4.2.3 Sample FTP Subcommands

There are approximately 50 FTP subcommands. I'll just mention the more popular ones here. Logically enough, both client and server don't share the same set of subcommands. Some of the ones they do share are slightly different for each. Table 12-3 shows the client and server versions of the subcommands. For more information, refer to sections 7.12 FTP Subcommands and 8.5 FTP Server Subcommands of the IBM manual *OS/400 TCP/IP Configuration and Reference V4R3.*

Table 12-3: Subcommands.

Client Subcommand	Description	Server Subcommand
?	Get general help	
	Add physical file member	ADDM
	Add physical file variable length member	ADDV
APPEND	Append a local file member to a remote file	APPE
ASCII	Local file types become ASCII	
BINARY	Local file types become BINARY	
CD	Change Directory	
	Create Library	CRTL
	Create Physical File	CRTP
	Create Source Physical File	CRTS
DELETE	Delete a file on the remote system	DELE
	Delete File	DLTF
	Delete Library	DLTL
EBCDIC	Local file types become EBCDIC	
GET	Copy a file from the remote to the local system	
HELP	Get specific help on an FTP command	HELP
LTYPE	Local data type	
MDELETE	Delete multiple files on the remote system	
MGET	Copy multiple files from the remote to the local system	
MKDIR	Make a directory	MKD
MODE	Set transmission mode	MODE
MPUT	Copy multiple files from the local to the remote system	
PASS	Enter your password	PASS
PUT	Copy a file from the local to the remote system	
PWD	Display current directory, folder, or library	PWD
QUIT	Disconnect and end the FTP session	QUIT
QUOTE	Pass a server subcommand to a server from a client. This is a handy way to pass a server subcommand to the server from the client.	

Table 12-3: Subcommands (continued).		
Client Subcommand	**Description**	**Server Subcommand**
RMDIR	Remove a directory	RMD
SUNIQUE	This is only in effect when the target computer is an AS/400. When the target file member is specified and it exists, this command toggles the option: <on> The existing member is replaced <off> A new member is created with a sequential numeric suffix to make it unique	
SYSCMD	Pass an AS/400 system command (not a server subcommand) to the remote AS/400	
TYPE	Set the data transfer type	TYPE
USER	Enter your user id	USER

12.4.2.4 A Sample Interactive FTP Session

Start the session from a workstation with the commands mentioned in section 12.4.2.2 Configuring the AS/400 as an FTP Server.

You will have to sign on to the remote system with a user ID and password. If that system takes the lead and asks you, just follow along. If not, type in the subcommands:

```
===> USER <your user id>
```

Wait for a response and then type:

```
===> PASSWORD <your password>
```

Wait for a response indicating you are logged in. It'll look like this:

```
<your user id> logged on.
```

I'll presume you know the name of the file you want transferred and its data type. ASCII is the default type for FTP files. If you want the file coming in converted to EBCDIC, type "EBCDIC" and press the Enter key to change the document. If you want the file to be in binary or if you don't want any translation, type "BINARY" and press the Enter key.

Change to the directory you want on the remote computer with the subcommand:

```
CD <directory name>
```

Doesn't it have the look and feel of an old PC? If you're ever stuck for a subcommand in FTP, try an old DOS command. It'll probably work.

If you are going to copy files, use the SUNIQUE subcommand to toggle how you want existing members handled. The default when the session starts is that SUNIQUE is off. Don't do anything if you want existing file members replaced when copied file members have the same name. If you want unique file members at all times, toggle this condition with the command:

```
SUNIQUE
```

On the other hand, the (REPLACE) option on the GET, PUT, MGET, and MPUT commands will dictate that similarly named "file.members" are replaced.

To get a file from the remote system, type:

```
GET <file name> <file name > (replace)
     Remote      Local
                  Optional     Optional
```

Either file (remote or local) can be qualified with the library and forward slashes or with periods and extensions as suffixes. File names should follow the convention of the file system in which they reside. Here are two examples:

- The GET /QDLS/MYLIB/PROGRAM.EXE command is for files that don't reside in the AS/400 library file system.
- The GET MASTLIBR/MASTFILE.MEMBXX command is for files that do reside in the AS/400 library file system. In this example, the suffix set off with a period determines the file member to get.

The REPLACE parameter is optional and, if specified, causes the new data to write over the old.

If you want, you can move a file from the local system to the remote system with the PUT subcommand. Here is its format:

```
PUT <file name> <file name>
    Local       Remote
                  Optional
```

The file name rules that applied to GET apply to PUT.

If you want to GET or PUT several files using generic naming, use the MGET and MPUT subcommands. The structure of these subcommands is the same as GET and PUT.

End the session with the QUIT subcommand. There are no additional parameters.

12.4.2.5 A Sample Batch FTP Session

An FTP session can run in batch mode so you can transfer large files unattended in the middle of the night. Actually, there isn't any rocket science here. You'll use a compiled CL program (CLP) that you will schedule to run and another CL source physical file member to contain the FTP session commands.

Here is a sample of the first program, the CLP, you schedule:

```
PGM
  OVRDBF INPUT TOFILE(<libr name>/QCLSRC) MBR(GOFTP)
  OVRDBF OUTPUT TOFILE(<libr name>/QCLSRC) MBR(FTPERR)
  FTP   RMTSYS
ENDPGM
```

FTP is an application program with an input file named INPUT and an output file for session messages named OUTPUT. This simple CLP overrides file input so it will take its subcommands from a source physical file member named GOFTP, located in <libr name>/QCLSRC. Also, all session messages, instead of going to a screen will be directed into a file named FTPERR located in <libr name>/QCLSRC (as directed in the example override to the output file).

The input file, GOFTP, will contain all the commands you would use during an interactive session (you may want to try this a couple of times before you really submit it to run at some odd hour). Here is a sample of what the file could contain:

```
PGM
  USER <your user profile on the remote system>
  PASS <your password on the remote system>
  CD RMTMSTLIB
  GET MASTFILE LCLLIB/RMTMSTF
ENDPGM
```

When you come in after this has run in batch, display the contents of the file FTPERR and you'll see all messages that were issued during the session.

12.4.3 SMTP

SMTP stands for Simple Mail Transfer Protocol and is used to route e-mail between different systems. The AS/400 uses SNADS (refer to chapter 10, section 10.8.3, SNA Distribution Services) to route mail to and from SMTP. The AS/400 then can be used as a gateway to other networks.

SMTP starts automatically when TCP/IP is started. If you do not plan to use it, disable the automatic start with this command:

```
CHGSMTPA  AUTOSTART(*NO)
```

Change it back at any time with the same command but substitute *YES for *NO.

If you are running TCP/IP with SMTP disabled and you want to bring it up, you can do so manually by typing on any command line:

```
STRTCPSVR *SMTP
```

Although SMTP is a routing protocol, you can send and receive SMTP individual mail through a client-based browser or Office Vision/400. You can also send/receive SMTP mail by using the command line on the green screen, but it's quite a chore. If you're a glutton for punishment or just love the command line, refer to sections 9.5, Sending a Message without Office Vision, and 9.6, Receiving a Message without Office Vision, in the IBM manual *OS/400 TCP/IP Configuration and Reference V4R3*.

If you're wondering if SMTP is up on your system, do a Work with Active Jobs (WRKACTJOB) command and look for four jobs that make up SMTP:

- QTSMTPSRVR—Server.
- QTSMTPCLNT—Client.
- QTSMTPBRSR—Bridge server.
- QTSMTPBRCL—Bridge client.

12.4.3.1 Configuring SMTP

If you haven't turned off SMTP autostart in TCP, when TCP starts on the AS/400, SMTP will start with TCP; and the first time, SMTP will configure itself.

If you aren't sure that this configuration is in place, check it by looking at the QSYSWRK subsystem. This is the only subsystem TCP/IP runs in. First, use the Display Subsystem Description (DSPSBSD) command. Then take Option 7 to display routing entries. Look for a routing entry with compare value of SMTPROUT.

Frankly, there is a way to manually configure SMTP but it is unnecessary work. Change the TCP/IP command so that SMTP will come up automatically with this command:

```
CHGSMTPA  AUTOSTART(*YES)
```

Then start TCP/IP and it will configure SMTP for you. You can turn off autostart afterward with the same command; just change *YES to *NO.

Whether SMTP was started automatically or not, you have some things to do to configure an SMTP server. These steps are:

- Update the system distribution directory.
- Update SMTP aliases.
- Configure SMTP to use a domain name server.

12.4.3.1.1 Update the System Distribution Directory

The *system distribution directory* names the user to whom mail will be sent, what system on which the user is located, and its address and name.

To work with the system distribution directory, type the command:

```
WRKDIRE
```

Because SMTP routes mail between systems, its system directory entries pertain to system-to-system information. Individual users are not listed. See section 12.4.4 for information about the POP3 server.

From the WRKDIRE screen, place a 1 on the option line and press the Enter key. You'll get a screen similar to the example shown in Figure 12-6.

```
                              Add Directory Entry

 Type choices, press Enter.

   User ID/Address . . . .   *ANY     TEST400
   Description . . . . . .   TCP Remote System
   System name/Group . . .   TCPIP                    F4 for list
   User profile  . . . . .                            F4 for list
   Network user ID . . . .

   Name:
     Last  . . . . . . . .
     First . . . . . . . .
     Middle  . . . . . . .
     Preferred . . . . . .
     Full  . . . . . . . .

   Department  . . . . . .                            F4 for list
   Job title . . . . . . .
   Company . . . . . . . .
```

Figure 12-6: Screen to add a directory entry.

Although you could name each user on each remote system, instead use *ANY for the user name. Doing so just means all mail destined for the remote address will be delivered to the system and that the system can determine the deliverability of the user ID.

Optionally, you could use *ANY for one of the systems on the list. This creates a system that receives all unknown (destination system unknown) mail. Remember two things:

- When setting up a remote user on a non-IBM platform that supports uppercase and lowercase letters for user profiles, this approach causes user profile names to fall under SNADs rules (which only passes uppercase letters).
- You'll have serious and unexpected problems if you use user ID *ANY and a host name the same as your local host name.

Be careful of using *ANY for the user profile and for the remote system address. It's a common way of providing routing for undeliverable mail, but you could be setting yourself up for a route-loop condition (messages go round and round the network forever). Here's what you have to do to avoid this problem (and still have *ANY for undeliverable mail):

- The system that's supposed to resolve undeliverable mail should not have an *ANY *ANY routing. (Remember, the system distribution directory entry will still have a system name and that will determine the system that gets this mail.)

Additionally, there are two things to be wary about the system configuration directory:

1. This figure is of the system distribution directory on a local AS/400. It's nice that you can get by with just forwarding all users to the remote system (thanks to the *ANY user ID). But the system distribution directory on the remote system must identify all its users.
2. The System name/Group field shows the local name. This name must agree with the name on the system distribution routing entries. If you don't remember setting one up, that's because one is set up for you automatically the first time SMTP starts. To find out the name you must use, enter the Display Distribution Services (DSPDSTSRV) command with a parameter 2: DSPDSTSRV 2

You'll get a screen similar to the one shown in Figure 12-7.

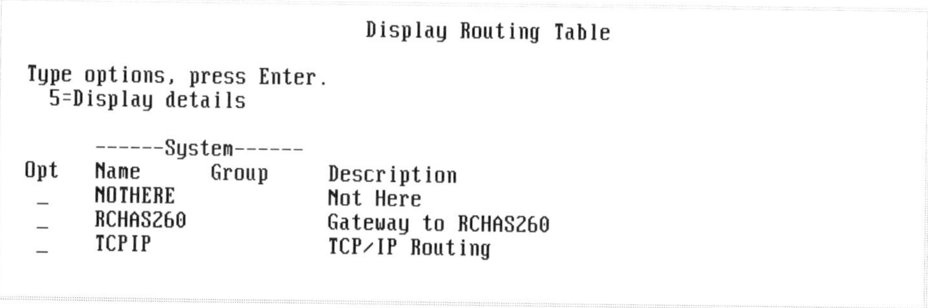

```
                              Display Routing Table

 Type options, press Enter.
   5=Display details

        ------System------
 Opt    Name      Group      Description
  _     NOTHERE              Not Here
  _     RCHAS260             Gateway to RCHAS260
  _     TCPIP                TCP/IP Routing
```

Figure 12-7: System Distribution Routing Entries.

The name you want is the first one (with the DESTINATION SYSTEM NAME/GROUP parameter). In this case, it's TCPIP (usually the generated name).

One thing that is new with the WRKDIRE entry is the RENAME option, invoked with command key 7. Previously, the only way to rename an existing entry was to delete it and re-add it. Now you can rename any directory entry.

A big deal to SMTP is mail routing. A lot of this stuff supports routing. You'll see shortly how you can specify a route to an individual. One thing that's kind of nice is that you can specify an alternate mail router to receive messages the AS/400 just can't figure out what to do with. To name this router, use the Change SMTP Attributes (CHGSMTPA) command and the MAILROUTER parameter. Here's a sample:

```
CHGSMTPA MAILROUTER(MAIL400.IBM.COM)
```

12.4.3.1.2 Update SMTP Name Table

The *SMTP name table* contains an AS/400 User ID and address (the system name) and a SMTP name and domain. Because the table makes a match between a very long SMTP and a "normal" AS/400 name, it is often called the *alias table*. This table is required whenever aliases are desired:

- The AS/400 needs to distribute mail from non-AS/400 hosts where user profiles might be otherwise too long or contain embedded special characters. An SMTP name consists of two components:
  1. User ID—up to 24 characters.
  2. Domain—up to 255.
- The user ID combined with the domain make up the SMTP name (which itself cannot be longer than 255 characters).
- A host's SMTP name is shorter than it's SNADS host name. A typical SNADS host name might be MDAWSON RMTSYS while the SMTP name could be MIKE.
- If a specific routing (referred to as *SMTP relay)* needs to be specified, this is done on the alias.

Although those are the rules, the convention is to routinely set up aliases. To set up an alias table, use the Work with Names for SMTP (WRKNAMSMTP) command. From that screen, take Option 1 to add a name and use Option 2 to change a name. Figure 12-8 shows an example of the resulting screen.

The screen shown in Figure 12-8 does several things. The User ID and Address are those of the remote, not the local, host. These are shorter fields than the SMTP User ID and domain because they are SNADS names (not SMTP). As such, they must also be in capital letters. Both must be filled in. In mail distribution, they are combined to form a "TO" address. When SMTP receives mail from a remote host, this address is parsed into a local User ID and host name (which should match the local name or the mail will be forwarded).

```
                       Add Name for SMTP
                                                System:   TEST400
 Type choices, press Enter.

   User ID . . . . . . . . .   MIKE      Character value, *ANY, F4 for list
   Address . . . . . . . . .   TEST400   Character value, F4 for list


   SMTP user ID  . . . . . .   MDAWSON
   SMTP domain . . . . . . .   TEST400.J2CA.COM



   SMTP route  . . . . . . .   @MINOT,@DENVER,MDAWSON@TEST400.J2CA.COM
```

Figure 12-8: Adding a name for SMTP.

The first two parameters make the SNADS name and the next two combined make the SMTP name. Notice how much larger the SMTP name can be than the SNADS name. If the User ID on a local host contains *ANY, then SMTP User ID must be left blank.

Although the SMTP domain name is just that—a domain name, like J2CA.COM—but for AS/400s, you concatenate the system name on the front. If the system name is TCPIP, the SMTP domain name becomes TCPIP.J2CA.COM.

In either case, the SMTP name also must be defined in a host table or name server so the router can find an Internet address to associate with it.

My AS/400 name is MIKE and my address is TEST400. My SMTP ID is MDAWSON and my SMTP Domain is TCPIP.J2CA.COM. The two of those concatenated together make the SMTP name: DAWSON@TCPIP.J2CA.COM.

Although I didn't have to, I also specified the route for my messages. I could have skipped the SMTP User and domain names and just specified my own route. In this case, maybe I am a part of a large network and I want a specific route to be used when routing my mail to me.

As in Figure 12-8, mail will come to me from a host named @MINOT, then a host named @DENVER, to the local host named @TEST400, and then to me at MDAWSON on domain J2CA.COM. That's how remote stations with mail addressed to MIKE in PHOENIX will route my mail to me.

Note the construction:

- Hosts are preceded with an at symbol (@).
- Hosts are separated from each other by a comma (,).
- The destination name is preceded by a host name (and itself preceded with an at symbol), followed by a colon (:) and the full, concatenated SMTP name.

By the way, it's a good idea to use the AS/400 user profile (refer to chapter 5) as the SMTP User ID.

This is another screen where *ANY is a valid entry for the *user ID* field. If *ANY is used, the SMTP user ID field should be left blank.

12.4.3.1.3 Configure SMTP to use a Domain Name Server

When you configured TCP/IP on your AS/400, you might have included a domain name server on it. If you did, that is the local domain name server and the default where SMTP will go to resolve unknown names and IP addresses.

Your AS/400 can only have a domain name server with local (to it and its LANs) names and IP addresses. It won't support an Internet-level domain name server. The ISP will offer that service. The domain name server on your AS/400 (with your local names) is referred to as the local domain name server. The one out on the ISP is the remote domain name server. Your AS/400 can access both.

To direct SMTP to a network-resident domain server, use the Change TCP/IP Domain (CHGTCPDMN) command. Figure 12-9 shows a sample of that screen.

The *host name search priority* tells the AS/400 which domain name server to use first when resolving domain names into IP addresses. *LOCAL (the default) will have the AS/400 access its own domain name server first. *REMOTE sends it to the ISPs first.

```
                    Change TCP/IP Domain (CHGTCPDMN)

 Type choices, press Enter.

 Host name . . . . . . . . . . .   TEST400

 Domain name . . . . . . . . . .   J2CA.COM

 Host name search priority . . .   *REMOTE      *REMOTE, *LOCAL, *SAME

   Internet address . . . . . . .  '9.1.2.68'
                                   *SAME
                                   *SAME
```

Figure 12-9: Directing SMTP to use a remote (not local) domain name server.

12.4.4 POP3 Server

POP stands for Post Office Protocol and the AS/400's TCP/IP support is for Version 3 of this standard. This allows the AS/400 to serve as a POP server for any client running POP mail on Windows, OS/2, AIX, and Macintosh.

While SMTP can receive users' mail, more typically you see SMTP routing mail and POP providing electronic mailboxes on the local host from which users can retrieve mail.

The AS/400's POP support includes support for Multipurpose Internet Mail Exchange (MIME). This allows transmission of video, image, audio, binary, and text mail.

To support POP, the AS/400 has to have several things running. For anyone serious about maintaining an Internet presence, SMTP and POP together make the mail standard.

POP itself doesn't have anything to do with SNADS or SMTP directly, but the AS/400 exchanges POP through the AnyMail/400 mail server framework. Because AnyMail/400 runs over SNADS and SMTP, they must be up when POP is running. Therefore, to support POP mail, the AS/400 must have up:

- SNADS.
- AnyMail/400.
- TCP/IP.
- SMTP.
- POP.

Clients accessing POP can be local workstations with any flavor TCP/IP support or AS/400 Client Access with MAPI on their client. The biggest difference between the two is that the standard TCP/IP client sends its mail to SMTP first and SMTP routes it either away from the local host or to the POP server (for local mail). The AS/400 Client Access workstations send their mail directly to the POP server for either local delivery or routing to SMTP and external routing from there. The key to all this working is our friend the system distribution directory.

12.4.4.1 Bringing up the POP Server

The sequence to bringing up a POP server is:

- Ensure SNADS is up. Because it is its own subsystem, use Work with Active Jobs (WRKACTJOB) and look for subsystem QSNADS to be there. If it is not, start it with the Start Subsystem (STRSBS) command:

```
STRSBS QSNADS
```

- Ensure the mail server framework (MSF) is up. Use Work with Active Jobs (WRKACTJOB) and look for subsystem QSYSWRK to be active with job(s) named QMSF running under it. If there are no such jobs, start one with the Start Mail Framework (STRMSF) command: `STRMSF`.

- If the clients connecting to the system are AS/400 Client Access and they are to connect to the POP server through IPX, make sure IPX is running.

- If the clients connecting to the system are AS/400 Client Access, issue the Start Host Server (STRHOSTSVR) command:

```
STRHOSTSVR *ALL
```

- Ensure SMTP is up. If it isn't up, start it. Refer to section 12.4.3.1.1 Update the System Distribution Directory for more information.

- Ensure you have system distribution directories set up. For basic information, refer to section 12.4.3 SMTP. For POP, though, you need a couple specific things:
  - ✔ An AS/400 system user profile for each local POP user.
  - ✔ The Mail Service Level parameter of each system distribution directory entry must be set to a 2 and the Preferred Address parameter set to:
    - ➢ 3 if you are using SMTP names.
    - ➢ 1 if you are using SNADS without a TCP/IP connection at all.
- If you are using SMTP addressing (and have set the Preferred Address to 3), press F19 from the Work with Directory Entries (WRKDIRE) (Figure 12-6) and enter the SMTP name. Remember to name all local users but specify *ANY for remote systems' users. Also, for the local users, make their AS/400 User ID the SMTP User ID. For more information, refer to section 12.4.3 SMTP.
- Ensure the connection is correctly specified in the POP application. Use the Change POP Attributes (CHGPOPA) command and check the Host Server Connection (HOSTSVRCNN) parameter. If you change any parameters on the CHGPOPA command, you'll probably want to end and restart the mail server (refer to the next bulleted item).
- Start the POP Server with the Start Mail Server Framework (STRMSF) command. If you need to end it, use the End Mail Server Framework (ENDMSF) command.

12.4.4.1.1 POP Server Commands

POP clients have their own set of verbs to communicate with POP servers. See Table 12-4.

Table 12-4: POP Server Commands.

Verb <parameters>	Description
USER <user ID>	Send the user ID
PASS <password>	Send the password
STAT	Check mailbox ("status")
LIST <msg # (optional)>	Check mail message statistics
RETR <msg #>	Retrieve message
DELE <msg #>	Delete message
RSET	Reset message delete status
TOP <msg #><lines>	Retrieve message header and data
UIDL <msg # (optional)>	Get message unique ID listing
NOOP	No operation
QUIT	Quit client session

12.4.4.2 Bringing up the POP Client

Because a workstation can use any browser to bring up POP, the specifics of this will vary. Needless to say, if your workstation client is Client Access for Windows, you don't have to do any of this. But if you don't have Client Access for Windows, you will have to do the following:

- Give the client the User ID and Host Name of the mail recipient. These will probably be entered separately through a GUI interface, but if they are entered together as a string, put an at symbol (@) between the two. Also:
  - ✔ The User ID will be the same as the AS/400 User ID.
  - ✔ The host name will be the system name concatenated with a period and the domain name. For example, if the domain name is J2CA.COM and the system name is TEST400, the host name will be TEST400.J2CA.COM.
- On some clients, you'll have to put in the host's IP address several times. Don't complain; just type away.

- The POP User (sometimes called the Account Name) should be the AS/400 User ID.
- The password must be the AS/400 password. (See why you've been using the AS/400 User ID?)

12.4.5 REXEC

The REXEC (Remote Executive) server allows any client to submit a system command to the AS/400. Embedded in that system command are the user's ID and password so the AS/400 can go through all its normal authorization approvals before executing the command.

Note that the commands that REXEC can submit must be capable of running in batch. Commands contain information on where they are allowed to run and one of these values must be *BATCH. To check, use the Display Object (DSPOBJ) command on any command.

12.4.5.1 Bringing up the REXEC Server

Unless you've disabled it, the REXEC server will start automatically when TCP is started. If you have disabled the REXEC server, or it is not running for any reason, you can start it with the Start TCP/IP Server (STRTCPSVR) command, with the SERVER parameter set to *REXEC as follows:

```
STRTCPSVR SERVER(*REXEC)
```

If it's already started, you can again start the REXEC server, but the system will start another server. If you're not sure if a REXEC server is running, look for jobs in the QSYSWRK subsystem. Each server will be named QTRXC*nnnn* (where *nnnnn* is a unique 5-digit number). To look at the subsystem, use the Work with Subsystem Jobs (WRKSBSJOB) command with the subsystem specified or the Work with Active Jobs (WRKACTJOB) command:

```
      WRKSBSJOB QSYSWRK
or
      WRKACTJOB
```

To change the AUTOSTART parameter (or others), use the Change Rexec Attributes (CHGRXCA) command.

Specify the End TCP/IP Server (ENDTCPSVR) command with the server attribute set to *REXEC, as follows:

```
ENDTCPSVR SERVER(*REXEC)
```

12.4.5.2 Rexec Client

REXEC clients use the Run Remote Command (RUNRMTCMD) command to send commands to the server. When connecting to an AS/400, the clients have one return connection. When connecting to UNIX, OS/2, Windows 95, or Windows NT, REXEC clients have two return connections.

What this means to you is that any printed output from the REXEC-submitted command will be sent back to the requesting client (that's one communication connection). Any error spool file will be sent back down the second connection (if there is one). If there is only one connection, the error will be sent over the first connection immediately after the command's output.

12.4.6 LPR/LPD

LPR stands for *Line Printer Requester* and LPD stands for *Line Printer Daemon.* These two applications are used to send/receive print files around a network.

LPR sends print files to remote systems (including to LAN-attached printers). You can send AFPDS printer files through LPR. However, some of the neat AFPDS things might be lost in print transformation.

LPD receives print files from remote systems. Although it will receive them, LPD will not convert ASCII print files.

The process that results from the combination LPR/LPD is referred to as *printer pass-through.*

12.4.6.1 LPR Configuration

LPR attempts to use the host and domain server names. While it's not a requirement for the names to be configured when TCP/IP is configured on the AS/400, doing so will make life better. LPR configuration also requires the names of remote systems to which it will be sending print files. Again, you can use the raw IP address, but the smart AS/400 person will have remote systems named in the host table. This allows you to use either the host or domain name when sending spool files.

To configure printer pass-through using LPR, you must first configure a remote output queue. Do this with the Create Output Queue (CRTOUTQ). Figure 12-10 has a sample of that command.

```
                      Create Output Queue (CRTOUTQ)

 Type choices, press Enter.

 Output queue . . . . . . . . . . > RMTSYS____      Name
   Library  . . . . . . . . . . .     *CURLIB___    Name, *CURLIB
 Maximum spooled file size:         _
   Number of pages  . . . . . . .   *NONE______     Number, *NONE
   Starting time  . . . . . . . .   ________        Time
   Ending time  . . . . . . . . .   ________        Time
               + for more values _
 Order of files on queue  . . . .   *FIFO__         *FIFO, *JOBNBR
 Remote system  . . . . . . . . . > RMTSYS______________________________
________________________________________________________________________
________________________________________________________________________
________________________________________________________

 Remote printer queue . . . . . . > LCLSYS______________________________
________________________________________________________________________
```

Figure 12-10: Prompted version of the CRTOUTQ command for creating a remote output queue.

As in the Figure 12-10, create the output queue with a name the same as the remote system (RMTSYS in this case). Name the specific print queue on the remote system. In this example, I named the remote print queue LCLSYS to show it is named after the system sending print files to it.

Connection type and destination type are mutually dependent on each other. Possible values for destination type and what they mean are listed in Table 12-5.

Table 12-5: Destination Type Values.	
Value	**Destination**
*OS400	An AS/400 running OS/400 of version V2R3 or later.
*OS400V2	An AS/400 running OS/400 of a version V3R1M0 and prior.
*S390	An IBM mainframe.
*NETWARE3	Any computer running version 3 of Netware.
*NDS	Any computer running version 4 of Netware.
*PSF2	A PC with PSF/2.
*OTHER	Something not defined. This can be UNIX machines, non-IBM machines, or System/36, System/38, or AS/400s running version 1 of OS/400.

Possible values for connection type depend on the destination type. Here they are:

- If the destination type is *OS/400, the connection type must be either *IP or *USRDFN.
- If the destination type is *OS/400V2, the connection type must be *SNA.
- If the destination type is *S390, the connection type must be either *SNA or *USRDFN.
- If the destination type is *PSF2, the connection type must be *IP.
- If the destination type is *OTHER, the connection type must *not* be *IPX.
- If destination type is *NETWARE3 or *NDS, the connection type must be either *IPX or *USRDFN.
- If the destination type is anything else, the connection type must be *IP.

Notice in Figure 12-10, one writer job is specified to autostart. Normally, the remote writer will just be up. To verify this, use the Work Active Job (WRKACTJOB) command and look for subsystem QSPL to be active.

If you did not specify any autostart jobs or the job ended for some reason, start it with the Start Remote Writer (STRRMTWTR) command. Just name the remote printer as the first parameter: STRRMTWTR RMTSYS.

12.4.6.2 LPD Configuration

LPD receives spool files from LPR on remote systems (most typically non-AS/400 hosts) and routes their contents to output queues from which they are printed.

LPD AS/400 jobs run in the QSYSWRK subsystem. Check the jobs running in this subsystem with the Work with Active Jobs (WRKACTJOB) command. LPD jobs are named QTLPD*nnnnn* (where *nnnnn* represents a unique numerical suffix).

LPD servers are automatically configured when you start TCP/IP unless you've set them to not autostart. You would have done that through the Change LPD Attributes (CHGLPDA) command, which also sets the number of servers to start.

The system comes with autostart set to *YES (LPD servers will start automatically). The number of servers that will start is set to two. Two is the optimum number of servers to have up for normal operation. If your AS/400 is supporting a lot of printing from remote non-AS/400 hosts, feel free to raise this number up to a maximum of 20.

If the LPD servers are not running, start them with the Start TCP Server (STRTCPSVR) command, which will bring up the number of servers specified on the LPD Attributes. If for any reason an LPD server is to be ended, use the End TCP/IP Server (ENDTCPSRV) command with the SERVER(*LPD) parameter specified.

Of the several LPD jobs running on an AS/400, only one is actively listening for incoming spool files at one time. When it gets a file, it sends the listening task to another LPD server while it starts translating and routing the spool-file request. After it finishes, it starts another LPD server and terminates itself. The problem a busy AS/400 will have is that its remote hosts could have to wait until a fresh LPD is ready to receive it. That's when to increase the number of LPD servers with the CHGLPDA command.

Spool files have attributes like fonts, lines per inch, page widths, and number of copies. Because these attributes do not come in with the spool file, the receiving AS/400 must get the attributes from somewhere. The first place it looks for attributes is under the User ID.

If the receiving system doesn't recognize the file's "owner," the next place it looks for attributes is in the print file called QTMPLPD. This file is included in the AS/400 in library QTCP. Any customer can accept these defaults, change them, or copy file QTMPLPD to another user library and modify them there. Controlling the library lists is a way of supporting different remote printer attributes on the same system.

12.4.7 SNMP

SNMP stands for Simple Network Management Protocol and is designed specifically for TCP/IP networks. SNMP is a weird little group of *SNMP managers, SNMP agents*, and information objects called *management information bases* (MIBs). Managers ask agents to do things for them, and agents do those things through the MIBs.

For example, if a manager wants to know the contact person for a remote host, the manager asks the agent who queries the remote's MIB that handles that (in this case, that MIB would be sysContact). Because the manager asked who it was, the agent READS the information and passes it back to the manager. If the manager had WRITE authority, it could have asked the agent to change the same MIB.

There are some MIBs to which agents don't have direct access. In these cases the agents use dedicated subagents. But they can be thought of as agents as far as we are concerned.

The set of managers and agents that works together is called the *community*. What defines the community is a table within an agent of the managers to which the agent will respond.

SNMP's two components, managers and agents, make a strange egalitarian community. Although the managers hold all the data, give users the information they need, and ask the agents to do the work, the agents determine what managers get to play and what access authorities each has.

In AS/400 terms, both SNMP managers and agents work through SNMP APIs, which you can reference in the IBM manual *System API Reference: UNIX-Type APIs*.

12.4.7.1 SNMP Manager

An SNMP Manager is a set of applications that collect data about the hosts and clients on the network. The SNMP manager is running when SNMP is started.

The manager contains a *trap manager* to handle traps. A *trap* is an event that causes an exception-type message. The trap manager receives traps, parses them out, and logs and forwards them. It can forward traps to other managers. The commands to run the trap manager within the SNMP manager are:

- Start Trap Manager (STRTRPMGR). This command has a parameter, FWDTRP, and valid values are *YES and *NO. This parameter determines if traps are to be forwarded to the trap manager specified on the agent. Keep the following tip in mind.

> **TIP:** Be careful of these parameters or you'll have two or more nodes in a *trap loop*, each forwarding traps to the others.

- End Trap Manager (ENDTRPMGR).

12.4.7.2 SNMP Agents

The SNMP agent carries out valid requests from the managers and accesses or changes data about the network nodes through MIBs.

12.4.7.2.1 Configuring SNMP Agents

Your AS/400 has one agent and one manager. They come with some defaults, but you probably need to change at least a couple of them. Agents contain information that define the:

- Community name.
- Table of valid managers.
- Access level of those managers.
- Logging level.

The command to add a community to the agent community list (yes, an agent can support multiple communities) is the Add Community for SNMP (ADDCOMSNMP) command. You can change communities previously named with the Change Community for SNMP (CHGCOMSNMP) command. Remove communities from the list with the Remove Community for SNMP (RMVCOMSNMP) command.

You can also get to these parameters by entering the Configure TCP/IP SNMP (CFGTCPSNMP) command and taking Option 2 (Work with Communities). That will give you a list of all the communities and you can take standard AS/400 menu options to manipulate them.

Valid managers are listed in the INTNETADR parameter. Be sure to use their IP addresses and not domain names. Each manager IP address is separated from its neighbor with a space. If your network is strictly local, you can use the generic *ANY as a single entry on this parameter and the agent will work with any manager on the network.

Name the access authority for attached managers with the OBJACC parameter. Possible values are *READ, *WRITE, *NONE, and *SNMPATR. The first two are logical enough; *NONE is used temporarily to logically remove a manager from its community without having to remove, rebuild, remove, and rebuild the whole community. *SNMPATR relies on the attributes of the SNMP for access rules.

The AS/400 comes with a default community name of "public." If your TCP/IP network is just the local workstations, this will do. However, if you're supporting anything more than that, you should probably change it.

Community names can consist of just about anything; even unreadable characters are permitted. But try to come up with names that mean something.

Two other parameters are LOGSET and LOGGET. Possible values for both are *YES, *NO, and *SNMPATR. These are nice for security logging.

That one command and those parameters will configure the agent. There are several attributes you can change within the agent. Change agent attributes with the Change SNMP Attributes (CHGSNMPA) command or type the Configure TCP/IP SNMP (CFGTCPSNMP) command and take Option 1. These agent attributes and their descriptions are listed in Table 12-6.

Table 12-6: Agent Attributes and Descriptions.

Attribute	Description
SYSCONTACT	The contact person of the system. Generally enter a phone number here, too.
SYSLOC	Plain language description of the system location.
SNDAUTTRP	*YES or *NO, send failed authentication messages to an SNMP manager.
AUTOSTART	*YES or *NO, automatically start the SNMP agent with TCP/IP. If this is set to *NO, STRTCPSVR must be used to start.
OBJACC	*SNMPATR, *READ, *WRITE, and *NONE set the access the manager will have to MIBs
LOGSET LOGGET	*YES, *NO, and *SNMP set whether SET and GET commands are logged.
LOGTRP	*YES and *NO state whether traps are forwarded or not.
TRPMGR	Names the SNMP manager(s) to receive forwarded traps.

12.4.8 Workstation Gateway (WSG)

Workstation Gateway (WSG) automatically transforms AS/400 application screens into 5250/Hypertext Markup Language (HTML). Therefore, any workstation running through a browser can get a "GUI-zed" presentation of any AS/400 green-screen application.

Any browser connected to the AS/400 through TCP/IP (local or remote) can get slower, but prettier application presentations through WSG. With WSG you can mix and match workstations. Some, attached via a browser, view AS/400 applications through GUI-colored glasses. Others can connect with 5250 and see the same applications in green screen.

Not all browsers are created equal and some may interpret the embedded configuration commands in 5250/HTML differently. But only the appearance changes; the screens all work. Two things to be aware of with WSG are that:

- Applications run through it run much slower than they do on locally attached workstations.
- Without a firewall, transactions are not encrypted over the net. This includes sign-on passwords.

12.4.8.1 WSG Configuration

There isn't much to WSG configuration. Use the Configure TCP/IP WSG (CFGTCPWSG) command to do this step:

- Change the Display Sign-on Panel to *YES.

Wasn't that hard? If you want users to sign on without seeing an AS/400 sign-on screen, refer to appendix I, section 10, in the IBM manual *OS/400 TCP/IP Configuration and Reference V4R3*. I'll warn you, though, if you don't really know API programming on the AS/400 and C/400, this is extremely difficult to do.

The WSG server uses virtual devices—if it needs a device, it just creates it. The system value QAUTOVRT enables and controls this virtual device creation. Check it with the Display System Value (DSPSYSVAL) command and change it if you need to with the Change System Value (DSPSYSVAL) command. Don't let it be equal to 0. To start with, set it to something like 50 or higher.

If you're past the learning stage and really want to support some workstations, do the following:

- Set QAUTOVRT to *NOMAX.
- Start the WSG server (refer to section 12.4.8.2 Starting WSG).
- Allow your users on and check the number of devices WSG created. Use the Work with Device Descriptions (WRKDEVD) command and count the number of controllers (named QPACTL*nnn*) and devices (QPADEV*nnnn*) and add the numbers together. That's the minimum number of devices WSG will require to support those users. Then reset QAUTOVRT to that number plus 10 percent for error.

From time to time, you might want to make changes to the WSG server. Do so with the Change TCP WSG (CHGTCPWSG) command. Soon after your network stabilizes, parameter changes to consider are the:

- Number of Clients per Server (NBRCLT). The default is 20; you might want to change it to any number from 1 to 50.
- Inactivity Timeout (INACTTIMO). This is the value in minutes a WSG server can be inactive before the AS/400 shuts it down. The default is 10 minutes.
- Data Request Timeout (DTARQSTIMO). This value is how many seconds the WSG server will wait for requested data from a client before taking the client offline. Keep the following tip in mind.

> ***TIP:*** This value doesn't account for network delays. If your network is very busy, increase this value or your users will get false error messages.

12.4.8.2 Starting WSG

While many other TCP/IP applications are shipped to start automatically, WSG is not. The customer must do some configuring first. The Change WSG Attributes (CHGWSGA) command sets WSG to automatically start. Here is a sample of it:

```
CHGWSGA AUTOSTART(*YES)
```

If WSG is not running but TCP/IP is, you can start it with the Start TCP Server (STRTCPSVR) command, specifying the *WSG value on the SERVER parameter:

```
STRTCPSVR SERVER(*WSG)
```

If the WSG server is already started when you issue the STRTCPSVR command, another will be started. Refer to your setting of NBRCLT in the preceding section (12.4.8.1 WSG Configuration). Adding another server will support this many more clients on your system.

If you need to end WSG server, the End TCP Server (ENDTCPSVR) command will do the trick. Like the start command, name the server with the *WSG value. Naming the parameter is optional but, if you don't specify it, all TCP/IP servers will end.

Don't skim the preceding paragraph too lightly. IBM doesn't ship WSG to start automatically for very good security reasons. Any customer should treat WSG as a potentially open door to the big bad world. End WSG server during any time periods you aren't supporting browser-equipped workstations. Don't just leave it up.

12.4.8.3 The WSG Access Log

Remember what you're doing with WSG. Most customers are allowing access to people who could be strangers. WSG keeps a log of all accesses. If you're brave (or really hurting for storage resources) you can turn this log off, but such an action might not get you too far through your next EDP audit.

The name of the log is QATMTLOG and it is shipped with MAXMBRS(*NOMAX) and SIZE(*NOMAX). You can change either or both of these with the Change Physical File Description (CHGFD) command. If you fix the size of the file, be careful. If the file fills up, the AS/400 will rename it to a name based on the date (QCYYMMDD). If it fills up again on the same day, logging will stop (but TCP and the WSG will keep on going).

You can view the contents of the file with either the Display Physical File Member (DSPPFM) command or through the PDM (Programmer's Development Menu).

12.4.8.4 The View from the Browser

To access an AS/400 from a browser-equipped workstation, just bring up the browser and type in:

```
http://host:port/WSG
```

Where *host* is either:

- The host IP address in the form 999.999.999.999 or
- The host domain name if the AS/400 has a domain name server or local host table.

Where *port* is 5061 (the default).

If you're thinking about changing the default port, refer to section 11.10.2 Accessing the Workstation Gateway from a Web Browser in the IBM manual *OS/400 TCP/IP Configuration and Reference V4R3.*

12.4.9 OS/400 TCP/IP Functions

The AS/400 also offers four miscellaneous functions for customers running its TCP/IP. They are:

- BOOTP.
- RouteD server.
- SLIP.
- TFTP Server.

12.4.9.1 BOOTP

BOOTP supports "thin clients" or client workstations with memory and logic but no media (hard or soft drives). When such a client connects to the AS/400, this service sends down a file to allow the client to boot up.

12.4.9.2 RouteD Server

RouteD stands for Routing Daemon and it supports the Routing Information Protocol (RIP). An Interior Gateway Protocol (IGP), RIP is the most popular routing protocol today. If the AS/400 is a TCP/IP server, it may have to route packets. If the network the AS/400 is on is an intranet (strictly local) and has redundant routes between nodes, try RIP for very fast dynamic routing of packets.

Remember, for security, the AS/400 cannot route packets out onto the Internet direct. RouteD support is strictly for intranet routing.

12.4.9.3 SLIP

SLIP (Serial Line Internet Protocol) gives the AS/400 dial-up TCP/IP support. SLIP isn't an application as much as it is a protocol to enable the dial-up. Once the connection is made, the user will run applications like Telnet, FTP, and SMTP.

SLIP enables a personal computer, AS/400, or any other computer to dial into an AS/400 (or vice versa, for an AS/400 to dial to any of those). SLIP must be installed and running on both computers when the connection is made.

SLIP communications is only asynchronous. As such, it will support popular modems (ZOOM, US Robotics, and Multitech) as well as IBM asynchronous modems.

On the AS/400, it is part of the base operating system starting with V3R2 and must work with a 2609 or 2612 communications adapter.

SLIP is driven with a *dialog script*. A dialog script is a source file member that specifies a series of prompts and responses. In other words, it's the handshake protocol between two computers. Because this handshake is not standard across all computers, the dialog script gives the customer some latitude to customize it.

Because this handshake can vary from manufacturer to manufacturer, you should work with the other vendor if you are connecting to a non-IBM host. For that reason, I won't attempt to show all the permutations of dialog scripts.

12.4.9.4 TFTP Server

TFTP (Trivial File Transfer Protocol) provides FTP support with no security checking. This protocol is usually used with BOOTP to provide thin-client support.

12.5 Connecting the AS/400 to the Internet

After all this, you're probably anxious to get connected to the Internet. Actually, that part is pretty routine. There's just one thing to be prepared for: When you talk to ISPs, be prepared for people who don't know about the AS/400.

Start with a phone call to a local Internet Service Provider (ISP). If you don't know any, sign on to the InterNIC at info@IS.Internet.net. They have a list of local ISPs around the country.

When considering ISPs, IBM provides ISP services through IBM Global Network (IGN). Contact your IBM representative or local branch office for more information.

An ISP will want to know what kind of support you want and you'll want to know what they offer. The primary ways you can connect to the Internet are:

- LAN-to-LAN. Your AS/400 is attached to a LAN. On the LAN is an IP Router that provides the Internet connection (the AS/400 doesn't). There are two primary ways of connecting the IP Router to the ISP:
    - ✔ Leased line (usually an E1 or T1).
    - ✔ Dial-up through a high-speed modem attached to the IP Router. This dial-up can be one-way or two-way (the AS/400 can only dial out to the ISP, but either can dial the other).
- Pure dial-up. Attach an asynchronous card and modem to your AS/400 and plan to dial into the ISP when you want Internet access. One common trick is to use the AS/400's existing ECS (Electronic Customer Support) modem (all AS/400s come with one).

Because an AS/400 cannot route messages to the Internet, the LAN-to-LAN connection is made with a hardware device (another node) on your LAN (an IP Router). IBM has a great router with model 2210. When considering any IP router, made sure it will support your LAN's protocol and the leased line or modem to the ISP.

If you opt for LAN-to-LAN dial-up, decide if you want SLIP or PPP (Point-to-Point Protoco)l as your protocol. You might not have a choice; many ISPs only offer PPP.

While SLIP is older and declining in popularity, it is very simple to use and ideal for simple two-node, dial-up links. In general, SLIP has gotten a bad reputation because it doesn't have much flow control and error-checking. With the AS/400, flow control and checking errors are not really problems as those functions are shifted to the host.

PPP is quickly becoming the darling of the Internet community. Because it has strong flow control and error-checking features, plus dynamic IP addressing, support of a large dynamic Internet environment is handled nicely.

With a LAN-to-LAN dial-up, the leased line, the modem, and the IP Router probably will be supplied by the ISP. Nevertheless, make sure. Also, ask how you'll be charged for service: a monthly fee based on usage or a flat rate. Will a modem be purchased outright? Check if "usage" means minutes, messages, or a flat rate combined with a per minute or per message charge.

Also, be able to tell the ISP how many hosts will be connecting. You'll want to make sure you'll have enough IP host-address space from the ISP for everyone.

The other popular option for Internet connectivity, direct AS/400 dial-up, uses an asynchronous adapter card, phone line, and modem (often the ECS modem itself). With this method, you can only dial out to the Internet and it can only support SLIP.

The direct dial-up method does seem limited. However, if you only want Internet access for limited reasons (file transfer or coast-to-coast communication without an expensive infrastructure are two examples), this is a very inexpensive and fast way to get connected. Also, security is simplified greatly for simple, on-and-off Internet connections.

12.5.1 Security on the Internet

Security is probably the hottest issue for most AS/400 Internet-bound customers. What's going to happen when you open the doors to your AS/400 to the big, bad world?

The first thing you do is go back to basic AS/400 security as discussed in chapters 5 and 6. The AS/400 has more built-in security than any computer. Some basic security measures you may want to put in place are:

- Set *PUBLIC access to all objects to *EXCLUDE. You'd be surprised at the authority levels many shops grant to the public.
- Think through and set the AS/400 system level security.
- Change the IBM-supplied default passwords to the following user IDs:
    - ✔ QSECOFR
    - ✔ QSYSOPR
    - ✔ IBM
    - ✔ QSVR
    - ✔ QSERV
- Give Internet User IDs as limited authority as possible.
- Use the user environment of the user profile (refer to chapter 5 for more information).
- Use the Change System Value (CHGSYSVAL) or Work with System Value (WRKSYSVAL) commands to set QLMTSECOFR to 1. This prohibits users with *ALLOBJ or *SERVICE authorities from Internet access.

- Use the password system values (refer to appendices A and B in this book) so users are forced to use complex passwords. Better yet, consider having the system generate passwords for Internet users.
- When FTP users' fail in a sign on attempt, message CPF2234 is written to the QHST log. Consider having a monitor program that, when it detects too many failed sign-on attempts, ends FTP (and maybe all TCP/IP) servers.
- Tighten up your ASP thresholds and what action is taken when they are reached. An Internet user might be flooding your system.
- Don't start servers you don't need.
- Restrict AS/400 command types such as RESTORE, START, and POWER DOWN from Internet-based users.
- Remove compilers from the system or restrict access to them severely.
- Don't allow IP forwarding. Change this with the Change TCP/IP Attributes (CHGTCPA) command and set the IPDTGFWD parameter to *no.
- Isolate the Internet AS/400 from any other network or segment in the following ways:
  - ✔ Don't allow Anynet/400 to run. Turn this off with the Change Network Attributes (CHGNETA) command:

    ```
    CHGNETA ALWANYNET(*NO)
    ```

  - ✔ Take all authority to the Start Pass Thru (STRPASTHR) command from any outside user.

Be aware of several other security issues.

- That User IDs and passwords are transmitted unencrypted—anyone can monitor a line for them.
- FTP users may only have *USE authority to your files but they can still copy the files to another computer's hard disk.
- Even though SMTP can route undeliverable mail by including an *ANY *ANY entry in the system directory, if you do this, someone can flood your system with computer-generated garbage messages. (Why? So they can delight in overflowing your DASD and crashing your system.)

- If you use POP and allow users who are not regular AS/400 uses to send, store, and retrieve mail, set the following parameters on their user profile through the Work with User Profile (WRKUSRPRF) command:

```
INLMNU(*SIGNOFF)
    INLPGM(*NONE)
```

- Most IP Routers provide some simple security by using *filtering packets*. Messages that aren't destined for the hosts it supports are discarded before they reach you. Remember, *packets* can be anything (not just mail messages). You are ahead of the game if incoming packets without valid addresses are discarded early.

I would hesitate to provide Internet access to my production AS/400. Instead, I would opt for a smaller, separate AS/400 that isn't normally connected to my production machine. I would also enforce strict one-way file transfers (from production to the Internet AS/400, never back again).

You can incorporate some interesting security features if you program user exits in FTP and WSG. However, I personally am not too excited about these for two reasons:

- They are difficult to write and probably impossible to maintain.
- It pits me and my staff against the dedicated efforts of hackers, and we just don't have time for it.

My solution to all that is to purchase Firewall/400. It's an excellant firewall that'll give superior protection.

Firewall/400 is a software package that runs on the Integrated PC Server (IPCS) and provides a *proxy-based firewall*. A proxy-based firewall is one that hides the secured part of the Internet from the unsecured. Like a gate guard, it'll screen out unknown users and undeliverable mail. It'll also protect individuals' true IP addresses from the riff-raff on the unsecured side.

The unusual thing about the AS/400 over other hosts is that, with its firewall running on the IPCS, the firewall is actually not running on the AS/400. There is no way anyone can circumvent the firewall and get loose inside the system.

Keep in mind that everything that goes over the Internet goes in the clear. You can encrypt transmissions coming in and going out from your AS/400, but you do so with encryption technology installed on both the AS/400 and any browsers accessing it. This is getting pretty common as more corporations do business over the Internet and two standards that are starting to emerge are:

- Secure Sockets Layer (SSL). The SSL protocol lies below HTTP, FTP, and Telnet, but above TCP/IP. The handshake that starts an individual session sets the encryption algorithm, which is not reset and cannot be determined later by anyone outside that two-party handshake. Also, the server (and optionally the client) is authenticated. In other words, it ensures clients are connected to the server they thought they were.
- Secure Hypertext Transfer Protocol (SHTTP). The SHTTP protocol is an extension to HTTP that provides built-in encryption of data and authentication of servers and clients. It also uses embedded signatures to detect any change to the data in transmission.

In the case of the AS/400, a firewall is a kind of a gateway in the sense that it resides in front of and apart from the host. (Other firewalls are part of the host.)

An emerging gateway-based security standard is SOCKS. SOCKS resides on the gateway (or Firewall/400) and enforces security issues more transparently to the users on either end. When discussing security, *transparency* isn't a user-friendly issue, it's a security issue. Hackers can't hack what they can't see going on.

12.6 References

AS/400 LAN, Frame-Relay, and ATM Support V4R2 (SC41-5405-01)

System API Reference: UNIX-Type APIs

AS/400 Wireless LAN Installation & Planning Guide (G571-0303)

IBM LAN Bridge and Switch Guide (SB24-5000)

Local Area Network Concept & Product: LAN Architecture (SC24-4753-00)

OS/400 Communications Configuration V4R1 (SC41-5401-00)

OS/400 Communications Management V4R2 (SC41-5406-01)

OS/400 TCP/IP Configuration and Reference V4R3 (SC41-5420-02)

Tips and Tools for Securing Your AS/400 (SC41-3300)

System Values (Alphabetical Order)

System Value	Description	Parameters: Values
QABNORMSW	Previous end-of-system indicator	0=Normal 1=Abnormal
QACGLVL	Accounting level	*JOB Job resource use is written to a journal. *NONE No accounting information is written to a journal. *PRINT Spooled and printer file resource use is written to a journal.
QACTJOB	Initial number of active jobs	1-32767
QADLACTJ	Additional number of active jobs	1-32767
QADLSPLA	Spooling control block additional storage	1024-32767
QADLTOTJ	Additional number of total jobs	1-32767
QALWOBJRST	Allow object restore option	*ALL All objects are restored regardless of security sensitive attributes. *NONE No objects with security sensitive attributes are restored. *ALWYSSTT - Programs with the system state attribute are restored. *ALWPGMADP - Programs with the adopt authority attribute are restored.
QALWUSRDMN	Allow user domain objects in libraries	Name of libraries that can contain user domain user objects
QASTLVL	User assistance level	*BASIC *INTERMED *ADVANCED
QATNPGM	Attention program	*NONE *ASSIST Library/program name

System Value	Description	Parameters: Values
QAUDCTL	Auditing control	*AUDLVL *OBJAUD
QAUDENDACN	Auditing end action	*NOTIFY *PWRDWNSYS
QAUDFRCLVL	Force auditing data	*SYS 1-100
QAUDLVL	Security auditing level	*SECURITY *AUTFAIL *DELETE *OBJMGT *CREATE *SAVRST *SPLFDTA *SYSMGT *SERVICE *PGMADP *JOBDTA
QAUTOCFG	Autoconfigure devices	0=Off 1=On
QAUTORMT	Autoconfigure of remote controllers	0=Off 1=On
QAUTOSPRPT	Automatic system disabled reporting	0=Off 1=On
QAUTOVRT	Autoconfigure virtual devices	0-32,500 or *NOMAX
QBASACTLVL	Base storage pool activity level	1-32767
QBASPOOL	Base storage pool minimum size (sizes in kilo-bytes)	256-2147483647
QBOOKPATH	Book and bookshelf search path for books. Default: /QDLS/QBKBOOKS/BOOKS	Directories to be searched
QCCSID	Coded character set identifier	1-65535
QCHRID	Graphic character set and code page	Character ID: 1-32767 Code page: 1-32767
QCHRIDCTL	Character identifier control	Character ID: 1-32767 *DEVD *JOBCCSID

System Value	Description	Parameters: Values
QCMNRCYLMT	Communications recovery limits	Recovery limit attempts: 0-99 Time interval in minutes: 0-120
QCNTRYID	Country identifier	Country abbreviation
QCONSOLE	Console name	Device description
QCRTAUT	Create default public authority	*CHANGE *ALL *USE *EXCLUDE
QCRTOBJAUD	Create object auditing	*NONE *USRPRF *CHANGE *ALL
QCTLSBSD	Controlling subsystem	Library/Subsystem name
QCURSYM	Currency symbol	Character
QDATE	System date	Date (refer to QDATFMT, next, for format)
QDATFMT	Date format	YMD MDY DMY JUL
QDATSEP	Date separator	Numeric code: 1=/ 2=- 3=. 4=, 5=blank
QDAY	Day	1-31
QDBRCVYWT	Database recovery wait indicator	0=Do not wait 1=Wait
QDECFMT	Decimal format	1=blank(Period for decimal, zero suppression) 2=J(Comma for decimal, one leading zero) 3=I(Comma for decimal, zero suppression)

System Value	Description	Parameters: Values
QDEVNAMING	Device naming conventions	*NORMAL *S36 *DEVADR
QDEVRCYACN	Device I/O error action	*MSG *DSCMSG *DSCENDRQS *ENDJOB *ENDJOBNOLIST
QDSCJOBITV	Time interval in minutes before disconnected jobs end	*NONE 5-1440
QDSPSGNINF	Sign-on display information control	0=Do not display 1=Display
QDYNPTRADJ	Dynamic priority adjustment. Only in effect for AS/400e models with QSYNPTRSCD set to '1'.	0=Interactive jobs' priorities will not be changed 1=Interactive jobs' priorities will be changed
QDYNPTYSCD	Dynamic priority scheduler. Automatically adjusts job priorities	0=Off 1=On
QFRCCVNRST	Force conversion on restore	0=Off 1=On
QHOUR	Current hour of the day	Hour (0-23)
QHSTLOGSIZ	Maximum history log records	1-32767
QIGC	DBCS version installed indicator	0=Not installed 1=Installed
QIGCCDEFNT	Double byte code font	Library/font name
QIGCFNTSIZ	Double byte coded font point size	
QINACTITV	Inactive job time-out (minutes)	*NONE 5-300
QINACTMSGQ	Inactive job message queue	*ENDJOB *DSCJOB Library/message queue name
QIPLDATTIM	Date and time to automatically IPL	*NONE or IPL date: MM/DD/YY IPL time: HH:MM:SS

System Value	Description	Parameters: Values
QIPLSTS	IPL status indicator	0=Operator panel IPL 1=Auto-IPL after power is restored 2=Restart IPL 3=Time of day IPL 4=Remote IPL
QIPLTYPE	Type of IPL to perform	0=Unattended IPL 1=Attended IPL with dedicated service tools 2=Attended IPL, console in debug mode
QJOBMSGQFL	Job message queue full action	*NOWRAP *WRAP *PRTWRAP
QJOBMSGQMX	Maximum size in megabytes of job message queue	8-64
QJOBMSGQSZ	Job message queue initial size (in kilobytes)	1-16384
QJOBMSGQTL	Job message queue maximum initial size (in kilobytes)	1-16384
QJOBSPLA	Spooling control block initial size(in bytes)	3516-32767
QKBDBUF	Type ahead and/or attention key option	*TYPEAHEAD *YES *NO
QKBDTYPE	Keyboard language character set	Language/Country abbreviation
QLANGID	Language identifier	Language abbreviation
QLEAPADJ	Leap year adjustment	0-3
QLMTDEVSSN	Limit device sessions	0=Do not limit 1=Limit

System Value	Description	Parameters: Values
QLMTSECOFR	Limit security officer device access	0=Do not limit 1=Limit
QLOCALE	Locale path name	*NONE Locale path name
QMAXACTLVL	Maximum activity level of system	*NOMAX 2-32767
QMAXSGNACN	Action to take for failed signon attempts	Numeric code: 1=Disable device 2=Disable profile 3=Disable device and profile
QMAXSIGN	Maximum sign-on attempts allowed	*NOMAX 1-25
QMCHPOOL	Machine storage pool size (in kilobytes)	256-2147483647
QMINUTE	Current minute of the hour	Minute (00-59)
QMODEL	Current system model number	System model number
QMONTH	Current month of the year	Month (1-12)
QPFRADJ	Automatic performance adjustment	0=No adjustment 1=Adjustment at IPL 2=Adjustment at IPL and automatic adjustment 3=Automatic adjustment
QPRBFTR	Problem log filter	Library/name of problem log filter
QPRBHLDITV	Problem log hold interval	0-999
QPRCFEAT	Processor feature	4 character processor feature code
QPRCMLTTSK	Processor multi-tasking	0=multi-tasking is off 1=multi-tasking is on

System Value	Description	Parameters: Values
QPRTDEV	Printer device description	Name
QPRTKEYFMT	Print header and/or border information	*PRTHDR *PRTBDR *PRTALL *NONE
QPRTTXT	Print text	text
QPWDEXPITV	Password expiration interval in days	*NOMAX (passwords don't expire) 1-366
QPWDLMTAJC	Limit adjacent digits in password	0=adjacent digits OK 1=adjacent digits not OK
QPWDLMTCHR	Limit characters in password	*NONE characters not allowed
QPWDLMTREP	Limit repeating characters in password	0=Can be repeated 1=Cannot be repeated 2=Cannot be repeated consecutively
QPWDMAXLEN	Maximum password length	1-10
QPWDMINLEN	Minimum password length	1-10
QPWDPOSDIF	Limit password character positions	0=Can be the same 1=Cannot be the same
QPWDRQDDGT	Require digit in password	0=Not required 1=Required
QPWDRQDDIF	Duplicate password control	Numeric code: 0=Duplicates allowed - or - Cannot be the same as any in the last 1=32 passwords 2=24 passwords 3=18 passwords

System Value	Description	Parameters: Values
QPWDRQDDIF	*(continued)*	4=12 passwords 5=10 passwords 6=8 passwords 7=6 passwords 8=4 passwords
QPWDVLDPGM	Password validation program	*NONE Library/program name
QPWRDWNLMT	Maximum time in seconds for PWRDWNSYS *IMMED	0-32767
QPWRRSTIPL	Automatic IPL after power restored	0=Not allowed
QRCLSPLSTG	Days to reclaim spool storage	*NONE *NOMAX 1-366
QRMTIPL	Remote power on and IPL	0=Not allowed 1=Allowed
QRMTSIGN	Remote sign-on control	*FRCSIGNON *SAMEPRF *REJECT *VERIFY - or -Library/Remote session sign-on program
QRMTSRVATR	Remote service attribute	0=Off 1=On
QSCPFCONS	IPL action with console problem	0=End IPL 1=Unattended IPL
QSECOND	Current second of the minute	Second (0-59)

System Value	Description	Parameters: Values
QSECURITY	System security level	10=Physical security only 20=Password security only 30=Password and object security 40=Password, object, and operating system integrity 50=Password, object, and enhanced operating system integrity (C2)
QSETJOBATR	Set job attributes from locale	*NONE - or - Job attributes option
QSFWERRLOG	Software error logging	*LOG *NOLOG
QSPCENV	Special environment	*NONE *S36
QSRLNBR	System serial number	System serial number
QSRTSEQ	Sort sequence	Library/name *HEX *LANGIDUNQ *LANGIDSHR
QSRVDMP	Service dump control	*DMPUSRJOB *DMPSYSJOB *DMPALLJOB *NONE
QSTRPRTWTR	Start print writers at IPL	0=Do not start 1=Start
QSTRUPPGM	Start-up program	*NONE Library/name
QSTSMSG	Display status messages	*NONE *NORMAL

System Value	Description	Parameters: Values
QSVRAUTITV	Server authentication interval in minutes	1-108000
QSYSLIBL	System part of the library list (can be many entries)	Sequence/library name
QTIME	Current time of day	Time in HH:MM:SS format
QTIMSEP	Time separator	Numeric code: 1=: 2=. 3=, 4=blank
QTOTJOB	Initial total number of jobs	1-32767
QTSEPOOL	Time slice end pool	*NONE *BASE
QUPSDLYTIM	Uninterruptible power supply delay time in seconds	*CALC *BASIC *NOMAX 0-99999
QUPSMSGQ	Uninterruptible power supply message queue	Library/message queue name
QUSRLIBL	Default user part of the library list	Sequence/library (may be many)
QUTCOFFSET	Coordinated universal time offset	-24:00 to +24:00
QYEAR	Current year	Year (0-99)

System Values (Functional Order)

Table B-1: Character Sets/Languages.		
System Value	**Description**	**Parameters**
QCCSID	Coded character set identifier	1-65535
QCHRID	Graphic character set and code page	Character ID: 1-32767 Code page: 1-32767
QCHRIDCTL	Graphic character set/code page control	*DEVD *JOBCCID Code page: 1-32767
QCNTRYID	Country identifier	Country abbreviation
QCURSYM	Currency symbol	Character
QDECFMT	Decimal format	1=blank (Period for decimal, zero suppression) 2=J (Comma for decimal, one leading zero) 3=I (Comma for decimal, zero suppression)
QIGC	DBCS version installed indicator	0=Not installed 1=Installed
QIGCCDEFNT	Double byte code font	Library/font name
QIGCFNTSIZ	Double byte code font size (in points)	*NONE 000.1 – 999.9
QKBDBUF	Type ahead and/or attention key option	*TYPEAHEAD *YES *NO
QKBDTYPE	Keyboard language character set abbreviation	Language/Country
QLANGID	Language identifier	Language abbreviation

Table B-2: Date/Time.		
System Value	**Description**	**Parameters**
QDATE	System date	Date (refer to QDATFMT, next, for format)
QDATFMT	Date format	YMD MDY DMY JUL
QDATSEP	Date separator	Numeric code: 1=/ 2=- 3=. 4=, 5=blank
QDAY	Day	1-31
QHOUR	Current hour of the day	Hour (0-23)
QLEAPADJ	Leap year adjustment	0-3
QMINUTE	Current minute of the hour	Minute (00-59)
QMONTH	Current month of the year	Month (1-12)
QSECOND	Current second of the minute	Second (0-59)
QTIME	Current time of day Time separator	Time in HH:MM:SS format Numeric code: 1=: 2=. 3=, 4=blank
QUTCOFFSET	Coordinated universal time offset	-24:00 to +24:00
QYEAR	Current year	Year (0-99)

Table B-3: Disaster.

System Value	Description	Parameters
QABNORMSW	Previous end-of-system indicator	0=Normal 1=Abnormal
QAUTOSPRPT	Automatic system disabled reporting	0=Off 1=On
QCMNRCYLMT	Communications recovery limits	Recovery limit attempts: 0-99 Time interval in minutes: 0-120
QDBRCVYWT	Database recovery wait indicator	0=Do not wait 1=Wait
QDEVRCYACN	Device I/O error action	*MSG *DSCMSG *DSCENDRQS *ENDJOB *ENDJOBNOLIST

Table B-4: IPL.

System Value	Description	Parameters
QIPLDATTIM	Date and time to automatically IPL	*NONE or IPL date: MM/DD/YY IPL time: HH:MM:SS
QIPLSTS	IPL status indicator	0=Operator panel IPL 1=Auto-IPL after power is restored 2=Restart IPL 3=Time of day IPL 4=Remote IPL
QIPLTYPE	Type of IPL to perform	0=Unattended IPL 1=Attended IPL with dedicated service tools 2=Attended IPL, console in debug mode
QPWRDWNLMT	Maximum time in seconds for PWRDWNSYS *IMMED	0-32767
QPWRRSTIPL	Automatic IPL after power restored	0=Not allowed

Table B-4: IPL (continued).		
System Value	**Description**	**Parameters**
QRMTIPL	Remote power on and IPL	0=Not allowed 1=Allowed
QSCPFCONS	IPL action with console problem	0=End IPL 1=Unattended IPL
QSTRPRTWTR	Start print writers at IPL	0=Do not start 1=Start
QSTRUPPGM	Start-up program	*NONE Library/name

Table B-5: Miscelleneous.		
System Value	**Description**	**Parameters**
QACGLVL	Accounting level	*JOB Job resource use is written to a journal *NONE No accounting information is written to a journal *PRINT Spooled and printer file resource use is written to a journal
QBOOKPATH	Book and bookshelf search path	Directories to be searched for books. Default: /QDLS/QBKBOOKS/BOOKS
QLOCALE	Locale path name	*NONE Locale path name
QMODEL	Current system model number	System model number
QPRCFEAT	Processor feature	System processor feature
QRMTSRVATR	Remote service attribute	0=Off 1=On
QSETJOBATR	Set job attributes from locale	*NONE - or - Job attributes option
QSPCENV	Special environment	*NONE *S36
QSRLNBR	System serial number	System serial number

Table B-5: Miscelleneous (continued).		
System Value	**Description**	**Parameters**
QSRTSEQ	Sort sequence	Library/name *HEX *LANGIDUNQ *LANGIDSHR
QSRVDMP	Service dump control	*DMPUSRJOB *DMPSYSJOB *DMPALLJOB *NONE
QSTSMSG	Display status messages	*NONE *NORMAL
QUPSDLYTIM	Uninterruptible power supply delay time in seconds	*CALC *BASIC *NOMAX 0-99999
QUPSMSGQ	Uninterruptible power supply message queue	Library/message queue name

Table B-6: Problem Reporting.		
System Value	**Description**	**Parameters**
QPRBFTR	Problem log filter	Library/name of problem log filter
QPRBHLDITV	Problem log hold interval	0-999
QSFWERRLOG	Software error logging	*LOG

Table B-7: Security.		
System Value	**Description**	**Parameters**
QALWOBJRST	Allow object restore option	*ALL All objects are restored regardless of security sensitive attributes *NONE No objects withsecurity sensitive attributes are restored *ALWYSSTT Programs with the system state attribute are restored *ALWPGMADP - Programs with the adopt authority attribute are restored
QAUDCTL	Auditing control	*AUDLVL *OBJAUD
QAUDENDACN	Auditing end action	*NOTIFY *PWRDWNSYS
QAUDFRCLVL	Force auditing data	*SYS 1-100
QAUDLVL	Security auditing level	*SECURITY *AUTFAIL *DELETE *OBJMGT *CREATE *SAVRST *SPLFDTA *SYSMGT *SERVICE *PGMADP *JOBDTA
QCRTAUT	Create default public authority	*CHANGE *ALL *USE *EXCLUDE
QCRTOBJAUD	Create object auditing	*NONE *USRPRF *CHANGE *ALL

Table B-7: Security (continued).		
System Value	**Description**	**Parameters**
QDSCJOBITV	Time interval in minutes before disconnected jobs end	*NONE 5-1440
QDSPSGNINF	Sign-on display information control	0=Do not display 1=Display
QFRCCVNRST	Force conversion on restore	0=Off 1=On
QINACTITV	Inactive job time-out (minutes)	*NONE 5-300
QINACTMSGQ	Inactive job message queue	*ENDJOB *DSCJOB Library/message queue name
QLMTDEVSSN	Limit device sessions	0=Do not limit 1=Limit
QLMTSECOFR	Limit security officer device access	0=Do not limit 1=Limit
QMAXSGNACN	Action to take for failed signon attempts	Numeric code: 1=Disable device 2=Disable profile 3=Disable device and profile
QMAXSIGN	Maximum sign-on attempts allowed	*NOMAX 1-25
QPWDEXPITV	Password expiration interval in days	*NOMAX (passwords don't expire) 1-366
QPWDLMTAJC	Limit adjacent digits in password	0=adjacent digits OK 1=adjacent digits not OK

Table B-7: Security (continued).		
System Value	**Description**	**Parameters**
QPWDLMTCHR	Limit characters in password	*NONE characters not allowed
QPWDLMTREP	Limit repeating characters in password	0=Can be repeated 1=Cannot be repeated 2=Cannot be repeated consecutively
QPWDMAXLEN	Maximum password length	1-10
QPWDMINLEN	Minimum password length	1-10
QPWDPOSDIF	Limit password character positions	0=Can be the same 1=Cannot be the same
QPWDRQDDGT	Require digit in password	0=Not required 1=Required
QPWDRQDDIF	Duplicate password control	Numeric code: 0=Duplicates allowed - or -Cannot be the same as any in the last 1=32 passwords 2=24 passwords 3=18 passwords 4=12 passwords 5=10 passwords 6=8 passwords 7=6 passwords 8=4 passwords
QPWDVLDPGM	Password validation program	*NONE Library/program name

Table B-7: Security (continued).		
System Value	**Description**	**Parameters**
QRMTSIGN	Remote sign-on control	*FRCSIGNON *SAMEPRF *REJECT *VERIFY - or -Library/Remote session sign-on program
QSECURITY	System security level	10=Physical security only
		20=Password security only
		30=Password and object security 40=Password, object, and operating system integrity 50=Password, object, and enhanced operating system integrity (C2)
QSVRAUTITV	Server authentication interval in minutes	1-108000

Table B-8: Spool File Control.		
System Value	**Description**	**Parameters**
QADLSPLA	Spooling control block additional storage	1024-32767
QJOBSPLA	Spooling control block initial size(in bytes)	3516-32767
QRCLSPLSTG	Days to reclaim spool storage	*NONE *NOMAX 1-366

Table B-9: System Configuration.

System Value	Description	Parameters
QALWUSRDMN	Allow user domain objects in libraries	Name of libraries that can contain user domain user objects
QASTLVL	User assistance level	*BASIC *INTERMED *ADVANCED
QATNPGM	Attention program	*NONE *ASSIST Library/program name
QAUTOCFG	Autoconfigure devices	0=Off 1=On
QAUTORMT	Autoconfigure of remote	0=Off 1=On
QAUTOVRT	Autoconfigure virtual devices	0-32,500 or *NOMAX
QCONSOLE	Console name	Device description
QCTLSBSD	Controlling subsystem	Library/Subsystem name
QDEVNAMING	Device naming conventions	*NORMAL *S36 *DEVADR
QHSTLOGSIZ	Maximum history log records	1-32767
QJOBMSGQFL	Job message queue full action	*NOWRAP *WRAP *PRTWRAP
QJOBMSGQMX	Maximum size in megabytes of job message queue	8-64
QJOBMSGQSZ	Job message queue initial size (in kilobytes)	1-16384
QJOBMSGQTL	Job message queue maximum initial size (in kilobytes)	1-16384
QPRTDEV	Printer device description	Name
QPRTKEYFMT	Print header and/or border information	*PRTHDR *PRTBDR *PRTALL *NONE

Table B-9: System Configuration (continued).		
System Value	**Description**	**Parameters**
QPRTTXT	Print text	text
QSYSLIBL	System part of the library list (can be many entries)	Sequence/library name
QUSRLIBL	Default user part of the library list	Sequence/library (may be many)

Table B-10: Performance.		
System Value	**Description**	**Parameters**
QBASACTLVL	Base storage pool activity level	1-32767
QBASPOOL	Base storage pool minimum size (sizes in kilobytes)	256-2147483647
QDYNPTYADJ	AS/400e only, if QDYNPTYSCD is on. Determines if interactive jobs will have their priorities adjusted	0=No Adjustment 1=Adjusted
QDYNPTYSCD	Enables dynamic priority scheduling	0=Dynamic priority scheduling off 1=Dynamic priority scheduling on.
QMAXACTLVL	Maximum activity level of system	*NOMAX 2-32767
QMCHPOOL	Machine storage pool size (in kilobytes)	256-2147483647
QPFRADJ	Automatic performance adjustment	0=No adjustment 1=Adjustment at IPL 2=Adjustment at IPL and continuously thereafter 3=Continuously after IPL
QTOTJOB	Initial total number of jobs	1-32767
QTSEPOOL	Time slice end pool	*NONE *BASE *NOLOG

Table B-11: Work Management.		
System Value	Description	Parameters
QACTJOB	Initial number of active jobs	1-32767
QADLACTJ	Additional number of active jobs	1-32767
QADLTOTJ	Additional number of total jobs	1-32767
QBASACTLVL	Base storage pool activity level	1-32767
QBASPOOL	Base storage pool minimum size (sizes in kilobytes)	256-2147483647
QMAXACTLVL	Maximum activity level of system	*NOMAX 2-32767
QMCHPOOL	Machine storage pool size (in kilobytes)	256-2147483647
QTOTJOB	Initial total number of jobs	1-32767
QTSEPOOL	Time slice end pool	*NONE *BASE *NOLOG

Glossary

activity level

The number of jobs in a subsystem that the system will allow to be active at one time.

adopted authority

A security feature where a running program takes on the authority of the program creator instead of the program user.

advanced peer-to-peer communications (APPC)

The protocol for communicating between two AS/400s.

advanced peer-to-peer networking (APPN)

The protocol for most AS/400 network computing. LAN communication runs under APPN.

authorities

In security, authorities are "permissions" for a person to access an AS/400 object.

authorization lists

A list of authorized users and their authorization level. This is a fast method of granting the same authorities to many objects.

automatic mode

When an AS/400 is IPLed, it will come up automatically, without operator intervention (unless there is a problem.)

base memory pool

Special shared memory pool that contains all unallocated memory available to all subsystems.

batch job

A program or set of commands that runs in the background in intervals and segments. It does not tie up a workstation while it runs. *See* interactive job; job.

bridged frame relay

A frame-relay network where the remote attachment is a bridge into a LAN.

broken chain

Journal receivers are sequentially numbered and should be accessed that way. A broken chain occurs when one or more receivers are missing.

carrier sense multiple access with collision detection (CSMA/CD)

The protocol used by Ethernet networks. Transmissions are made when the network thinks the line is not busy. If it detects another transmission made at the same time (a collision occurs), it will attempt to resend both after waiting a random amount of time.

channel service unit (CSU)

Half of the attachment device into a frame-relay network. *See* data service unit (DSU); CSU/DSU.

class-of-service

User-defined preferences for each link and node on a network. The AS/400 will take these preferences into consideration when routing network transmissions. The result should be transmission routing that the user prefers.

concentrator

A communication device that allows multiple devices to be used where one would normally be used. For example, a single wire may support one workstation. If a concentrator is attached to that wire, it may support up to seven workstations.

control points

Information kept on network node servers about the adjacent links and nodes. Used to calculate optimum routing of transmissions.

controller

A device to control sending and receiving information to DASD or workstations. Controllers are connected to IOPs.

data link connection identifier (DLCI)

A unique number to identify each permanent virtual circuit (PVC) on a frame relay physical connection.

data service unit

Half of the attachment hardware into a frame-relay network. *See* data service unit (DSU); CSU/DSU.

data striping
AS/400's method of writing data to disk.

DDI network
Direct Data Interchange network protocol. Uses two counter-rotating rings.

destination service access points (DSAP)
The SAP of the remote (the receiving) computer. *See* service access points (SAP); source service access points (SSAP).

device Any apparatus connected to an AS/400 (printer, workstation, tape drive, etc.)

device attachment (DA) card
Used to connect remote workstations to a DDI network.

device configuration
The description and simple operating characteristics of a device.

direct frame relay
Frame relay consisting of two or more AS/400s running APPC/APPN.

domain name
In Internet addressing, the easy way of addressing a node.

DSU/CSU
The device used to attach into a frame-relay network. Think of the DSU/CSU as a modem.

end nodes
Nodes on a network that do not participate in routing transmissions beyond themselves. They can only send and receive their own transmissions.

Ethernet
A LAN that supports one of two standards: Ethernet Version 2 or the IEEE 802.3 standard. *See* carrier sense multiple access with collision detection (CSMA/CD).

faulting

When the AS/400 is running a job and it unexpectedly finds a page missing from memory, it finds the page on disk and restores it. Usually a symptom of an out-of-capacity AS/400 or a poorly tuned one.

file A collection of records. *See* physical file; logical file.

frame handler (FH)

A intermediate (not end) node on a frame-relay network.

frame relay

A packet-switching protocol that is similar to X.25 that uses established data communications networks.

frame size

In frame relay, the size of each frame or packet that the network can handle.

general shared pools

A memory pool sharable among subsystems.

initial program load (IPL)

The AS/400 way of referring to bootstrapping the system.

interactive

AS/400 terminology for online.

Internet

A collection of networks for the public to use for business, recreation, reference and other purposes.

interoperable

An IBM term referring to how sharable data between operating system releases are. If two releases are interoperable, saved data from one can be restored on another.

IOP (input-output processor)

The last piece of AS/400 communications equipment before the controller. Disk data being written goes through an IOP and then a DASD controller. Outgoing screen data goes through an IOP then a workstation controller.

job

On an AS/400, a job is a program or set of programs run as a unit. When a user signs onto the system, he or she starts an interactive job that doesn't end until her or she signs off. *See* interactive jobs; batch jobs.

job queue

A queue—like a bank teller line—where jobs wait their turn to run.

journaling

A feature you turn on that records every operation against one or more files and many system operations. Great security and disaster-recovery tool.

journal identifier

A label put on a file that it is currently being journaled.

journal receiver

The repository for data being journaled (record before-images and after-images, file open and close, etc.).

list management rights

The capability to create, change, and delete authorization lists.

logical file

A file with no data; just a key index.

low-entry nodes

See end nodes.

machine pool

The memory pool reserved for machine tasks.

manual mode

When an AS/400 is IPLed, it will stop to give the operator a chance to do something before it is fully operational.

members

An AS/400 file can consist of one or more members, each one of which can be processed as a complete file. All AS/400 files contain at least one member.

memory pools

An amount of memory set aside for use by one or more subsystems.

native support
An indication that IBM supports something used by the AS/400, such as a communications protocol, without using emulation.

network nodes
Intelligent nodes on a network that not only send and receive their own transmissions, they can receive and reroute transmissions for other nodes. Network nodes build control-point information about the links and nodes attached to them.

network node server
A network node capable of administering its own traffic, other traffic on the network, and transmissions to and from end nodes or low-entry nodes. Network nodes become network node server through the Change Network Attributes (CHGNETA) command. Up to five network node servers are allowed per APPN application.

network topology database
The aggregate knowledge about the network accumulated by all network nodes' control-point information. If a link or node goes down, adjacent network nodes will reconfigure this network topology database.

nodes Devices that can send and receive into the network.

normal mode
See automatic mode.

object Everything on the AS/400 is an object. The object type determines what the object really is (for example, a file or a device).

object type
See object.

OS/400 The name of the AS/400 operating system.

outfile Many informational commands can send their output to physical files referred to as outfiles.

output queue
Output scheduled for a printer will wait in an output queue until it has a chance to be printed.

paging Efficient use of memory by keeping little-used sections, or pages, on a disk until they are needed.

permanent virtual circuit (PVC)
In frame relay, a single physical cable can support up to 256 virtual circuits, each one of which is referred to as a permanent virtual circuit (PVC) and is identified by a data-link connection identifier (DLCI).

physical file
A file that actually contains records. *See* file; logical file.

physical interfaces
The connector used on network cabling.

pool *See* memory pools.

pool identifier
In a subsystem, the relative number of the memory pools it will use.

preset address
The unique address assigned by the manufacturer to LAN adapter cards.

private pool
A memory pool dedicated to one subsystem that cannot be shared by other subsystems.

Program Temporary Fix (PTF)
An added feature or a solution to an operating-system problem. PTFs are released sporadically.

public authority
Permission for any user without specific authorization to access an object.

resource name
Used in the AS/400 for all LAN connections merely as an addressing method. A concatenation of the adapter and port of that adapter the object will use.

restricted state
An AS/400 with only the controlling subsystem (QCTL) active.

route addition resistance
A user can indicate a preference that the network should or should not use a particular route for transmissions.

route congestion
A way of indicating user preference of transmission routing. When APPN determines that a route is congested, it will start to route transmissions away from the congestion. APPN concludes that congestion happens when the link is 90 percent full. Users can lower the percentage-full number and can start routing away from the link sooner.

save file A special file that contains the output from a save operation. You cannot use this file directly like others, but you can copy it to tape or restore it.

save-while-active
A special AS/400 feature that allows files to be saved while users are accessing them.

server node *See* network server node.

service access points (SAP)
Simple, two-digit addressing used at the adapter level on an AS/400. These addresses can be assigned by the user or the user can allow the AS/400 to assign them. *See* source service access points (SSAP); destination service access points (DSAP).

service providers
For Internet and frame-relay networks, companies provide access into the public-use networks. You will be a subscriber to them.

session When an interactive user signs onto the system, he or she has created a session. Many terminals allow multiple sessions where the user can acquire another sign display and sign on again, creating a second session.

shared pool
Memory pools are sharable among subsystems.

SNA-direct connection
In frame relay, the SNA systems can connect directly to the frame handler.

source service access points (SSAP)

The SAP of the source (the sending) computer. *See* service access points (SAP); *see* destination service access points (DSAP).

special authorities

Associated with a user profile to allow users such as system operators—who don't have any access to some objects—to work with objects and do routine system functions such as save and restore.

special IP addressing

In TCP/IP, some addresses (all bit 1s or all bit 0s) take on special meaning.

special shared pools

Machine pools and base pools are set up by IBM. Customers have limited control over the pools.

specific authorities

The user profiles grant some authority to each object. Specific authorities reside with the objects.

spooled output file

Printed output from jobs or programs do not usually go directly to a printer on the AS/400. They are held as spooled output files until directed to an output queue to which a printer is attached.

storage pool

See memory pool.

subsystem

A run-time environment for specific types of jobs. All interactive jobs run in an interactive subsystem. All batch jobs run in a batch subsystem.

switched

Theoretically a line is switched if devices attach by dialing up. However, with the AS/400's automatic configuration, any line or device unknown to the AS/400 can be configured as soon as its presence is detected. These lines/devices are referred to as switched.

symbols

In DDI networks, frame sizes are often referred to in double-byte or symbols.

TCP/IP

See transmission control protocol/Internet protocol.

terminal equipment (TE)

On frame-relay networks, the end AS/400s.

thrashing

The point where an AS/400 spends more time faulting and paging than it does working on jobs or programs. Usually, only a symptom of a very out-of-capacity AS/400 or one that is very poorly adjusted.

token ring

A LAN protocol that supports the IEEE 802.5 standard. A token—an object or message—passes data over a ring topology.

transceiver

On an Ethernet network, a device that connects any nodes into the cable.

transmission control protocol/Internet protocol (TCP/IP)

The standards allowing computers to exchange information. AS/400s and workstations can be connected with the TCP/IP protocol.

user Generally, the person working on a workstation attached to the AS/400 or receiving reports from the AS/400. However, in the AS/400, some tasks have their own pseudo user. For example, ODBC jobs typically are represented by their own user (who is not the person making the ODBC request).

user profile

A user is made known to the AS/400 through an object, called a user profile, that contains basic information about who the person is and what they are authorized to do on the system.

vary on/vary off

Essentially, you can turn devices on and off from any workstation attached to an AS/400. This is a soft turn on or off that is similar to, but not really the same as, switching mechanical switches on and off.

workstation

AS/400 terminology for a display station.

writer AS/400 terminology for a printer.

INDEX

B

C

D

E

F

G

H

I

J

K

L

M

N

O

P

Q

R

S

T

U

V

W

FAXABLE ORDER FORM

Fax to: 760-931-9935

BILL TO:

Name ______________________________

Title ______________________________

Company ______________________________

Address ______________________________

City ____________ State ________ Zip ____________

YTOAZ

SHIP TO (if different from above):

Name ____________ Title ____________

Company ______________________________

Address ______________________________

City/State/Zip ______________________________

ITEMS ORDERED:

Item No.	Page	Description	Price	Quantity	Total Price

Subtotal	
Add 7.75% sales tax (CA Residents Only) or 6.25% sales tax (TX residents only)	
Shipping/Handling—$6.25 per book (UPS ground continental U.S. only)	
Total	

ADDITIONAL INFORMATION:

Daytime Phone (required to process order):

(______) ________ - ________

Fax (______) ________ - ________

Email ______________________________

* Note: All prices are U.S. only. Please call for orders and prices outside the U.S. Prices Subject to change.

BILLING INFORMATION:

☐ Payment Enclosed (Make check payable to Midrange Computing.)

CREDIT CARD: ☐ VISA ☐ MasterCard ☐ AMEX ☐ Discover

Card # ______________________________

BILL ME, P.O. # ______________________________

Signature (required) ______________________________

VISA MasterCard American Express Cards Discover Novus